S104 Exploring science
Science: Level 1

**The Open University**

# Life

Prepared by Diane Butler, Michael Gillman, Judith Metcalfe and David Robinson

D1347640

This publication forms part of an Open University course S104 *Exploring science*. The complete list of texts which make up this course can be found on the back cover. Details of this and other Open University courses can be obtained from the Student Registration and Enquiry Service, The Open University, PO Box 197, Milton Keynes MK7 6BJ, United Kingdom: tel. +44 (0)845 300 60 90, email general-enquiries@open.ac.uk

Alternatively, you may visit the Open University website at http://www.open.ac.uk where you can learn more about the wide range of courses and packs offered at all levels by The Open University.

To purchase a selection of Open University course materials visit http://www.ouw.co.uk, or contact Open University Worldwide, Michael Young Building, Walton Hall, Milton Keynes MK7 6AA, United Kingdom for a brochure. tel. +44 (0)1908 858793; fax +44 (0)1908 858787; email ouw-customer-services@open.ac.uk

The Open University
Walton Hall, Milton Keynes
MK7 6AA

First published 2008

Edited and designed by The Open University.

Typeset by SR Nova Pvt Ltd, Bangalore, India.

Printed and bound in the United Kingdom by Halstan Printing Group, Amersham.

ISBN 978 1 8487 3166 0

2.1

# Contents

# Chapter 1
# Introduction

As you will recall from Book 1, the part of the Earth that is capable of supporting life is called the biosphere. Now that you know something of the processes that shape the biosphere, it is a good time to look at life on Earth. Perhaps the most fascinating feature of life on Earth is the huge variety of plants and animals that it supports. Many of these are easily seen, but there are others that we are only dimly aware of or never encounter at all, for example most of the animals in the soil or the microscopic plants and animals in the sea. The size range of life on Earth is impressive too. The smallest form of life is the virus, which may be 20 nm in size (1 nm is $1 \times 10^{-9}$ m) and 100 times smaller than a bacterium, but there are trees that are 112 m tall and a blue whale may be 33 m in length. You might also be struck by the immense variety of some forms of life. There are only a dozen or so different whales, but 40% of all insects are beetles – and there are 350 000 different ones. But underlying the astonishing variety – or diversity – of life is a much less diverse framework. Not only is the fine structure of organisms surprisingly consistent, but a lot of the chemistry of life is consistent as well. The fact that uniformity underlies diversity in living organisms is central to the study of life on Earth.

Imagine that you are walking through the rainforest in Brazil – or more likely through a garden or shopping centre – and you see a plant like the one in Figure 1.1. If you touch the flower it might well feel warm and perhaps be much warmer than its surroundings. This is not what you would expect and is unusual among plants.

■ Bearing in mind what you have already studied in earlier books, why might the flower be warm?

□ Chemical energy may be converted to heat energy as a result of a chemical reaction. Such a reaction is an exothermic one. So, you might reasonably deduce that an exothermic reaction is taking place within the flower.

You will be familiar with the heat that you dissipate even when sitting still. This is also as a result of chemical reactions. Cold can stimulate a particular reaction that liberates a lot of heat energy from the chemical breakdown of fats. The chemical reaction by which the flower warmed was found to be very much like that in humans, with the plant breaking down fats via a similar series of reactions, liberating heat. The breakdown process for fats, and other sources of energy for life, is referred to as respiration and the chemical pathways involved in respiration are ubiquitous in the natural world. The details of the chemistry of the stages of respiration are covered in Chapter 6 of this book.

The observation of the warmth of the flower should lead you to another and potentially much more difficult question, 'Why is this flower warm, when most are not?' A biologist would ask this question in a more formal way, so that rather than asking, 'Why is the flower warm?' would ask, 'What advantages does the warmth bring to the flower?' The reason for rephrasing the question in this way,

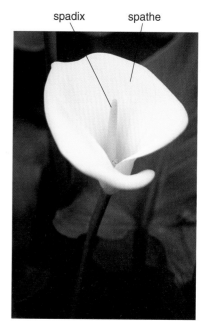

spadix    spathe

**Figure 1.1**  An Arum lily in flower. This is the species of lily most often found in cultivation in the UK. The central flower spike contains the male and female flowers and is called the spadix. The surround of the spadix looks like a petal but is actually a different structure, which is called the spathe.

is to put it into an evolutionary context. New characteristics that arise that confer an advantage to an organism are more likely to be retained in a population. You will read more about the mechanisms of evolution in Chapter 14.

The flower of the Arum lily is actually a group of flowers, so is more properly called an inflorescence. It is made up of lots of small flowers (florets), both male and female, arranged on the central flower spike – the spadix (Figure 1.1). The male flowers are usually above the female ones. The flowers of some lily species, for example in Brazil, are pollinated by beetles, which are attracted in large numbers to each flower spike. The peak temperature of the flower coincides with the period of 18–24 hours of female receptivity. One possibility for this is that the rise in temperature triggers the release of a volatile chemical that attracts the beetles. The petal-like surround closes up the spadix after about 12 hours, trapping beetles inside where, as they blunder around in the warmth feeding and mating, they transfer pollen to the female flowers. After a further 12 hours, the flower opens and the beetles depart, picking up male pollen as they go. The temperature inside the flower is close to the preferred temperature for the beetle.

■ Considering the information that you now have about the Arum lily flower, try to answer the question, 'What advantages does the warmth bring?'

☐ For the plant, the warmth of the flower appears to be a mechanism for attracting beetles, resulting in both pollination of the female florets and dispersion of the pollen from the male florets. The beetles appear to reap a reward from the food sources within the flower, and perhaps also from the warmth of their temporary prison. They can also mate.

This is a close link between the beetle and the plant, with each being beautifully adapted to its particular lifestyle. Very detailed study is required to explain how that link came about. The most significant unifying concept in biology is that of evolution by natural selection. In any particular environment – a fast-running river or stream, for example – only those animals that are well suited to that environment will prosper and reproduce successfully. Should the speed of the river change, then animals that are suited to the new speed will survive and others will not. The change in river speed has 'selected' a particular subset of the animals. Natural selection offers the best explanation of how individual animals and plants have, over time, become adapted to a particular habitat or lifestyle. The key to natural selection is variation, but variation within an interbreeding group of animals. Animals that can interbreed and produce offspring that can themselves interbreed are said to be in the same species. You will know from everyday experience that individuals within species differ from one other. These variations become significant if some individuals are more successful than others and make a greater contribution to the future generations. You will explore the processes of evolution in much more detail later in this book; you will also consider the ways in which characteristics of one individual are inherited in subsequent generations.

You might not have posed this question yourself, but another question raised by the warm Arum lily flowers is whether the relationship between the flowers and the beetles has developed recently. The surprising answer is that plants that show this characteristic are all in ancient groups that started to appear about 180 million years (180 Ma) ago and they have all been around since the Jurassic (200–145 Ma) and Cretaceous (145–65 Ma) Periods. (You will learn more about periods of geological time in Book 6.) Similarly, the beetles first appear during the same periods. Thus it seems likely that the close relationship between the two also dates from the same time. 180 million years might seem to you to be a very long period over which there has been relatively little change, but there are animals that have existed with very little change since the first period of geological time, the Cambrian (542–488 Ma) Period. For example, a brachiopod is a type of shelled animal that has changed very little over time. Compare the fossil and present-day forms of the brachiopod shown in Figure 1.2. They are very similar.

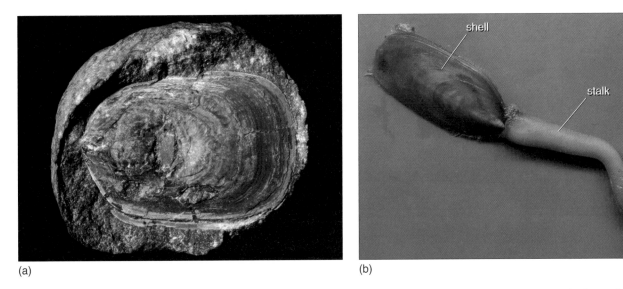

(a)                                                                              (b)

**Figure 1.2**    (a) The brachiopod *Lingulella* from the Cambrian Period; (b) the brachiopod *Lingula* from the Pacific Ocean.

Evolution can produce large changes in short periods of time. For example, it was only 7 Ma ago that the human ancestral line diverged from that of chimps. When it comes to viruses and bacteria, observable changes in their characteristics occur over periods of a few years, or sometimes even more rapidly. So the rate of evolution is highly variable.

The pearly shells of *Nautilus* (Figure 1.3a) can quite often be found in seaside shops that sell souvenirs. The animals live in tropical seas and, although they have remained largely unaltered for over 150 Ma, their relatives the ammonites had three periods of extensive expansion, with large numbers of new species appearing. Each period of expansion was followed by a drastic reduction in numbers. After the final period of expansion, all the ammonites disappeared around 65 Ma ago. There are close similarities between the ammonites and *Nautilus*, as you can see in Figure 1.3, and it is interesting that *Nautilus* survives but the similar looking ammonites are all extinct. You will learn more about extinction in later chapters.

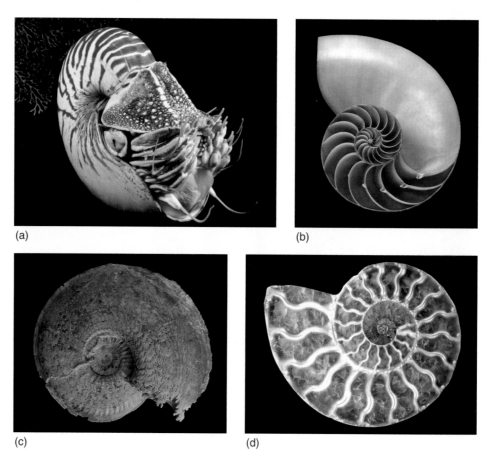

(a)          (b)

(c)          (d)

**Figure 1.3**   (a) A live *Nautilus*; (b) *Nautilus* shell sectioned to show the internal chambers. (c) An ammonite showing the external zigzag lines that mark the internal divisions between the chambers. (d) A section through an ammonite to show the internal chambers.

Just because animals look alike does not necessarily mean that they are very closely related. Consider the three animals pictured in Figure 1.4. They are obviously moles and you might pick out differences in the colour of their fur, but they do not look obviously different. However, these moles are not closely related. The mole in 1.4a is the common mole from Europe; the mole in 1.4b is not closely related to the common mole and comes from South Africa; the mole in 1.4c is even more distantly related, being a marsupial, and is found in Australia. Marsupial mammals have a pouch, in which the young suckle and grow and they are only distantly related to other mammals. Over time, these unrelated animals that have all adopted a burrowing lifestyle have come to look like each other. What is the biological explanation for this? As you read on through the book, you will be able to develop your own explanation. You will return to the moles in Chapter 15.

(a)

(b)

(c)

**Figure 1.4**   Three different moles (see text for explanation).

Modern biology takes an integrative approach towards the study of the natural world. New laboratory techniques, the rapid advances in molecular biology and the introduction of new technologies into field studies have all contributed to integrative biology. Scientists can, for example, track animals with the help of satellite tags, use molecular techniques to find out who is related to whom, project backwards to work out an evolutionary history, monitor activity and calculate energy budgets. This drawing together of information from different sources is a very powerful research process. You will meet other examples of this integrative approach later in the book.

This chapter started with the biosphere, the part of the Earth capable of supporting life. But what is the scientific definition of life? This is the subject of the next chapter.

## 1.1   Planning your study of Book 5

You will have already realised that this is a very thick book! Take a look at the Study Calendar to see the number of weeks set aside for the study of Book 5 and how the chapters and activities fit into each of the allotted weeks. You need to think carefully about how you will divide up your time to ensure that you maintain a reasonable pace through the material. As with previous books of the course, it is strongly recommended that you spend time planning your study, and that you construct your own personal study timetable.

On first examination of the book you will notice that the chapters are of uneven length. This is intentional, and you should take this into account when you plan your study timetable. Inevitably you will find some chapters more difficult than others; many students find biochemistry topics (Chapters 5 and 6) to be quite challenging and you may need to allow more time to study these parts of the book. Don't be afraid to keep moving through this material if you find it difficult and try not to become 'bogged down' – you will find that your understanding develops gradually. It is a good strategy to return to problematic concepts at a later date, as more recently studied topics can help the ideas fall into place. You will find that the Book 5 activities are very good at supporting your learning of these difficult concepts.

In planning your detailed study schedule there are some activities in Book 5 that are worth thinking about ahead of time. In Chapter 2 (Activity 2.1) you will conduct an experiment that will take a few days to run to completion, so do plan ahead and make sure you have all the equipment you need. In addition, this book has several quite lengthy computer-based activities. These are in Chapter 2 (Activity 2.2), Chapter 3 (Activity 3.1), Chapter 4 (Activity 4.3, Part 1), Chapter 7 (Activities 7.1 and 7.2), Chapter 8 (Activity 4.3, Part 2), Chapter 10 (Activity 10.1) and Chapter 14 (Activity 14.1). It's important that you study these activities at the correct time, so ensure you organise computer access (if that is a problem) well in advance. You are advised to complete all the computer-based activities; these are designed to complement and augment the biology developed in the book and you may well be assessed on material that is only found within a computer-based activity.

Another important item to plan into your study of Book 5 is the set of online activities that will take place in your tutor group forum. Chapters 2 and 3 have online activities associated with them and, in order to participate fully in your tutor group discussion, you must make sure you complete the preparatory tasks in good time and post your findings to the forum when appropriate.

In addition to developing your knowledge and understanding of biology, this book will help you to develop and practise other important skills. Many of the book's activities are based around extracting and assimilating information that can then be presented in a variety of ways, for example as diagrams, flow charts, tables, lists or short accounts. The book emphasises a very important skill, which is the ability to relate knowledge and concepts both within and between different sections of the book and with other books of the course, particularly Book 4. By completing these activities in full and making use of the comments at the end of the book, you will be able to improve your understanding of the concepts and develop your written communication skills and information literacy skills.

Finally, before you move on to Chapter 2, think about how you will cope with the huge number of new words (many of which look unpronounceable!) and terms that you will meet in Book 5. Biology is a subject with its own specialist vocabulary and most people find it difficult to keep track of the large number of new words they encounter. You might want to consider keeping your own glossary. Whatever strategy you employ, be assured that *most* of these long and difficult words really do become second nature in the end.

# Chapter 2
# What is life?

Look around any garden or park and it is easy to pick out the living from the non-living (Figure 2.1). The trees, flowers, birds and people are living, whereas the parked cars, pathways and lake are non-living. To answer the question, 'What is life?' should simply be a matter of listing those things (i.e. qualities) that living things share with each other, but which they do not share with non-living things. Unfortunately, such a list is not easy to compile, as you would discover quickly if you tried to specify what flowers, humans and birds have in common.

**Figure 2.1**   A view of parkland.

There are, however, three qualities that these organisms, and all other organisms, do share. They form the subject matter for this section, and indeed for much of biology.

> The qualities possessed by all living organisms are *reproduction*, *growth* and *metabolism*. These three shared qualities are called **attributes of life**.

## 2.1   Life arises from the living

Before you go on holiday, it is always a good idea to empty your teapot (and coffee cup and fruit bowl). If you do not, then when you return you will find a fine cottony mat of material growing on the tea (or coffee or fruit). The material

**Figure 2.2**   Close-up of a fungus (*Rhizopus stolonifer*) growing on a carrot (magnification about ×10). *Rhizopus stolonifer* is the scientific name of this particular fungus. The use of scientific names is explained in Section 3.2.

will be floating on the surface of the tea and it will probably be white with flecks of black (although different types have different colours, including green and orange). If you are away for only a few days, then the cottony mat will scarcely be visible; but if you are away for a week or two, the mat will be very conspicuous. The material arises from organisms (known as moulds or *fungi*, singular: *fungus*) growing on the tea. Figure 2.2 shows a fungus growing on the surface of a carrot.

■   What quality of fungi suggests that they are living organisms?

☐   The quality that suggests that fungi are living organisms is growth; the longer they are left, the bigger they get.

The observation that they apparently appear from nothing raises the question, 'Where do fungi come from?' You may well know the answer, but the question provoked considerable debate during the 19th century. There were those scientists, championed by the Frenchman Félix-Archimède Pouchet (1800–1872), who thought that the fungus arose from whatever it grew on, e.g. from within the tea or the rotting fruit. Such scientists accepted that fungi would be created over and over again, without parents, provided only that the conditions were right, i.e. wherever it was warm and damp and there was something for them to grow on (e.g. tea, fruit or bread). Therefore, as fungi are living organisms, they also accepted that life could be repeatedly created. Pouchet and like-minded scientists supported the theory of *spontaneous generation*, the idea that certain forms of life could arise spontaneously.

Other scientists disagreed. They could not accept that life was being created over and over again. Instead they supported the theory that fungi arose from minute fungal particles carried in the air. These particles eventually settled onto surfaces and, if those surfaces were suitable (e.g. tea or bread), then the fungal particles would begin to grow and produce visible fungus. These scientists supported the view that life arose only from material that was already living; in other words, spontaneous generation did not occur.

The argument in favour of the small airborne particle hypothesis was clinched in 1867 by another French scientist, Louis Pasteur (Figure 2.3). Pasteur conducted a meticulous series of experiments that led him to the final, conclusive experiment described here. He believed that the fungi that grew on suitable surfaces must either have been present already, or have arrived there from the air. He therefore devised an experiment that did two things. First, fungi had to be eliminated from the suitable surface before starting the experiment. Second, it was necessary to prevent any new fungal particles arriving on the surface from the air. Under these very specific conditions in which no fungal particles were present, no fungi should grow on the surface.

**Figure 2.3**   Louis Pasteur (1822–1895), after whom the process of pasteurisation is named.

■   What would it mean if fungi did grow on the surface under these conditions?

☐   It would mean that spontaneous generation did occur.

Pasteur decided to use a liquid (a solution of sugar in water plus a small amount of brewers' waste) rather than a solid because he knew from previous experiments that the liquid could support fungal growth, but that boiling it would eliminate any fungal particles present. He devised a flask to prevent particles settling onto the mixture from the air. This had a special neck that he could stretch and bend into a long, thin 'U' after the mixture had been put into the flask (Figure 2.4). He reasoned that the thin neck would allow air to be in contact with the mixture, but would reduce the movement of air, so that any fungal particles in the air would be trapped in the bottom of the 'U'.

Pasteur found that fungi did not grow on or within the solution; it remained clear of life. This seemed to indicate that when life was eliminated from the solution and the air above it, nothing would grow in the solution. But there is another reason why nothing might grow.

■ What other possible reason could there be for nothing growing in the solution?

☐ The conditions in the flask may no longer be suitable for fungal growth.

■ How could the conditions in the flask be tested for their suitability for fungal growth?

☐ Some fungal particles could be introduced to see if they can grow.

Pasteur introduced fungal particles by tipping the flask so that some of the sugar solution ran down into the 'U' and then tipping it back into the body of the flask (Figure 2.5). By doing this he was also hoping to prove that living particles were indeed trapped in the 'U'. As a consequence of the tipping, fungi grew in the solution.

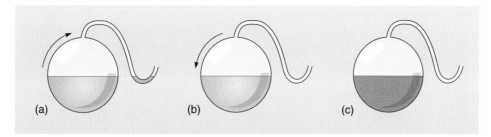

**Figure 2.5** (a) The flask is tipped so that solution runs down into the 'U' and then back into the body of the flask (b). (c) After 3 weeks the mixture is clouded with fungi.

Pasteur proved two things with his experiments:
- boiling a liquid would kill any life that might be in it
- life would grow on suitable surfaces or in suitable solutions only if living particles arrived from elsewhere, i.e. spontaneous generation did *not* occur.

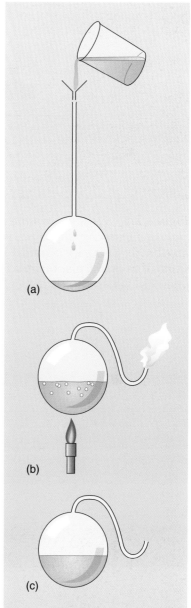

**Figure 2.4** Pasteur's conclusive experiment: (a) the sugar solution is introduced to the flask; (b) the neck of the flask is bent and the solution boiled. (c) After 3 weeks there is no evidence of fungal growth in the flask.

You will now have the opportunity to investigate fungal particles in the air for yourself in Activity 2.1.

---

### Activity 2.1    Investigating fungal particles in the air – Part 1

We expect this activity will take you approximately 30 minutes (spread over several days).

In this activity you will carry out your own investigation into the fungal particles in the air around you and share your findings with other students in your tutor group forum.

The aim of this investigation is to estimate the density of fungal particles in a room (e.g. the kitchen) by exposing an appropriate growth medium (tomato soup) to a known volume of air and then seeing how many fungi grow on it.

Equipment

*Non-kit items*

- small can of cheap tomato soup
- rectangular plastic container
- means of labelling plastic container
- cling film
- ruler or other measuring device.

Introduction

Density tells you the mass of a substance per cubic metre; however, you can also consider density as expressing the number of 'things', e.g. fungal particles per cubic metre. The basic idea of this investigation is to allow fungal particles in the air to settle on the tomato soup and then to estimate the density of particles in the air by counting the number of fungi growing on the surface of the soup. Since it would be very difficult to expose the soup to exactly 1 m³ of air, the strategy you will use is to expose the soup to a known (smaller) volume of air in the rectangular container and then use maths to work out the number of particles per cubic metre.

The design of the investigation

Among other things, you will need to think about how to make sure that a known volume of air is in contact with the soup, and that no fungal particles are introduced from elsewhere.

Spend a few minutes thinking about precisely how you will carry out this investigation using the equipment listed above. It may help you to think of questions such as:

- What size container do I need?
- Why was it suggested that a rectangular container be used rather than (say) a cylindrical one?
- How do I make sure that only air and soup are in the container at the start of the investigation?
- How do I make sure that nothing else gets inside the container once the investigation is under way?
- How do I measure the volume of air in the container?

- Where should I leave the container for the duration of the investigation?
- How long should I leave it?
- How do I make sure that no one disturbs it?
- What records should I keep of the investigation?
- What should I do with the container and its contents afterwards?

You should read the comments on this activity at the end of this book and the safety warning below before proceeding.

**Safety warning**

Read the whole of this section before starting the activity and make sure that you have read the section on 'Practical activities' in the *Course Guide*.

When carrying out practical activities, you should always take care to observe the simple safety precautions highlighted in the course book. Very often, as in the case of this activity, these precautions will seem quite obvious and just a matter of using common sense. However, that does not mean that you should ignore the safety instructions. The Open University has a duty to give advice on health and safety to students carrying out any activities that are described in the course. Similarly, *you* have a duty to follow the instructions and to carry out the practical activity having regard for your own safety and that of other people around you. Whenever you do practical activities you should think about the hazards involved, and how any risks can be minimised.

**Important safety precautions**

Take note of the following safety precautions, which apply to all practical activities:

- Keep children and animals away while you are working.
- Clear your working area of clutter. Put all food away. Ensure there is nothing to trip on underfoot.
- Always wash your hands thoroughly after a practical activity.
- Any household items used should be thoroughly cleaned before returning them to domestic use.

Practical procedure

Wash the container thoroughly and allow it to dry upside down. When it is dry, open the can of soup and quickly pour the contents into the container. Immediately cover the container with the cling film. Label the container so that it is clear what it is and who is responsible for it; ensure that the label says 'NOT TO BE EATEN'. Record the date and time, and where the container is to be kept for the duration of the investigation. *Make sure that the container is kept out of reach of young children and pets at all times.*

You need to calculate the volume of air between the surface of the soup and the cling film. Measure the width and length of the container (these will be approximate measurements as the corners of the container are likely to be rounded). If you use a translucent container, you will be able to measure the distance from the surface of the soup to the cling film from the outside. If you cannot see the level of the soup through the side of the container, wait until the end of the experiment and then take the measurement after peeling back the cling film a little before re-attaching it. You should not do this during the course of the investigation, as this would allow more fungal particles to enter.

Record your measurements, being careful to use the same unit for each one you make. Don't forget to note down which unit you used (e.g. cm).

Carefully place the container in a warm location where it will not be disturbed.

Without lifting the cling film, inspect the surface of the soup every day or two. On each occasion count and record the number of separate areas of fungal growth you can see. You might also like to write a brief description of the fungal areas. Are there different types of fungus growing on the soup?

Data collection can cease once it is clear that the number of areas of fungal growth is no longer increasing between inspections, but this may well take a few days or longer. You will find instructions on what to do next in Part 2 of this activity near the end of this chapter.

---

Pasteur's findings helped establish that all life on Earth today comes from already living organisms; this fact is captured in the phrase 'the life cycle'. To explain what is meant by the life cycle, and how it fits in with Pasteur's findings, two of the three attributes of life – reproduction and growth – must be considered.

## 2.2    Reproduction and growth: the life cycle

**Reproduction** is the process by which organisms produce offspring. This simple statement belies a hugely complex sequence of events that usually begins with one organism finding a mate and ends with the birth of at least one new organism. Needless to say, there is tremendous variation in exactly how different kinds of organism produce their offspring. Some of this variation is discussed in later sections, but here you are concerned with things that organisms have in common. Two aspects of reproduction are universal. The first is that the offspring produced are initially small compared with their parents (Figure 2.6).

The offspring, therefore, have to grow. The period of **growth** varies between organisms, from minutes (for some bacteria) to centuries (for some trees). The size to which different organisms grow also varies. However, *all* offspring, and hence *all* organisms, have to grow.

The second universal aspect of reproduction is that only mature organisms are able to reproduce. Generally speaking, if an organism grows for long enough, it will be able to reproduce.

Putting these two aspects together: reproduction is followed by the growth of the offspring, which then reproduce to produce offspring themselves, which then grow … and so on. The

**Figure 2.6**    Size difference between adult and offspring: a strawberry frog (*Dendrobates pumilio*) carrying one of its tadpoles on its back.

repetition of reproduction followed by growth followed by reproduction is called the **life cycle**, and it is usually depicted as a circle (Figure 2.7).

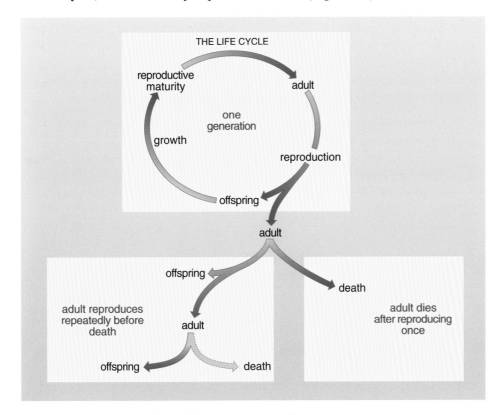

**Figure 2.7** A generalised life cycle (see text for explanation).

The circle represents the passage of time. Starting with 'offspring' and moving in a clockwise direction, the offspring grow and mature to become adult and then they themselves reproduce. One turn around the cycle represents the period of time from the birth of offspring to those offspring producing offspring of their own. In the generalised life cycle illustrated here, and in most depictions of life cycles, the adult drops out of the cycle between 'reproduction' and 'offspring'. In fact, the adults may go on to reproduce again, possibly several times until prevented from doing so by death or old age. The point is that one turn around the cycle covers the phases of life of that type of organism that are necessary to produce the next generation. The **generation time** is the time it takes a particular type of organism to go once around its life cycle. You will learn more about life cycles, and the extent to which they differ in detail between organisms of different types, in Section 4.4. For now, you need to remember only that life cycles are universal to organisms and that one cycle is equivalent to one generation.

Question 2.1

Approximately how many years difference (if any) are there between the duration of the life cycle, the generation time and the length of life for humans?

The unusual feature of the fungal life cycle that fooled Pouchet is that fungal particles retain indefinitely their ability to grow. The particles are spores, which are special structures produced by fungi that serve a similar function to seeds in plants. The spores could sit in Pasteur's 'U' bend for hundreds of years without losing their ability to grow.

■ Under what conditions did Pasteur's experiments show that fungal spores lose their ability to grow?

☐ When they are subjected to the heat of boiling water. (In fact, the spores of a few types of fungi will survive even boiling water.)

When the spores are in *favourable conditions* they will begin to grow. The concept of favourable conditions is an extremely important one in biology. Different organisms require different conditions of, for example, humidity and temperature in order to grow. What makes one type of organism different from another are the conditions in which it grows; each type of organism has a specific set of conditions in which it grows best. Thus, one type of fungus grows best on bread, another on rotten fruit and yet another on damp wallpaper.

■ Several different materials on which fungi grow have been mentioned. What do these materials have in common?

☐ They are made of, or incorporate, once-living material.

Fungi of one sort or another will grow on almost anything that was once living – collectively called organic matter. Yet other fungi are able to grow on organic matter that is still living; one such is the common fungus *Tinea pedis* that causes cracks in the skin between the toes and itching, the condition known as athlete's foot.

The organic matter is the source of both material and energy for the fungus. Material is needed for the production and growth of new body parts, for repairing damage and for making new organisms (i.e. offspring). Energy is required for growth and for other processes that are essential for life. Material and energy are therefore essential requirements in all organisms for maintaining life, for growth and for reproduction. For example, as a tadpole changes from a pond-living, swimming organism to a land-based, hopping frog it requires material from which to make new legs and new skin. As a land-based frog, it continues to grow. Energy is required, not just to enable the tadpole to swim or the frog to hop, but also for the construction of new bone, muscle and skin from raw material.

So far, the discussion of the life processes of growth and reproduction has focused on whole organisms of different types (e.g. fungi and frogs). The whole organism is relatively easy to relate to, because that is what is usually seen. Next you will look briefly at the level of the molecules that make up organisms, a level that provides a somewhat different perspective on life processes.

## 2.3   Metabolism

All organisms are composed of combinations of chemical substances, i.e. molecules. Water is the major constituent of all organisms. The bulk of the rest of the material of which an organism is made contains carbon. So water and carbon-based substances constitute an organism's biggest requirements. The way in which organisms obtain their carbon-based materials separate them into two groups: the *autotrophs* and the *heterotrophs*.

**Autotrophs** (from the Greek *auto* meaning 'self' and *troph* meaning 'feed') make their own carbon-based material starting with carbon dioxide. You met the chemical reaction for this process in Book 1, Section 7.3.1:

$$\text{carbon dioxide} + \text{water} \longrightarrow \text{organic carbon} + \text{oxygen} \tag{2.1}$$

■ What is missing from this chemical reaction?

☐ The reaction requires the input of energy.

■ Where does the energy come from and what is this process called?

☐ The energy comes from the Sun and the process is called photosynthesis.

Photosynthesis is part of the carbon cycle. Solar energy is captured in very small structures called *chloroplasts* in the leaves of plants. Carbon dioxide effectively reacts with water to produce simple, carbon-based, organic molecules, i.e. sugars. Nearly all living organisms depend either directly or indirectly on photosynthesis for their supply of organic molecules. (There are a few bacteria, called chemoautotrophs, which produce sugars using different reactions that do not require solar energy.) Sugars serve two important roles. First, other organic molecules can be made from them. Second, they serve as a store for some of the Sun's energy. However, before considering how the energy is released from storage, you need to look briefly at heterotrophs.

**Heterotrophs** (from the Greek *hetero* meaning 'other' and *troph* meaning 'feed') cannot make sugars by photosynthesis, so they rely on other organisms for their carbon-based materials. Essentially, heterotrophs either eat plants (**herbivores**), eat other animals that have eaten plants (**carnivores**) (Figure 2.8) or eat both plants and animals (**omnivores**).

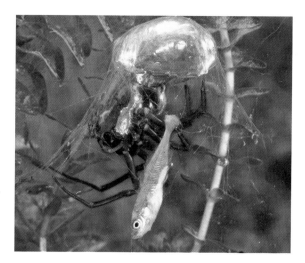

**Figure 2.8**   A carnivorous heterotroph (the water spider, *Argyroneta aquatica*) with a source of carbon-based materials (a stickleback, *Gasterosteus aculeatus*).

All animals are heterotrophs, which means that all the animals you see around you are ultimately dependent on plants for their carbon-based materials.

■ Are fungi heterotrophs or autotrophs?

☐ Fungi are heterotrophs because they rely on other organisms (e.g. leaves of the tea plant, fruit and human skin) for their carbon-based materials.

However an organism obtains its organic molecules, whether by photosynthesis or by eating them, these molecules undergo a series of chemical transformations that result in the production of the hundreds of different substances needed for life. The sum total of all these transformations is the organism's **metabolism**. Each type of organism has its own particular metabolism suited to its carbon source(s) and the substances it needs to make for body maintenance, repair and new growth. Maintenance involves the destruction of old material and its replacement with new. For example, in an average adult human up to 2.5 million red blood cells are destroyed every second and are normally replaced at the same rate (so that all the red blood cells you have in you now will have been entirely replaced in four months time). Skin, muscle and internal organs are all also subject to a continuous programme of replacement for which metabolism is responsible. In addition, organisms get injured and damaged; making new bark (in the case of trees) or new skin (in the case of humans) to repair such damage also involves metabolism.

■ Heterotrophs obtain their carbon-based materials ultimately from plants. From where do they obtain their energy?

☐ From the same source: the carbon-based materials also supply energy.

We can now return to the process by which energy stored in organic molecules is released. The specific process is respiration and it is effectively the reverse of photosynthesis. Note that respiration at this level, the molecular level, is not the same as breathing. It is unfortunate, but quite common in biology, that one word has two different meanings. The process of **respiration** releases the energy stored in organic molecules in a series of highly controlled, very small steps. The end result is the production of carbon dioxide and water, so this process is an important part of the carbon cycle, as you saw in Section 7.3 of Book 1. The chemical reaction for respiration is:

$$\text{organic carbon} + \text{oxygen} \longrightarrow \text{carbon dioxide} + \text{water} \qquad (2.2)$$

■ What is missing from this chemical reaction?

☐ The energy that is released.

■ Is respiration part of metabolism?

☐ Respiration involves the conversion of organic molecules into carbon dioxide and water. Thus, it is a chemical transformation occurring inside an organism and is therefore part of metabolism.

The energy released by respiration is used to drive other parts of metabolism, to enable other chemical transformations to take place, and to enable animals to move. Moreover, respiration is just as important to autotrophs as it is to heterotrophs.

Question 2.2

Why do autotrophs need respiration, rather than simply using the Sun's energy directly to 'drive' metabolism?

**Figure 2.9**  The brine shrimp (*Artemia franciscana*), an organism that produces spore-like cysts that seems to be able to survive for some considerable time without metabolism (magnification ×5).

Organisms live over a period of time – centuries in the case of some trees. During its lifetime, an organism will exhibit each of the attributes of life. However, at any particular moment an organism might not be growing (e.g. as an adult) or it might not be reproducing (e.g. as a juvenile). The one attribute of life that nearly all organisms reveal nearly all of the time is metabolism, although it is difficult to detect in seeds and even more so in fungal spores. In fact, only one organism, the brine shrimp (*Artemia franciscana*) (Figure 2.9), has ever been found that appears to be able to survive a period of time without metabolising at all.

Question 2.3

An adult male mayfly neither grows nor feeds, but flies around searching for a female with which to mate.

(a)  Does the adult mayfly metabolise?

(b)  All organisms have to grow, so how can the adult mayfly not grow?

(c)  Is the adult mayfly an autotroph or a heterotroph?

(d)  Apart from the adult mayfly, give an example of an organism that is neither growing nor photosynthesising.

Question 2.4

You want to grow some mould on a piece of bread. You seal the bread in a clear plastic bag to stop it drying out. Do you think it makes any difference whether you put the bread in a dark cupboard or leave it on a table in the light? Explain your answer.

Question 2.5

It was stated earlier that metabolism 'is difficult to detect in seeds and even more so in fungal spores'. What might scientists measure to show that metabolism is taking place in fungal spores?

## 2.4   From individual feeding and reproduction to population change

So far you have generally considered individual organisms in isolation. You have seen that they need to feed and that through their metabolism the resultant energy is used in various ways, in particular for growth and reproduction. As the numbers of individuals of a species reproduce and multiply, we move into a new realm of biological investigation – the population. A **population** is a collection of individuals of the same species. The definition of population may be refined to include all those individuals in a given area that have the potential to interbreed (assuming they are reproductively mature).

Populations of different species that occupy the same area may interact. (This shorthand of saying 'different populations interact' means that the individuals of those populations interact.) These interactions fall into three broad categories: populations feed on each other, or they compete with each other, or they benefit each other. The feeding interactions include populations of plants (autotrophs), populations of plant-feeders (herbivores) and populations of herbivore-feeders (carnivores) – the carnivores may also be food for higher carnivore groups. Interactions between plants and herbivores, or herbivores and carnivores, are often referred to as **predator–prey** interactions. There will be less concern here with competition between populations and mutualistic (beneficial) interactions, but they are important. Competition may occur for a variety of resources, including breeding areas and food, whilst mutualistic interactions like the Arum lily and the beetles you were introduced to in Chapter 1, include pollination (which usually also involves some feeding).

Feeding interactions between populations become increasingly interesting as more links in the **food chain** are considered. The term food chain is self-explanatory: starting with autotrophs (usually plants), energy and nutrients are transferred through a chain of individuals (and therefore populations) from herbivores to different levels of carnivores. The composition of complex food chains is considered in Chapter 7, but for now the focus is on the feeding interactions between three populations: plant, herbivore and carnivore. The plant will be represented by a species of grass, which is fed on by a population of snowshoe hares, which are in turn eaten by a population of lynx. These interactions are played out over large areas of northern USA and Canada. The interactions between these populations should help you understand more complex systems.

In order to study the interactions between the lynx and its prey, you should now do Activity 2.2, which uses a computer model.

---

### Activity 2.2   Population Dynamics: Investigation of predator–prey dynamics (lynx and snowshoe hare)

We expect this activity will take you approximately 1 hour.

In this computer-based activity you will investigate the population dynamics between a predator and its prey. You will look at the survival rates and reproductive rates of the lynx (*Lynx canadensis*) in relation to its prey, the snowshoe hare (*Lepus americanus*), and will use a computer model to make predictions about the future size of the predator population under different environmental circumstances.

There are no comments on this activity.

---

You will conclude this examination of the attributes of living organisms by returning to the investigation you began in Activity 2.1 Part 1. In Part 2 of the experiment you will report your findings to your tutor group forum and discuss your results with other students.

---

### Activity 2.1 (continued)   Investigating fungal particles in the air – Part 2

We expect this activity will take you approximately 40 minutes.

Once it is clear that the number of fungal patches on your soup is not increasing, work through Part 2 of this activity entitled 'Analysis of results' and post your final results to your tutor group forum. Read the instructions on the course website for guidance about what information to include and how to present it.

For safety reasons, it is recommended that both the container and its contents be disposed of straight away – without removing the cling film – just as you would dispose of any other contaminated food. If you want to keep the container, make sure that it is immediately washed extremely thoroughly.

## Analysis of results

Since each area of growth probably represents one fungus, which will have arisen from one fungal particle, you can now work out the density of fungal particles in the sample of air above the soup.

To find the volume of air, multiply your three measurements together. You are multiplying three lengths together, so your units will become cubic (e.g. cubic centimetres). To convert from cubic centimetres ($cm^3$) to cubic metres ($m^3$), divide by $10^6$ (because there are $100\ cm \times 100\ cm \times 100\ cm$, or $10^6\ cm^3$, in $1\ m^3$).

You can write your result as 'so many fungal particles' per 'so many cubic metres', for example 6 fungal particles per $6.8 \times 10^{-4}\ m^3$.

However, it is more useful to know how many fungal particles there are in $1\ m^3$, so that your results can more readily be compared with those of other students.

In the example given above, there are:

6 fungal particles per $6.8 \times 10^{-4}\ m^3$

$$= \frac{6\ particles}{6.8 \times 10^{-4}\ m^3}$$

$$= \frac{6}{6.8 \times 10^{-4}}\ fungal\ particles\ per\ m^3$$

$$= 8.8 \times 10^3\ fungal\ particles\ m^{-3}$$

So to find the density of fungal particles in the air, you divide the number of particles by the volume of air containing that number.

Calculate a value for the density of fungal particles measured in your experiment, and then write a conclusion to your investigation that includes this result.

The sample of air above the soup came from one particular location (e.g. the kitchen), so if you know the volume of air in that location, you could work out the total number of fungal particles in the air in that location.

## Thinking critically about your results

The result obtained for this investigation relies on a number of assumptions. You will discuss these assumptions with other students and with your tutor in your tutor group forum. Why, do you suppose, is the density of fungal particles obtained almost certainly an underestimate of the true density?

## Thinking of possible further investigations

This investigation may have set you wondering what would happen if you tried a slightly different investigation. You may even be thinking of other experiments you would like to carry out, in order to investigate fungal particles more fully. Spend a few minutes thinking about what else you might like to find out – and how you would go about it. Try to formulate your thoughts as questions to be answered experimentally. Again, you will have an opportunity to discuss your thoughts with other students and your tutor.

Note that, although reference has been made to 'fungal particles', they are more correctly called 'fungal spores'.

There are no comments on this part of the activity.

## 2.5   Summary of Chapter 2

All living organisms have three attributes in common. Reproduction is the process by which an organism produces offspring. All organisms grow, both to increase in size and to repair damage. All organisms obtain the materials and energy they need through the chemical transformations of metabolism.

Autotrophs make their own organic molecules, the vast majority using photosynthesis. Heterotrophs obtain organic molecules from other organisms. Originally this material was produced by autotrophs.

All organisms release energy from organic molecules by the process of respiration.

The life cycle depicts all the stages an organism must go through from birth to parenthood, the duration of which is the generation time. During the life cycle, organisms are either growing and becoming mature, or they are mature and seeking to reproduce. Many organisms live for longer than one generation.

The three attributes of life are not necessarily evident at all stages of an organism's life.

A population is composed of individuals of the same species. Populations are linked together by feeding interactions to form a food chain.

In Activity 2.1 you have thought about experimental design and carried out a simple experiment to evaluate the number of fungal spores in air. Through discussion with your tutor and other students, you have been able to compare your experimental procedure and your results and come to some conclusions about the nature of practical work in science.

In Activity 2.2 you made use of a computer model to manipulate characteristics of interacting populations in order to draw conclusions about predator–prey relationships.

# Chapter 3
# Diversity: the spice of life

You saw in Chapter 2 that all living organisms share three fundamental attributes: the processes of reproduction, growth and metabolism. You will see, in Chapter 4, that all living organisms are also united in their construction since they are composed of one or more of the basic units known as cells. While most multicellular organisms are composed of huge numbers of individual cells, altogether there are only a few hundred different types of cell.

In contrast to this impressive display of *unity*, this section is concerned with *diversity*. Specifically, it is concerned with the manifestation of life in an enormous number (millions) of different types of organism (i.e. different species). Among the knowledge and skills emphasised in this section are therefore those that relate to classification, since it is important to be able to 'see the wood for the trees' among this great variety of species.

## 3.1    Species

You are probably familiar with the expression 'the human species'. But what does the word 'species' mean? It means that members of our species (*Homo sapiens*) possess one or more characters in common that make it sensible (a) to group or classify humans together and (b) to distinguish humans from other species. In the present context, the term **character** is used to mean a characteristic or trait. All other species must likewise have some distinguishing character(s). (Incidentally, the word 'species' is both singular and plural: one species, several species.)

■   From general knowledge, what two characters are generally implied about organisms that are said to belong to the same species?

☐   Most obviously, members of the same species tend to be quite similar to one another in, for example, appearance and behaviour. Perhaps less obviously, members of the same species are capable of producing offspring that clearly belong to the same species – and *only* the same species – as themselves.

You probably understand why a particular organism belongs to one species rather than another, but in practice it is remarkably difficult to give a precise definition of the word 'species'. This is not dissimilar to the situation you encountered when trying to pin down the precise meaning of the word 'life' in Chapter 2.

Of the two characters of **species** suggested above, many biologists prefer to give priority to the ability of organisms of a particular species to produce offspring, all of which are members of the same species as themselves. Such biologists emphasise the **reproductive isolation** of species from one another. Two adult humans of the opposite sex are usually capable of mating and producing more humans (their offspring). This is true also of pairs belonging to other familiar species, such as the common chimpanzee (*Pan troglodytes*), the domestic horse (*Equus caballus*), the donkey (*Equus asinus*), the lion (*Panthera leo*) and the tiger (*Panthera tigris*). However, as members of different species, a human and a common chimpanzee are not capable of producing offspring together.

Consider what happens when mating takes place between a horse and a donkey. The offspring of a female horse mated to a male donkey is a mule, while that of a female donkey mated to a male horse is a hinny. Does this mean that horses and donkeys are not truly separate species after all? In fact, mules are infertile (i.e. they are incapable of producing offspring themselves) and hinnies have considerably reduced fertility. Thus, although a horse mated to a donkey can produce offspring, those offspring represent reproductive 'dead ends'. Similarly, although lions and tigers are distinct species, they too have been known to produce (relatively infertile) offspring together, but only in captivity when separated from members of the opposite sex of their own species. In fact, a number of animal species are known to interbreed even in the wild. Some even produce what appear to be fully-fertile hybrids (in this context, the offspring of a mating between two distinct species is called a hybrid). Nevertheless, hybridisation between species in the wild occurs only under rather limited circumstances, for instance where the geographical ranges of two similar species overlap only slightly. Because hybridisation between species is considerably more common in plants than in animals, it is particularly difficult to define plant species in terms of reproductive isolation.

These various exceptions mean that biologists have to qualify the preferred basis for defining species. Organisms are said to belong to different species if adults of the opposite sex are never capable of producing *fully fertile* offspring under *natural conditions* or if hybridisation is *extremely* rare for most of the population of that organism. Unfortunately, all sorts of operational difficulties can complicate attempts to classify organisms into distinct species. For instance, if similar-looking animals live in different parts of the world, how could it be established with certainty whether or not they belong to the same species? One way would be to move one or both of them to the same location. However, if they fail to interbreed there, is it because they belong to different species or is it because the prevailing conditions are insufficiently natural for one or both of them? Moreover, it is obvious that the fertility test cannot be applied to establish whether or not a fossil and a living animal, or two fossil animals, belong to the same species or to decide whether two plants that reproduce without sex (e.g. by producing bulbs) belong to the same species.

In practice, therefore, most organisms are classified into one species or another on the basis of their appearance and/or their behaviour (e.g. the songs of different bird species), rather than on whether or not they can interbreed. This allows fossil as well as living organisms and non-sexual as well as sexual organisms to be classified into species. The trouble is that many perfectly valid species (e.g. different groups of animals that are *known* not to breed together) look virtually identical even to experts, while sometimes members of the same species can look very different from one another. The warblers (*Phylloscopus* species) are a group of similar-looking birds which include species that coexist in the same habitat but are known not to interbreed. Even an experienced birdwatcher would have a major problem distinguishing a chiffchaff from a willow warbler by its appearance (Figure 3.1). So, how do birds know which is the right mate? (You will find the answer in the next section.) Variation within species is illustrated by domestic and

(a)

(b)

(c)

(d)

**Figure 3.1**   Representative species of three bird families: (a) goldfinch (*Carduelis carduelis*); (b) tree sparrow (*Passer montanus*); (c) willow warbler (*Phylloscopus trochilus*); (d) chiffchaff (*Phylloscopus collybita*).

agricultural animals, although the reason for the large amount of variation here is undoubtedly human interference. However, there are many wild species that are described as **polymorphic** because they exist in a number of highly distinctive types with different appearance or *morphology* (Figure 3.2). There are also species in which the sexes are strikingly different from one another, a phenomenon known as **sexual dimorphism** (Figure 3.3). In each case, if you did not know about the breeding behaviour of the animals concerned, you might well assume that they belonged to different species.

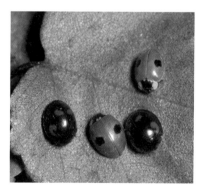

**Figure 3.2**   The two-spot ladybird (*Adalia bipunctata*) comes in both a 'typical' and a dark (or melanic) form.

(a)

(b)

**Figure 3.3**   (a) Male and female elephant seals (*Mirounga angustirostris*) differ greatly in size, while (b) male and female peafowl (*Pavo cristatus*) have strikingly different plumage.

## 3.2    Recognising and labelling species

Biologists would like to be able to classify all living (and fossil) organisms into one or another species. Ideally this would be on the basis of their reproductive behaviour, but generally it is on the basis of their appearance and/or other aspects of their behaviour. Intrinsic to this procedure is, first, recognising species as distinct entities and, second, giving these entities unique names. It is important to realise that a labelled category (such as a species) should not have been designated in the first place, and individual organisms cannot be placed consistently into one category rather than another unless significant differences between organisms that belong to different species can be reliably identified.

You probably already know that the scientific name of our own species is *Homo sapiens*. You may also know that this Latin name is generally translated as 'thinking man' (with the immodest implication that humans are better at thinking than other species and the inaccurate implication that males are somehow more significant than females). What you may not fully appreciate as you see and hear this scientific name bandied about is that it is not just a fancy alternative to the word 'human'. Rather, its use implies acceptance of all sorts of knowledge about how the human species relates to other species, knowledge that may be commonplace to our generation, but which would have been (quite literally) unthinkable in earlier times.

Consider someone who decides to take up birdwatching as a hobby. They would not, of course, be starting from scratch. Several distinctive species (e.g. the robin), as well as some distinctive categories of birds (e.g. wildfowl and gulls), would already be familiar. However, the novice would soon be able to distinguish between far more species and also classify many more species into groups that are widely accepted as 'natural'. For instance, they would learn to distinguish between blue tits, great tits and coal tits and also realise that tits form a group (or family) of species distinct from other groups such as finches (Figure 3.1a), sparrows (Figure 3.1b) and warblers (Figure 3.1c and d). With perseverance, the birdwatcher will develop the knowledge and skills needed to distinguish (often instantly) between the 300 or so bird species regularly found in the British Isles, sometimes on the basis of extremely subtle differences in their plumage or call.

Is it possible, however, that agreement about what constitutes a particular bird species, or which species form 'natural' groups (families), exists only because of uncritical acceptance of the published opinions of 'experts'? An expedition to the Arfak Mountains of New Guinea in 1928 by the American biologist Ernst Mayr (1904–2005) provided an opportunity to test this possibility. Before setting out, Mayr studied the relevant bird collections in European museums. When he arrived in New Guinea, he hired local hunters to collect specimens of all the different birds they knew of in the region. Mayr found that the Arfak hunters recognised 136 distinct types of bird. The match between these types and the species recognised by European biologists on the basis of museum specimens was almost perfect. In fact, the Arfak hunters lumped together just one pair of very similar species. The very high level of agreement between two such different cultures strongly suggests that our division of organisms into distinct species is a true reflection of the natural world.

Of course, birds are a rather conspicuous, well-studied group of species. Moreover, only about 9000 species of bird have been described in total, of which about 500 have been seen in the British Isles at some time. Many other groups are far less familiar, and some of these are known to include *many* species (e.g. almost a million species of insect have been described). It is hardly surprising, therefore, that while all known bird species have a common name (in English and several other languages) that can easily be looked up, this is *not* true of the majority of species.

■ Why does *every* known species not have a common name in, for example, English?

☐ Inevitably, many species will be much more familiar to people who live in countries where English is not the main language. These species may, therefore, have been given common names in other languages. However, it is hardly a practical proposition to give a million insect species, many of which are rather inconspicuous, different common names in *any* everyday language.

■ What advantages are there in *every* fully described species (i.e. even those that *do* have common names) having a unique label that is used by scientists throughout the world?

☐ Referring to a species by a single label accepted throughout the world is *essential* for scientific communication. If biologists in different countries referred to a species only by its common name in their own language, biologists elsewhere would not know whether the species was the same as one they were studying.

Incidentally, the problem of a species having different common names can apply even within a single language and/or country. For instance, *Galium aparine*, a common British plant widely known as either cleavers or goosegrass, has at least 20 other common names.

Another advantage of species having unique scientific names is that sometimes the same common name is used to describe different species in different parts of the world. You might think that the 'Christmas card' robin (*Erithacus rubecula*) is sufficiently familiar and distinctive to be referred to safely by its common name. However, when North Americans use the word 'robin', they usually mean *Turdus migratorius*, a much larger thrush that also happens to have a reddish breast.

## 3.3    Classifying species

So far the focus has been on the division of organisms into species. You will now move on to look at the classification of species into larger groups (e.g. bird species into families).

An important reason for classifying species is to help in the sorting of the vast number of different species known to exist. While there may be a few people who can identify all 9000 or so known bird species, there is surely no one who can do this for the one million or more known species of insect. In order to systematically record all the information known about (say) insects, and efficiently retrieve that information when needed, insects have to be classified into a succession of categories between insects (a group of a million species) at one end of the spectrum and individual species (a million single-species groups) at the other.

Classifying anything (whether birds, insects, volcanoes or library books) depends on recognising similarities between individuals to enable them to be grouped together, and differences to enable one group to be distinguished from another. There are, of course, many ways in which species could be classified. For instance, you could distinguish between species that (at least some) humans consider edible and those considered inedible. Alternatively, you could for example group together species generally regarded as pests, those known to be poisonous or sources of medicine, and those that make good pets. The basis of such classifications is how useful (or otherwise) the species are to humans, but they do not tell us much about what the organisms are like. However, there is a much more fundamental basis for classifying species, which is that species do seem to cluster into 'natural' groups.

Most people would be in agreement about certain 'natural' groupings of species. For example, birds are obviously distinct from mammals, fishes and insects. All birds share a number of major characters (e.g. they all have feathers and beaks) that are distinct from the characters of any other group (mammals, fishes and insects do not have feathers and beaks). Among birds, more specific characters allow smaller groupings to be distinguished, such as waterfowl, birds of prey and songbirds. Among songbirds, tits are distinct from finches, warblers, sparrows, etc. Certainly the broadest of these 'natural' groupings of species has been recognised since at least the time of the ancient Greeks, while a 'natural' classification had been worked out in considerable detail by early in the 19th century. Indeed, thousands of species were fitted into a 'natural' classification, still largely accepted by biologists today, before people knew *why* there were 'natural' links between species. The process now known to be responsible for species falling into such 'natural' groups is evolution.

During the course of evolution, a group of ancestral vertebrate animals (i.e. animals with backbones) gave rise to several distinct subgroups of vertebrates (e.g. birds and mammals). Each of these gave rise to further subgroups (e.g. ancestral birds evolved into waterfowl, birds of prey, songbirds, etc.), which gave rise to further subgroups (e.g. ancestral songbirds evolved into tits, finches, sparrows, etc.), and so on until the level of the individual modern species was reached, e.g. the blue tit (Figure 3.4). In their 'natural' classification of living (and, indeed, extinct) species, biologists aim to reflect this 'top down' splitting of groups of organisms into ever smaller groups and, in so doing, to trace the course of evolution. Figure 3.5 shows the blue tit species 'nested' into successively larger groups of organisms (i.e. tit species, songbird species, bird species and vertebrate species).

You may be wondering why, after emphasising the importance of scientific names, both common and scientific names are still being used here. This is primarily because by launching straight into a complete use of scientific names many of you would be completely unfamiliar with the groups of organisms. Instead, the use of scientific names is phased in so that you can follow the thread of the argument.

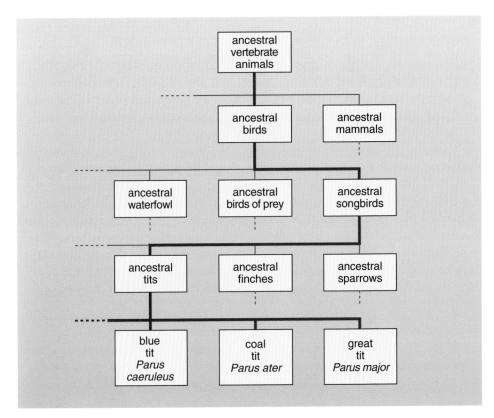

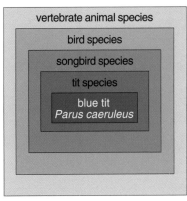

**Figure 3.5**  Diagram showing how the blue tit fits into successively larger groups of vertebrate species.

**Figure 3.4**  Schematic diagram to show how a group of ancestral vertebrate animals gave rise successively to several distinct subgroups of vertebrates during the course of evolution.

In this regard you should note that 'songbirds' (which includes the warblers and the tits) are not the only birds that make calls. Thus, the common name 'songbird' is misleading, which is why the scientific name Passeriformes (also known as passerines), used to cover all 'songbirds', is preferable.

■ All blue tits are very similar to one another, which is one of two main reasons why they are recognised as a particular species. What is the other main reason?

☐ Blue tits breed with one another to produce more blue tits, but they do not breed with other species.

Blue tits also share many features with other species of tit. If they did not, we would not recognise the category 'tit'. Note that this similarity is reflected in them being placed in the same genus (*Parus*, Figure 3.4). However, a blue tit has fewer features in common with a coal tit or a great tit than it does with other blue tits. Similarly, tit species have fewer features in common with other songbird species than they do with one another; songbird species have fewer features in common with other types of bird species than they do with one another, and so on.

■ Why do the members of successively larger, and therefore more inclusive, groups necessarily have fewer and fewer features in common?

□ Because they are ever more distantly related to one another, their common ancestor having lived that much longer ago. For example, first cousins (who share the same grandparents but have different parents) are likely to possess fewer characters in common than brothers and sisters (who share the same parents).

Importantly, while the number of features shared decreases as you move up the classification hierarchy, the features that are shared become increasingly more fundamental to the recognition of what constitutes a 'bird'. A blue tit is recognised as a blue tit because it has a particular blue and yellow colouring, but it is recognised as a bird because of its more fundamental characteristics. If you were asked to classify a blue tit, an owl and a blue and yellow fish, you would have no hesitation in grouping the blue tit and the owl together on the basis of their shared fundamental characters of beaks and feathers (among other things).

Pioneer biologists were able to fit species into a 'natural' system of classification because they recognised patterns in the way species shared some features and not others. Only some time later was it realised that most of these patterns exist as a direct consequence of the evolutionary relationships between species. Each species had descended from a line of ancestral species, some of which gave rise to many descendant species, which therefore tend to have features in common.

The study of classification has been revolutionised by the application of molecular techniques and the use of statistical models to determine the likelihood of any one evolutionary tree. These trees are often referred to as **phylogenetic trees** or simply **phylogenies** (singular phylogeny) and this terminology is used here. The branching structure of the phylogenetic tree indicates the probable splitting of an ancestral group into two or more descendant groups. The evolutionary relationships of many species are now determined by similarity in sections of their molecules rather than their similarity in terms of physical structure. This has helped to resolve many important controversies, such as showing that chimpanzees are the nearest living relatives of humans (Figure 3.6). An important guiding principle is that of **parsimony**. Essentially this means finding the simplest possible explanation of how the evolutionary tree is constructed. (The principle of parsimony, seeking the simplest explanation, has a general application across all branches of scientific study. However, it is also true to say that the simplest explanation is not always the correct one.) The statistical analysis also allows the likelihood of whether a given group of end points (e.g. species) have the same or different common ancestors to be determined. All the species that are derived from the same common ancestor are said to belong to the same **clade** and to be **monophyletic**.

■ Do humans and chimpanzees comprise a clade?

□ Yes, because they have a single origin as indicated by point A in Figure 3.6.

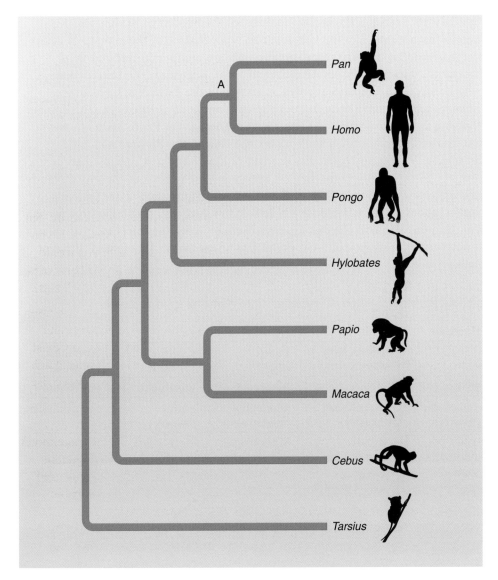

**Figure 3.6**    Phylogeny of humans (*Homo*), chimpanzees (*Pan*) and other primates.

Having considered the basis of a 'natural' or an evolutionary classification of species, you will now take a brief look at the classification scheme itself. At the very broadest level, organisms are grouped into three **domains**:

- Archaea
- Bacteria
- Eukarya.

These domains reflect the type of **cell** from which the species is constructed. The structural detail of cells, which are the building blocks of all organisms, is described in Chapter 4. Two of the domains – the **Archaea** (pronounced 'are-key-ah') and the **Bacteria** – include all the **Prokarya**, which are organisms composed of the simplest cell types that exist; these types of cells are referred to as **prokaryotes** (prokaryotes are commonly referred to as 'bacteria', which combines Archaea and 'true' Bacteria). The third domain, which includes all the **eukaryotes**, is known as the **Eukarya**. Cells of the Eukarya are fundamentally more complex than those of Prokarya. The domain Eukarya is further subdivided into four **kingdoms**: the **Protoctista** (formerly, but less accurately, known as Protista), the **Fungi**, the **Plantae** and the **Animalia**. Within any particular domain or kingdom most species share just a few key features; otherwise they are rather diverse (i.e. most are only distantly related to one another). Much of the following information about domains and kingdoms is summarised in Table 3.1, to which you might like to refer as you read on. You will see that the classification refers to unicellular organisms (composed of just one cell) and multicellular organisms (composed of many cells).

**Table 3.1** Summary of information about the classification of organisms into domains and kingdoms.

| Domain | Archaea | Bacteria | Eukarya | | | |
|---|---|---|---|---|---|---|
| Kingdom | | | Protoctista (protoctists) | Fungi (fungi) | Plantae (plants) | Animalia (animals) |
| Cell type | prokaryotic | prokaryotic | eukaryotic | eukaryotic | eukaryotic | eukaryotic |
| Number of cells | unicellular (mostly) | unicellular (mostly) | unicellular (mostly) | multicellular (mostly) | multicellular (mostly) | multicellular |
| Feeding method | some autotrophic, some heterotrophic | some autotrophic, some heterotrophic | some autotrophic, some heterotrophic | heterotrophic | autotrophic (almost all) | heterotrophic |

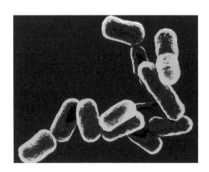

**Figure 3.7** *Escherichia coli*, a rod-shaped bacterium commonly found in the gut (magnification ×14 000). False colour has been added to the image to enhance the visibility of the bacterial cells.

All members of the domains Archaea and Bacteria are, by definition, prokaryotic and most of them are unicellular (Figure 3.7).

Prokaryotes are perhaps the most widely dispersed of all organisms, some being capable of living in even the most extreme of environments, such as hot volcanic springs and strong solutions of acid or salt (brine). Some prokaryotes are autotrophic and others are heterotrophic. Although some cause serious diseases in humans, including tuberculosis, leprosy and typhoid, we are also dependent on them because of the crucial part they play in the carbon cycle. They were the first living organisms to arise on Earth about 4 billion years ago, and they had it to themselves for about 2 billion years.

Members of the kingdom Protoctista (referred to informally as protoctists) are also mostly unicellular, although their cells are eukaryotic (Figure 3.8). Again, some are autotrophic and others are heterotrophic. Protoctists are responsible for many diseases in humans, including amoebic dysentery and malaria. Protoctists come in such a wide variety of forms that classifying them together in a single kingdom may say more about our lack of knowledge about them than about the evolutionary course they followed.

The final three kingdoms (which, of course, are referred to informally as fungi, plants and animals), include the vast majority of multicellular eukaryotic organisms. As such, they will be more familiar to you than the mostly unicellular organisms already discussed. While almost all multicellular organisms belong to one of these three kingdoms, some fungi and plants exist as both unicellular and multicellular types. Unfortunately, in biology there is usually an exception to every rule.

Question 3.1

Which two characters would allow you to distinguish fairly reliably between fungi, plants and animals? FOOD SOURCE, MOBILITY

In order to show how organisms are classified within kingdoms, the focus will be on the animal kingdom because it is the one with which you are likely to be most familiar. Similar principles apply in the case of other kingdoms, but generally speaking more detailed knowledge is required to appreciate the relevant distinctions. The classification scheme will be illustrated with two particularly familiar animals: the domestic cat (*Felis catus*) and the domestic dog (*Canis familiaris*). You will find it useful to refer to Figure 3.9 as you read on.

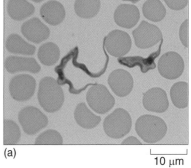
(a)　　　　10 μm

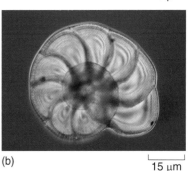
(b)　　　　15 μm

**Figure 3.8**   Examples of protoctists: (a) *Trypanosoma* (in human blood), which causes the disease 'sleeping sickness'; (b) a foraminiferan (*Operculina ammanoides*), shells of these organisms are an important constituent of some carbonate rocks (Book 6).

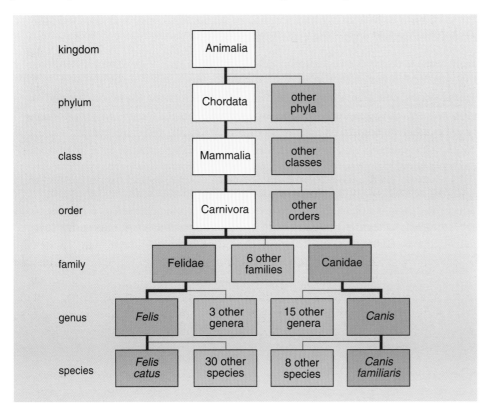

**Figure 3.9**   The scientific classification of the domestic cat (*Felis catus*) and the domestic dog (*Canis familiaris*).

The **phylum** (plural: phyla) (pronounced 'file-um' and 'file-ah', respectively) is the broadest division within a kingdom. Different phyla represent fundamentally different body plans. Almost 100 living phyla are recognised across the three domains. The animal kingdom is divided into 20–30 living phyla by most experts. It is an unfortunate fact of life that experts do not agree on the number of different phyla. The problem stems primarily from whether a particular body plan is regarded as 'fundamentally' different from other body plans or less than 'fundamentally' different. But it is exacerbated by the enormous range in the number of species encompassed by different phyla, however these are defined. With about one million living species, no biologist would hesitate to grant phylum status to the distinctive arthropods (i.e. animals with external skeletons and jointed legs, such as insects, spiders and lobsters). Other important animal phyla with many species are the molluscs (e.g. snails) and the chordates (mainly animals with backbones, such as ourselves). However, many biologists are reluctant to call even quite distinctive groups of animals separate phyla if they contain just a few species. As animals with backbones, domestic cats and dogs are classified together as members of the kingdom Animalia and of the phylum Chordata.

Each phylum is divided into a number of *classes*. Among the classes into which the chordates are subdivided are those into which fishes, amphibians, reptiles, birds and mammals are classified. Because they are warm-blooded, possess fur, give birth to live young and produce milk, domestic cats and dogs are still classified together within the class Mammalia.

Each class is divided into a number of *orders*. Cats and dogs remain classified together within the order Carnivora. Of course, the words 'carnivore' and 'carnivorous' describe a way of life. Most members of the Carnivora are indeed carnivorous, although the bamboo-eating giant panda (*Ailuropoda melanoleuca*) is yet another biological exception. On the other hand, there are many carnivorous animals that are not members of the mammalian order Carnivora, for example some members of the order Insectivora.

Each order is divided into a number of *families*. Within the order Carnivora, domestic cats and dogs are classified into two different families (the Felidae and the Canidae, respectively) which exist alongside six others (including the bear family, the Ursidae).

Finally, there are the two levels of classification that together form the basis of each species' binomial (or 'two part') scientific name, the **genus** (plural: genera) (pronounced 'jean-us' and 'jen-er-ah', respectively) and the species. *Felis* is one of four genera within the Felidae; the genus contains 31 species, including *Felis catus* and the wild cat (*Felis silvestris*). *Canis* is one of 16 genera within the Canidae, which contains nine species, including *Canis familiaris* and the wolf (*Canis lupus*).

## 3.4  The use of scientific labels for organisms

This section begins by considering some of the issues surrounding scientific labels for organisms. The main reason why every organism is given a scientific name is to facilitate international communication within the scientific community.

For example, a scientist might have carried out some research and published a paper with the title 'Beziehungen zwischen Hunden (*Canis familiaris*) und Katzen (*Felis catus*) im Rahmen vom Stadtmilieu'. Even if unable to read German, a scientist could immediately see that the paper concerned two particular animal species. If those species were relevant to the scientist's own work, translation of the paper's title and summary, and then perhaps the entire paper, could be arranged. But without the use of species' scientific names in this way, comparatively few scientists would realise the potential relevance of papers written in languages other than their own.

To help you become familiar with the use of organisms' scientific names, they are used in this book just as you might come across them in scientific papers. Where an organism has a widely used common name, its scientific name is usually given in parentheses the first time the species is referred to, but not used thereafter. Where several species belong to the same genus, the genus is often abbreviated after the first use to just its initial letter followed by a full stop, provided there is no ambiguity, e.g. 'the domestic horse (*Equus caballus*) and the donkey (*E. asinus*)'. If a species does not have a common name (e.g. the common gut bacterium, *Escherichia coli*), its scientific label has to be used throughout (abbreviated to *E. coli* after the first use). Where an author wants to refer to all the species in a genus (or does not want to distinguish between species), then the genus name is used by itself and never abbreviated to just its initial letter, e.g. the fly genus *Drosophila*.

Doubtless you will have noticed that the scientific names of genera (whether abbreviated or not) and species are always printed in *italics*. If possible (e.g. when using a computer), you should use italics for genera and species labels. If this is not possible (e.g. in handwriting), you should underline the labels. Thus, '*Felis catus*' and 'Felis catus' are equally acceptable; however, 'Felis catus' and 'Felis catus' should be avoided. Note that the names of genera always start with a capital letter, as do those of families, orders, classes, etc. However, the names of species never do, even when the species has been named after a person (e.g. Bonelli's warbler, *Phylloscopus bonelli*). It is surprising how often scientific names are used incorrectly in newspapers and magazines.

Finally, you may have noticed that gardeners use 'scientific-looking' names for plants. Beware! Sometimes the names used really are the species' scientific names – however, there are many exceptions. For instance, plants that gardeners call 'geraniums' belong to the genus *Pelargonium*; on the other hand, *Geranium* is the scientific name of the genus that includes bloody cranesbill (*G. sanguineum*).

## Question 3.2

Figure 3.10 shows how *Felis catus* can be 'nested' within successively broader, more inclusive, levels of classification. Produce a similar diagram for *Canis familiaris*.

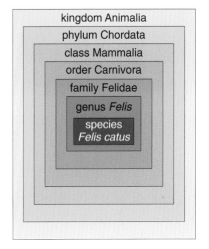

**Figure 3.10**   Diagram to show how *Felis catus* can be 'nested' within successively broader levels of classification.

## 3.5  Biodiversity

The word 'biodiversity' is widely used these days by biologists, the popular media and even politicians. It is, however, rarely defined clearly. Most commonly, **biodiversity** refers to the fact that the Earth contains a very large number of animal, plant and other species, and that these species are extremely diverse in size, appearance and behaviour. You will recall from Section 3.3 that the classification scheme was devised partly to help cope with biodiversity in this sense. Sometimes the word is also used to encompass the diversity of ecological systems.

Since biologists have been carefully documenting the Earth's living organisms for many years, it may well come as a surprise to you to learn that no one really knows how many species there are. The basic problem is that there are so many species on Earth that biologists have barely begun the task of documenting them. A secondary problem is that no central archive exists at present, so even the number of species that have been recorded and labelled has to be estimated. The current construction of the *Encyclopedia of Life* on the internet may go some way to solving this problem; this website aims to bring together all the available information into a freely accessible site.

According to the American biologist Edward O. Wilson in his book *The Diversity of Life* (1992), about 1 413 000 species have been fully described, labelled and classified. Of these, 73% are animals and 18% are plants. The total number of known species in 2007 is about 1.75 million. This is likely to be a major underestimate of the actual number of species; for example, the number of fungi species that have been described is likely to be less than 10% of the global number, which is estimated at 1.5 million. Within the animal kingdom, arthropods have by far the largest number of species (Table 3.2).

**Table 3.2**  Numbers of described species in the different animal phyla.

| Animal phylum | Number of described species |
| --- | --- |
| Arthropoda (e.g. insects) | 1 113 400 |
| Mollusca (e.g. snails) | 81 000 |
| Chordata (e.g. fishes, amphibians, reptiles, birds and mammals) | 59 800 |
| Platyhelminthes (e.g. tapeworms) | 12 200 |
| Nematoda (i.e. unsegmented worms) | 12 000 |
| Annelida (i.e. segmented worms) | 12 000 |
| Cnidaria and Ctenophora (e.g. jellyfish) | 9 000 |
| Echinodermata (e.g. starfish) | 6 100 |
| Porifera (e.g. sponges) | 5 000 |
| other phyla, each with relatively few species | 9 300 |

Within the arthropod phylum, the insect class is the largest and, within that class, the beetle order predominates (Table 3.3). No wonder the British biologist J. B. S. Haldane (1893–1964), on being asked what one could conclude as to the nature of the Creator from a study of creation, famously responded 'An inordinate fondness for beetles'. The first number given in Table 3.3 is the current (2007) number of species; the numbers in brackets are the estimates for the late

1990s. You can see how much knowledge of certain groups has increased in that time (it is assumed that evolution accounts for a relatively small proportion of the observed increase in numbers of species).

**Table 3.3** Numbers of described species within subgroups of the phylum Arthropoda in 2007. (Numbers in brackets are the numbers of species described in the late 1990s.)

| Arthropod class | Number of described species |
|---|---|
| class Insecta | 904 000 (751 000) |
| order Coleoptera (beetles) | 350 000 (290 000) |
| order Lepidoptera (butterflies, moths) | 142 000 (112 000) |
| order Hymenoptera (ants, bees, wasps) | 130 000 (103 000) |
| order Diptera (two-winged or true flies) | 120 000 (98 500) |
| orders Homoptera and Hemiptera (true bugs) | 80 000 (82 000) |
| other insect orders | 82 000 (65 500) |
| class Arachnida (e.g. spiders) | 73 400 |
| other arthropod classes | 50 000 |

Documenting the Earth's plants and animals is the fundamental activity of a branch of biology called *taxonomy*. The first taxonomist, the Swedish biologist Carolus Linnaeus (Figure 3.11), described 9000 species of animals and plants. Since then, knowledge of various groups of organisms has advanced at different rates. The two best-documented groups are birds and mammals, whose current totals are about 9000 and about 4000 species, respectively.

There are two major ways that new species are discovered. Some discoveries arise from exploration of parts of the world that have not previously been explored, revealing organisms that are quite new to science; for example, multitudes of small nematodes (unsegmented worms) have been found in previously unsampled oceanic sediments. Other new species are animals and plants that have been known for some time, but have not been differentiated from very similar species. For example, in 1996 the British pipistrelle bat (*Pipistrellus pipistrellus*) was divided, initially, on the basis of differences in the very high-frequency calls they use for navigation, into two distinct species (*P. pipistrellus* and *P. pygmaeus*). Many species are very similar to one another and can only be distinguished on the basis of detailed research, which takes a long time to complete. For birds and mammals discoveries of new species are now rare, but they continue to be made for less well-known groups such as insects. Thus, while it is estimated that the world inventory of bird species now increases by only about 0.05 species per year (i.e. one new species every 20 years) on average, those for insects, arachnids, fungi and nematodes are increasing at a much more substantial rate.

**Figure 3.11**   Carolus Linnaeus (1707–1778), as he is usually known (although originally called Carl Linné and later ennobled as Carl von Linné), was the first taxonomist. He described 9000 species of animals and plants in the tenth edition of his book *Systema Naturae* (1758). As well as cataloguing many species for the first time, Linnaeus also devised the system of classification and binomial labelling of species.

### 3.5.1   Estimating species numbers

While the number of species already documented and described is known with *reasonable* accuracy, the *total* number of living species can only be estimated. Such estimates are made using simple arguments based on the relative abundances of organisms already known and a variety of assumptions – the validity of which may be open to question. Thus, while the estimates are useful for getting an indication of the numbers involved, the results obtained should be treated with caution.

To take one example of such an estimate, the catalogues of known bird and mammal species indicate that for both these fairly completely described groups, there are twice as many species living in the tropics as in temperate regions of the Earth. In contrast, most insect species that have been described so far are from temperate regions. On the assumption that insects, like birds and mammals, are in reality twice as numerous in the tropics, it has been estimated that the Earth contains 3–5 million insect species.

■ For which groups of organisms do you suppose that estimates of species numbers are most likely, and least likely, to be accurate?

☐ The estimates are most likely to be accurate for birds and mammals. Since new species are only rarely described for these groups, it appears that most species have already been described (which is hardly surprising, given that most are fairly conspicuous). It is for groups like insects, arachnids and nematodes, in which the rates at which new species are still being discovered are relatively high, that there is greatest uncertainty about how many species there are altogether.

One technique used to estimate species numbers is to sample a new region of the world and determine the proportion of species in the sample that have already been described.

## Question 3.3

True bugs are members of two insect orders (Table 3.3). A study of these bugs in Indonesia revealed 1690 species, of which 63% were new to science. Assuming that the percentage of previously unknown bug species is similar throughout the world, use information from Table 3.3 to estimate the total number of bug species on Earth.

A study of beetles in Panama by the American biologist Terry Erwin used similar methods to estimate the total number of arthropod species living in the world's tropical forests. Erwin and his team blew a fog of fast-acting insecticide from ground level into the tops of individual trees at dawn when there was very little wind. For the next five hours they collected the 'rain' of dead and dying arthropods in funnels arranged beneath the trees. Finally, the specimens were sorted and sent to specialists for identification. Erwin found that 163 species of beetle lived exclusively in the crowns of one species of tree that he considered to be typical of the tropics.

■ Using Erwin's estimate that beetles represent about 40% of all described arthropods, roughly how many arthropod species inhabit only the crowns of this particular species of tree?

☐ $163 \times \dfrac{100\%}{40\%}$ or about 400 arthropod species.

■ Erwin reckoned that there are about $5 \times 10^4$ species of tropical tree. He also believed that most arthropod species are confined to a single tree species. Roughly how many species of arthropod live in the crowns of tropical trees?

☐ About $400 \times 5 \times 10^4$ species, i.e. about $2 \times 10^7$ arthropod species.

■ Finally, Erwin reckoned that about half as many arthropod species live on the ground as in the crowns of tropical trees. What would his total be for the number of arthropod species inhabiting tropical forests?

☐ About $10^7$ species live on the ground (half of $2 \times 10^7$ species), so the total number of species would be about $(2 \times 10^7) + 10^7$, i.e. $3 \times 10^7$ or 30 million arthropod species.

## Question 3.4

One of the problems of estimating species numbers in this sort of way is that quite a few assumptions have to be made. What do you consider to be the six most important assumptions made by Erwin?

Another method that has been used to estimate species numbers is based on the fact that organisms vary in body size and that larger organisms are less numerous than smaller ones. As a general rule, a tenfold reduction in body size between one group of species and another group usually means that the smaller species will be 100 times more numerous than the larger species. For obvious reasons, biologists probably know most of the world's larger species, so their numbers can be estimated quite accurately. From the number of large animals already documented, it has been estimated by this method that there is a total of $10^7$ species of land-dwelling animals. This is in marked contrast to Erwin's estimate.

It should now be clear that making estimates of the number of living species is a very imprecise process, which depends on assumptions that may or may not be true. It is thus not surprising that such estimates vary enormously.

## 3.5.2 Species turnover

Current popular and scientific interest in biodiversity has arisen primarily because biodiversity on Earth is seriously threatened. We live at a time when plant and animal species are becoming extinct at a very high rate, often as the direct or indirect result of human activities. However, the extinction of species is not a recent phenomenon. Extinction is an integral part of the evolutionary process and it has been occurring ever since life on Earth began to evolve. Nor can extinction be regarded as a rare or an unusual event; indeed, it is the fate of most species to become extinct and the vast majority that have ever existed are now extinct. The 30 million or so species alive today are believed to represent only a tiny fraction of the total number that have existed since life began on Earth.

Evolution is a process of change, in which new species are constantly appearing, and older species are disappearing. Thus, there has always been a turnover of species on Earth. However, the rate at which this turnover has occurred has not been constant over time; it has been much faster during certain periods of the Earth's history than during others. These periods of accelerated species turnover, called *mass extinctions*, are discussed in Book 6. In the view of many biologists, we are currently witnessing a mass extinction event caused by human activity in which the rate of species extinction is so high that it is likely to have a more profound effect on the Earth's biodiversity than *any* of the previous mass extinctions.

It is largely from the study of fossils that we know about life on Earth in the past, and hence can make some kind of estimate of former rates of species turnover. The fossil record contains an even more diverse range of organisms than the variety of living species. Some fossil remains are of species that bear little or no resemblance to living species, whereas others clearly resemble living species and may be their evolutionary ancestors. An important distinction must therefore be made between the true extinction of a species, representing the end of the line for that species (or even a whole group of species if it leaves no descendent species), and the gradual replacement over time of one species by a descendent species. Ammonites (Chapter 1, Figure 1.3) are an example of the end of the line, since they appear to have left no descendants when they became extinct 65 Ma ago. On the other hand, although the dinosaurs are usually thought of as having become extinct at the same time, this may not be strictly true, as living birds probably descended from a group of related reptiles. One of the features of the era of rapid extinction that we are currently witnessing is that the species that are becoming extinct are not leaving descendant species.

Attempts have been made to estimate the number of species in various groups of organisms that have inhabited the Earth, and thus to arrive at a figure for the average time for which individual species exist. Given the fact that there is considerable variation in estimates of the number of living species, it is not surprising that estimates of species longevities, from origin to extinction, are very vague indeed. For example, estimates of the number of bird species that have existed on Earth since the time of one of the earliest known fossil species, *Archaeopteryx*, about 125 Ma ago, range from $1.5 \times 10^5$ to $1.6 \times 10^6$. While these estimates are wildly different, both suggest that the 9000 or so species of birds estimated to be alive today represent only a very small proportion of the total number of species that have existed. From figures such as these, it has been estimated that the average longevity of a bird species is about half a million years. A similar figure has been estimated for mammals. However, average species longevities are believed to be much longer for most other animal groups. Why species turnover rates should be higher for birds and mammals than for other groups of animals is a question that biologists have not yet been able to answer.

### 3.5.3   Why does biodiversity matter?

Biodiversity on Earth is threatened because innumerable animal, plant and other species are being driven to extinction by the destruction of their natural habitats, hunting, pollution and a number of indirect effects of human activities. These processes are generated by the needs of a rapidly expanding human population for resources, primarily space in which to live and land on which to grow food.

These effects are exacerbated by the market-driven economies of the developed world, which exploit the whole world for the raw materials needed to make a wide range of products. Among the arguments that have been advanced against this overexploitation of the Earth's resources are those based on ethics, aesthetics, biology and economics. There are many who argue that the reduction of biodiversity will eventually threaten the continued existence of the human species. For example, deforestation is helping to alter the composition of the Earth's atmosphere (Book 1, Section 7.6), a process that, if not checked, threatens all forms of life. Pollution is causing a thinning of the ozone layer in the upper atmosphere, exposing the Earth's surface to increasing levels of ultraviolet radiation which is harmful to living things (Book 1, Section 4.3). Finally, humans are largely dependent on other living species as sources of food and medicines and we simply do not know what vital resources may be lost when species become extinct.

In Book 4, Chapter 16, you encountered the drug aspirin and studied the chemistry of drug action. Aspirin was first isolated from plant material; people over the centuries have found that extracts of willow bark help to ease aches and pains, and this example shows what an important resource other species of living things can be in our search for effective medicines. Many such medicines originate from plants and it is highly likely that there are many others. The information in Box 3.1 on medicinal plants, taken from the WWF (the global conservation organization) website, illustrates the importance of conserving biodiversity.

## Box 3.1  Medicinal plants

Why should you care about plants? Well, if you've ever had a headache, been ill, or had an operation you may well have used medicines that originated from plants. Plants have been the most important source of medicine throughout human history.

We already know of dozens of plants that are vital to modern western medicine, and there are thousands more used in traditional and herbal remedies. Below are a few examples.

| Plant | Medical use |
| --- | --- |
| rosy periwinkle | Chemical extracts enable four out of five children with leukaemia to recover. |
| foxglove | Extracts regulate the heartbeat of people with heart ailments. |
| Curare | Produces a muscle relaxant used in surgery. |
| white birch | Some tests have shown it may be effective in killing melanoma (skin cancer) cells. |
| velvet bean | Used in the treatment of Parkinson's disease. |
| Himalayan yew | Produces taxol, which is used to treat several forms of cancer. |
| willow | Extracts inspired the development of aspirin. |
| cinchona tree | Quinine is extracted from the bark and used to treat malaria. |
| wild yam | Extracts are modified to produce oestrogen, which is used in birth control pills. |

In the laboratory, scientists have been able to copy and manufacture some plant medicines such as aspirin, but in other cases such as the rosy periwinkle, this is not possible – which means the plant is the only source of the medicine. Some plant extracts, such as those from the wild yam, are modified by scientists to produce the final medicinal product.

Many of the chemicals used for medicines are produced by plants or bacteria as a defence mechanism against predators or disease. As all plants are potential food sources and can suffer from diseases, all plants are sources of biologically active chemicals which could be useful as medicines. New plant-derived medicines are most likely to be found in rainforests, as these areas are richest in plant diversity.

(WWF, June 2007)

It is important to note that many of the plants listed on the WWF website are not used in their natural plant form. However, this does not diminish their value. Without the knowledge of the structures of the plant chemicals, many of which have evolved as defence compounds, pharmaceutical companies would not have been able to manufacture the anaesthetics, pain-killers, anti-malarials and anti-cancer agents in use today.

### Activity 3.1   Biodiversity and conservation

We expect this activity will take you approximately 1 hour.

In this activity you will make use of the internet to search for information concerning one particular phylogenetic group. Here you will be concerned with the evolutionary relationships between the species in the group, the geographical spread of these species and their conservation status. For this activity you will be working online with other members of your tutor group.

Now go to Activity 3.1 on the course website.

There are no comments on this activity.

## 3.6   Summary of Chapter 3

While, in principle, species can be defined on the basis of their reproductive isolation from other species, in practice, species are more usually recognised on the basis of their physical (and sometimes behavioural) features.

Species are placed within a scheme of classification that biologists believe reflects the course of evolution.

At the broadest level of classification, species can be placed in one of three domains: the Archaea and Bacteria (both prokaryotes, which are mostly unicellular); and the Eukarya (unicellular or multicellular eukaryotes). The domain

Eukarya is further divided into four kingdoms: the Protoctista (protoctists – mostly unicellular eukaryotes); the Fungi (fungi – mostly multicellular, heterotrophic eukaryotes); the Plantae (plants – mostly multicellular, autotrophic eukaryotes); and the Animalia (animals – multicellular, heterotrophic eukaryotes).

The domains are divided into about 100 phyla.

An organism's binomial scientific label, which is important for international scientific communication, is a combination of its genus and species labels (e.g that for modern humans is *Homo sapiens*).

Biodiversity refers to the very large number of animal, plant and other species, and to their great diversity.

About 1.75 million species have been described but there may be the same number again that are either undescribed or are yet to be discovered.

The vast majority of species that have ever lived are now extinct, and only a few have left descendant species.

The average longevity of bird and mammal species may be about half a million years, but the average species longevity is probably much greater in most other animal groups.

Many biologists believe that, as a consequence of environmental impacts such as habitat destruction and pollution caused by humans, the current rate of species extinction is comparable with the highest rates detectable in the fossil record (i.e. during so-called mass extinctions).

The loss of biodiversity matters for ethical, aesthetic, biological and economic reasons.

Activity 3.1 gave you the opportunity to collaborate with fellow students online by researching and discussing a topical issue related to biodiversity and conservation.

# Chapter 4
# The cell: unity within diversity

Virtually all organisms are composed of cells; they are the basic unit of life. Some organisms can be single cells but others are composed of huge numbers of cells – they are **multicellular organisms**. It is difficult to give an exact figure for the number of cells in such an organism because there are usually too many to count. As a guide, though, it has been estimated that your brain alone contains somewhere in the region of $10^{10}$ cells. Whether an organism is composed of one cell or many, all cells have many fundamental characteristics in common. They are the smallest units of living things that show the three attributes of life: reproduction, growth and metabolism. At a fundamental level, cells have the individual capability to obtain energy from their environment; to use this energy to sustain life processes including the manufacture of new components for growth and to transmit information to offspring during reproduction.

The cell is an elegant and universal solution to a particular problem. The problem is that metabolism requires the intimate association between many different molecules; yet molecules have a tendency to drift about and become separated. Hence, the right molecules may be too far apart to interact with each other when needed. Metabolism – and thus life – would stop and start, depending on the proximity of particular molecules. The solution used by all organisms is to constrain the molecules needed for metabolism in small 'bags' made of sheet-like structures called membranes. Thus constrained, the molecules remain relatively close together. The small amount of living material in each 'bag', including its enclosing membrane, is called the cell.

Cells are found in an enormous variety of sizes and shapes; they can range from the smallest bacteria with a length of 2–10 μm (1 μm is $1 \times 10^{-6}$ m) to human cells typically with a diameter of 10–50 μm and plant cells, which are larger still, with typical diameters of 50–100 μm. But more startling is their sheer variety; in a multicellular organism, there are many types of cell, each suited to a wide variety of different functions within the organism. However, despite this variety, there is an underlying similarity between all cells; the cell, therefore, exemplifies unity within diversity. This chapter begins by considering the structure of cells, identifying the structural components that all cells have in common. It then investigates cell diversity, and looks at how the structure of cells is related to their function. The chapter continues with an examination of a hypothesis that provides a unifying concept to account for the evolutionary relationships of all types of cell. Finally, it takes a first look at cell division, explores how multicellular organisms can arise from a single cell and how organisms reproduce themselves.

## 4.1    Cell structure

You will begin your investigation of cell structure by considering basic cell types. Recall from Chapter 3 that 'cell type' was used as a basis for the classification of organisms into distinct domains. In fact, all cells are divided into two distinct groups on the basis of the location within the cell of their genetic material. This is the material that stores all the information necessary for reproduction, growth and metabolism and is copied from parent to offspring during reproduction. In fact, the genetic material is the molecule **deoxyribonucleic acid (DNA)**. You will return to look at DNA in detail in Chapter 10 but for the moment you are only concerned about its location in the cell. In some organisms, DNA is contained within a **nucleus** (plural nuclei); these are prominent structures found inside each cell. Organisms with nuclei are known as eukaryotes; their cells are known as *eukaryotic* cells and they belong to the domain Eukarya. Not all organisms have nuclei, however. Organisms that do not have nuclei, and whose DNA is therefore free within the cell, are known as prokaryotes (and their cells are described as *prokaryotic*). All prokaryotes are single-celled organisms.

■ Which two domains consist of organisms with prokaryotic cells?

□ Archaea and Bacteria.

While some eukaryotes also consist of single cells, others consist of many cells. Two of the most familiar types of eukaryotic cells are animal cells and plant cells. You will now examine each of these cell types in turn, beginning with animal cells. In Section 4.2, you will investigate the other important types of eukaryotic cells, the fungi and the protoctists.

Look at Figure 4.1, which shows views through a microscope of two 'slices', or sections, of material taken from different parts of the body of a mammal. Note that both are not only made up of many cells, but also have areas without cells. The presence of the scale bar will help you deduce the actual size of the individual cells. If you were to examine material from other parts of an animal, say from bone, brain or muscle, you would see that these too are composed of cells.

■ What features are common to the cells in both Figures 4.1a and b?

□ Each cell contains a round or ovoid, dark object. This is the nucleus of the cell. You will also notice in Figure 4.1 that each cell is separated from its immediate environment by a **cell membrane** and that this membrane encloses a grainy material (stained light pink in Figure 4.1) called the **cytoplasm** (pronounced 'sigh-toe-plaz-um').

Several key features that typify a eukaryotic cell have now been identified: each has an outer boundary cell membrane, which encloses the cytoplasm and the nucleus. These features are shown in diagrammatic form and labelled in Figure 4.2 to help you identify them.

Virtually all cells are too small to be seen by the unaided eye; although giant squids have nerve cells nearly 1 mm in diameter. Therefore, in order to visualise cells and examine their external form and internal details, they have to be enlarged, or magnified, using microscopes. There are two principal types of microscopy, which differ in the ways that images are viewed: light microscopy and electron microscopy.

In light microscopy, the object to be examined is illuminated by placing it in a beam of light. The beam of light passes through the object and then through a series of lenses, which magnify the object. The beam of light then reaches the eye of the observer; the magnified image is viewed directly by the eye. Using this

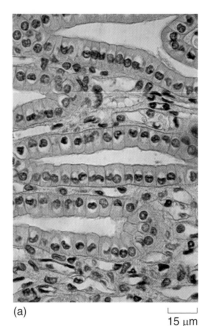
(a)                    15 μm

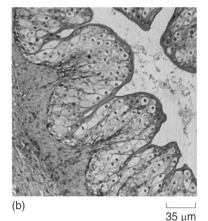
(b)                    35 μm

**Figure 4.1**   Sections of cells from (a) a kidney and (b) a ureter (the tube through which urine passes from the kidney to the bladder); both are from a mammal. Note that the colours are not the natural colours of the cells shown, but result from treatment of the cells with coloured stains.

technique, certain living cells can be examined: those of unicellular organisms and those from very thin sections of multicellular organisms. Whatever the source of the material, it has to be thin enough for light to pass through it. So, for example, you cannot examine the cells in your finger or from a large piece of a plant leaf by simply placing the finger or leaf under the microscope because light cannot travel through such material.

Most cells in their natural state are almost invisible under a light microscope. More detail can be seen by staining the cells with dyes, although this treatment immobilises and kills them. For example, a thin slice (called a section) can be cut from a plant leaf or a part of an animal, and this section can be treated with dyes that preferentially stain particular parts or features of the cell. The images in Figure 4.1 have been taken using a light microscope and are called *light micrographs*. The cells shown in Figure 4.1 are from thin sections that have been treated with a stain that specifically adds colour to cell nuclei. Only the large-scale structure of cells (i.e. their size and shape) can be observed in living cells examined by light microscopy, which can enlarge, or magnify, an image up to 1500 times. The scale bar on the photograph shows just how small the cells actually are; the kidney cells in Figure 4.1a are less than 15 μm wide.

Greater magnification is needed to study the detail of individual features within cells; this is achieved using electron microscopy. Objects can be enlarged up to a million times by an electron microscope – nearly 700 times greater than the maximum possible with a light microscope. Unfortunately, because of the need to dry and stain the material for examination by electron microscopy, only dead cells can be observed. In an electron microscope, a beam of electrons is fired at the object (rather than shining a beam of light through it, as in light microscopy). The electrons that are transmitted through the section, or reflected off its surface, are collected and viewed on a screen. Figure 4.3a is an electron microscope image (an *electron micrograph*) showing a section of an animal cell and parts of other cells that surround it. Electron micrographs can be difficult to

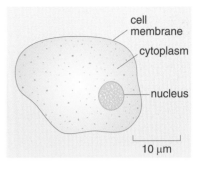

**Figure 4.2**   A generalised eukaryotic cell showing the cell membrane, the cytoplasm and the nucleus.

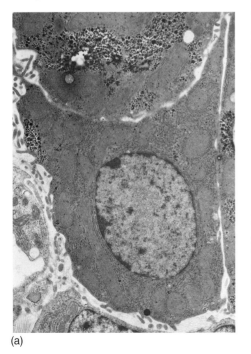

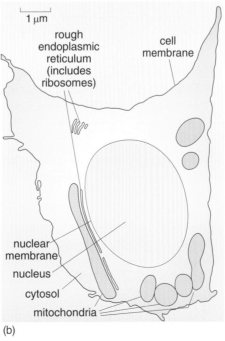

**Figure 4.3**   (a) An electron micrograph of part of a section of chick (*Gallus domesticus*) liver. One complete cell can be seen and parts of the adjacent cells are also visible. (b) Drawing of the cell in (a) with the key features identified.

interpret to the untrained eye, although if you compare this with Figure 4.1 you will appreciate how much more detail can be seen using electron microscopy – surface features of cells as well as internal structures can be identified.

To help you make sense of the electron micrograph, Figure 4.3b shows a drawing of the same cell as that in Figure 4.3a with the key features highlighted. It is important to realise that this shows just one section through a cell, so all that you are seeing is a two-dimensional slice of a three-dimensional object.

The cell membrane is an extremely thin, yet very complex, structure – notice how in Figure 4.3b it appears to be highly folded and convoluted. Its main function is to constrain the molecules involved in metabolism, thereby maintaining the right environment for the cell's metabolism. The membrane does this by restricting the movement of molecules from the inside of the cell to the outside, and vice versa. The latter restriction serves to protect the contents of the cell from harmful or unnecessary molecules.

Although most substances cannot cross the cell membrane, it is not a total barrier to the movement of substances. Rather than being *completely permeable* (which means allowing any substance to pass through), the cell membrane is **selectively permeable**, which means that it exerts some control over which substances can pass through it. Molecules of some substances (e.g. oxygen, carbon dioxide and water) move freely from one side of the cell membrane to the other by *diffusion*, which is simply the process by which molecules tend to move from areas where they are plentiful to areas where they are scarce. Sugars do not diffuse across the cell membrane. Instead, cells have special molecules in their membranes that assist in the process of moving sugar into and out of the cell. You will meet cell membranes again in Chapter 5 where there is a little more explanation about how the movement of some substances is restricted while others can cross the membrane easily.

The most prominent feature of the cell in Figure 4.3 is the nucleus, which contains the DNA, the genetic material. The nucleus, like the cell itself, is bounded by a membrane, the *nuclear membrane*. You know (from the presence of a nucleus) that this is a eukaryotic cell.

■ How many membranes separate the DNA of a eukaryote from the cell's surroundings?

☐ There are two membranes: the nuclear membrane separating the DNA from the cytoplasm and the cell membrane that encloses all the cell's contents, including the nucleus.

The nucleus is the largest of several membrane-bound cell components, called **organelles**. Outside the nucleus other organelles can be seen. The most prominent of these are the **mitochondria** (pronounced 'my-toe-kon-dree-a'; singular mitochondrion). These vary in size and shape, being either spherical or sausage-shaped, but in Figure 4.3 they are shown in section and appear mainly as circles. Not only do mitochondria have an outer membrane, but they also have a highly convoluted internal membrane. The mitochondrion is often described as the powerhouse of the cell. This is because it is within this organelle that energy is transferred to a form that can be used by the cell, as will be described in Chapter 6.

Another structure composed of membranes is identified in Figure 4.3b, namely **rough endoplasmic reticulum**. This is membrane material organised into sack-like or sheet-like structures. Rough endoplasmic reticulum has a granular appearance because of the attachment to its surface of many small, roughly spherical particles known as **ribosomes** (pronounced 'rye-bo-zome-s'). It is on the ribosomes that protein synthesis takes place. You will learn about this process in Chapter 11.

Membranes are key features of cell organelles and serve as partitions between different regions of the cell; thus a cell can be viewed as a series of separate but linked compartments. The partitioning enables some cell functions to be restricted to particular parts of the cell, as will be revealed when you examine cell metabolism in Chapter 6. Mitochondria and ribosomes are therefore two examples of cell compartmentation: energy metabolism within the mitochondria and protein synthesis on the ribosomes attached to the rough endoplasmic reticulum.

All the material outside the nucleus and contained within the cell membrane is the *cytoplasm*. It includes all the organelles, internal membranes and ribosomes. The gel-like liquid that remains when rough endoplasmic reticulum, mitochondria and all other subcellular structures have been removed is termed the **cytosol** (Figure 4.3b).

■ The scale bar in Figure 4.3b represents a length of 1 μm ($10^{-6}$ m). What is the approximate horizontal diameter of the nucleus shown in Figure 4.3a? Give your answer in both micrometres and metres.

☐ The nucleus is about three times wider than the scale bar, so it is about 3 μm, i.e. $3 \times 10^{-6}$ m, in diameter.

So far, we have looked at the principal features of a typical animal cell. Let us now consider a plant cell, as shown in Figure 4.4.

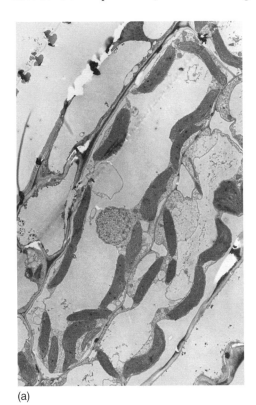

(a)

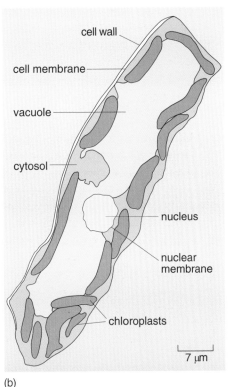

(b)

**Figure 4.4** (a) Electron micrograph of a section of part of a maize (*Zea mays*) leaf. (b) Drawing of one of the cells in (a) with the key features identified.

■ What features are common to both the animal cell in Figure 4.3 and the plant cell in Figure 4.4?

□ Cell membrane, cytosol, nucleus, and nuclear membrane. (Rough endoplasmic reticulum and mitochondria are also present in plant cells, but are not visible in Figure 4.4.)

Having identified the similarities between an animal and a plant cell, the two types of cell will now be contrasted.

■ Which of the features labelled on the drawing of the plant cell (Figure 4.4b) are absent from the animal cell in Figure 4.3b?

□ Cell wall, chloroplasts and vacuole.

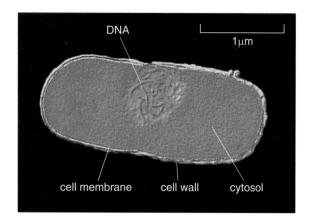

**Figure 4.5**   Electron micrograph of a section through a prokaryotic cell, the bacterium *E. coli*.

These three features are found in most plant cells. The rigid **cell wall** occurs just outside the cell membrane. It is made of fibres of cellulose (described in Book 4, Section 15.3) embedded in a gel-like matrix, and helps to maintain the shape of the cell. The **chloroplasts** are organelles that, like mitochondria, are bound by a membrane, but they also have complex internal membranes. These are the organelles where photosynthesis occurs, a process that is discussed in Chapter 6. Finally, occupying most of the cell volume, there is a **vacuole** filled with a watery solution and bounded by a membrane. The large permanent vacuole provides structural support for the cell; it also acts as a store for water, other small molecules and ions, as well as waste products. Vacuoles can also occur in animal cells, but here they are generally small and transitory.

The two types of cell considered so far are both eukaryotic cells. The third basic cell type is the prokaryotic cell shown in Figure 4.5.

■ What is the main feature that distinguishes the prokaryotic cell (Figure 4.5) from the eukaryotic cells shown in Figures 4.3 and 4.4?

□ The prokaryotic cell lacks a nucleus.

The prokaryotic cell also lacks membrane-bound organelles such as mitochondria and chloroplasts. So, inside the cell membrane there are no clearly defined structures. Ribosomes are present in the cytosol, but are not associated with rough endoplasmic reticulum.

■ How long is the cell shown in Figure 4.5?

□ About 2.5 μm.

Prokaryotic cells are generally smaller than eukaryotic ones. In the examples chosen here, the prokaryotic cell is even smaller than the animal cell nucleus.

■ What feature is common to the prokaryotic cell (Figure 4.5) and the plant cell (Figure 4.4), but absent from the animal cell (Figure 4.3)?

☐ A cell wall; both the plant cell and the prokaryotic cell are bound by a cell wall, but the animal cell is not.

As in plant cells, cell walls help to maintain the rigid shapes of prokaryotic cells, in contrast to animal cells which can readily change their shape.

Question 4.1

(a) Summarise and compare the basic features of animal cells, plant cells and prokaryotic cells by completing Table 4.1. For each of the cell features listed, indicate with a tick or a cross whether it is present or absent in each of the three cell types.

**Table 4.1** Comparison of three basic cell types.

| Cell feature | Cell type | | |
| --- | --- | --- | --- |
| | Animal | Plant | Prokaryote |
| cell membrane | | | |
| cell wall | | | |
| chloroplasts | | | |
| cytoplasm | | | |
| cytosol | | | |
| mitochondria | | | |
| nucleus | | | |
| nuclear membrane | | | |
| organelles | | | |
| ribosomes | | | |
| rough endoplasmic reticulum | | | |
| large vacuole | | | |

(b) Which of the three cell types, animal, plant or prokaryote, has the largest number of the cell features listed in Table 4.1?

Question 4.2

List six eukaryotic cell features that are composed of, or are bounded by, membranes.

## 4.2   Cell diversity: variations on a theme

Cells come in an immense variety of sizes and shapes. Having looked at the structural features that cells have in common, you will move on to consider how diverse they are and then explore diversity across the range of living organisms, in order of increasing complexity. You will begin with a very brief look at prokaryotic cells (members of the domain Bacteria) and will then look in turn at examples from the four kingdoms of the domain Eukarya: Protoctista, Fungi, Plantae and Animalia (Section 3.3). What is important here is the diversity of cell form, and the relationship between form and function in multicellular organisms. You are not expected to memorise the various cell features illustrated in Figures 4.7–4.10.

Before looking at true cells, a brief consideration of *viruses* is appropriate. Viruses cause many diseases of plants and animals. For example, the tobacco mosaic virus produces brown blotches on the leaves of tobacco plants and the pox virus causes cowpox in cattle. Viral damage to crop plants can result in loss of yield and the effects of viral disease on livestock can also have serious economic consequences. Familiar viral diseases of humans in the western world include the common cold, influenza, mumps and acquired immunodeficiency syndrome (AIDS).

Each virus particle consists of genetic material contained within a protein coat. Viruses are not free-living because they are incapable of independent reproduction or replication, and can reproduce only when inside a host cell. Outside of their host cells viruses are inert, capable of neither reproduction nor metabolism. Viruses are therefore not cells. These parasitic particles are small, significantly smaller than the smallest known cells (Figure 4.6).

**Figure 4.6**   Virus size and structure: (a) the size of a typical virus particle compared with a typical animal cell and its nucleus, and a typical bacterial cell; (b) an electron micrograph of influenza virus particles.

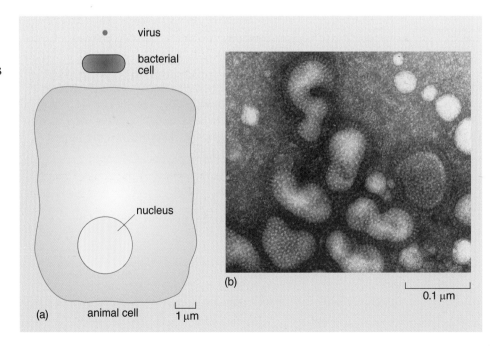

The simplest types of true cells are prokaryotic, from the domains Archaea and Bacteria. The term bacteria is used to encompass organisms from both these domains. Most bacteria are unicellular and usually spherical or rod-shaped (such as the one illustrated in Figure 4.5). Despite their apparently simple cellular structure, bacteria are incredibly successful at colonising any environment on Earth – from soil to acidic water near 100 °C to radioactive waste to the bodies of other organisms. They are the most ubiquitous of all organisms on the planet; you will return to an examination of their ancestry in Book 8 where you will consider how life might have begun on Earth.

You will now consider the more diverse eukaryote domain, beginning with protoctists. Cell diversity within protoctists is illustrated in Figure 4.7. The vast majority of organisms in this kingdom are unicellular (although some do have multicellular stages within their life cycle). Many of these can move and hence are described as *motile*. Some protoctist cells, such as that shown in Figure 4.7a, are covered in numerous small, hair-like structures termed cilia (pronounced 'silly-a'; singular: cilium). Others have one, or two, whip-like projections known as flagella (pronounced 'fla-jell-a'; singular: flagellum), which are longer than cilia; a unicellular protoctist with two flagella is shown in Figure 4.7b. This contrasts with the protoctist shown in Figure 4.7c, which moves by pushing out projections of cytoplasm. This capacity to change shape illustrates that some protoctist cells do not have cell walls. (In fact, this is true for the majority of protoctists.)

Cells of fungi are illustrated in Figure 4.8. A relatively small number of fungi are unicellular, such as the bakers' or brewers' yeast shown in Figure 4.8a. These cells can exist on their own, and as they grow and divide (by a process called *budding*) the new cells either remain loosely attached or become separated. Most fungi, though, are multicellular organisms, as shown in Figure 4.8b. In these fungi, different cell types with different functions occur in the same organism, i.e. the cells are *specialised*. Most fungi consist of long, thin filaments comprising large numbers of cells linked together. Most of the smaller cells shown in Figure 4.8a are reproductive structures, which will separate off, be dispersed, and begin their separate life cycles. A characteristic feature of the cells of most fungi is that, like prokaryote and plant cells, they have rigid cell walls.

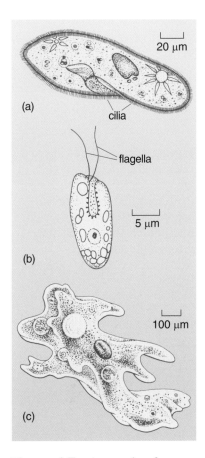

**Figure 4.7**   A sample of protoctists showing the range of cell shapes: (a) *Paramecium* sp.; (b) *Chilomonas* sp.; (c) *Amoeba* sp. (For these organisms the species has not been defined, hence the genus name is followed by sp., which is the abbreviation for species.)

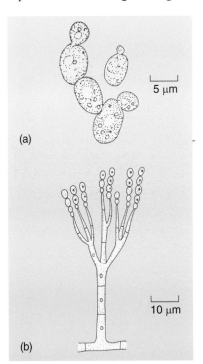

**Figure 4.8**   Cell shapes and organisation found in fungi: (a) a budding yeast (bakers' or brewers' yeast, *Saccharomyces cerevisiae*); (b) a filamentous fungus (*Penicillium* sp., which synthesises the antibiotic penicillin).

Members of the plant kingdom are principally complex, multicellular organisms. An individual plant contains a wide range of specialised cells, a few examples of which are illustrated in the section through a leaf shown in Figure 4.9. Two main cell types can be seen. The cells in the outer layers of the leaf (top and bottom of the section) are different from the cells inside the leaf. These outer cells have thickened cell walls; in fact, they have a waterproof outer coating that prevents

**Figure 4.9** (a) Drawing of the internal arrangement of cells in a beech leaf (*Fagus sylvatica*). (b) Beech leaf torn to reveal source of cells in (a). (c) Light micrograph showing section through the same leaf.

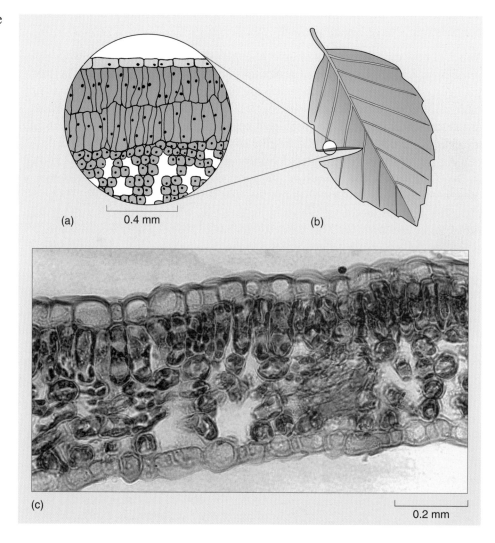

(a)    0.4 mm    (b)

(c)    0.2 mm

water loss from the plant. The cells on the inside of the leaf contain chloroplasts and carry out photosynthesis. The two main cell types shown in Figure 4.9a and c, therefore, have different roles, or functions. In contrast to the cells that make up leaves, the cells in plant stems are extremely long and narrow. This is consistent with their principal function, which is the transport of materials, such as water, ions and sugars, through the stem.

Finally, this review of cell diversity looks at the specialised cells of animals, a few of which are shown in Figure 4.10 – which should be sufficient to give you an idea of the diversity found in animals. Figure 4.10a shows red blood cells; these have the very regular appearance of concave disks. Their primary function is to transport oxygen around the body via the bloodstream. In contrast, muscle cells (Figure 4.10b) do not exist singly, but as with the liver cells in Figure 4.3, are part of a continuous structure made up of many cells of the same type, called a *tissue*. Muscle cells are long and thin and, since they can contract, the actions of these cells bring about movement. The cells in Figure 4.10c are from the lining of the windpipe, or trachea. The cilia on their surfaces move mucus up into the throat, thus preventing inhaled particles, which become trapped in the mucus, from reaching the lungs. Finally, Figure 4.10d shows two types of cell of markedly different shape and

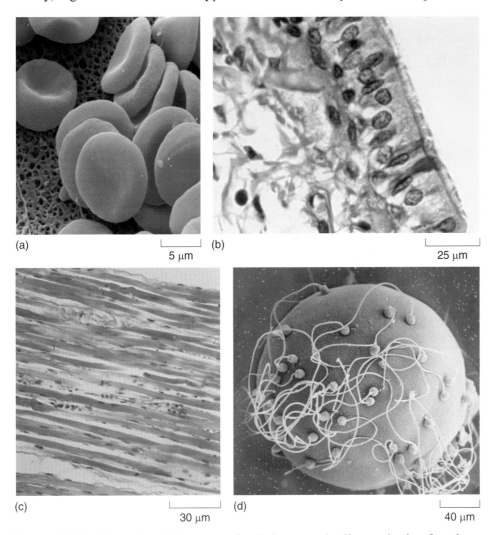

(a)     5 μm     (b)     25 μm

(c)     30 μm     (d)     40 μm

**Figure 4.10** Examples of the range of cell shapes and cell organisation found in animals: (a) human (*Homo sapiens*) red blood cells; (b) a section of the layer of ciliated cells lining the trachea (windpipe) of *R. norvegicus*; (c) a section of heart muscle cells from a rat (*Rattus norvegicus*); (d) a number of spermatozoa, each with a single flagellum, on the surface of an ovum from a mollusc (*Mya* sp.).

size: many sperm on the surface of an egg. Sperm and eggs are the specialised types of cells involved in reproduction and you will learn more detail about their role later in this chapter. Each sperm is a single cell with a flagellum that enables it to swim and so make contact with the egg (also a single cell). Note that the structure of each specialised type of cell is closely related to the function it carries out.

Despite this apparent diversity, all the types of cell illustrated have the same basic features that were elaborated in Section 4.1 – there is unity within diversity. Indeed, the unity of structure found at the level of organelles and other intracellular structures is echoed in the very molecules that make up cells. All cells are constructed of the same sorts of biochemical material and these chemicals of life are the subject of Chapter 5.

Question 4.3

Examine Figure 4.11, which shows a unicellular organism, and then answer the following questions.

**Figure 4.11**   An electron micrograph of a unicellular organism. For use with Question 4.3.

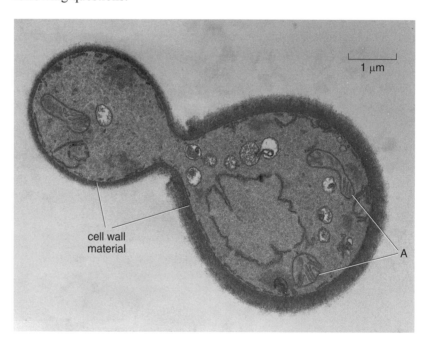

(a) Is this a prokaryotic or a eukaryotic cell? Justify your answer.

(b) Identify the structures labelled A, giving a reason for your answer. (You will find it helpful to compare these features with those shown in Figure 4.3.)

(c) Is this organism an animal, a bacterium, a fungus, a plant or a protoctist? Again, you should justify your answer. (This is not an easy question, so do not worry if you cannot come to a definite conclusion.)

## 4.3   The origin of eukaryotes: endosymbiosis

Even though there is a wide diversity of cell types, they all fall into two principal groups: prokaryotes and eukaryotes. In this section you will examine a hypothesis, proposed in the 1970s by the American biologist Lynn Margulis

(Figure 4.12), which provides a unifying concept to account for the evolutionary relationships of cells of all domains and kingdoms.

It is believed that the earliest eukaryotic cells had a nucleus, but no other organelles, and that mitochondria and chloroplasts were acquired later, by an interesting route. Margulis proposed that both types of organelle were originally free-living bacteria, which were engulfed by eukaryote 'host' cells. The association between the host cell and its bacterial 'lodgers' must have been mutually beneficial (with each partner performing a useful function for the other) and eventually the bacterial partners must have become completely integrated into, and dependent upon, the host cell. A useful term that describes this process is *endosymbiosis* ('endo-' meaning inside and 'symbiosis' meaning living together). The so-called **endosymbiotic hypothesis** provides a plausible explanation for the evolutionary origin of modern-day eukaryotic cells.

Figure 4.13 shows the proposed pathway for the evolution of eukaryotic cells from a universal ancestor. This ancestor gave rise to three different cellular lines (1–3) that represent the three domains. As you have already seen, there are two different prokaryote domains: the Bacteria (1) and the Archaea (2). Bacteria of the Archaea domain, like those of the Bacteria domain, are single celled with no internal membranes and only a single naked loop of DNA inside the cell. However, there are also many important differences that suggest the Archaea have more in common with eukaryotic cells: aspects of the chemistry of their protein synthesis is similar to that of eukaryotes and many of their cellular structures, such as the cell wall, are made from different substances to those used

**Figure 4.12**   Lynn Margulis, working at the University of Massachusetts, USA, suggested in 1970 that mitochondria and chloroplasts originally evolved as separate organisms – bacteria – which then merged with their host cells. Both these organelles have two important attributes that support Margulis's endosymbiotic hypothesis: they reproduce by dividing and they contain DNA. The hypothesis has since become widely accepted by the scientific community.

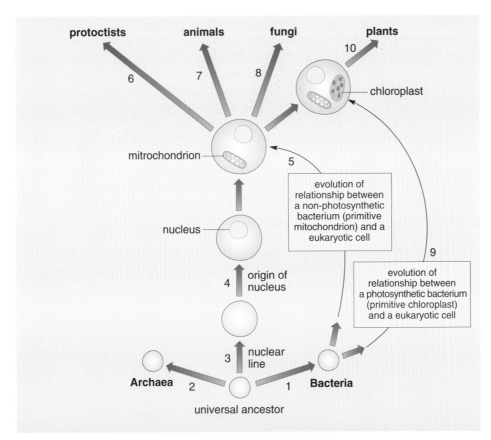

**Figure 4.13**   The origin of eukaryotic cells as accounted for by the endosymbiotic hypothesis.

in the Bacteria. The third major evolutionary line, the Eukarya domain, arising from the universal ancestor was the nuclear line (3), which gave rise to a primitive eukaryotic cell, i.e. one with a nucleus (event 4). Event 5 was the evolution of a relationship between a primitive eukaryotic cell and a non-photosynthetic bacterium (a primitive mitochondrion), giving a cell with a nucleus and a mitochondrion. From here protoctists (6), animals (7) and fungi (8) evolved.

Another major evolutionary route (9) involved a relationship between a relatively primitive eukaryotic cell (containing a nucleus and a mitochondrion) and a photosynthetic bacterium (a primitive chloroplast). This is the origin of a photosynthetic eukaryotic cell, from which further evolution (10) gave rise to plants.

There are many endosymbiotic relationships known to exist today; for example, unicellular green plants live inside the cells of coral (an animal). Evidence supporting the endosymbiotic hypothesis for the evolution of eukaryotes is the fact that mitochondria and chloroplasts still retain traces of their free-living ancestry in the form of genetic material (DNA) and ribosomes, both of which are similar to those found in modern bacteria. In addition, both mitochondria and chloroplasts reproduce by dividing.

## 4.4    The eukaryotic cell cycle

The cells in a multicellular organism all arise by cell division from a single cell, called the *zygote*. For now, the zygote can be defined very simply as 'the first cell of an organism' although this definition will be refined in due course. All the cells of a multicellular organism are descendants of the zygote and normally they all contain exactly the same genetic material. Recall that the genetic information of the cell consists of molecules of DNA which effectively store the genetic instructions for the functioning and development of the cell; it is vital that each progeny cell produced during cell division contains an exact copy of this full set of instructions. For an explanation of how this comes about, you need to consider the cell cycle.

The principles of the **cell cycle** are the same for all organisms, although there are subtle differences between prokaryotes and eukaryotes. For simplicity, only the eukaryotic cell cycle (Figure 4.14) will be considered here. The zygote grows until it is sufficiently large to undergo cell division, during which it divides to produce two **progeny cells**. The zygote itself effectively disappears, leaving only the two progeny cells. The two progeny cells now grow until they too are sufficiently large to divide, and then they each produce two progeny cells. The sequence progeny cell–growth–cell division (boxed in Figure 4.14) is repeated again and again. Figure 4.15 illustrates this sequence in an alternative way.

**Figure 4.14**   A sequence of cell divisions. Each cell produces two progeny cells when it divides. The letter A represents the start, and the letter B the end, of one cell cycle.

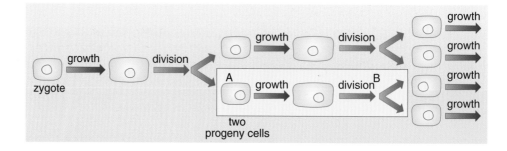

The cell cycle can take anything from a few hours to many weeks to complete. The rate at which a cell proceeds through the cycle depends on many factors, including the type of organism, the type of cell and its size, and the environment in which the cell is growing. There is also variation in the duration of cell division itself. For instance, cells in the roots of many plants take about 12 hours to divide, those in the gut of a mouse take about 17 hours and those in human skin take about 24 hours to divide.

It is important to appreciate that the cell cycle is continuous. Nevertheless, for convenience of explanation, it can be divided into four phases (Figure 4.16). The longest phase, and the one with the most variable duration, is when most of the cell's increase in size takes place. This phase, which is referred to as **growth I**, can be speeded up or slowed down quite considerably, depending upon the prevailing conditions, and so it has the greatest influence on how long the cell cycle takes to complete. In dormant organisms (e.g. plant seeds or the fungal spores you encountered in Activity 2.1), cells are usually held in this phase until conditions are suitable for them to grow. After growth I, the DNA molecules within the cell's nucleus are copied, during the **replication** phase, to produce two identical sets of DNA molecules. A second, shorter, growth phase, **growth II**, follows. These three phases, growth I, replication and growth II, are collectively referred to as **interphase**. The cycle finishes with **cell division**, which comprises two short, but crucial, episodes. In the first, called mitosis (which is considered in detail in Section 4.4.1), one copy of each DNA molecule is distributed to each end of the parent cell. In the second, the parent cell makes a new membrane across its middle and, in so doing, divides to create two progeny cells, each with a set of genetic material identical to that of the parent cell.

Within the nucleus, DNA molecules are attached to other molecules (mainly proteins) to form structures known as **chromosomes**. During interphase most DNA exists as very long, thin threads; this makes it very difficult to see chromosomes

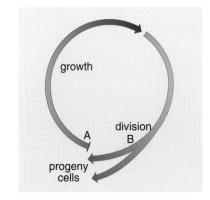

**Figure 4.15**  The cell cycle in outline. The letters A and B correspond to the same points in the cycle as shown in Figure 4.14.

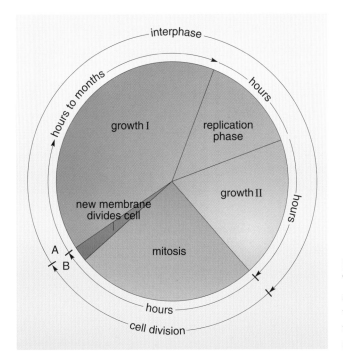

**Figure 4.16**  The eukaryotic cell cycle in detail. The duration given for each of the four phases is very approximate and varies according to the conditions in which the cell finds itself. The letters A and B correspond to the same points in the cycle shown in Figures 4.14 and 4.15.

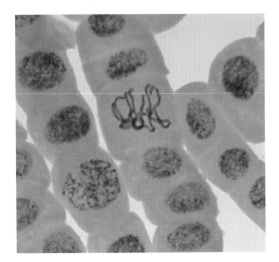

even through a microscope. During mitosis, however, the DNA becomes tightly coiled, which makes the chromosomes very much more conspicuous (Figure 4.17).

The number of chromosomes in a cell is characteristic of each type of organism. For example, a human cell has a set of 46 chromosomes, some of which are long and some of which are short. In any other cell from the same human (or another human of the same sex) there would also be a set of 46 chromosomes identical in size and shape to the first set. In humans, 44 chromosomes are matching twins, i.e. there are 22 pairs of chromosomes. These matching chromosomes are called **autosomes**. Eukaryotes, such as humans, in which the autosomes normally exist as pairs, are referred to as being **diploid**. The remaining two chromosomes, known as the **sex chromosomes** because they determine whether someone is male or female, do not always have a matching twin. Females do have a matching pair of X chromosomes, but males have one X and one Y chromosome that do not match.

**Figure 4.17**   Chromosomes are conspicuous during mitosis, particularly when special dyes are used to make them stand out from the background. This photograph shows chromosomes in a cell of the broad bean, *Vicia faba* (magnification ×2000).

Question 4.4

(a)  During growth phase I are there (i) more, (ii) fewer, (iii) about the same number or (iv) exactly the same number of chromosomes as molecules of DNA in the nucleus?

(b)  Is a DNA molecule (i) shorter, (ii) longer, (iii) about the same length or (iv) exactly the same length during mitosis as it is during interphase?

---

**Activity 4.1   Analysing and improving a description of the cell cycle**

We expect this activity will take you approximately 15 minutes.

A good way to improve your writing skills is to critically analyse someone else's writing, for both accuracy and clarity, and then to improve upon it. In this activity, you will do this with a description of the cell cycle.

Read the following short description of the cell cycle.

*The cell cycle, which takes different amounts of time, consists of growth and division. Growth takes place twice. These are called growth 1 and growth 2. There are also two parts to division. These are mitosis and cell division. Also there is replication in the middle of intophase.*

(a) List any inaccuracies contained in the description.

(b) Jot down any ways in which the description is less clear than it might be.

(c) Have a go at producing a better description of the cell cycle in about twice the number of words used in the original description.

Now look at the comments on this activity at the end of this book.

---

### 4.4.1   Mitosis

Each progeny cell must have a complete set of the parent cell's chromosomes so that each has a copy of all the organism's genetic information. The process by which this is achieved is known as **mitosis** (pronounced 'my-toe-sis'). For simplicity, mitosis is described here for a diploid cell with just four chromosomes (i.e. two pairs of matching chromosomes). However, the same principles would apply if there were 18, 46 or any other number of chromosomes in the cell.

Mitosis begins when the DNA molecules in the nucleus become tightly coiled or condensed, so making the chromosomes visible using a microscope. As each DNA molecule made a copy of itself during the replication phase of interphase (Figure 4.16), the four chromosomes consist of eight rather than four DNA molecules at this stage. Somewhere along its length, each DNA molecule is joined to its copy. This point of attachment is called the **centromere**, and its position is characteristic of each chromosome. In this state of attachment, each DNA molecule of a pair (plus its associated protein molecules) is called a **chromatid** (Figure 4.18).

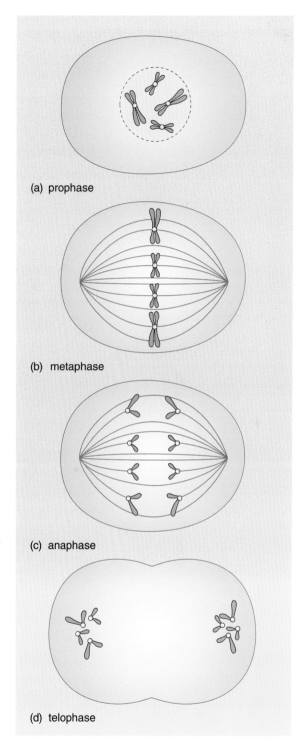

(a) prophase

(b) metaphase

■ For any particular autosomal chromatid, how many of the other chromatids in the same cell have exactly the same size and shape? (Look at Figure 4.19a.)

☐ Three, the one that is attached to it and the two that make up the chromosome's twin chromosome.

■ The common fruit-fly (*Drosophila melanogaster*), which is seen hovering around fruit in the summer months, has eight chromosomes. How many chromatids are there in one of its cells at the start of mitosis?

☐ At the start of mitosis, a fruit-fly cell has 16 chromatids.

(c) anaphase

Once started, mitosis is a continuous process. During the earliest phase of mitosis (known as **prophase**), the membrane that usually surrounds the chromosomes disappears, so that the cell no longer has a nucleus. The loss of the nuclear membrane is necessary to allow unrestrained movement of the four chromosomes within the cell; each chromosome now consists of a pair of identical chromatids joined together at the centromere (Figure 4.19a).

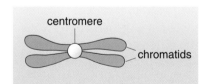

**Figure 4.18** Drawing of a chromosome to show the two chromatids joined at the centromere.

(d) telophase

**Figure 4.19** The phases of mitosis: (a) prophase: the four chromosomes each consist of two chromatids attached at a centromere; (b) metaphase: the four chromosomes are aligned across the centre of the cell with threads attached to their centromeres; (c) anaphase: the pairs of chromatids separate in each of the four chromosomes, giving rise to eight separate chromosomes that are drawn to opposite ends of the cell; (d) telophase: four chromosomes arrive at each end of the cell.

Delicate threads anchored at one or other end of the cell become attached to the centromeres. During the next phase (known as **metaphase**) these threads exert tension on the chromosomes, eventually aligning them across the middle of the cell (Figure 4.19b).

The chromatids then separate, so that each becomes a chromosome in its own right. One member of each former pair of chromatids is drawn to one end of the cell, while its partner is drawn to the other end. This phase of mitosis is known as **anaphase** (Figure 4.19c).

Once the chromosomes reach one or other end of the cell, the threads that were attached to them disappear. There is now a set of four chromosomes clustered at one end of the cell and an equivalent set of four chromosomes clustered at the other end (Figure 4.19d), a phase of mitosis known as **telophase**.

The DNA molecules then start to become uncoiled. At the same time, a nuclear membrane forms around each chromosome cluster so that the cell temporarily contains two nuclei. Mitosis has now finished but, to complete the cell cycle, the cell itself must divide in two.

The division of the cytoplasm between the two new progeny cells is achieved by the production of a new membrane exactly where the chromosomes aligned across the middle of the cell during metaphase. (The start of this process is visible in Figure 4.19d.) Once the new membrane divides the cell, cell division is complete; one cell has become two. These two cells are now in interphase.

Each of the two new cells contains an identical copy of the genetic material. However, each of the two new cells is half the size of the original cell just before mitosis began. A period of growth, during which the cells increase in size (i.e. the 'growth I' and 'growth II' phases of the cell cycle) and the DNA molecules replicate, is therefore required before the new cells can themselves undergo mitosis and cell division.

### Activity 4.2   Drawing a diagram of mitosis

We expect this activity will take you approximately 15 minutes.

In this activity you will draw a diagram to help you to remember what happens in the various phases of mitosis. The choice of type of diagram is left entirely up to you.

Since mitosis is an important concept, which you will need to remember in some detail, it is suggested that you close the book before beginning this activity. Draw a diagram that helps you to visualise the order of the different phases of mitosis and what occurs in each phase. Then look at the relevant pages of the book, amend your diagram to ensure that it is accurate, and add anything you think might be useful. Two possible diagrams are given in the comments at the end of this book. However, it does not matter if your diagram is very different, as long as it helps you.

What else could you do to help you remember the order in which the phases of mitosis occur?

Now look at the comments on this activity at the end of this book.

Question 4.5

How many chromosomes would you expect to see in a human cell during anaphase?

Question 4.6

Explain why each of the following statements is incorrect:

(a)  There are always two chromosomes in every diploid cell.

(b)  There are always two chromatids in every chromosome.

(c)  Each chromosome has its own nucleus.

(d)  Mitosis is part of interphase.

(e)  A cell with no nucleus must be prokaryotic.

As you know from Section 4.2, most multicellular organisms contain lots of different types of cells. All these many and varied cells originated from other cells by the process of mitosis and cell division. Figure 4.20a illustrates four of the few hundred different types of cell from the human body and Figure 4.20b shows the relative sizes of three human cells and a bacterial cell.

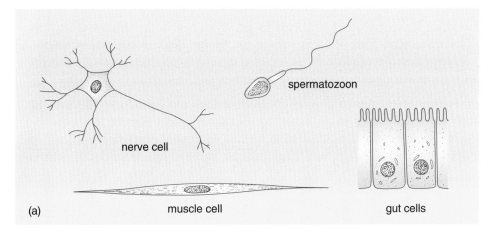
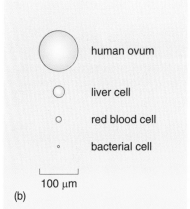

**Figure 4.20**  (a) Four different sorts of cell from the human body (not to scale). (b) Diagram to show the relative sizes of four different cells.

Your skin cells provide protection from the external environment, your nerve cells help you to sense your surroundings and your muscle cells enable you to move. The cells of multicellular organisms each do a few things very well; they are said to be *specialised*. When they become specialised, some types of cell lose the ability to divide. Red blood cells are very good at carrying oxygen around the body, but they cannot divide. Since red blood cells are continually being destroyed in large numbers, other cells have to do the dividing for them in order to replace the lost cells. The cells that specialise in dividing to produce red blood cells are found in the bone marrow.

All this specialisation raises the question, 'How is it achieved?' After all, since all the cells in a multicellular organism are all derived ultimately from the zygote. Mitotic cell division ensures that each cell contains exactly the same genetic information as that present in the zygote. But some of this information is about how to make skin cells, some of it is about how to make nerve cells, some of it is about how to make muscle cells, and so on. If a cell were to 'obey' all the instructions present in its DNA, it could not become specialised. Therefore, only some of the genetic information present in every one of an organism's cells is 'switched on' in any particular cell at any particular time.

### Activity 4.3    Mitosis, meiosis and recombination – Part I

We expect this part of the activity will take you approximately 30 minutes.

You will now have an opportunity to consolidate your understanding of the process of mitotic cell division by observing the sequence of events in living cells and an interactive animation of the process (DVD screens 1–5).

There are no comments for this part of the activity. In Section 8.5.2 you will return to this activity to study a second type of cell division, meiosis.

## 4.5    Reproduction

The ability to reproduce, the process by which all new organisms are created, is a fundamental attribute of living organisms. At the simplest level, many single-celled organisms reproduce by undergoing mitosis to produce two independent cells; for multicellular organisms reproduction is a little more complicated.

Essentially, there are two ways in which organisms can reproduce. They can do so alone, out of their own resources, by **asexual reproduction**, or they can do so with another organism of the same species, by **sexual reproduction**. Each of these ways has advantages and disadvantages, some of which are discussed here.

### 4.5.1    Asexual reproduction

When a cell divides by mitosis, it produces two identical progeny cells. Of crucial importance here is the fact that the DNA of each progeny cell is an identical copy of that of the parent cell. The two progeny cells, which contain identical DNA, are referred to as **clones**. In unicellular organisms (i.e. most prokaryotes and protoctists), these two progeny cells would be two new organisms. In multicellular organisms, cell division leads to growth; the organisms consist of more and more cells, and so get bigger. The point is that all the cells in multicellular organisms are clones of the original zygote. If some of those cells are used to produce a new organism, then that new organism is often referred to loosely as a 'clone' of the original organism. This section continues by looking at some examples of natural clones in plants and then considers artificial cloning procedures that are now used in animals.

Some multicellular organisms are able to direct cell division and so produce a new organism 'on the side' (often literally). This type of reproduction, in which an organism reproduces on its own, is known as asexual reproduction. Asexual reproduction is illustrated here with the strawberry plant, *Fragaria ananassa* (Figure 4.21).

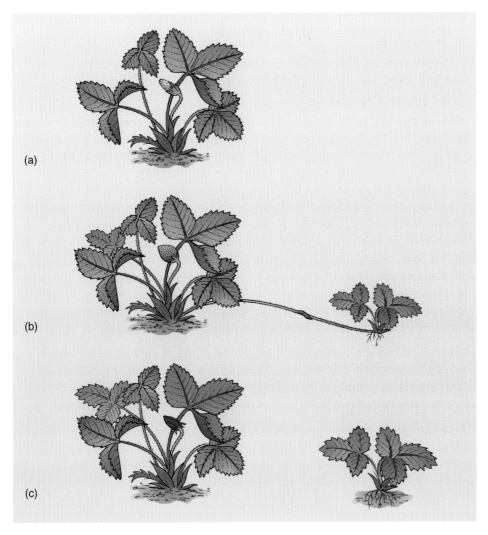

(a)

(b)

(c)

**Figure 4.21**  Asexual reproduction in the strawberry plant (*Fragaria ananassa*): (a) a mature parent plant; (b) the same parent plant showing a runner and a developing plant; (c) the runner has now disappeared, leaving the parent plant and the asexually produced offspring.

During asexual reproduction, the mature strawberry plant produces long, thin shoots called runners. The runners grow out from all sides of the plant keeping close to, but just above, the ground. When a runner is 5–10 cm long, leaves begin to form at its end (Figure 4.21b). These leaves will eventually be part of a new plant. The runner keeps growing away from the parent plant, but the longer it gets, the less able it is to keep the new leaves at its tip above the ground. So, when the runner is 10–15 cm long, it sags sufficiently for the tip to come into contact with the ground. When such contact is made, roots grow down into the soil. The roots and leaves at the tip of the runner are not a new plant yet, because they remain connected to the parent plant by the runner. However, once the roots have become established, the runner joining the parent to its offspring withers and breaks, leaving two separate plants (Figure 4.21c). The original plant has reproduced.

■   Is the new strawberry plant, formed at the end of a runner, a clone of the parent plant?

☐   The new strawberry plant is indeed a clone of the parent. The cells of the new plant arose by mitosis of cells in the parent plant and so contain identical DNA to that in the cells of the parent plant.

Many plants use asexual reproduction and some of these produce clones that cover vast areas. For instance, the bamboo forests of China (Figure 4.22) originate in this way.

Selective breeding of agricultural animals has been used over hundreds of years to improve yields of food products such as meat and milk. Animals with desirable traits are bred together to produce offspring that share the characteristics of each parent. This type of selection can be rather hit or miss and many of the animals produced do not live up to the breeders' expectations. More recently, scientists are investigating laboratory techniques to produce cloned mammals – so-called 'reproductive cloning'. Once again, the main driver is to improve livestock by producing large numbers of cloned agricultural animals from elite animals. In this case, only one 'parent' animal is required: an individual that possesses all the desirable characteristics of a specific breed. By using artificial cloning methods, the scientists can be sure that any offspring that are produced will be completely identical to their parent with no 'rogue' traits appearing in the next or subsequent generations – a common occurrence with selective breeding methods.

Dolly, the cloned sheep, was introduced to the world in February 1997. What made Dolly special is that she was cloned from another sheep. Scientists in Scotland took an ovum (i.e. an unfertilised egg) from a ewe (sheep 1) and discarded its nucleus (Figure 4.23).

At the same time, they extracted the nucleus from a cell taken from the udder of another ewe (sheep 2). They then inserted the nucleus from the udder cell of sheep 2 into the denucleated egg (nucleus removed) from sheep 1, thus

**Figure 4.22**   A species of bamboo (*Phyllostachys pubescens*). Bamboo is a kind of grass that reproduces in much the same way as the strawberry, except that bamboo runners are much thicker, run underground and each one can produce several new plants.

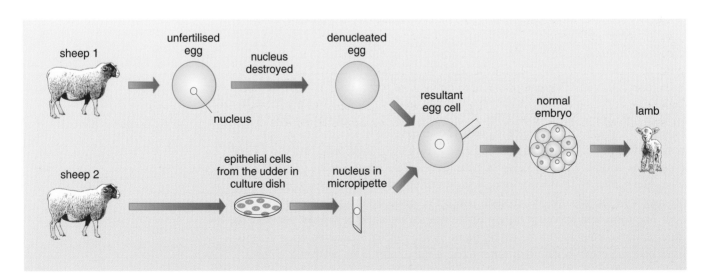

**Figure 4.23**   The cloning procedure used to produce Dolly. An unfertilised mature ovum is taken from sheep 1 and subjected to ultraviolet light to destroy the nucleus. The nucleus from an udder taken from sheep 2 is then injected into the ovum. The embryo is implanted into the uterus of sheep 3 and the result is Dolly.

producing the equivalent of a zygote. Floating in a liquid designed to support metabolism, this cell was allowed to undergo several mitotic divisions before the resulting cluster of cells (or *embryo*) was placed in the uterus of a third sheep, the surrogate mother. Five months later Dolly was born. Although the scientists attempted the process 277 times, Dolly was their first complete success.

■ Is Dolly best described as a clone of the donor of the ovum, a clone of the donor of the nucleus, or a clone of the surrogate mother?

☐ Dolly is best described as a clone of the donor of the nucleus. This is because all the DNA in the nuclei of all her cells is identical to the DNA in the donated nucleus as a consequence of repeated mitotic cell division.

However, a word of caution: while Dolly's nuclear DNA is certainly cloned from the donated nuclear DNA, the cytoplasm of the 'zygote' came from the ovum donor. Therefore, it was not truly a clone of either original cell. Moreover, as Dolly developed in a different environment to both these donors – in the uterus of the surrogate mother – she would not be expected to be completely identical to either.

Since Dolly's birth, scientists have sought to emulate the cloning procedure, in other animals as well as human embryos, and to improve its efficiency. It is still proving difficult, despite extensive modifications of the cloning technique, to produce large numbers of cloned animals and there is a cloud over the long-term health prospects of the few cloned animals that make it through gestation and birth. Dolly died in 2003 at the age of 6½ years, a relatively poor lifespan for a sheep of her breed. Her untimely death immediately provoked speculation that her premature ageing (she suffered from arthritis) was a consequence of the age of the cell she was cloned from; in other words, that she was 6 years old already 'at birth' as the egg that donated the nucleus was taken from a 6-year-old animal. Since Dolly's early demise several other species have been cloned but again the success rate is poor.

The jury is still out on whether cloning will deliver significant beneficial results in agriculture and attention is now focusing on the use of cloned embryos to produce genetically matched human cells in order to replace tissues lost to disease or injury: so-called 'therapeutic cloning'. In therapeutic cloning, an embryo is created specifically for the purpose of harvesting stem cells; these are the embryonic cells that can give rise to any sort of cell type in the human body. In Section 4.2, you learned how different cells in an organism ultimately take on specialised functions. Stem cells have yet to take on a specialised role in the developing embryo and if removed from the embryo they can be cultivated in the laboratory. Ultimately, stem cells may be implanted into individuals suffering from specific diseases such as muscular dystrophy (a muscle-wasting disease that results in insufficient muscle cells) or with injuries such as spinal cord damage in the hope that the embryo-derived cells will multiply and take on an appropriate specialised function. The nuclear transfer techniques pioneered in the production of Dolly are vitally important in the field of therapeutic cloning. In the latter the nucleus to be implanted into a denucleated ovum (usually taken from an egg donated by a woman undergoing *in vitro* fertilisation (IVF)) comes from the disease sufferer, the ultimate recipient of the stem cells. The embryo develops from the equivalent of a zygote and stem cells are harvested from it. The stem cells derived from the cloned embryos are genetically identical to the recipient of the stem cells. This is significant as the recipient's body would be likely to 'reject' any implanted cells with a different genetic make-up. This is a common problem for all transplanted human tissue and requires constant drug therapy to reduce the risk of rejection. Therapeutic cloning can therefore deliver a ready-made supply of cells to replace those lost to disease but the technique is not uncontroversial, not least because the created human embryo is always destroyed by the harvesting process.

Question 4.7

Describe what is meant by the term 'clone'.

## 4.5.2   Sexual reproduction

Sexual reproduction requires the involvement of two individual organisms belonging to the same species. Each produces special types of cell, called gametes, which fuse together to form a zygote from which the offspring grows (Section 4.4). This subsection begins by outlining the type of cell division that results in the production of gametes.

The only type of cell division that has been considered so far is that which involves mitosis.

■   What does mitosis ensure in terms of chromosomes?

☐   It ensures that each progeny cell contains chromosomes that are exact copies of those of the parent cell in every respect.

There is a second type of cell division, involving a process known as *meiosis* (pronounced 'my-oh-sis'), which ensures that each progeny cell contains exactly *half* the chromosomes of the parent cell.

■   In humans, how many chromosomes would there be in a progeny cell produced by meiosis?

☐   Since human cells normally contain 46 chromosomes, there should be 23 chromosomes in a progeny cell produced by meiosis.

In fact, the progeny cells do not contain just *any* 23 of the 46 original chromosomes. Recall that human cells are diploid, containing 22 pairs of autosomes and two sex chromosomes (Section 4.4). The progeny cells contain one member of each of the 22 pairs of autosomes plus one of the two sex chromosomes. In order to achieve this very precise outcome, the process of meiosis is rather more elaborate than that of mitosis. However, here you are concerned only with the results of meiosis; you will return to the details of the meiotic process in Chapter 8.

The cells produced by meiosis, which contain one sex chromosome and one member of each pair of autosomes, are said to be **haploid** rather than diploid. Some organisms (e.g. some fungi, algae and insects) spend a large part of their life cycle with all their cells in the haploid state. Other organisms (e.g. mammals) use haploid cells only for sexual reproduction. In such sexually reproducing organisms, haploid cells constitute an extremely special group because only haploid cells directly contribute DNA to the next generation. The haploid cells are called **ova** (singular *ovum*, sometimes called an egg) in female animals and **spermatozoa** (or sperm, for short; singular *spermatozoon*) in male animals. The equivalent terms in plants are *ovules* and *pollen grains*. Collectively, the haploid cells involved in reproduction are known as **gametes**.

Sexual reproduction requires that a sperm fuses with (or *fertilises*) an ovum. Although some animal species and many plant species are hermaphrodite (i.e. they produce both male and female gametes), the sperm and ova usually come from different individuals if fertilisation is to occur. Moreover, those two individuals must be of the same species. If they are not, then either fertilisation will not occur at all or the resulting hybrid offspring will have much reduced fertility (Section 3.1).

When a sperm fertilises an ovum, the result is a single cell called a **zygote** (this is a more accurate definition and replaces that given in Section 4.4). After fertilisation, the chromosomes present in the sperm and those present in the ovum are brought together in the zygote.

■ Is the zygote haploid or diploid?

☐ The zygote is diploid. The zygote contains a haploid set of chromosomes from the sperm and a haploid set from the ovum, making a diploid set of chromosomes in all.

The strawberry plant, which was used to illustrate asexual reproduction, also reproduces sexually. In sexual reproduction the plant produces flowers (Figure 4.24a), which are quite complex structures (Figure 4.24b). Some strawberry plants have flowers that produce both ovules and pollen grains. Others have only either female (i.e. ovule-producing) flowers or male (i.e. pollen-producing) flowers. Whatever the precise arrangement, fertilisation requires that a pollen grain from one flower gets to the ovule of another flower. The pollen is carried from one flower to another attached to the body of an insect (such as a bee). Even if a pollen grain gets carried to a flower of the same species, it may not fertilise an ovule. Only pollen that attaches to a particular small part of the flower, the stigma, will do so (Figure 4.24b). Soon after it arrives on a stigma, a pollen grain grows a tube down to the ovule. The pollen nucleus moves down

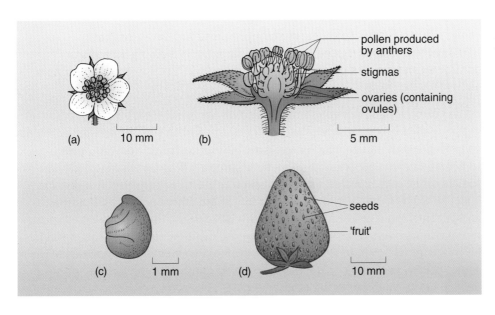

**Figure 4.24**   The strawberry plant: (a) the flower; (b) the flower cut in half and magnified to show the detail (the petals have been removed); (c) the seed; (d) seeds on the surface of the strawberry 'fruit'.

the tube to enter the ovule. The resulting zygote grows into a seed by repeated mitotic divisions. The seed of the strawberry is very small (Figure 4.24c) and is usually seen on the outside of the familiar 'fruit' (Figure 4.24d). The seed may eventually grow into a new individual plant, provided it encounters favourable conditions. The complete sexual reproduction cycle of the strawberry is shown in Figure 4.25. Most other flowering plants undergo sexual reproduction in a similar way.

**Figure 4.25**   The sexual reproduction cycle in the strawberry plant.

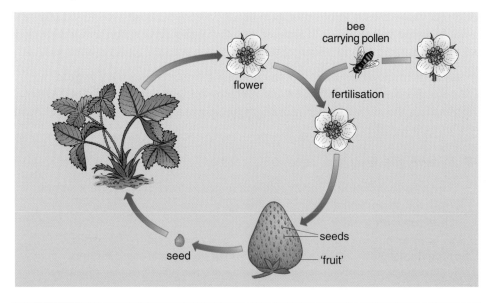

## Activity 4.4   Drawing a flow diagram

We expect this activity will take you approximately 15 minutes.

This activity asks you to draw a flow diagram showing, at the cellular level, the sequence of events in sexual reproduction described in the text.

As in Activity 4.2, it does not matter what sort of flow diagram you draw to show the sequence of events in sexual reproduction, provided that it helps you understand and remember. Start by looking back through Section 4.5, making notes if necessary. Then draw a diagram to show the order in which the different events in sexual reproduction occur.

Now look at the comments on this activity at the end of this book.

It is clear that, compared with asexual reproduction, sexual reproduction in plants is much more complex, involving specialised organs (i.e. flowers) and cells (i.e. ovules and pollen grains). It also involves the wasteful business of getting pollen from one flower to the stigma of another. For animals the problems of getting sperm into contact with ova are no less complex. Some animals (e.g. many fishes) use water to carry their gametes. When a male is near to a female of the same species, they squirt their respective sperm and ova into the water so that there is *external* fertilisation. On the other hand, most land-based animals, including insects, birds and mammals, require the male to squirt sperm into the female so that fertilisation is *internal*. Just how risky such mating can be is illustrated by spiders. Male spiders are usually smaller than females of the same species. In order to mate, the male has to climb onto the female, whereupon he is in grave danger of being eaten!

You have seen that sexual reproduction has a number of disadvantages over asexual reproduction. Yet sexual reproduction is used by many species. An important question taxing the minds of contemporary biologists is, 'What is so advantageous about sexual reproduction that so many organisms use it?' Although the answer remains unclear at present, there is likely to be great significance in the fact that DNA from two individuals is combined in the offspring to produce a different combination of chromosomes than in either parent.

### Question 4.8

Select *six* words from the following list and use each selected word *once* to correctly complete sentences (a) and (b).

meiosis, mitosis, haploid, diploid, spermatozoon, ovum, pollen, stigma, zygote

(a)  A male _____ fertilises a female _____ to produce
a _____  _____.

(b)  Gametes are _____ and are produced by cell division that
involves _____.

### Question 4.9

(a)  Why should the term 'zygote' not be used in connection with asexual reproduction?

(b)  Why is the zygote not a clone of the male contributing the sperm in sexual reproduction?

---

## Activity 4.5   Comparing and contrasting sexual and asexual reproduction

We expect this activity will take you approximately 15 minutes.

Draw up a table that compares and contrasts the characteristics of sexual and asexual reproduction. You should remember from Book 2, Activity 8.3 that if you compare and contrast two things you describe their similarities and their differences.

Do this activity without referring to the text and find out what you can initially remember. Start your table with the more obvious similarities and differences. However, do not forget to also include other features such as how the two types of reproduction differ at a cellular level. Indicate in your table, by use of different columns, those entries that indicate similarities between the two types of reproduction and those that indicate differences.

Now look at the comments on this activity at the end of this book.

---

### 4.5.3   Choosing between modes of reproduction

Some animal species are actually capable of both sexual and asexual modes of reproduction. The tiny, soft-bodied, pond-dwelling animal *Hydra* can reproduce asexually by budding. The cells on the trunk of *Hydra* sometimes divide in such a way as to form a bud on the side of the trunk (Figure 4.26). The bud grows out from the side of the parent animal until it becomes a small, but complete, version of the parent. Once fully formed, the offspring separates from the parent.

■ Is the new *Hydra*, formed by budding, a clone of the parent?

□ The new *Hydra* is indeed a clone of the parent. Its cells arose by mitosis of cells in the parent and so contain identical DNA to that in the cells of the parent animal.

**Figure 4.26** Asexual reproduction through budding in *Hydra* (magnification ×5).

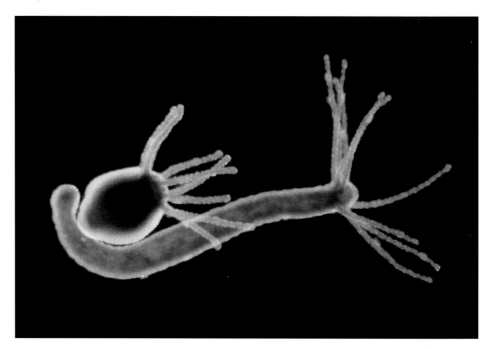

Alternatively, *Hydra* can reproduce sexually by developing large numbers of gametes (ova and sperm) and releasing them into the water. These gametes fuse with the gametes of other *Hydra* to form zygotes, which in time develop into new *Hydra*. What therefore influences which mode of reproduction *Hydra* uses? *Hydra* reproduce asexually or sexually depending on the environmental conditions experienced at the time. Figure 4.27 shows the life cycle of *Hydra*. Asexual reproduction occurs when environmental conditions are good. If conditions should deteriorate, for example the pond begins to dry up in summer, *Hydra* will reproduce sexually and the large numbers of zygotes produced will form into drought-resistant spores capable of withstanding the drought and ready to regenerate once conditions improve.

The advantage of asexual reproduction is that it allows the DNA of a successful organism to be passed on intact to its offspring. So when environmental conditions are stable, it makes sense to produce organisms that share the same characteristics as their parents. Once conditions change, it is worthwhile to divert resources to the production of gametes, increasing the probability that the offspring will differ from the parents (as a result of the combination of DNA from two individuals) and perhaps be more able to survive the deteriorating conditions. In the case of *Hydra*, two strategies assist the survival of the species in adverse conditions: firstly, the production of spores means that the species will survive the imminent threat of drying out; and secondly, the variation in the offspring, which is a consequence of combining DNA from two parents, will mean that there is a chance that some of the offspring will be better suited to survive in the new environmental conditions the offspring find themselves in.

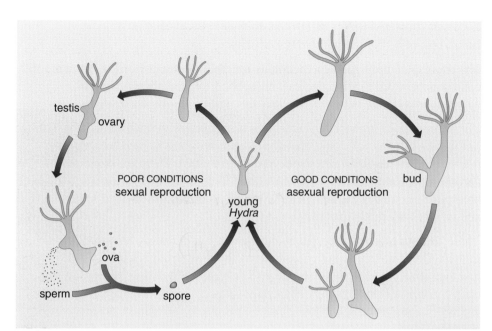

**Figure 4.27**  The life cycle of *Hydra*.

To illustrate how versatile some organisms can be with regard to reproduction, consider the spiny stick insect *Extatosoma tiaratum* (Figure 4.28). The female stores sperm from the male after mating which she uses to fertilise her ova. Eventually this sperm supply runs out and in the absence of further available males to mate with the female can resort to asexual reproduction. She then lays unfertilised eggs which develop into diploid progeny. Sexual reproduction may be best given the opportunity, but any type of reproduction is better than none!

## 4.6   Summary of Chapter 4

The cell is the smallest living unit capable of reproduction, growth and metabolism. All living organisms are composed of one or more cells, and are either prokaryotes or eukaryotes. At one time or another, all organisms exist as a single cell – the zygote. Some organisms remain as single cells throughout their lives. On the other hand, multicellular organisms are single-celled only as zygotes. Viruses are not cells, but can only reproduce inside a host cell.

**Figure 4.28**  The spiny stick insect (*Extatosoma tiaratum*), which is about 12 cm long.

The cell is surrounded by a cell membrane, which constrains the cytoplasm and is selectively permeable. Membrane-bound cell structures – chloroplasts, mitochondria and nuclei – are called organelles. A eukaryotic cell has a number of characteristic features, the most important of which are: a cell membrane, cytosol, mitochondria, a nucleus, nuclear membrane, and ribosomes present on rough endoplasmic reticulum. In addition to these features, a plant cell has a cell wall, chloroplasts and a large fluid-filled vacuole.

Prokaryotic cells differ from eukaryotic cells in that they lack organelles, so chloroplasts, mitochondria and nuclei are absent. Prokaryotic cells are bound by cell walls.

Each cell contains DNA. The DNA is enclosed in a nuclear membrane in eukaryotic cells, but not in prokaryotic cells.

The endosymbiotic hypothesis accounts for the evolutionary origin of eukaryotic cells; it is believed that the nucleus, mitochondrion and chloroplast had independent origins, but came together through symbiotic associations.

Chromosomes comprise DNA molecules associated with other molecules. During mitosis the DNA is fully coiled, enabling chromosomes to be seen under the microscope (particularly when special dyes are used). There are two types of chromosomes: autosomes, which are paired in diploid eukaryotic cells; and sex chromosomes, which are designated X and Y in humans (and other mammals) and may or may not be paired.

There are four phases to the cell cycle: growth I, replication, growth II and mitosis. DNA molecules are copied during the replication phase of the cell cycle and then shared equally between the two progeny cells during mitosis, so that each contains a complete copy of the DNA present in the original cell. Mitosis is a continuous process, but four phases – prophase, metaphase, anaphase and telophase – can be recognised.

Cells of living organisms exhibit a wide diversity of form, within which there is unity of structure in terms of the basic cell features. The cells in multicellular organisms are specialised to perform different functions. Specialisation results from each cell 'obeying' only some of the instructions contained in its DNA.

Asexual reproduction leads to the production of offspring whose chromosomes are identical to one another and to those of their parent; they are clones.

Present scientific research is focusing on novel techniques to produce cloned organisms (reproductive cloning) or cloned cells (therapeutic cloning).

In sexual reproduction, half the male parent's chromosomes are combined with half the female parent's chromosomes to produce offspring with a different combination of chromosomes.

Gametes (i.e. ova and sperm in animals; ovules and pollen grains in plants) are haploid, containing unpaired chromosomes. When gametes fuse at fertilisation, the resulting zygote is diploid and contains paired autosomes plus a sex chromosome from each parent (where sex is determined in this way, e.g. in humans).

Sexual reproduction is complex, wasteful and can be risky compared with asexual reproduction. There must therefore be some compensating advantage, probably related to DNA from two individuals being brought together in their offspring.

During your study of Chapter 4, you have been able to practise your science communication skills in several different ways. This has included analysing and rewriting a short description of the cell cycle (Activity 4.1), drawing a summary diagram to describe the complex process of mitosis (Activity 4.2), drawing a flow diagram to outline the sequence of events in sexual reproduction (Activity 4.4) and constructing a table to bring out the similarities and differences between two related processes – sexual and asexual reproduction (Activity 4.5).

# Chapter 5
# The chemistry of life: biological molecules

If the similarities in the cell structure of different organisms and different cell types are impressive, the similarities in cell chemistry and biochemistry are even more so. This underlying 'chemical unity' is hardly surprising, given the evolutionary relationships between cells as proposed by the endosymbiotic hypothesis (Section 4.3). All organisms are organised cellular assemblages of similar chemicals: they comprise both soluble and insoluble, organic and inorganic molecules and ions.

The description of cells in Chapter 4 was based mainly on observations of dead cellular material. But it is important to remember that living cells are complex 'molecular factories', with many different processes going on at once. So at a given moment, a cell may be replicating its genetic material (DNA) between cell divisions, building large molecules, taking in small molecules and ions from outside the cell membrane, breaking down complex molecules and creating new cell parts. Such activities require energy (which is released inside the cell, largely from sugars) and, directly or indirectly, involve metabolism – the sets of chemical reactions that take place inside cells.

Since the 19th century, organic chemists have been assiduously isolating and identifying the great range of molecules found inside cells. In more recent years, with the rapid growth of biochemistry, more and more information about cell metabolism has been revealed.

■ Bearing in mind that biochemical research is expensive, what reasons would you suggest, from your general knowledge, for large resources being made available for this kind of work?

☐ Biochemical knowledge lies at the heart of modern medicine and agriculture, and vast international industries depend on continuing research in biochemistry.

A living cell is composed of a restricted set of elements, four of which (carbon, hydrogen, nitrogen and oxygen) make up nearly 99% of its dry mass (i.e. the material that remains when all the water is removed). This composition differs markedly from the average composition of the Earth's crust and is evidence of a distinctive type of chemistry associated with life. Chapters 5 and 6 look at this special chemistry, beginning here in Chapter 5 with a description of the types of molecules found in living organisms – both within cells and in the surrounding extracellular space. As you learned in Chapter 4, structures have functions in the living world, and so this section may provide some answers to the question, 'How do the structures of molecules relate to their biological functions?'

## Activity 5.1    Revision: chemical compounds

We expect this activity will take you approximately 30 minutes.

This activity is designed to help you revise material from earlier in the course. Try to complete the activity before you check back to Book 4, Chapters 12, 14 and 15.

For each item in the list below, write a sentence that defines what the item is, and give an example.

carboxylic acid  *ORGANIC – CARBOXYL Group*  $-\overset{O}{\underset{O-H}{C}}$  *(COOH)*

amine  *ORGANIC – AMINO Group (—NH₂) : R – N⟨ᴴ⟨H*

amino acid  *ORGANIC : CARBOXYLIC + AMINO*

catalyst  *ACCELERATES A CHEMICAL REACTION*

enzyme  *ORGANIC CATALYST*

covalent bond  *STRONG BOND, ELECTRON SHARING (CH₄)*

condensation reaction  
*BETWEEN 2 DIFFERENT MONOMER. WATER CREATED.*

ester  *ORGANIC, ESTER Group  $-C\overset{=O}{\underset{O-}{}}$*

hydrolysis  
*OPPOSITE OF CONDENSATION. WATER CONSUMED.*

monomer  
*SMALL MOLECULE THAT FORMS A POLYMER.*

polymer  
*LARGE MOLECULE CHAIN FROM CONDENSATION REACTIONS.*

The comments on this activity at the end of this book include some hints about revising material you have already studied during the course in preparation for this book and for the final assessment of S104.

## 5.1    Substances of life

What are cells made of? This section gives an overview of the molecules found in cells. By far the greatest contributor to cell mass is water. Nearly all of the other molecules in a cell are compounds of carbon. As described in Book 4, carbon is outstanding among all the elements for its ability to form very large molecules in which carbon atoms are linked by strong covalent bonds to each other and to hydrogen, oxygen, nitrogen and phosphorus atoms.

Apart from water, proteins are the compounds present in mammalian cells in the largest proportion (Table 5.1), followed by lipids (fats and oils) and polysaccharides (pronounced 'polly-sack-a-rides', literally 'many sugars'). Nucleic acids are present in smaller proportions; you have already met one of these – DNA – as the genetic material (Section 4.1). Polysaccharides, nucleic acids and proteins are all biopolymers, that is, polymers synthesised by living organisms from small-molecule 'building blocks', or monomers. Although lipids share some of the features of biopolymers, they are not generally regarded as such, for most exist as large aggregates of individual, relatively small, lipid molecules. All biopolymers and lipids are synthesised inside the cell itself. Some biopolymers, such as the major components of wood and bone, are secreted by cells and are so tough that they last long after the cells that made them have died. The small proportion of organic molecules that remains free in solution inside the cell includes amino acids and sugars. Only about 1% of body cell mass comprises inorganic ions, e.g. calcium, sodium, potassium, magnesium, chloride and bicarbonate ions.

**Table 5.1**  Chemical composition of a typical mammalian cell.

| Compound | Mass as proportion of total/% |
| --- | --- |
| water | 70 |
| proteins | 18 |
| lipids (fatty substances) | 5 |
| polysaccharides (made of sugars) | 2 |
| nucleic acids | 1 |
| small organic molecules | 3 |
| inorganic ions | 1 |

A comparison between Table 5.1 and a table of nutritional information on a snack bar (Book 4, Figure 15.1) reveals remarkable similarities. As you will recall from Book 4, food products also contain proteins, lipids (fats) and polysaccharides (listed on food packets as 'carbohydrates', which also includes sugars). The food we eat – cereals, such as maize, wheat or oats, fruit, vegetables and meat – was once living material, and this similarity emphasises the uniformity between the chemical components of all organisms.

Through the remainder of this section each of the main chemicals of life will be considered in turn, beginning with the lipids and then moving onto the three classes of biopolymer: polysaccharides, nucleic acids and proteins. Some of this information will be familiar to you from Book 4, Chapter 15, and some activities are included to help you revise the functional group approach to food molecules taken there. By the end of this section, you should have a better understanding of the chemical components of living cells in addition to the role these chemicals play in foodstuffs. However, before beginning your exploration of biological chemicals, it is worth taking a moment to look at the properties of certain chemical groups in relation to their interaction with water. You will notice from the chemical composition of the typical mammalian cell that there is a lot of water about – cells are made of around 70% water. The cell is said to be an 'aqueous environment' and consequently the way in which water affects the chemicals that are found inside and make up cells is highly significant.

A particular biological molecule assumes a specific shape in the watery environment of the cytosol. To understand how this happens you need to look further at both the functional groups and other parts of the molecule. You will recall from Book 4 that functional groups are the parts of organic molecules that determine the chemical reactions they can undertake; apart from alkenes these are parts of the molecule that consist of elements other than just carbon and hydrogen. The remainder of the molecule merely consists of hydrocarbon chains of various sizes. Organic molecules can be divided into **hydrophilic** (water-loving) and **hydrophobic** (water-fearing) parts. Some biological molecules have only hydrophobic or hydrophilic parts within them although others may contain both types.

Parts of organic molecules with hydrophobic properties tend to be long hydrocarbon chains or benzene ring structures. Following on from the convention introduced in Book 4, these groups cannot be referred to as functional because they do not generally determine the chemical properties of the molecules that contain them; however, their presence does impact on other characteristic properties of the molecules in which they are present. Molecules such as lipids and oils, which contain only hydrophobic parts, will not interact with water molecules and so form large droplets or aggregates in a watery environment. These aggregates are held together by hydrophobic interactions between the hydrophobic parts on adjacent molecules. On the other hand, molecules with only hydrophilic groups, such as the functional groups amino ($NH_2$) and hydroxyl (OH), will interact freely with water, forming hydrogen bonds (Book 4, Section 4.2.3) with individual water molecules. Molecules such as sugars fall into this category and the presence of large numbers of OH groups mean that they can easily dissolve in water.

Complex biological molecules in the cell, such as proteins (Figure 5.1), often have hydrophobic and hydrophilic regions within them; such molecules automatically bend or fold up so that the hydrophobic parts become tucked away towards the interior of the molecule, out of contact with the water. Here they interact with one another, thereby strengthening the three-dimensional shape of the molecule. The hydrophilic groups are exposed on the surface of the molecule, forming hydrogen bonds with individual water molecules, further stabilising the structure. The hydrogen bonds formed between hydrophilic groups and water molecules and the hydrophobic interactions between adjacent hydrophobic

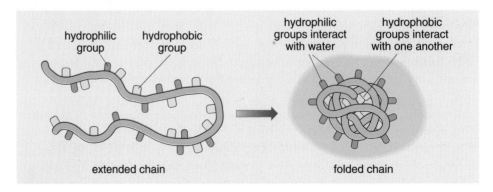

**Figure 5.1**   A biological molecule (in this case a globular protein) folding in water.

groups are both types of intermolecular interactions. These are typically weak interactions compared with the strong bonds that hold atoms together in molecules, but are vitally important in determining the shape biological molecules take up within living cells. The shapes of these molecules are essential for their correct functioning in the cell.

## 5.1.1 Lipids

**Lipids** are the fatty components of living organisms, and include (among others) all the substances you might already think of as fats or oils. They are the major components of margarine, cooking oil, butter, and the white fat associated with meat. All of these lipids originated from animals or plants, which gives a hint of how widespread and important these compounds are in living things. As you will recall from Book 4, Section 15.1, the terms 'fat' and 'oil' simply describe whether a lipid is solid (a fat) or liquid (an oil) at room temperature.

It is important to stress that lipids are *not* biopolymers; their average molecular mass is very much smaller than that of proteins, polysaccharides and nucleic acids. Chemically, lipids are a rather varied group of compounds, but with one outstanding property in common: all lipids are hydrophobic. They, therefore, tend to separate from water and from all water-soluble, hydrophilic compounds, and to group themselves together as large hydrophobic aggregates.

■ What type of weak interactions hold the molecules in lipid aggregates together?

□ Hydrophobic interactions (and van der Waals forces; Book 4, Section 4.2.1).

Because of the weak interactions between the molecules, lipids tend to be *fluid* aggregates that can easily change shape. To demonstrate this readiness to change shape, try pressing with your thumb on a packet of butter at room temperature; it dents. A material like this with a certain amount of fluidity can be extremely useful in certain situations – as you will see shortly.

The large proportion of hydrophobic groups is the most basic chemical characteristic of lipids, and underpins the crude definition of a lipid as a substance that is insoluble in water and soluble in hydrophobic solvents, such as chloroform. As you will remember from Book 4, Section 15.1, the simplest lipids are the fats and oils, collectively called **triacylglycerols**, which serve mainly as energy storage compounds. Being insoluble in water is extremely useful when it comes to forming a barrier that separates one cell from another, as in the case of phospholipids, which make up cellular membranes.

## 5.1.2 Triacylglycerols

Triacylglycerols are the commonest lipids in living organisms. Recall that these molecules are esters of long-chain carboxylic acids, called **fatty acids**, and an alcohol called **glycerol**. A fatty acid molecule has two distinct parts: a long hydrocarbon chain and a carboxylic acid group. An ester is formed by a condensation reaction between the OH of an alcohol (R—OH) and the COOH of a carboxylic acid (R—COOH), where R is the hydrocarbon chain (e.g. $CH_3-CH_2-CH_2-$ etc.) The condensation reaction between acetic acid ($CH_3-COOH$) and methanol ($CH_3-OH$) can be written as:

$$CH_3-C\overset{O}{\underset{OH}{\big|\big|}} \quad + \quad HO-CH_3 \quad \longrightarrow \quad CH_3-C\overset{O}{\underset{O-CH_3}{\big|\big|}} \quad + \quad H_2O \qquad (5.1)$$

| acetic acid | methanol | methyl acetate |
|---|---|---|
| (carboxylic acid) | (alcohol) | (ester) |

Since glycerol has three OH groups it can form three ester bonds, one with each of the carboxylic acid groups at the ends of three fatty acid molecules. One of the ways in which naturally occurring fatty acids differ is in the length of the hydrocarbon chain. The name triacylglycerol, which is often abbreviated to **TAG**, is derived from its constituent parts: *tri* means three, fatty acids are *acyl* groups, plus *glycerol*. Figure 5.2 is a simplified representation of a triacylglycerol molecule, showing the glycerol 'core' and the long, hydrophobic, hydrocarbon 'tails' of the three fatty acids.

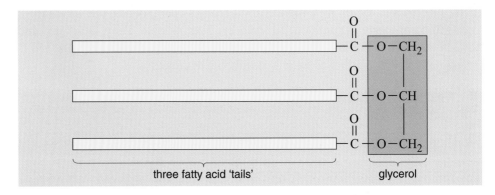

**Figure 5.2**   Pictorial representation of a triacylglycerol molecule showing the central core (glycerol) and the three long hydrophobic fatty acid 'tails'.

In both animals and plants, TAGs are used mainly for energy storage. In animals, TAGs are stored in a specialised tissue called *adipose tissue*, commonly called simply fat. Under the microscope the individual adipose tissue cells can be seen, with the fat itself stored as a globule inside a vacuole in the cytosol. Many people living in western societies have a much greater proportion of fat than most wild animals; even a fairly thin human, for example, has a layer of adipose tissue immediately below the skin over certain parts of the body such as the thighs, upper arms and belly. In certain plants, one of the main TAG stores is the seeds, from which, for example, olive oil, maize (corn) oil and groundnut oil are obtained. These stores of TAGs, like polysaccharide energy stores, can be readily mobilised, and then broken down to provide energy (see Section 6.3).

### 5.1.3   Phospholipids

**Phospholipids**, like TAGs, are long-chain fatty acid esters of glycerol, but one of the glycerol OH groups is esterified by a phosphorus-containing group with a negative charge (instead of a third fatty acid group), as shown in Figure 5.3.

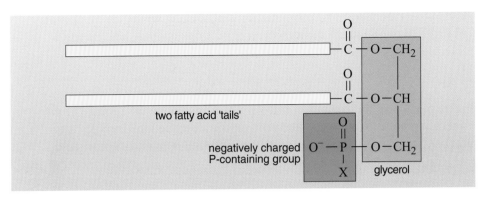

**Figure 5.3**  Pictorial representation of a phospholipid, where X may represent a variety of different groups depending on the phospholipid in question. (Compare this figure with Figure 5.2.)

Charged groups are extremely hydrophilic, which accounts for the major difference in properties between phospholipids and TAGs. As in TAGs, the fatty acid hydrocarbon chains in phospholipids may be very long, with at least 14 $CH_2$ groups (sometimes 24 or more), making them strongly hydrophobic.

You will return to phospholipids at the end of this chapter to take a closer look at the role these molecules play in the composition of cell membranes.

## 5.2  Introducing biopolymers

In Book 4, Chapter 15, you were introduced to two important classes of **biopolymer**, namely polysaccharides and proteins. Nucleic acids are also biopolymers. All biopolymers are made by linking together large numbers of monomers by covalent bonds. The monomer units are different in each class of biopolymer: they are amino acids in proteins, sugars (commonly glucose) in polysaccharides, and nucleotides in nucleic acids. Even though there is a limited repertoire of these monomer units, as you will see, each biopolymer within a class can have unique properties. This section explores some general properties of biopolymers, in particular the functional groups of the monomer units and the bonds that link these units together.

Any number from a few hundred to several thousand monomers can be linked together in a single biopolymer chain. Consequently, biopolymers are enormously large molecules – often called *macromolecules*, where 'macro' simply means large. The relative molecular mass of a biopolymer may run into thousands or even millions, compared with only 18 for water ($H_2O$) and 180 for a simple sugar like glucose ($C_6H_{12}O_6$). Macromolecules have the same functional groups as small molecules and it is these functional groups that largely govern their behaviour.

■ In Book 4 polymers were likened to long trains, formed by coupling together large numbers of railway carriages. The 'couplings' that monomers have are functional groups that allow them to form covalent bonds to other monomers. How many such groups must each monomer have for polymerisation to take place?

☐ Each monomer needs at least *two* functional groups for polymerisation.

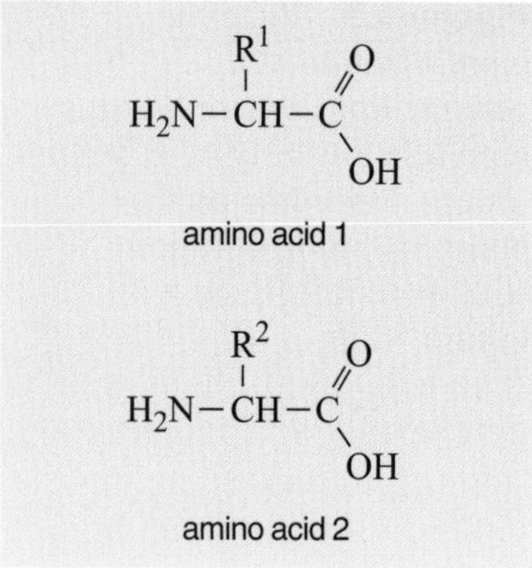

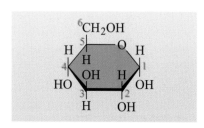

**Figure 5.4**  Formulae of two amino acids, for use with Question 5.1.

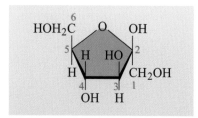

**Figure 5.5**  The structural formula of the monosaccharide glucose. The ring carbon atoms (C-1 to C-5) are not shown. (You do not need to remember this structure.)

**Figure 5.6**  Structural formula of the monosaccharide fructose. Again the ring carbon atoms (C-2 to C-5) have been omitted. (You do not need to remember this structure.)

Biopolymers are formed by condensation reactions, in which the functional groups from two separate monomers react with one another, eliminating a molecule of water and forming a covalent bond (Book 4, Section 14.2).

### Question 5.1

Figure 5.4 shows the formulae of two amino acids. Draw the formula of the molecule produced in the condensation reaction between the carboxylic acid group (COOH) of amino acid 1 and the amino ($NH_2$) group of amino acid 2.

As you learnt in Book 4, biopolymers can be broken down into monomers again, by breaking the covalent bonds between them. This is accomplished by hydrolysis ('splitting with water'); which is the reverse of condensation. For example, in the hydrolysis of the molecule shown in the answer to Question 5.1, the OH part of a water molecule becomes attached to one monomer (amino acid 1) and the H atom to the other (amino acid 2).

## 5.3   Polysaccharides

The first important group of biopolymers considered are the polysaccharides. The monomers of which polysaccharides are composed are known collectively as **monosaccharides** (mono means 'one'), each of which is a type of sugar molecule. Sugars are water-soluble, sweet-tasting compounds, molecules of which contain a number of OH groups, usually known as hydroxyl groups. Sugars are particularly important in biology because they provide energy. The most familiar monosaccharide sugar is glucose, and a well-known disaccharide (di means 'two') is sucrose, or table sugar. The term carbohydrate, commonly used on food packaging, encompasses both polysaccharides and sugars.

Figure 5.5 shows the ring structure of the glucose molecule. This type of diagrammatic representation is known as a Haworth projection and you were introduced to this for the first time in Book 4, Section 15.3. The numbers 1–6 in blue denote the carbon atoms, referred to as C-1, C-2, etc. Five of the carbon atoms (C-1 to C-5) and one oxygen atom form the ring; C-1 to C-4 each have an OH group and a hydrogen atom attached, and C-5 has a $CH_2OH$ group and a hydrogen atom attached.

■   Count the number of carbon, hydrogen and oxygen atoms and then write out the molecular formula of glucose.

☐   You should find your totals match the molecular formula $C_6H_{12}O_6$.

Figure 5.6 shows the formula of another common monosaccharide, fructose (often called 'fruit sugar' because of its presence in ripe fruit). Although both glucose and fructose have the same molecular formula, $C_6H_{12}O_6$, you can see that there are differences between them; for example, the fructose ring has one carbon atom fewer. The disaccharide sucrose is made up of one molecule of glucose and one molecule of fructose.

In contrast to sugars, polysaccharides are usually insoluble. The commonest are energy-storage substances (starch in plants and glycogen in animals) and support molecules (cellulose in plant cell walls). All three of these polysaccharides are polymers of glucose.

■ Suggest how monosaccharide monomers are joined together to form polysaccharides – and conversely, how polysaccharides can be converted back to the monosaccharides from which they were formed.

☐ Monosaccharides are joined together by covalent bonds formed during sequential condensation reactions; polysaccharides are broken down again into monosaccharides by hydrolysis.

Figure 5.7 shows the reaction between two glucose molecules, specifically between the OH group on C-4 of one glucose molecule and C-1 of the other. This is a condensation reaction; a molecule of water is produced and a **glycosidic linkage** is formed between the glucose monomers.

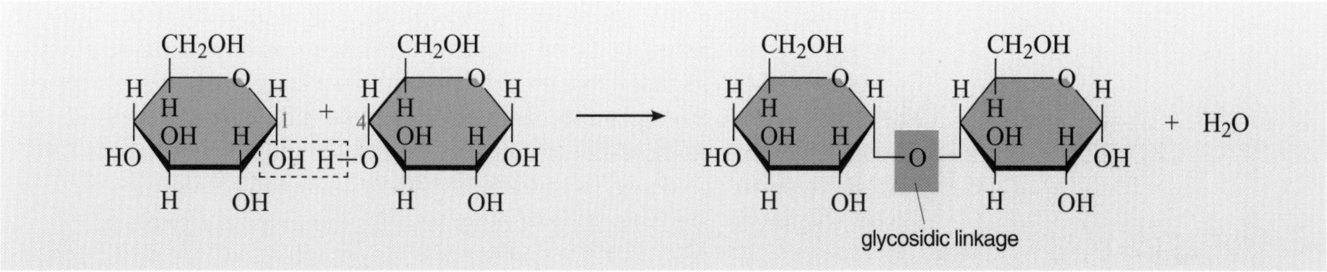

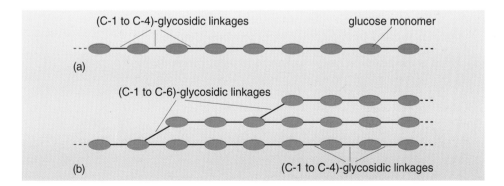

**Figure 5.7**   Formation of a glycosidic linkage between two glucose molecules. (Note that the bonds from the O atom to C-1 and C-4 in the glycosidic linkage are not actually bent.)

Figure 5.8 shows the simplified structure of two glucose polymers; each oval represents a glucose monomer, and the lines between them denote the glycosidic linkages. Cellulose (Figure 5.8a) is a typical fibrous polysaccharide, with extended unbranched chains, each at least 500 monomers long. The chains can pack side by side to give a very tough fibre, which is strengthened by many

**Figure 5.8**   Simplified diagram of two polymers of glucose: (a) cellulose; (b) amylopectin, the main component of starch. The abbreviations C-1 to C-4 and C-1 to C-6 identify the carbon atoms involved in the glycosidic linkages.

hydrogen bonds between adjacent overlapping chains. Try breaking a thread of cotton – which is almost pure cellulose – and you can test this fibrous strength for yourself. Cellulose is the most abundant organic macromolecule on Earth. This is because it is the major component of the extracellular matrix that forms the rigid supporting framework of the cell walls in all plants (shown in Figure 4.4).

Another polysaccharide composed solely of glucose is amylopectin (Figure 5.8b), which is the main component of the familiar food material, starch. Individual molecules of amylopectin vary in size, the larger ones consisting of over 20 000 monomers. However, here the glucose monomers are not all linked between C-1 and C-4; there are occasional branch points where there are also links between C-1 and C-6. A consequence of this branching is that adjacent glucose chains cannot get close enough to reinforce one another by parallel stacking as in cellulose, and this means that starch could not function as a support material. However, its open bush-like structure is ideal for packing into a small space whilst still allowing access for the enzymes that release the glucose monomers from storage when energy is required. In fact, starch is the major fuel reserve of plants. It is commonly stored in chloroplasts in the cells of leaves and stems of all green plants, and is also present in large quantities in other organelles of non-photosynthesising cells, particularly in below-ground parts of the plant; for example, the cells that make up potatoes contain a large proportion of starch. The major glucose storage molecule in most animals is the polysaccharide glycogen which is contained in granules in the cytosol of liver and muscle cells. Like amylopectin, glycogen has a branched structure and the molecules can vary in size, the larger ones consisting of more than 20 000 glucose monomers.

■ Why is glycogen a better storage molecule for glucose – why not simply store glucose in cells?

□ Glycogen is insoluble and so 'stays put' inside the cell until the glucose is required.

The molecular structure of polysaccharides – and hence their physical and chemical properties – are closely related to their biological role. The same is true for nucleic acids and proteins, the subjects of the next two sections.

Question 5.2

(a) How many water molecules are formed when a trisaccharide ('tri' denotes three) is formed from its constituent monosaccharides?

(b) What is the principal polysaccharide in plant cell walls?

(c) When one mole of sucrose molecules are hydrolysed, how many moles of fructose and glucose molecules are produced?

(d) What is the main energy-storage polysaccharide of animals?

## 5.4   Nucleic acids

The most abundant **nucleic acid** is DNA. In eukaryotes, DNA molecules, together with proteins, are organised into distinct chromosomes, which are present in the cell nucleus (Section 4.4). In prokaryotes the DNA is present in the cytosol and is not associated with proteins.

Like polysaccharides, nucleic acids are condensation polymers. In this case the monomers are called nucleotides, and these are linked together into chains, which can be hydrolysed back to their constituent nucleotide monomers. The biological importance of nucleic acids depends on their nucleotide sequence. This acts as a code, with different sequences representing different messages, and hence nucleic acids are often referred to as informational macromolecules. The sequence of nucleotides within DNA *is* the genetic message. The structure of DNA and how it conveys this message is the subject of Chapter 10.

# 5.5   Proteins

Although nutritional information on food packets lists 'protein' as if it were a single substance; it is, in fact, a whole *class* of substances and there are hundreds of thousands of different protein molecules in living organisms. All life is based on proteins. As Table 5.1 showed, proteins are the major organic constituents of cells. To see why proteins are so important, you need to recall some of the points introduced in Section 4.1 about the structural differences between eukaryotic cell types. Although cells of a multicellular organism have many features in common, there are also characteristic structural and hence functional differences between the different types; in the course of development, cells become specialised for carrying out only some of the range of functions required for the survival and reproduction of the whole organism.

These similarities and differences between cells arise from differences in the proteins they contain. Figure 4.10 showed a selection of different, specialised animal cells. These cells contain some proteins that are common to all cell types, for example those in the mitochondria, but they each contain some proteins that are specific to that cell type. Such proteins determine the specialised functions of that cell and hence whether it is part of the blood system, muscle or liver tissue, for example.

There may be tens of thousands of different types of proteins in any organism. Each different protein has its own specialist job to do and each type of protein has its own unique structure.

## 5.5.1   Fibrous and globular proteins

Proteins are remarkably versatile with respect to the structures that they form. They fall into one of two classes: fibrous and globular. The **fibrous proteins** are usually very elongated, with roughly linear structures in which two, or three, almost identical polymer chains wind around one another like the strands of a rope, to form a spiral, or helix.

All fibrous proteins are made within cells, but many are then secreted outside the cell into the extracellular space where the individual molecules come together into double or triple helices. Most animal tissues are composed not only of cells but also of extracellular space, which is filled with a network of macromolecules permeated by fluid. This network is called the extracellular matrix and is made

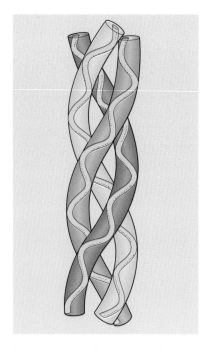

**Figure 5.9**   Structure of collagen, a fibrous protein. A collagen molecule is a triple helix: three polymer chains (which themselves are helical) coiled around each other and held together by weak, non-covalent interactions.

up of a variety of proteins and polysaccharides. The matrix plays a very important role because it determines many of the physical properties of the tissue. One of the most abundant fibrous proteins in the extracellular matrix of vertebrates (such as humans) is collagen (Figure 5.9), which accounts for 25% of all body protein. Collagen has great tensile strength and is found particularly in the skin and tendons of vertebrates.

Hair and fingernail protein, or keratin, is formed from hundreds of closely packed pairs of intertwined helices. Myosin, which consists mainly of fibrous protein, is present in enormous quantities in muscle cells, and hence is a major component of meat (which is mostly muscle).

Individual molecules of these fibrous proteins are extremely thin and long. For example, the collagen triple helix molecule is 1.5 nm wide, and hundreds of micrometres in length. However, the molecules are always packed side by side into small groups – of up to 200 triple helices – to form fibrils, as shown in Figure 5.10a and b. Fibrils are then bundled together to make larger structures called fibres (Figure 5.10c), and the fibres in turn may be bundled together into yet larger aggregates. So fibrous proteins are mostly used in large numbers to build up body structure. The controlled aggregation of hundreds of parallel fibrous molecules ultimately produces something very strong and tough, such as the skin or the tendons of vertebrates mentioned above. Hence fibrous proteins are important for providing support.

In contrast to the fibrous proteins, the **globular proteins** are compact and roughly spherical in shape. This shape is achieved by the polymer chain winding round and round itself, rather like a ball of string, as shown in Figure 5.11 for myoglobin, the oxygen-binding protein found in muscle. Globular proteins usually have more specialised roles than fibrous proteins. Most importantly, they rely for their activity on specialised 'pockets' built into the protein surface. These specialised pockets, or binding sites, are precisely shaped so that each provides an exact fit with one particular type of molecule.

The binding of a globular protein to a specific molecule serves a number of different functions. For instance, for a particular receptor protein that forms part of the cell membrane, the molecule with which it has an exact fit is the hormone (Book 4, Section 16.2.2), or other molecule, that it recognises. A receptor protein can receive messages from specific hormones only if it has a binding site that

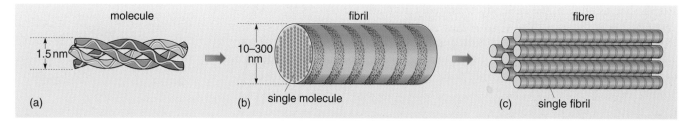

**Figure 5.10**   (a) A collagen molecule, up to 200 of which are packed together to form fibrils (b), which themselves pack together to form fibres (c).

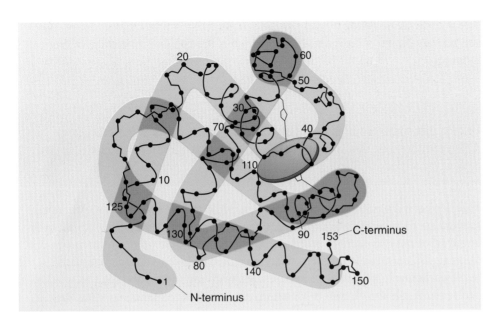

**Figure 5.11** Structure of myoglobin, a globular protein that is present in muscle and is responsible for binding oxygen. The black dots (some of which are numbered) are amino acid monomers. The blue 'folded sausage' shows the higher-order structure (Section 5.5.2) and the red disc is the binding site for oxygen.

the hormone fits into exactly, as shown in Figure 5.12. In insects, for example, female sex hormones can stimulate a male of the same species even if he is 2 kilometres downwind – because he has receptor proteins on the cells of his antennae that have specific binding sites for that particular hormone molecule. Humans are not sexually aroused by insect sex hormones because they lack the right receptor proteins! In enzyme proteins, which are biological catalysts (such as trypsin and cyclo-oxygenase discussed in Book 4, Section 16.2), the specific binding site is known as the **active site**, and its shape determines the molecule that it can bind (the substrate) and the reaction it catalyses (Figure 5.12b).

To explore this subject of protein binding sites with which specific molecules interact, consider another type of globular protein, the antibodies. Antibody proteins are produced by certain types of white blood cells, which are part of the body's immune system. They are produced in response to attack from viruses and bacteria, for example, and can be induced by immunisation against specific diseases. For instance, the polio vaccine stimulates white blood cells to make antibodies against the polio virus. Antibodies are very large globular proteins, and in this case, each has a binding site that exactly matches part of the surface structure of a polio virus, as illustrated in Figure 5.13. By 'locking' the virus onto its surface as shown, the antibody effectively prevents the virus from entering cells and reproducing. (The virus is then destroyed by further processes in the blood.) Having once met and overcome the polio virus, the body can make a rapid response to any future polio infection by rapidly synthesising more of this same polio virus antibody. However, to be similarly prepared against, say, tetanus (caused in this case by a bacterial infection), the body must be immunised specifically against the tetanus bacterium. The important point here is that the body becomes immune to specific diseases only by producing antibody protein with a specific binding site, one that precisely fits the surface structure of the invading organism. Such binding specificity is found in all globular proteins.

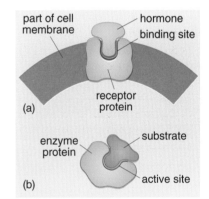

**Figure 5.12** Specific binding sites (a) on the surface of a receptor protein within the cell membrane, and (b) on an enzyme protein. The binding site of an enzyme is called the active site.

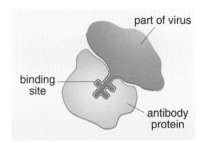

**Figure 5.13** A specific binding site for a virus on an antibody protein molecule.

The precise shape of the binding site is unique to each type of globular protein and confers on it a unique specificity, which is the basis of its precise biological function.

### 5.5.2   Primary and higher-order structure of proteins

Having met some proteins with very different structures and therefore very different functions, you will now explore how these structures are built up and look at the structural features that proteins have in common. To do this, consider myoglobin, the protein shown in Figure 5.11.

Muscles need a plentiful supply of oxygen while they are working to produce movement. (The reasons for this will become clear in Chapter 6.) Myoglobin is one kind of oxygen-storage protein, and is largely responsible for the red colour of meat. This protein is found in many muscles, including those of humans, but is particularly abundant in the muscles of diving mammals, such as whales and seals. While the animal is breathing in air, oxygen is taken up from the bloodstream by the muscles, and concentrated by binding to myoglobin. The myoglobin releases oxygen while the animal is under water, when the blood does not contain enough oxygen to meet the muscles' demands.

In Figure 5.11 the myoglobin molecule is represented as a long, contorted, blue 'sausage'. The string of black dots within the blue 'sausage' represents the chain of amino acid monomers. The amino acids are linked together by condensation reactions between amino ($NH_2$) and carboxylic acid (COOH) functional groups, and as you saw in the answer to Question 5.1, the result of each condensation reaction is an amide bond, known as a peptide bond (Figure 5.14).

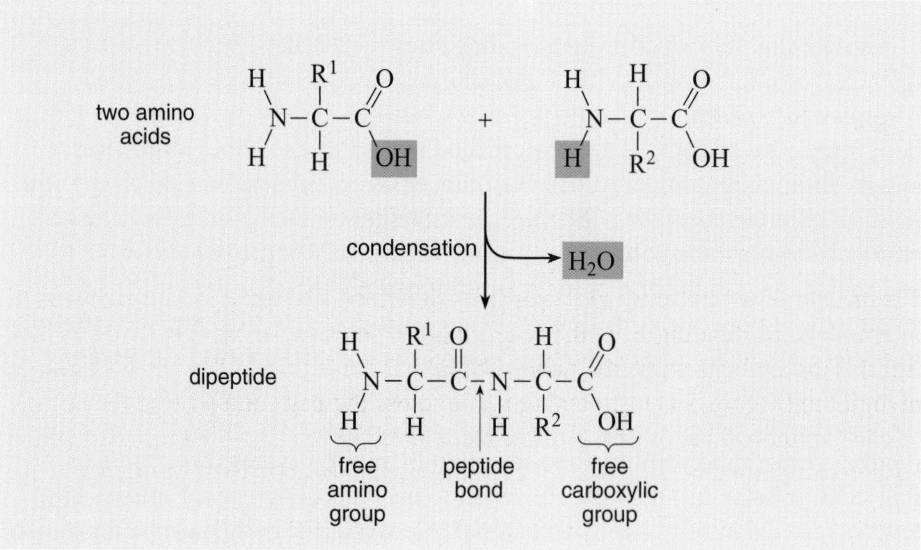

**Figure 5.14**   The formation of a peptide bond from two amino acids.

There is always a free amino group at one end (conventionally drawn as the 'left-hand' end of the chain) and a free carboxylic acid group at the other, 'right-hand' end; these ends are known respectively as the N-terminus and the C-terminus of the protein chain.

There are 20 different amino acids commonly found in proteins. The two amino acid structures shown in Figure 5.14 represent the general formula of amino acids. You will notice that both amino acids in Figure 5.14 are identical except for the group designated $R^1$ or $R^2$. Recall from Book 4, Section 15.2 that amino acids differ from each other only in the type of R group they contain.

You have already met several different amino acids in Book 4; Table 5.2 gives the full and abbreviated names and R group formulas of six additional amino acids. However, there are many thousands of different proteins, each with a particular biological function, and it is clear that there must be an enormous variety of structures. How can this be, given that they are all polymers of only 20 different amino acid monomers? The answer is that when several hundred of the 20 different types link up to form a protein chain, there is a huge number of possible sequences. Some amino acids may not be used at all in a protein whereas others may occur many times. Every different protein is unique because it has its own unique sequence of amino acids along its length.

**Table 5.2** Six amino acids commonly found in proteins. (You do not need to memorise the structures in this table.)

| Name and pronunciation | Standard abbreviation | Formula of R group | Name and pronunciation | Standard abbreviation | Formula of R group |
|---|---|---|---|---|---|
| glycine ('gly-seen') | Gly | H | alanine ('alla-neen') | Ala | $CH_3$ |
| phenylalanine ('fee-nile-alla-neen') | Phe | $CH_2$ (benzene ring) | aspartate ('ass-part-ate') | Asp | $O=C(O^-)$, $CH_2$ |
| lysine ('lye-seen') | Lys | $\overset{+}{N}H_3$, $(CH_2)_4$ | serine ('seer-een') | Ser | OH, $CH_2$ |

The structure of a protein can be partially described by listing its entire sequence of amino acids, reading from the N-terminus to the C-terminus (i.e. from left to right). This analysis would be rather like taking the black chain of amino acids of myoglobin (Figure 5.11), stretching it out across the page and writing the name of each amino acid above each of the black dots. Recall from Book 4 that this sequence of amino acids is known as the **primary structure** of the protein.

Chains of amino acids are often called polypeptides. Biochemists use the terms protein and polypeptide rather loosely and interchangeably. Here too both terms are used. When a protein is synthesised in a cell, the linear polypeptide chain folds as it is produced. The biological activity of this newly formed molecule depends on its three-dimensional, folded structure, and when considering a polypeptide chain as a three-dimensional structure it is generally referred to as a protein.

The primary structure of myoglobin appears to give no clues about the overall shape of the protein, nor whether it has any specific binding sites. Yet, amazingly, there is enough information in the primary structure alone for it to fold spontaneously into a particular three-dimensional shape, called its **higher-order structure**. All polypeptide chains with the same amino acid sequence fold in the same way provided the conditions are the same. So every molecule of myoglobin finishes up with the same convoluted higher-order structure outlined by the blue 'sausage' in Figure 5.11. Thus primary structure determines higher-order structure.

This general rule that primary structure determines higher-order structure is true for all proteins (and indeed for all biopolymers), but is particularly important for globular proteins, such as enzymes and antibodies – and indeed any protein that depends on having a surface binding site that fits exactly the molecule(s) with which it interacts. The surface geometry of a protein is even more irregular than it appears in Figure 5.11; it is pitted with crevices and depressions and covered with protuberances, all of exact shape and size. Every pit and protuberance occurs in just the same position on every molecule of that particular protein. As discussed above, this precise shape, or higher-order structure, determines the specificity of biological activity, or function, of the protein molecule.

The important relationships between primary structure, higher-order structure and the biological function of proteins can be summarised in the following way.

> Primary structure determines higher-order structure, which determines biological activity.

Question 5.3

Give an example of a protein molecule that can intertwine with two similar molecules to form a triple helix. What is the biological function of this protein?

Question 5.4

The higher-order structure of protein X in humans has a binding site into which the hormone adrenalin fits exactly.

(a)  What is the most likely biological function of protein X?

(b)  Suppose that certain individuals produce a protein X that has a small change from the normal amino acid sequence. Is this change likely to affect the response of their cells to adrenalin?

What exactly is the link between primary and higher-order structure? Why does a protein with a particular primary structure always have the same three-dimensional shape? The answer lies in the weak, non-covalent interactions that hold the polymer chain together in a particular shape. In the schematic model of myoglobin (Figure 5.11), for example, you can see a relatively straight stretch of the molecule (amino acids 125–150) lying on top of the rest of the protein, which is folded. This straight section does not flap about because it is held down by weak interactions that tether it to the underlying lengths of folded protein.

Similarly, there are weak interactions holding all the other lengths of polymer chain in place. The strength of these weak interactions is very much less than the strength of covalent bonds but, if there are enough of them, weak interactions can stabilise a particular folding pattern very effectively.

■ Look at the generalised formula for an amino acid in Figure 5.4. How many functional groups does it have? Which of them are still available for reaction once the amino acid is polymerised to form a polypeptide chain?

☐ An amino acid has a minimum of two functional groups: COOH and $NH_2$. Each amino acid also has a side chain referred to as R and can consist of a variety of different groups, some of which may be simple hydrocarbon chains, while others may be additional functional groups such as hydroxyl groups (OH). When the amino acid is part of a polypeptide chain, only the R group is available for interaction.

The biological activity of a protein depends critically on the shape of the whole molecule which in turn depends crucially on its R groups. Look at the formula of the R group for each of the six amino acids listed in Table 5.2. What is significant here is the range of different chemical structures, and hence properties, of the amino acid R groups. For example, in glycine, R is a single, unreactive hydrogen atom; some R groups are hydrophobic (e.g. the $CH_3$ group of alanine); some are large and bulky as well as being hydrophobic (e.g. in phenylalanine); some are charged (e.g. the negatively charged aspartate R group and the positively charged lysine R group) and others are hydrophilic (e.g. the OH in the $CH_2OH$ group of serine).

The higher-order structure of a globular protein is held together by weak interactions between different R groups of the folded chain. This requires the two R groups to be compatible (i.e. they must have the right chemical structures for a weak interaction to form between them). There are R groups all along the polypeptide chain, and this will fold to bring together as many weak interacting pairs as possible, so that an exact and highly specific higher-order protein structure always results.

Different proteins have different primary structures (different combinations of monomers in a different order) so there are different opportunities for weak interactions. The same is true for the other types of biopolymer; nucleic acids and polysaccharides also rely on weak interactions to stabilise their higher-order structure. To understand this effect, you need to look more closely at the nature of weak interactions. You have already met two types – hydrophobic interactions and hydrogen bonds (Section 5.1). In Figure 5.1, *all* the hydrophilic groups are on the surface of the folded molecule. However, this is an oversimplification. When a biopolymer folds in water, many of the hydrophilic groups will be in the interior of the molecule, away from the surrounding water, and instead of interacting with water molecules will form weak interactions (hydrogen bonds and ionic interactions) with each other. The three types of weak interactions are illustrated in Figure 5.15.

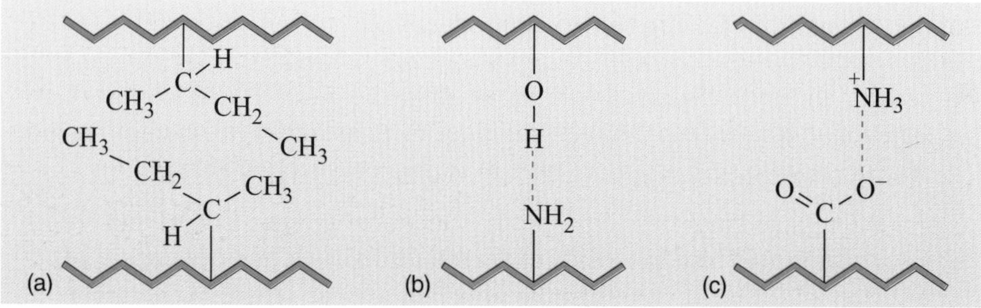

**Figure 5.15**    Weak interactions in biopolymers. The zigzag bars represent polymer chains. (a) A hydrophobic interaction formed between two hydrophobic groups, such as the hydrocarbon chains shown here. (b) A hydrogen bond, which is formed when two electronegative atoms (here O and N) each bond weakly with an H atom. (c) An ionic interaction, which is due to the attraction between oppositely charged groups. Here, a positively charged ammonium group and a negatively charged carboxylate group.

### Activity 5.2    Revision: weak interactions

We expect this activity will take you approximately 20 minutes.

The purpose of this activity is to revise your understanding of the three types of weak interactions, all of which play a role in forming and maintaining the higher-order structure of proteins. Each amino acid has a different R group – the group that sticks out from a polypeptide chain and is free to interact with other R groups after the peptide bonds have been formed between the carboxylic acid group of one amino acid and the amino group of the next amino acid. The R groups of eight amino acids are shown in Figure 5.16.

(a)  For each R group, identify which of the other seven R groups it could interact with, and name each type of interaction.

(b)  If each of these amino acids occurred in the same protein in a cell, identify where the R groups would be found in relation to the structure of the protein molecule as a whole.

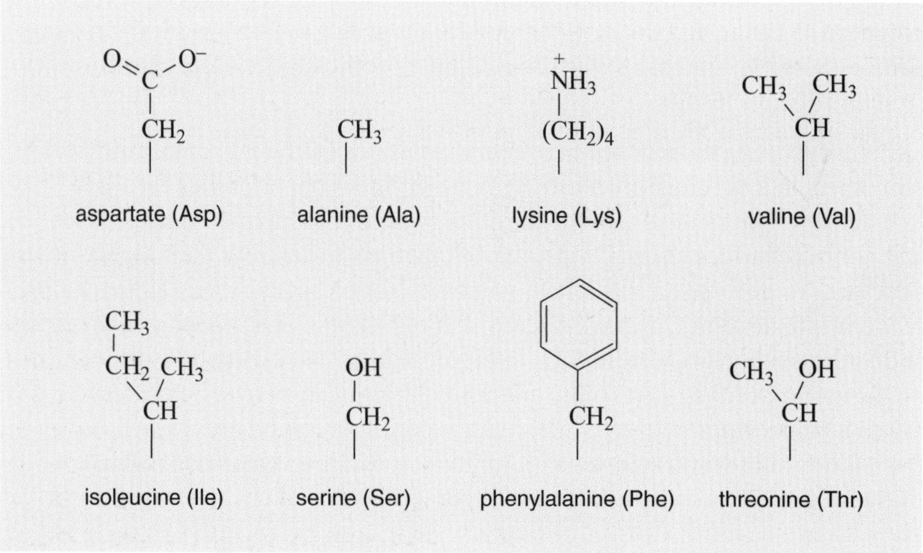

**Figure 5.16**    The R groups of eight amino acids.

The comments on this activity at the end of this book provide a full explanation of the types of weak interactions that can be formed between the various combinations of R group.

Having seen where the three types of weak interaction are likely to be formed, it is time to revisit the link between the structure of a globular protein and its function. The important point is that proteins tend to fold up in a way that maximises opportunities for weak interactions. If all molecules of a particular protein fold in this way, they all finish up with the same shape – the same higher-order structure.

Weak interactions also play a significant role in fibrous proteins, such as collagen and keratin, which consist of several intertwined helices. For example, a collagen molecule is strengthened by hydrogen bonds that run between its three helices, at right angles to the polypeptide chains. Newly formed collagen is fairly deformable, but over the years the hydrogen bonds between the helices are supplemented by much stronger, covalent bonds, thereby making the collagen fibres much tougher. This change is one reason why skin loses its suppleness with age.

So the key to understanding the relationship between the structure and function of proteins are weak interactions.

Question 5.5

Which of the following statements are true? Explain why any are false.

(a)  All proteins yield amino acids when they are hydrolysed.

(b)  A molecule of any protein contains all 20 of the common amino acids.

(c)  A polypeptide chain containing 100 amino acid monomer units has 100 peptide bonds.

---

## Activity 5.3    From amino acid sequence to functional protein

We expect this activity will take you approximately 30 minutes.

This activity will allow you to understand and remember how the primary structure of a protein determines its higher-order structure. This activity follows on from some of the scientific communications activities in Chapter 4 and allows you further opportunities to develop your writing skills by planning the content of a short account.

Assume that you have had an email from a fellow student, Sam, who cannot see how a particular primary structure of a specific globular protein determines its higher-order structure. Your task is to explain this in a written response. Sam doesn't know about biopolymers in living organisms, but understands different functional groups and the structure of polymers as presented in Book 4.

You are not expected to actually write your response to Sam but rather plan what you would say to him in the form of a bullet-point list. This list should comprise the main points that you would make in your answer – producing a list in note form of the information you would include in a written account is a very good first step when planning an answer.

It is suggested that you close this book before compiling your list, and then look at the relevant pages of the book and amend your answer.

One possible list is given in the comments on this activity at the end of this book.

---

In the next two sections, you will consider two very different roles for proteins in the living cell, beginning with an examination of enzymes – one of the most important groups of biological molecules – and then further investigating the role of proteins in the cell membrane.

Question 5.6

List the key structural similarities of the three types of biopolymer that have been discussed: polysaccharides, nucleic acids and proteins.

## 5.6    Enzymes are globular proteins

Enzymes are all globular proteins and they act as biological catalysts, speeding up chemical reactions in living organisms to a rate that is suitable to sustain life. The presence of enzymes allows the cell to carry out highly complex chemical transformations at moderate temperatures – about 37 °C for humans.

Enzymes are effective in exceedingly small amounts; even a few nanograms ($10^{-9}$ g) can make a spectacular difference to the rate of a reaction. This can be demonstrated in the laboratory using hydrogen peroxide ($H_2O_2$), which breaks down according to the following equation:

$$2H_2O_2 \longrightarrow 2H_2O + O_2 \tag{5.2}$$

Normally, a solution of hydrogen peroxide is fairly stable, breaking down only slowly. But if a tiny drop of blood – which contains the enzyme catalase – is added, the reaction speeds up at least a million times, the solution fizzing vigorously due to the large quantities of oxygen produced. In the video sequence *Features of reactions* (Book 4, Activity 9.1) you saw the catalytic effect of raw liver on the decomposition of hydrogen peroxide; this was due to the catalase present in the liver cells. What these demonstrations show is that enzymes are very powerful catalysts and without them chemical reactions would not proceed at a suitable rate to sustain life.

Question 5.7

In order for a reaction to occur, the reactant molecules must encounter each other. Write a short sentence to explain why each of the following three changes increases the rate of a chemical reaction in a test tube: (a) increasing the concentration of reactants; (b) increasing the temperature; (c) adding a catalyst.

Hydrogen peroxide is a toxic substance that is produced as a by-product of many metabolic reactions inside cells; its breakdown into harmless molecules by catalase, therefore, serves a protective function in the body. Different enzymes in cells catalyse different reactions. The great majority of enzymes occur inside the cells of an organism. Some, however, are secreted by cells into the surrounding medium; for example, digestive enzymes are secreted into the gut (Book 4, Section 15.3). Whatever the process, every reaction in metabolism is catalysed by an enzyme. There is a different enzyme for every single step (reaction) in the many multi-step chemical interconversions that take place in the cell. This means that any living organism is capable of making literally hundreds of different enzymes. Most enzymes have names that relate to the reaction they catalyse and end in -*ase*; for example, cellu*lase* hydrolyses cellulose. However, a few enzymes that were discovered a long time ago have arbitrary names, such as the digestive enzymes trypsin and pepsin.

## 5.6.1 Enzyme specificity

One of the most distinctive features of enzyme catalysis is *specificity*, which is the ability of the enzyme to interact specifically with one particular molecule (or type of molecule) and to catalyse one particular reaction (or type of reaction).

■ Which structural features of globular proteins account for enzyme specificity?

☐ Each protein has a different amino acid sequence (primary structure) and therefore folds into a different three-dimensional shape (higher-order structure) that determines its biological activity. The higher-order structure includes a binding site – called the active site in enzymes – which has a different shape in each enzyme, so that only one specific molecule, or type of molecule, will fit it. A molecule that binds to the enzyme active site and undergoes a chemical reaction there is known as the **substrate** of that enzyme. For example, the substrate of trypsin is the protein being digested.

■ What is the substrate of the enzyme catalase, which was referred to above?

☐ Hydrogen peroxide.

Many enzymes require such an exact fit between enzyme and substrate that even small structural changes in the substrate will not be tolerated. A good example of this is the enzyme hexokinase, which catalyses the first reaction of glucose catabolism. Only glucose, out of the vast collection of other small molecules in the cell, fits precisely enough to bind effectively to the active site of the hexokinase molecule. Because of this specificity, the presence (or absence) of a particular enzyme determines which one of several possible reactions actually occurs in the cell. Consequently, enzymes play an essential role in the organisation and control of metabolism.

Enzyme specificity is of crucial importance in the organisation and control of metabolism.

Question 5.8

Which of the following statements about enzymes are true?

(a) Amylase is a protein.

(b) Without enzymes, life as we know it would not exist.

(c) All globular proteins are enzymes.

(d) Most enzymes catalyse a specific chemical reaction.

### 5.6.2   How do enzymes work?

The catalase example shows that enzyme-catalysed reaction rates may be many times higher than those of uncatalysed reactions. Nevertheless, it is important to remember that, however miraculous their effects may seem, enzymes still obey the ordinary laws of physics and chemistry. Like other catalysts that operate in non-biological systems, enzymes are subject to the following restrictions:

1   They cannot catalyse a reaction that would not otherwise take place. They can only speed up reactions that are already happening. (It may *seem* as if the reaction does not start until the enzyme is added, but this is only because the uncatalysed reaction is extremely slow.)

2   They cannot change the equilibrium position of a reaction (see Book 4, Section 10.6).

3   They are not used up during a reaction; they may be reused over and over again.

You know from Book 4, Section 10.4, that catalysts work by lowering the energy barrier for a chemical reaction. Figure 5.17 compares the energy change of an uncatalysed reaction with that of the same reaction catalysed by an enzyme.

**Figure 5.17**   The energy changes associated with the reaction A $\longrightarrow$ B, with and without the enzyme present. The peak of the upper curve indicates the top of the energy barrier for the uncatalysed reaction. Similarly, the lower curve shows the much lower energy barrier of the enzyme-catalysed reaction.

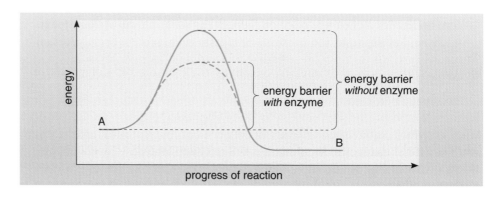

How do enzymes achieve their great powers of catalysis? The key feature is the binding of the substrate to the enzyme to form an **enzyme–substrate complex** (ES for short). The substrate does this by forming weak interactions with groups at the active site, as shown in Figure 5.18. Here the substrate molecule fits into a three-dimensional cavity on the enzyme surface, and this provides the ideal environment for the reaction to take place. It is ideal because the parts of the substrate to be chemically changed are placed next to parts of the enzyme protein able to catalyse this change. This fit is crucial to the whole catalytic reaction. Only if the substrate fits absolutely correctly – like a key fitting into a lock – will the parts to be chemically modified be correctly aligned. Binding of substrate to enzyme (to form the ES complex) greatly reduces the energy barrier of the reaction. In many cases, this is related to the distortion of bonds in the substrate, which occurs on binding (compare Figures 5.19a and b). These bonds, now under strain, are more readily broken, so the reaction is facilitated. After the reaction has taken place, the product(s) are then released from the active site (Figure 5.19c). Thus the analogy with a key in a lock is rather limited – because the key (substrate) does not become distorted by being inserted into the lock (enzyme), and then does not emerge either in pieces or with a different shape (as product(s))!

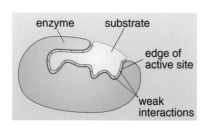

**Figure 5.18**   Enzyme action: binding of substrate to the enzyme.

The enzyme is then free to bind again with more substrate. The whole process can be summed up in the general equation:

$$E \;+\; S \;\rightleftharpoons\; ES \;\rightleftharpoons\; E \;+\; P \qquad (5.3)$$

enzyme    substrate     enzyme–substrate     enzyme    product(s)
complex

### 5.6.3 How temperature affects enzyme activity

Now you have an understanding of how enzymes work and how their structure relates to their function, it is interesting to consider a factor that affects the rate of enzyme-catalysed reactions, namely temperature. It has already been mentioned that enzymes catalyse chemical reactions at very moderate temperatures, but now you will investigate how they operate over a range of temperatures and see if their catalytic activity varies.

Consider one of the digestive enzymes in the human gut. Amylase is an enzyme secreted by the salivary glands, which hydrolyses the minor component of starch, amylose, to maltose (a disaccharide). In order to examine how the rate of the chemical reaction catalysed by amylase is affected by temperature, several experiments need to be conducted over a range of different temperatures. In Book 4, Section 10.1, you were introduced to the definition of reaction rate as a change in a physical quantity over a certain time period.

■ To investigate the rate of the amylase-catalysed reaction breaking down starch to maltose, what physical quantity could be measured as the reaction progressed?

☐ The increase in the concentration of maltose with time.

The chemical reaction can be set up at a range of temperatures and the amount of maltose formed in a set period of time can be measured. The larger the amount of maltose produced in a fixed time period, the faster the reaction rate. A graph of reaction rate against temperature (Figure 5.20) could then be plotted. It is highly likely that for whatever enzyme and reaction was chosen, the graph would look something like the one shown in Figure 5.20.

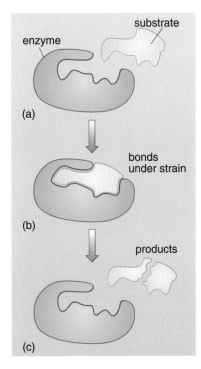

**Figure 5.19** Enzyme action: catalysing a reaction. Note here the distortion of the substrate in (b) and its breakdown into products, which then leave the active site (c).

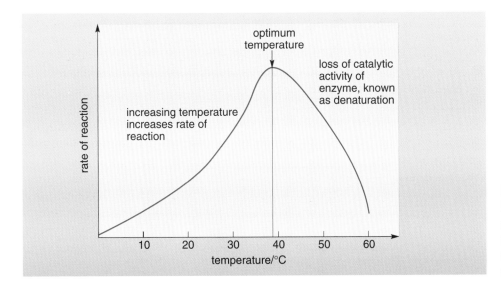

**Figure 5.20** Graph to illustrate the rate of reaction of an enzyme-catalysed reaction against the temperature of the solution in which the reaction occurs.

You will notice that the graph has several distinct phases. At comparatively low temperatures, as temperature increases the rate of reaction increases. At a certain specific temperature, the curve levels off at a maximum value for reaction rate, and then further increases in temperature actually slow the reaction down.

■ Look at Figure 5.20. At what temperature does the activity of this enzyme reach a maximum?

☐ Around 38 °C.

From Book 4, Section 10.2 you know that increasing the temperature increases the rate of a chemical reaction because more collisions occur between the reactant molecules (due to their increased kinetic energy) and more of the reacting molecules have sufficient kinetic energy to react. This feature explains why the rate of reaction initially seems to increase with temperature but it does not account for the levelling off of the graph and the final downturn. From your understanding of protein structure, can you explain why this curve should be characteristic of enzyme-catalysed reactions? Recall that the higher-order structure of proteins is dependent on weak interactions such as ionic interactions, hydrophobic interactions and hydrogen bonds. It is the action of these bonds in maintaining the three-dimensional shape of the protein that allows the protein to behave as an enzyme.

■ Which specific part of the enzyme has to be exactly the correct shape to bind it to its substrate?

☐ The active site.

As temperatures increase, the weak interactions holding the enzyme's active site in exactly the correct shape to fit its substrate break down and consequently the higher-order structure of proteins is progressively destroyed. This process is called **thermal denaturation** and accounts for the levelling off of the curve as the activity of the enzyme is reduced. Most enzymes have an optimum temperature at which they operate at peak activity; commonly this occurs between 35 °C and 45 °C. Organisms need to maintain their body temperatures within specific limits to maintain optimum reaction rates for their metabolic processes.

■ At what temperature would you expect the enzymes of the human body to have their optimum activity?

☐ 37 °C.

Question 5.9

Why is prolonged cooling or overheating so dangerous for the human body?

Some organisms, such as mammals and birds, rely on complex regulatory mechanisms that allow them to maintain constant body temperature. For these organisms, the internal temperature is maintained within tight limits to ensure that chemical reactions are occurring at an optimum rate. Other organisms, such as fish, reptiles and amphibians, do not regulate their core temperature and remain at the same temperature as their surroundings. For some organisms, this temperature may be very extreme indeed. Antarctic fish seem to cope well with a body temperature of –2 °C, while so-called thermophilic ('heat-loving') bacteria thrive in pools of water at near 100 °C. Clearly the enzymes responsible for metabolism in these two types of organism have widely different optimum temperatures. You will look more closely at the changes to enzymes at the molecular level that make catalytic activity possible in these extreme conditions in Chapter 15.

## 5.6.4 Coenzymes

Some enzymes do their catalytic work without help from other substances. Others require the help of small organic molecules called **coenzymes**. Coenzymes are so called because they work in cooperation with enzymes and can be used many times over. Since they bind to the active site of the enzyme alongside the substrate, a more appropriate name might be 'cosubstrate'. However, because coenzymes are continuously recycled, they are not substrates in the true sense. Coenzymes play a vital role in enzyme-catalysed reactions, as you will see in the example below.

Many enzyme-catalysed reactions involve the removal of (usually two) hydrogen atoms from the substrate molecule, a process called **dehydrogenation**. To understand the part played by coenzymes in metabolism you will look at one particular reaction: the transfer of two hydrogen atoms (which is represented as 2H) by a coenzyme called **NAD** (short for nicotinamide adenine dinucleotide – but you only need to remember the abbreviated name).

■ In which types of chemical reaction would you expect NAD to take part, if its role is to transfer hydrogen atoms?

☐ Oxidation and reduction reactions, since these involve the removal and addition of hydrogen, respectively.

As you will see in Chapter 6, one particular carbon compound accumulates in muscles when they are worked hard, i.e. when exercised vigorously. This compound is called lactic acid, or lactate. (Organic acids are present in the cell as the corresponding negative ion; for this reason, the term lactate rather than lactic acid is used here.) Lactate has to be removed from muscles so that they can go on working efficiently. There is a specific enzyme, lactate dehydrogenase (LDH), which catalyses the oxidation of lactate to pyruvate.

LDH is inactive on its own. To catalyse the dehydrogenation (hydrogen removal) reaction it requires the coenzyme NAD, as well as the substrate lactate – hence the idea of a 'cosubstrate' mentioned above. The active site of LDH, which binds both lactate and NAD, is shown in Figure 5.21. The NAD molecule collects two hydrogen atoms from lactate and is reduced to NAD.2H in the process, as shown in the figure. The equation for this reaction is:

$$C_3H_6O_3 + NAD \underset{}{\overset{LDH}{\rightleftharpoons}} C_3H_4O_3 + NAD.2H$$

$$\text{lactate} \qquad\qquad\qquad \text{pyruvate}$$

(5.4)

Notice that this is a *reversible* reaction. In fact, many enzyme-catalysed reactions can proceed in both directions, like the LDH-catalysed reaction here.

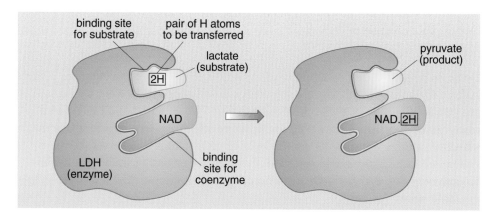

**Figure 5.21**   The coenzyme NAD binds to the enzyme lactate dehydrogenase and is reduced to NAD.2H by collecting two hydrogen atoms from the substrate, lactate, which is thereby converted to pyruvate.

The reduced coenzyme, NAD.2H, can then take part in another reaction, in which the hydrogen atoms are removed and it is thereby converted back to NAD; the coenzyme is thus recycled. Coenzymes are often called group transfer molecules because they 'shuttle' back and forth between reactions, picking up groups of atoms and then passing them on. This continual recycling of coenzymes explains why they need only be present in extremely small quantities in the cell.

There are just a few different coenzymes, each of which functions in a particular type of reaction. Thus one coenzyme can serve many different enzymes, provided these all catalyse the same type of reaction – oxidation or reduction in the case of NAD. Four of the coenzymes are listed in Table 5.3.

**Table 5.3**   Some coenzymes: their roles in group transfer and the vitamins from which they are derived.

| Coenzyme | Full name | Group transferred | Vitamin source |
|---|---|---|---|
| NAD | nicotinamide adenine dinucleotide | 2H | niacin (vitamin $B_3$) |
| FAD | flavin adenine dinucleotide | 2H | riboflavin (vitamin $B_2$) |
| CoA | coenzyme A | $CH_3CO$ (acetyl) | pantothenate (vitamin $B_5$) |
| NADP | nicotinamide adenine dinucleotide phosphate | 2H | niacin (vitamin $B_3$) |

Although the full names of coenzymes need not be remembered, the initials by which they are conventionally known are important. You will see from Table 5.3

that many of them are derived from *vitamins*, which most animals, including humans, are unable to synthesise for themselves. (Most plants cells, on the other hand, can synthesise all the vitamins they need.)

■ What can you conclude from the fact that the vitamin niacin, needed to produce NAD, cannot be made in the human body?

☐ Niacin must be obtained from food.

Look at the nutritional components listed on any cereal packet for other examples of vitamins. Given the vital role of coenzymes in metabolism, it is hardly surprising that vitamin deficiency has very serious consequences for health. For example, deficiency of niacin in humans can lead to pellagra (a skin, gut and nerve disorder). As noted above, without this particular vitamin the coenzyme NAD cannot be made.

### Question 5.10

(a) An enzyme catalyses the dehydrogenation of compound $BH_2$ to B, a reaction in which the coenzyme NAD also participates. What happens to NAD in this dehydrogenation reaction?

(b) The enzyme also has some effect on the substrate $JH_2$, but at a rate of only 10% of that with $BH_2$ as substrate. What is the probable reason for the lower activity of the enzyme with $JH_2$?

## 5.7 Biological membranes

Now you will consider how two types of biological molecule can be used to build an important cellular structure – the cell membrane. Biological membranes are composed of both phospholipids *and* proteins. However, it is the phospholipids that give membranes their unique sheet-like, bilayered structure and many of their functional properties. The structure of phospholipids was briefly mentioned in Section 5.1.3; recall that, like TAGs, they are long-chain fatty acid esters of glycerol, but one of the glycerol OH groups is esterified by a phosphorus-containing group with a negative charge (instead of a third fatty acid group, Figure 5.3).

Charged groups are extremely hydrophilic, which accounts for the major difference in properties between phospholipids and TAGs. As in TAGs, the fatty acid hydrocarbon chains in phospholipids may be very long, with at least 14 $CH_2$ groups (sometimes 24 or more), making them strongly hydrophobic. The immediate external environment for cells is always aqueous (watery) and this has implications for the molecules making up the surface of the cell. Hydrophobic groups, such as fatty acid tails, will try to orientate themselves away from this aqueous environment; whereas hydrophilic groups, such as the negatively charged phosphorous-containing group, will try to get as close to the water as possible.

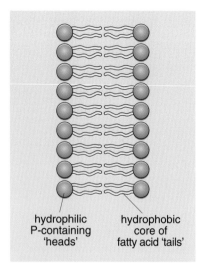

**Figure 5.22**   A phospholipid bilayer.

■ Describe how phospholipid molecules might aggregate together in a watery environment.

☐ The hydrophilic phosphate-containing groups will be on the *outside* of the aggregate, in contact with water molecules, while the hydrophobic chains will avoid water, coming together and interacting with one another on the *inside* of the aggregate.

When there are large numbers of phospholipid molecules, the result is a double-layered structure, a *phospholipid bilayer*. As shown in Figure 5.22, this arrangement brings the phosphate-containing 'heads' of the phospholipids into contact with water, while the fatty acid 'tails' are concealed in the interior, held together by hydrophobic interactions, so forming a hydrophobic 'core'. The phospholipid bilayer of a cell membrane (shown in Figure 5.23) is a very effective barrier, preventing hydrophilic molecules from passing freely into or out of the cell. Membranes define the boundaries of organelles, as described in Section 4.1, restricting various cellular functions to particular compartments of the cell. The movement of small molecules (such as glucose) and ions across membranes is controlled by special *transport* proteins that are embedded in the phospholipid bilayer, as shown in Figure 5.23. *Receptor* proteins are also found embedded in membranes (Figure 5.12a).

**Figure 5.23**   A biological membrane; a typical membrane thickness is about 10 nm. Some of the membrane proteins traverse the membrane and others are on its surface.

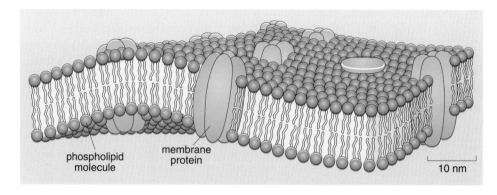

All the cells described in Chapter 4 contain all the biological polymer types that have been discussed in this section (proteins, polysaccharides and nucleic acids) and lipid aggregates. Thus the unity of structure observed at the level of cells and organelles occurs also at the molecular level. In Chapter 6, you will explore this molecular unity further, when the chemical reactions that go on inside cells are described.

Question 5.11

Which of the small molecules (i)–(vi) below are likely to be among the starting material(s) for the synthesis of each of the three compounds: (a) myoglobin, (b) TAGs and (c) glycogen?

(i) glucose; (ii) alanine; (iii) glycerol; (iv) fructose; (v) lysine; (vi) palmitic acid.

Question 5.12

Which type(s) of biopolymer or lipid provide each of the following functions in cells?

(a) support; (b) energy storage; (c) catalytic activity; (d) carry genetic information; (e) cell compartmentation.

## 5.8   Summary of Chapter 5

Proteins, polysaccharides and nucleic acids are condensation biopolymers, in which the monomer units are amino acids, monosaccharides and nucleotides, respectively. The monomer units are linked together by covalent bonds.

The primary structure of a biopolymer describes the type of monomers and the order in which they are linked. The primary structure of a biopolymer determines its higher-order structure (its shape), which in turn determines its biological activity.

Weak interactions (hydrophobic interactions, hydrogen bonds and ionic interactions) are crucial for the maintenance of the biologically active structure of proteins, polysaccharides, nucleic acids and lipids.

Lipids are not biopolymers but occur as large molecular aggregates. This group includes fats and oils, collectively termed triacylglycerols (TAGs). TAGs serve as energy stores in animals and in the seeds of some plants. The phospholipids contain two fatty acid chains and also a hydrophilic phosphorus-containing group, and in water form a bilayered structure with the hydrophobic fatty acid chains on the inside and the hydrophilic groups on the outside. Biological membranes are made up of a phospholipid bilayer with proteins embedded in it or attached to its surface.

Polysaccharides serve as energy-storage molecules in animals (glycogen) and plants (starch) or support molecules, particularly in plants (cellulose).

Nucleic acids are informational molecules.

The relationships between primary structure, higher-order structure and biological function are particularly obvious in proteins. The unique primary structure of a protein results from its amino acid sequence. There are two general types of protein: fibrous proteins, such as collagen; and globular proteins, such as enzymes, antibodies and receptor proteins. The relationship between structure and function is very precise, especially in globular proteins, where the specific higher-order structure provides a binding site (called the active site in enzymes) specific for molecules with which the protein interacts.

Enzymes are biological catalysts which increase the rate of a reaction, but they cannot alter the equilibrium position of a reaction, or initiate reactions that do not already take place. An enzyme binds a specific substrate(s) at the active site to form an enzyme–substrate complex, the reaction occurs and the product(s) are then released.

Coenzymes transfer small groups of atoms (e.g. pairs of H atoms) between different molecules in the cell.

During your study of Chapter 5, you have been able to practise your science communication skills by producing a summary list of the scientific content that you would include in an account (Activity 5.3). In addition, you will have had the opportunity to revisit, revise and integrate scientific concepts from previous books of S104 (Activities 5.1 and 5.2) and incorporate these concepts into the new material covered in Chapter 5.

# Chapter 6
# Energy for life

In this chapter, the processes by which living things obtain the energy they need for life are examined. You will look in detail at the vital energy transformations that maintain organisms and how energy is made available to living cells for the fundamental processes of life: metabolism, growth and reproduction.

In Section 2.3 you met the concept of metabolism to describe the sum total of all the chemical reactions that occur in living things. There it was established that organisms have two broad requirements – a source of carbon-based materials and a source of energy, and that these requirements differ between autotrophic organisms and heterotrophic organisms. Starting with the process of photosynthesis, autotrophs can manufacture all the biological molecules they require from basic chemical raw materials, i.e. carbon dioxide and water. The Sun supplies the energy for photosynthesis and solar energy is converted ultimately into chemical energy in the form of sugars. Heterotrophs, on the other hand, derive both their supply of carbon-based substances and their energy supply from the food they eat, by consuming either plants and/or other animals.

Photosynthesis is therefore one of the most important chemical processes in nature because by harnessing solar energy it supplies the biological molecules on which autotrophs and, in turn, heterotrophs depend. This chapter begins with an overview of the process of photosynthesis and then considers the fate of the carbon-based molecules produced. Plants use some of these molecules as building blocks to manufacture the complex molecules (storage carbohydrates such as starch, proteins and TAGs) investigated in Chapter 5. Alternatively, large proportions are used to supply chemical energy for reactions taking place in the cell.

As you are aware from Book 1 (Section 7.3), energy is released from organic molecules by the process of respiration. In this chapter you will consider how the organic molecules manufactured by photosynthesis are made available (via feeding and digestive processes) for respiration in heterotrophic organisms and then investigate the process of respiration in more depth. The commonest source of energy in cells is glucose; you will be concerned only with the main principles of the complex series of reactions required to break glucose down in aerobic (with oxygen) conditions and in anaerobic (without oxygen) conditions. You will briefly examine how cells can also release energy from molecules other than glucose. A final consideration of the similarities between respiratory and photosynthetic processes concludes this chapter.

## 6.1    Energy in biological systems

Living things require a constant input of energy from their environment in order to sustain life. All organisms obtain this energy from the oxidation of fuel molecules in the process called respiration and, in addition, autotrophs may obtain energy directly by harnessing it from light. The energy derived from these two sources must be converted into a suitable chemical form before organisms can use it for the processes of life. This is a chemical store or carrier of energy and it takes the form of a molecule, adenosine triphosphate (**ATP**). The simplified structure of ATP is shown in Figure 6.1. It consists of an organic part – a **base** plus sugar combination called adenosine – and a short chain of three phosphate groups; hence the name *tri*phosphate. One of the phosphate groups can be easily removed by hydrolysis to give **ADP** (adenosine *di*phosphate) and an inorganic phosphate ion, which is usually written as $P_i$.

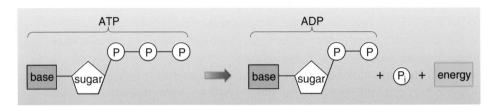

**Figure 6.1**    The breakdown of ATP (adenosine triphosphate) to ADP (adenosine diphosphate) and $P_i$ (inorganic phosphate). (Note that the term base has a different meaning here than in Book 4: you will return to this type of base again, in a different context, in Chapter 10.)

In the conversion of ATP to ADP and $P_i$, a large amount of energy is *released*. Similarly, in the synthesis of ATP from ADP and $P_i$, the same amount of energy is *absorbed*. During an energy-releasing process, such as the oxidation of fuel molecules in respiration or the absorption of light by plants in photosynthesis, the cell transforms the energy either in the fuel molecule or from light into chemical energy stored in ATP. These two simultaneous processes – energy release and ATP synthesis – are said to be *coupled*, as shown in Figure 6.2.

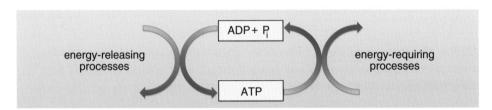

**Figure 6.2**    ATP acts as a molecular link between the various cellular processes that release energy and those that require energy. The energy from energy-releasing processes is coupled to the energy-requiring process of ATP synthesis.

What is important to the cell is that the 'reverse' coupling can take place. Figure 6.2 also shows how the conversion of ATP to ADP + $P_i$ releases energy and this reaction is coupled to energy-requiring processes. ATP therefore acts as an energy transfer molecule in the cell.

ATP is only a short-lived energy store, or energy carrier, which is never allowed to accumulate in the cell. It is rapidly recycled so there is a continuous turnover of ADP + $P_i$ to ATP and vice versa occurring constantly in the cell. In fact, in a typical cell a molecule of ATP is consumed within a minute of its formation.

## 6.2   Photosynthesis as a biosynthetic pathway

The wealth of biological molecules introduced in Chapter 5 are all manufactured in cells by a variety of different interlinked chemical processes. The process of building small organic molecules and combining them into the complex molecules that make up the cell is known as **biosynthesis**.

Photosynthesis is an example of biosynthesis: in this case, a process that builds up organic molecules (sugars) from inorganic molecules (carbon dioxide and water). Once manufactured, these simple sugar molecules can in turn be built up inside the cell into increasingly more complex molecules such as polysaccharides, proteins or lipids. Biosynthesis also produces numerous specialised substances, such as lignin (the material that makes the wood of trees hard) and pigments (for example, those that produce the brilliant colours of flower petals and the green pigment chlorophyll in chloroplasts).

An important feature of all biosynthetic processes is that they require energy. Chemical reactions in cells typically take place in multiple stages, an orderly sequence of linked chemical reactions called a **metabolic pathway**. Each chemical reaction in a pathway is catalysed by a specific enzyme and the product of each reaction is referred to as an **intermediate**. In biosynthetic metabolic pathways, energy in the form of ATP is usually required for each of the reactions in the sequence; however, in photosynthesis things are a little more complicated. The metabolic pathway is actually composed of two discrete phases. The first phase is referred to as the **light reactions**; here solar energy is used to manufacture ATP. The second part of the pathway, the **dark reactions**, which are not dependent on light, consume the ATP produced in the light reactions in order to supply the energy required to make glucose from water and carbon dioxide.

There is, therefore, no direct link between the Sun's energy and the chemical reactions that combine carbon dioxide and water. Instead ATP acts as an intermediary substance. ATP can be thought of as energy currency; converting ADP to ATP is collecting energy income, in this case from solar energy, and this energy is then spent on the various processes that require energy when ATP is converted back to ADP.

The first concern to be addressed, therefore, is how the photosynthesising plant cell produces ATP from $ADP + P_i$ using light energy during the light reactions of photosynthesis.

### 6.2.1   ATP production in chloroplasts during photosynthesis

The chloroplast is the site of the photosynthetic reactions, which produce glucose from carbon dioxide and water, releasing oxygen as a by-product.

$$6CO_2 + 6H_2O + \text{solar energy} \longrightarrow C_6H_{12}O_6 + 6O_2 \qquad (6.1)$$

Equation 6.1 shows the reaction for photosynthesis giving glucose as the organic compound produced. Chloroplasts lie in the cytosol, are bounded by an outer membrane and also have internal membranes. The internal membranes are folded back on themselves many times to form stacks called **grana** (singular: granum), as shown in Figure 6.3.

**Figure 6.3** (a) Electron micrograph of a chloroplast from a cell of a leaf of the Busy Lizzy (*Impatiens* sp.) showing the stacks of internal membranes, or grana, and the space between the grana, known as the stroma. The dark, oval structures are starch grains. (b) Diagram of a chloroplast showing internal 'energy-exchange' membranes – the thylakoids and stromal lamellae.

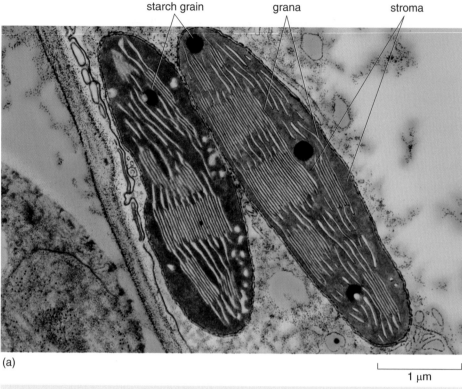

starch grain          grana          stroma

(a)

1 μm

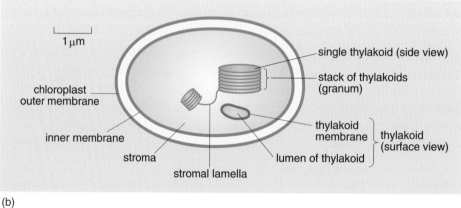

1 μm

chloroplast outer membrane

inner membrane

stroma

stromal lamella

single thylakoid (side view)

stack of thylakoids (granum)

thylakoid membrane

lumen of thylakoid

thylakoid (surface view)

(b)

Each granum consists of a stack of flattened sacs called **thylakoids**. The light-capturing machinery for photosynthesis, including the all-important light-absorbing chlorophyll molecules, are embedded within the surface membranes of the thylakoids and it is in these membranes where ATP is generated using energy captured from the Sun. The space inside the thylakoid is known as the thylakoid lumen.

■ Why is it important that the chloroplast contains so many membranes?

☐ To increase the surface area of the chloroplast capable of capturing incident solar energy.

Surrounding the thylakoid membranes is the **stroma** of the chloroplast; this is a fluid-filled space and is the site of the biosynthetic processes that manufacture sugar molecules. This type of compartmentation is a characteristic feature of cells (introduced in Section 4.1) and is important for the functioning of the chloroplast.

First you will look at the process by which ATP is generated in the chloroplast. Chlorophyll molecules can absorb photons of light. As light strikes the chlorophyll molecule, a photochemical reaction takes place whereby energy from light is used to split the hydrogen atoms in water into their constituent electrons and protons. Equation 6.2 shows how the protons and electrons in each hydrogen atom are separated from each other and from the oxygen atom.

$$H_2O \longrightarrow 2H^+ + 2e^- + \tfrac{1}{2} O_2 \qquad\qquad (6.2)$$

(Note that, for convenience, we may sometimes use fractions to balance equations – in this case, $\tfrac{1}{2}$.)

The released electrons are immediately transferred to a protein embedded in the thylakoid membrane called an electron carrier, the protons are released into the lumen of the thylakoid membrane and the oxygen is ultimately released from the cell as a by-product. So light energy is used to transfer electrons from water to a specific membrane protein in the thylakoid. You will now follow the fate of these transferred electrons and find the link to ATP production.

This first electron carrier is actually one of several membrane proteins; collectively these make up a photosynthetic **electron transport chain** or **ETC**. These are arranged in sequence repetitively along all the thylakoid membranes in every chloroplast (Figure 6.4). The electron carriers can readily accommodate extra electrons. Those carriers that bind electrons more tightly than other carriers are said to have a higher *electron affinity*. Carriers are arranged in the thylakoid membrane in order of increasing electron affinity. In this way, they form a chain that transports the

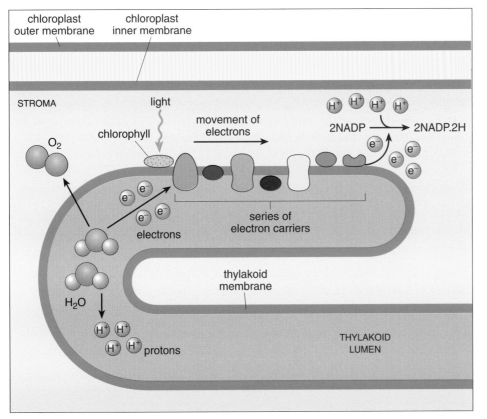

**Figure 6.4**  The photosynthetic electron transport chain consists of a series of protein electron carriers (shown here as coloured structures arranged in a line) embedded in the thylakoid membranes of the chloroplast. The carriers are arranged in order of increasing electron affinity. Solar energy captured by chlorophyll splits water into hydrogen and oxygen and the hydrogen into its constituent electrons and protons. Electrons are then transferred along the carrier system and the protons remain in the thylakoid lumen.

electrons released from water. The electron affinity of the first carrier is high enough to accept a pair of electrons from water. The second carrier removes the electrons from the first, and so on down the chain.

Once the moving electrons reach the end of the carrier system they have to be removed, otherwise electron transport would come to a halt. The ETC therefore relies on a substance that is capable of accepting the electrons from the final carrier. In Section 5.6.4, you learnt about coenzymes, which are group transfer molecules that can collect atoms from one reaction and shuttle them to another. In this case, the coenzyme **NADP** (nicotinamide adenine dinucleotide phosphate) accepts the electrons from the ETC and combines them with protons from the stroma to produce NADP.2H, the reduced form of this coenzyme; the NADP molecule has therefore accepted the equivalent of two hydrogen atoms. The NADP.2H molecules formed during this process will be vitally important for the synthesis of glucose, which occurs during the dark reactions of photosynthesis.

$$2H^+ + 2e^- + NADP \longrightarrow NADP.2H \tag{6.3}$$

As Equation 6.3 shows, each NADP combines with two electrons from the ETC and two protons from the stroma to form NADP.2H. One oxygen atom is released for every water molecule undergoing this photolytic (literally, 'splitting by light') process. Overall the reaction can be summarised as:

$$NADP + H_2O + solar\ energy \longrightarrow NADP.2H + \tfrac{1}{2}O_2 \tag{6.4}$$

■ How many water molecules must undergo photolysis in order to produce one molecule of oxygen?

☐ Two, since each water molecule contains only one oxygen atom.

This still leaves the question of exactly how ATP is synthesised from ADP. As electrons move along this electron transport chain, energy is released. This energy is not harnessed directly into the production of ATP. In fact, two processes are coupled together here: first, *electron transport*, which brings about the reduction of NADP to NADP.2H by water; and second, *phosphorylation*, which is the associated production of ATP from ADP and $P_i$. The synthesis of ATP hinges on the differences in concentration of protons ($H^+$ ions) in the two compartments of the chloroplast, the lumen of the thylakoid (the inside) and the stroma (the area outside the thylakoid). The transport of electrons from water along the ETC has a marked effect on the concentration of protons on either side of the thylakoid membrane separating these two compartments. Three processes achieve this difference in proton concentration:

1   The protons from the hydrogen in the water molecules are left behind in the lumen when the electrons begin their journey along the ETC. This increases the number of protons on the lumen side of the thylakoid membrane.

2   Protons are removed from the stroma side of the thylakoid membrane when two protons combine with NADP and two transported electrons to form NADP.2H. This reduces the number of protons on the stroma side of the thylakoid membrane.

3   The second electron carrier protein in the ETC is actually a mobile carrier that shuttles across the thylakoid membrane, collecting protons from the stroma side of the membrane and depositing them on the lumen side.

This means that a proton concentration gradient is formed across the thylakoid membrane, with a high concentration of protons in the lumen and a low concentration in the stroma, as shown in Figure 6.5.

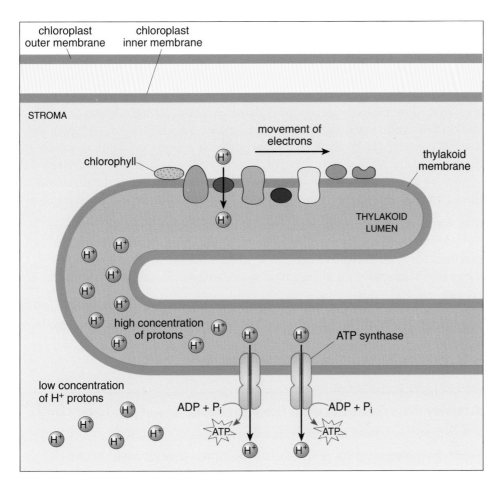

**Figure 6.5** Light-induced movement of electrons causes an increase in the concentration of protons in the thylakoid lumen and a decrease in the concentration of protons in the stroma. Electron transport energy is therefore stored as a transmembrane proton gradient. Protons can then flow back into the stroma down their concentration gradient through special channel proteins. These proteins are also ATP synthase complexes and, as protons flow through them, ATP is synthesised from ADP and $P_i$.

Energy from electron transport is now effectively stored, because there is a proton concentration gradient between the stroma and the lumen. This energy can be released, simply by allowing protons to move in the reverse direction, i.e. down their concentration gradient, from high to low concentration. This movement of protons can only occur in one part of the thylakoid membrane; protons are allowed to flood back into the stroma through a channel protein, which is also an enzyme, called **ATP synthase** (Figure 6.5). This movement of protons down the concentration gradient from lumen to stroma supplies energy to synthesise ATP from ADP and $P_i$. As the name ATP synthase suggests, this enzyme catalyses the formation of ATP from ADP and $P_i$. Thus the energy released in the transfer of electrons along the ETC to NADP.2H is used to accumulate protons in the thylakoid lumen, thereby being stored as a proton concentration gradient; as the protons flood back through the ATP synthase channel, this energy is used to convert ADP + $P_i$ to ATP.

■  What may be the consequences for ATP production if the thylakoid membranes were damaged so that $H^+$ ions could move across them without restriction?

☐  It would be impossible to build up a proton concentration gradient as $H^+$ ions would tend to move freely across the thylakoid membrane, equalising their concentrations on either side. This would mean that protons would not flow through ATP synthase channel proteins and ATP would not be formed.

This storage and flow of protons is analogous to a water storage system for producing electricity. In such a system, electricity is used in off-peak periods to move water from a lower-level reservoir to a higher-level reservoir, where it is stored. This process transforms electrical energy into the gravitational energy of water. During peak hours, the water is allowed to flow down from the higher-level to the lower-level reservoir through turbines (large water wheels) coupled to electricity generators. So in this process, the stored gravitational energy of the water is converted back to electrical energy (Book 3, Section 5.4). In this analogy, the stored water is the protons that are concentrated on one side of the thylakoid membrane as a result of electron transport, the higher reservoir is the thylakoid lumen, the lower reservoir is the stroma, and the turbine is the ATP synthase.

The formation of ATP in this way is called **photophosphorylation** (meaning *light*-driven phosphorylation). These initial reactions of photosynthesis, the light reactions (or more correctly the light-dependent reactions, since they can only take place in the presence of light), are summarised in Equation 6.5:

$$ADP + P_i + NADP + H_2O + \text{solar energy} \longrightarrow ATP + NADP.2H + \tfrac{1}{2}O_2 \quad (6.5)$$

The products of the light reactions, NADP.2H and ATP, do not appear in the overall equation for photosynthesis (Equation 6.1) since they will be used up in the pathway that builds sugar from carbon dioxide.

### Activity 6.1    Summarising the light reactions of photosynthesis

We expect this activity will take you approximately 30 minutes.

When describing complex processes in biology, it is usual to resort to using diagrams to help explain a sequence of events. When writing your own summaries or accounts to answer assignment questions, you will find it very useful to include diagrams; they can save you a lot of words, but it is vital that they are fully integrated into your writing. Diagrams that are merely added on and are not referred to in the text of your answer will not serve much purpose. It is therefore useful to think about how to properly incorporate diagrams in your writing.

This activity will allow you to practise using a fully labelled diagram to explain a complex biological process in a short written account.

Figure 6.6 summarises the main events in the light reactions of photosynthesis in the chloroplast but has some important labels missing. Complete the labelling in Figure 6.6 and then write a short summary account of about 200 words that refers explicitly to Figure 6.6 and describes:

• the key sequence of events in the light reactions
• the products of the light reactions.

You will find it useful to work through the detail of the diagram, picking out the main events in order. Write about each of these main events, referring to the diagram to summarise the process.

Compare your answer with the comments on this activity at the end of this book.

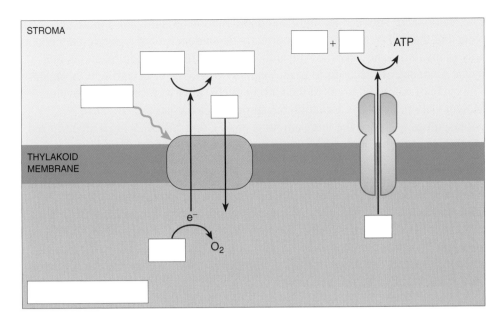

**Figure 6.6** Summary diagram: the light reactions.

## 6.2.2 The dark reactions and carbon dioxide fixation

This next subset of photosynthetic reactions, the *dark reactions* (or light-independent reactions), take place exclusively in the stroma of the chloroplast.

The products of the light reactions, ATP and the reduced coenzyme NADP.2H, are said to drive the dark reactions. ATP produced in the light reactions provides the energy for the process; NADP.2H provides the reducing power to convert carbon dioxide to a carbohydrate. This conversion is called 'fixing' of carbon. You will recall from Book 4, Section 14.2.2, that adding hydrogen to a molecule is termed reduction and removing hydrogen is termed oxidation. Converting carbon dioxide to carbohydrate is a reduction reaction, since hydrogen is added to carbon dioxide. This hydrogen has to come from somewhere and indeed is supplied by NADP.2H synthesised during the light reactions.

■ When one substance in a reaction is reduced what happens to the other substance?

☐ It must be oxidised, since reduction and oxidation can only take place together. Here carbon dioxide is reduced to glucose and NADP.2H is oxidised to NADP.

NADP.2H will be oxidised back to NADP where it can then be reused to accept further electrons from the ETC operating on the thylakoid membrane. You will now look in more detail at the dark reactions and how ATP and NADP.2H are utilised.

The relationship between the light and dark reactions is shown in Figure 6.7. Note that the dark reactions are not directly dependent on light, nor do they occur only in the dark. They use the ATP and NADP.2H from the light reactions in a cyclic sequence of reactions to reduce carbon dioxide, so converting it to sugars. The cycle of reactions is called the **Calvin cycle** (after its principal discoverer, Melvin Calvin, in 1945). Equation 6.6 summarises the dark reactions of photosynthesis. Notice the large amounts of ATP and NADP.2H that are required to produce each molecule of 3C sugar phosphate from carbon dioxide.

$$3CO_2 + 9ATP + 6NADP.2H \longrightarrow 3C \text{ sugar phosphate} + 9ADP + 8P_i + 6NADP \quad (6.6)$$

As shown in Equation 6.6 and Figure 6.7, the first carbon compound to be produced in the chloroplast is a 3C sugar phosphate. The designation '3C' refers to the number of carbon atoms in the carbon 'backbone' of the molecule. This 3C sugar phosphate is transported to the cytosol. Here, some is used directly as an energy source, but much of it is converted into glucose phosphate and fructose phosphate, which are both 6C sugars.

**Figure 6.7** The relationship between the light and dark reactions of photosynthesis. The reactions of carbon fixation are collectively called the Calvin cycle.

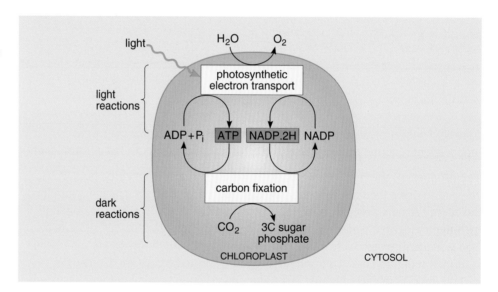

Glucose and fructose phosphates in the cytosol then combine to produce the disaccharide sucrose, with the loss of their phosphate groups. Sucrose is the major form in which sugar is transported between plant cells. It is easily transported from the leaves (where most of it is made) to the rest of the plant. As well as sugars, both fatty acids and amino acids are synthesised in the plant cells from the 3C sugar phosphate product of the dark reactions. Most of the 3C sugar phosphate molecules that remain in the chloroplast are converted to glucose molecules, which are then polymerised into starch. A starch grain is visible in the chloroplast in Figure 6.3a. As you learnt in Section 5.3, starch, like glycogen, is a large biopolymer that serves as a sugar reserve. The production of starch occurs in daylight.

■   What is the other product of photosynthesis, besides sugar?

☐   Oxygen (see Equation 6.1).

In fact, almost all the Earth's supply of atmospheric oxygen comes from photosynthesis. Without the evolution of photosynthetic autotrophs, the Earth's atmosphere would have remained anaerobic (literally, 'without air'; this will be discussed in more detail in Book 8).

As you saw in Section 4.2, most of a plant's chloroplasts are located in the inner layers of cells of the leaves. How can the carbon dioxide needed for photosynthesis get to the chloroplasts in these cells? Carbon dioxide enters the leaf through small pores in its surface. These pores, called **stomata** (singular: stoma), are shown in Figure 6.8. Stomata can open to allow the exchange of gases (oxygen and carbon dioxide) and close to reduce water loss from the plant. This opening and closing of stomata is controlled by pairs of guard cells that surround them (Figure 6.8).

Not surprisingly, photosynthesis is subject to stringent controls by the cell, ensuring that light and dark reactions keep in step and that the plant makes maximum use of the available light and carbon dioxide. An understanding of the mechanisms of control of photosynthesis is very important for maximising plant growth and crop production, particularly in countries where many people go hungry. Currently, there is a great deal of interest in the mechanism of the light reactions, since this is the stage that uses a truly renewable energy source – solar energy. In the long term, the key components of photosynthesis may perhaps be assembled artificially into light-driven fuel cells.

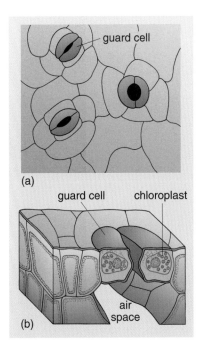

**Figure 6.8**   (a) Diagram of leaf surface showing three stomata, each of which is surrounded by two guard cells. (b) One of these stomata has been cut and is viewed from the side. Guard cells can change in size and so alter the size of the stoma.

## Question 6.1

State two reasons why photosynthesis is a vital process for life on Earth.

## Question 6.2

In what way are the dark reactions dependent on the light reactions of photosynthesis?

## Question 6.3

Chloroplasts isolated from spinach can be broken open and then separated into membranous material and soluble components, which will be called M and S, respectively. Both M and S are biochemically active. Which of the following features apply to each of these two chloroplast components: (a) contains chlorophyll; (b) converts carbon dioxide to sugar; (c) produces oxygen from water?

## 6.3   The link between photosynthesis and respiration

You have seen how photosynthesis enables plants to harness solar energy and convert it into the energy-rich molecules of ATP and NADP.2H during the light reactions. The ATP then supplies the energy while the reduced coenzyme molecules supply the reducing power for the conversion of carbon dioxide to organic carbon in the dark reactions. The first sugar produced is a 3C sugar phosphate, but this may be built up further into glucose or fructose phosphates and further converted to sucrose or to starch. Alternatively, the sugar phosphate molecules may be converted to amino acids (in order for the plant cell to construct proteins) or to fatty acids (for TAG synthesis). In fact, all the other biological molecules in plants are derived from the carbon dioxide that the plant 'fixed' during photosynthesis. All these 'building up' type chemical reactions are examples of biosynthesis. Photosynthesis is a special type of biosynthetic process; it is one where the energy used for the biosynthesis steps (the dark reactions where glucose is made) is derived from the ATP manufactured in the light-driven steps (the light reactions).

Manufacturing all other complex molecules from the products of photosynthesis requires energy and again this energy must be supplied in the form of ATP. However, this time the ATP will not be generated from the capture of solar energy – that can only occur in the chloroplast in order to fix carbon dioxide – but by the breakdown of glucose molecules (or indeed other substances like fats and proteins) in glucose oxidation. By converting solar energy into chemical energy in glucose the plant has a method of storing energy until that energy is required, at which point it re-oxidises the glucose in order to release the chemical energy it contains and converts it back to carbon dioxide and water. This is the reverse process to photosynthesis and the term cellular respiration is used to fully describe the reaction. You will return to a comparison of photosynthesis and respiration in a short while. In the meantime, you will look at the process of respiration in more detail. Bear in mind that the respiratory process is exactly the same in both autotrophs and heterotrophs. All organisms must respire to release energy from fuel molecules, no matter if they made the fuel themselves (plants) or acquired it by eating another organism (animals).

### Question 6.4

Biosynthesis reactions require energy in the form of ATP. What is unique about the way this ATP is supplied for the biosynthesis of glucose during photosynthesis compared with all other cellular biosynthetic reactions?

### 6.3.1   Respiration

The complete oxidation of glucose is represented by the equation:

$$C_6H_{12}O_6 + 6O_2 \longrightarrow 6CO_2 + 6H_2O \qquad (6.7)$$

Glucose oxidation is another example of a metabolic pathway, but this time, in contrast to photosynthesis, complex organic molecules are broken down to simple inorganic molecules. These types of reactions are called **catabolism** and in all cases energy is released. The definition of metabolism can therefore be defined as the sum total of all the biosynthetic and catabolic reactions that take place in living cells. Effectively there must be a balance between the amount of energy released by catabolic processes and the amount of energy required by biosynthesis. ATP acts as the molecular link transferring chemical energy between cellular processes that release energy and those that require energy. You know that in photosynthesis the ATP needed to drive the biosynthetic part of the pathway, the dark reactions, is synthesised using energy derived from the Sun during the light reactions, but in respiration the energy to phosphorylate ADP comes from the chemical energy contained in glucose molecules.

It is through the production of ATP that the energy originally derived from the oxidation of glucose (or TAGs) is released in a conveniently packaged form for immediate use. This happens in all living organisms.

## 6.3.2    The efficiency of respiration

You can think of glucose as a fuel for living processes and this prompts the question, 'How good a fuel is it?' How efficient is the process of respiration fuelled by glucose compared with, say, a car fuelled by petrol? This question is best answered by looking at the way that energy is released during respiration, and specifically during the oxidation of glucose.

When glucose is oxidised completely to carbon dioxide and water, a very large amount of energy is released – about 2900 kJ mol$^{-1}$. If this oxidation takes place outside the cell, e.g. by burning glucose on a spoon, all this energy is released in a single step, mostly in the form of heat, as shown in Figure 6.9a. The release of so much energy in one step in a living cell would disrupt the cell's delicate structure. Furthermore, there is no single biochemical process that could make use of so much energy at one go. In living cells, this energy is released piecemeal, by means of a series of small steps, as shown in Figure 6.9b. The energy released comes in small, manageable quantities that can be coupled to the production of ATP from ADP and P$_i$.

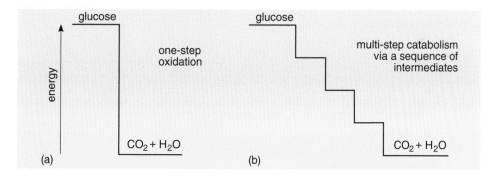

**Figure 6.9**    Glucose oxidation to carbon dioxide and water: (a) one-step oxidation outside the cell; (b) multi-step oxidation inside the cell, which occurs via a sequence of intermediates. (The number of intermediates is much greater than shown here.) Notice that the total amount of energy released is the same in (a) and (b).

So what is the energy-carrying capacity – or energy 'value' – of ATP? The conversion of ADP + P$_i$ to ATP absorbs quite a large amount of energy (about 30.6 kJ mol$^{-1}$) and, conversely, the conversion of ATP to ADP + P$_i$ releases the same amount of energy. The complete oxidation of one mole of glucose to carbon dioxide and water produces around 30 moles of ATP.

You may be wondering why chemical interconversions in cells follow such complex pathways. As you saw above, this means that energy is parcelled out, bit by bit, and efficiently transferred to ATP. In fact, cellular respiration is remarkably efficient.

■ If 30 moles of ATP are produced for each mole of glucose completely respired (to carbon dioxide and water), and about 30.6 kJ are required to produce each mole of ATP, what percentage of the chemical energy available from glucose oxidation is transferred into the chemical energy of ATP?

☐ A total of $30 \times 30.6$ kJ $= 918$ kJ of chemical energy are transferred to ATP. Since 2900 kJ are released in the complete oxidation of one mole of glucose, the percentage of the chemical energy in glucose that is transferred to ATP is:

$$\frac{918 \text{ kJ}}{2900 \text{ kJ}} \times 100\% = 32\%$$

■ What happens to the rest of the energy?

☐ It is lost as heat.

So the efficiency with which the energy from sugar is transferred to ATP is about 32%. You can now answer the question that was posed at the beginning of this section, 'How efficient is the process of respiration compared with a car fuelled by petrol?' The answer is that it is considerably more efficient, since a car at best transforms 20% of the chemical energy stored in petrol to mechanical energy. If animals were so inefficient at transferring the energy stored in food into energy stored in ATP they would need to eat voraciously most of the time.

In the next section, you will look at how heterotrophic organisms obtain the food they need from other organisms.

Question 6.5

When a person runs, what change occurs in the amount of ATP in their muscles?

Question 6.6

Which of the following statements about metabolism are true?

(a) The conversion of ADP + $P_i$ to ATP is coupled to energy-requiring reactions in the cell.

(b) ATP is a carrier of chemical energy.

(c) All the ATP produced in the cell by catabolic pathways is used in biosynthetic pathways.

(d) Energy derived from the oxidation of glucose is packaged as ATP and used within minutes.

### 6.3.3   Raw materials for catabolism

It has already been mentioned that glucose respiration occurs in all cells. It is quite clear where plants get the raw materials for respiration from: they make the necessary glucose and oxygen themselves during photosynthesis. During daylight hours plants are photosynthesising and respiring at the same time. As photosynthesis proceeds at a faster rate than respiration, the net effect is to remove carbon dioxide from the atmosphere and release oxygen to the atmosphere. More glucose is therefore synthesised during the day by photosynthesis than is consumed by respiration. At night, in the absence of light, plants are only respiring and so they become consumers of oxygen and net producers of carbon dioxide, like heterotrophs.

Moving on to heterotrophic organisms, how do they obtain the necessary raw materials? The simple answer is from their food. Heterotrophs eat either autotrophs or other heterotrophs and make use of the more complex molecules formed by autotrophs; the products of the metabolism of plants are the starting point for the metabolism of animals.

The tissues of animals such as ourselves are constantly being replaced from raw materials in food; as the poet Walter de la Mare put it, 'whatever Miss T eats turns into Miss T'. Less poetically, this can be restated as: 'cows convert grass into meat and milk'. In order to use the molecules in food and transform them into cellular substances, the food molecules – mainly biopolymers and TAGs – have to be broken down into small molecules by means of digestion. Animals obtain their raw materials by digesting the complex molecules eaten as food, as shown in Figure 6.10.

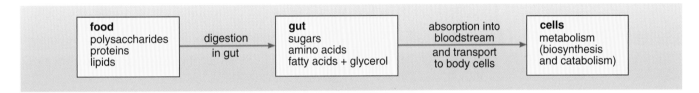

**Figure 6.10**   The steps from digestion of food to metabolism in cells.

Plants will have utilised the glucose made during photosynthesis to manufacture a whole range of organic molecules. When animals eat they consume plant cells and hence the diet can contain a 'mixed bag' of biological molecules. This can include sugars such as glucose and fructose, polysaccharides such as starch or cellulose, plus lipids and proteins. Large multicellular animals have specialised organs in which this occurs, such as the gut in humans.

Apart from mechanical processes, such as chewing and churning around in the stomach and intestine, digestion is largely a matter of hydrolysis. As you saw in Section 5.2, hydrolysis is the reversal of the condensation reactions by which small organic molecules were linked together in the first place. In Book 4, Chapter 15 you were introduced to the digestive enzymes (proteins in the gut that hydrolyse the components of food): lipids (fats) are hydrolysed to fatty acids and glycerol, polysaccharides are hydrolysed to sugars, and proteins are hydrolysed to amino acids. Examples of digestive enzymes include: amylase in saliva, which hydrolyses starch; pepsin in the stomach and trypsin in the intestine, both of which hydrolyse proteins; and lipases in the intestine, which hydrolyse lipids.

The small organic molecules resulting from digestion then have to reach individual cells. This is a very important step. In large multicellular animals, such as humans, there are specialised transport systems, like the blood, which carry nutrients from the gut to within a few micrometres of the cell membrane. The cell membrane is selectively permeable (Section 5.7) and the transfer of molecules across it – the final stage of getting the molecules into the cell – requires specific membrane transport proteins and the expenditure of energy. When the products of digestion are inside the cell, their metabolism can begin.

## 6.4    Glucose oxidation

The focus of this section is the metabolism of just one of the products of digestion: glucose. This is the commonest source of energy in cells, and almost all cells that live in an aerobic (oxygen-containing) environment get substantial amounts of their energy through this process. You saw in Section 6.2.1 that energy is required to fuel the huge number of biosynthetic reactions necessary to maintain life and to drive various other activities of life, such as muscular movement. The breakdown of glucose involves a complex series of chemical reactions and only the main principles are dealt with here.

### Question 6.7

Imagine a molecule of glucose, originally produced by photosynthesis, then used for storage within a plant cell. Outline what must happen to this glucose molecule before it can be broken down inside a cell of an animal that consumes the plant.

### 6.4.1    Overview of glucose oxidation

This section gives a brief overview of the complex process of glucose oxidation (respiration) in the cell, which is described in detail in Sections 6.4.2–6.4.5. You will find it helpful to bear in mind the basic information given here as you study these later sections. You need to remember the names and key features of the overall process and where the component pathways occur in the cell.

Recall from Section 6.3.2 that the oxidation of glucose takes place in many small, enzyme-catalysed steps. In fact, there are four distinct stages in the breakdown of glucose to release energy, each of which comprises many separate chemical reactions. These stages operate in succession to bring about its complete oxidation to carbon dioxide and water:

$$C_6H_{12}O_6 + 6O_2 + 30ADP + 30P_i \longrightarrow 6CO_2 + 6H_2O + 30ATP \tag{6.8}$$

(Equation 6.8 is a repeat of Equation 6.7, but with the associated ATP production; note that the value for 30 ATP molecules per molecule of glucose completely oxidised is approximate and depends on the type of cell in question.)

The four stages of glucose oxidation are shown in Figure 6.11. They are glycolysis, the link reaction, the tricarboxylic acid cycle (abbreviated to TCA cycle) and electron transport coupled to oxidative phosphorylation. This figure summarises the important information on glucose oxidation; the details are explained in later sections, but for now you will consider how the component pathways illustrated relate to the overall equation of glucose oxidation given in Equation 6.8.

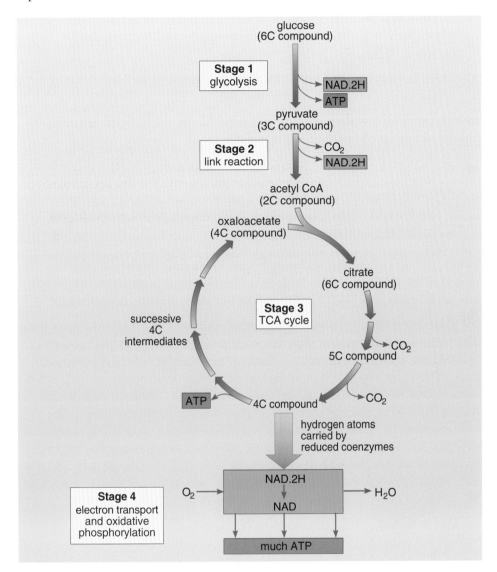

**Figure 6.11** The glucose oxidation pathway showing the four distinct stages of the process, the changes that occur in the carbon backbone, and the points at which the end-products carbon dioxide and water are released. (The term 'carbon backbone' refers to those carbon atoms linked together in the glucose molecule.) The information given in this diagram is important and by the time you have completed your study of glucose oxidation you should be able to explain it.

Notice from Figure 6.11 that the first three stages break down sequentially the carbon backbone of glucose (a chain of six carbon atoms, 6C), and release the carbon as the end-product, carbon dioxide.

1  **Glycolysis** (pronounced 'gly-kolli-sis') brings about the splitting of each 6C glucose to two molecules of a 3C (a chain of three carbon atoms) intermediate.

2  The **link reaction** converts each molecule of the 3C end-product of glycolysis to a 2C intermediate (with the release of a 1C compound, carbon dioxide).

3  The **tricarboxylic acid cycle (TCA cycle)** completes the breakdown of the carbon chain to 1C, i.e. to carbon dioxide.

In addition to the breakdown of the carbon backbone, the 12 hydrogen atoms of glucose are removed in a stepwise manner.

■  What type of molecule would be able to accept the hydrogen atoms removed from glucose?

☐  A coenzyme like NADP that accepts the hydrogen atoms removed from water during photosynthesis.

In fact, the coenzymes that accept hydrogen atoms from glucose in glucose oxidation are NAD and FAD (Table 5.3). The hydrogen atoms from Stages 1–3 are carried mainly as NAD.2H, the majority of them deriving from the TCA cycle.

The fourth and final stage of glucose oxidation is **electron transport** coupled to **oxidative phosphorylation**. It is during this stage that NAD.2H is oxidised back to NAD (or FAD.2H back to FAD) and the hydrogen atoms are transferred to molecular oxygen, producing the end-product water. You have already met one example of an electron transport system: you will recall that during the light reactions of photosynthesis, electrons move along a carrier system and are eventually picked up by NADP. These two different systems are compared in more detail later in this section.

■  Look at Figure 6.11 again. Which item has not yet been mentioned?

☐  ATP produced.

Recall that when glucose is oxidised on a spoon, all the energy appears as heat, whereas in the living cell some appears as heat and some as chemical energy in the ATP molecules formed from ADP and $P_i$. Figure 6.11 shows that most of the ATP is formed during Stage 4, and that this process is intimately linked to the oxidation of NAD.2H back to NAD.

So there are four distinct stages to glucose oxidation, but where in the cell does each of them occur? Figure 6.12 shows a cell with a mitochondrion in the cytosol. This figure also shows that each of the four stages of glucose oxidation occurs in a specific compartment within the cell. Only Stage 1, glycolysis, occurs in the cytosol. The remaining three stages of glucose oxidation take place in the mitochondrion. This organelle has an outer membrane as well as a convoluted inner membrane packed inside it. The inner membrane separates the mitochondrion into an inner fluid-filled centre, called the **matrix**, and a space between the inner and outer membranes, called the **intermembrane space**.

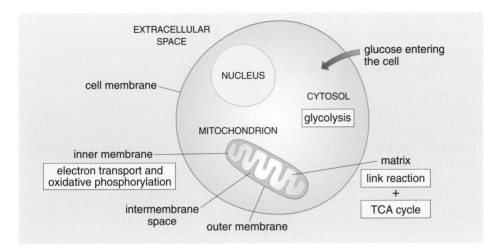

**Figure 6.12**    The location of each of the four stages of the glucose oxidation pathway in the cell. (The mitochondrion is much enlarged relative to the nucleus in order to show its internal structure.)

■ Name another organelle that illustrates this sort of compartmentation.

☐ The chloroplast – remember different chemical reactions take place in the stroma (dark reactions) and on the thylakoid membranes (light reactions).

Like the chloroplast, in the mitochondrion there is also a division of labour by the physical separation of internal compartments. Both Stages 2 and 3 of glucose oxidation – the link reaction and the TCA cycle – occur in the matrix. Stage 4, the coupled processes of electron transport and oxidative phosphorylation, takes place at the inner mitochondrial membrane. It is here that most of the ATP is produced in the cell. By the end of Section 6.4 you should appreciate the role of the mitochondrion in glucose oxidation, and why it is called the 'powerhouse of the cell'.

Different kinds of cell have different numbers of mitochondria within them – there are sometimes more than a thousand per cell. If you look back at Figure 4.3 you can see many mitochondria in the electron micrograph of a single mammalian liver cell. The more work a cell does, of whatever kind (e.g. biosynthesis or movement), the more mitochondria it contains. Thus, for example, a human skin cell contains fewer mitochondria than a human liver or muscle cell. Skin cells are relatively passive metabolically, liver cells are involved in much biosynthesis, and muscles are involved in the transformation of much chemical energy into kinetic energy. Thus the ATP requirements of cells and tissues can vary, and consequently the number of mitochondria they possess also differs.

Each of the four stages of glucose oxidation (Figure 6.11) will now be considered in turn, beginning with glycolysis.

## 6.4.2    Stage 1: glycolysis

Consider a glucose molecule that has just entered the cell. The first stage of glucose breakdown – the process of glycolysis (literally 'sugar splitting') – takes place in the cytosol. Here are found all the necessary enzymes. Glycolysis comprises a number of steps, and these are outlined in Figure 6.13. The pathway

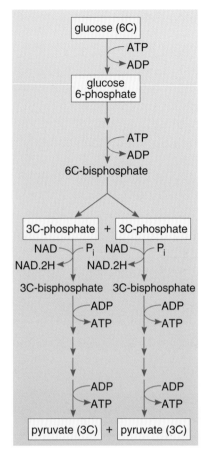

**Figure 6.13** Stage 1 of glucose oxidation: glycolysis. Note that the shorthand term '6C-bisphosphate' means a six-carbon compound with two phosphate groups, whereas 'glucose 6-phosphate' is glucose with a phosphate group on its carbon atom 6 (Figure 5.5 shows the carbon atom numbering in glucose).

begins with the 6C glucose molecule (shown at the top of the figure) and ends with two molecules of a 3C intermediate called **pyruvate** (pronounced 'pie-roo-vate'), shown at the bottom of Figure 6.13. Altogether there are eight intermediates between glucose and pyruvate, each formed from the preceding one by a different enzyme-catalysed reaction. Only the main reactions will be considered, starting with the splitting of the glucose carbon backbone.

Before glucose can be split under the conditions that exist in the cell, it has to be 'activated', so that energetically 'strong' bonds – like the C—C bonds holding the 6C backbone together – are weakened and hence more readily broken in the enzyme-catalysed reactions that follow. Activation is a complex process, but it can be brought about simply by placing charged groups near the bonds to be broken. Phosphate is one such group (Figure 5.3). All the intermediates of glycolysis have at least one phosphate group.

The first step in glycolysis is to phosphorylate (add a phosphate to) glucose, converting it to glucose 6-phosphate. The phosphate group is donated by ATP, and the reaction is catalysed by the enzyme hexokinase. There then follows a second phosphorylation step, which produces a doubly activated bisphosphate sugar (6C-bisphosphate in Figure 6.13; 'bis' here means two). This is then split into two 3C sugar phosphate molecules (3C-phosphate in the figure).

It may seem odd to use up two molecules of ATP right at the beginning of glycolysis, if the whole point of glucose oxidation is to generate ATP. But if you look again at Figure 6.13, you can see that this initial investment of ATP is justified by events later in the glycolytic pathway, where two reactions generate ATP, again from ADP. In fact, four ATP molecules are formed because each of the two 3C sugar phosphate molecules follows the same route to pyruvate; that is, the second half of the pathway happens twice for each molecule of glucose. In addition, as Figure 6.13 shows, some NAD is reduced to NAD.2H.

The important points to remember about glycolysis are that some of the energy stored in glucose has been tapped off into ATP and the reduced coenzyme NAD.2H. Most of the energy, however, is still stored in the two pyruvate molecules produced at the end of glycolysis.

Question 6.8

Complete Table 6.1 to summarise the key inputs and outputs and processes involved in glycolysis. You should include the number of molecules of substrate, the number of carbon-containing products and the number of any other products produced for each molecule of glucose moving along the pathway.

**Table 6.1** Summary of glycolysis.

| Reaction or metabolic pathway | Part of cell/ mitochondria located in | Begins with (principal substrate) | Carbon-containing end-products | Other products |
|---|---|---|---|---|
| glycolysis | | | | |

## 6.4.3   Stage 2: the link reaction

The two pyruvate molecules produced in glycolysis now move from the cytosol to the mitochondrion, passing through both outer and inner membranes and into the matrix (see Figure 6.12). It is here that the link reaction takes place.

In this reaction, one carbon atom is lost from the 3C pyruvate molecule as carbon dioxide, leaving a 2C fragment – the very reactive **acetyl** (pronounced 'asset-ile') group. This is transferred directly from pyruvate to a coenzyme called **coenzyme A** (**CoA** for short) (which was listed in Table 5.3). On combining with an acetyl group, the CoA molecule becomes **acetyl CoA**. At the same time, one molecule of NAD is reduced to NAD.2H. These simultaneous reactions are summarised in Equation 6.9.

$$\text{pyruvate} + \text{CoA} + \text{NAD} \longrightarrow \text{acetyl CoA} + CO_2 + \text{NAD.2H} \qquad (6.9)$$

The important point to remember about the link reaction is that the 2C acetyl group still contains some of the energy originally trapped in the glucose molecule and it is this group that is fed into the TCA cycle. In addition, some NAD.2H has been produced and this is eventually oxidised in the mitochondrion in Stage 4.

### Question 6.9

Complete Table 6.2 to summarise the key inputs and outputs and processes involved in the link reaction. You should include the number of molecules of substrate, the number of carbon-containing products and the number of any other products produced for each molecule of glucose moving along the pathway.

**Table 6.2**  Summary of the link reaction.

| Reaction or metabolic pathway | Part of cell/ mitochondria located in | Begins with (principal substrate) | Carbon-containing end-products | Other products |
|---|---|---|---|---|
| link reaction | | | | |

## 6.4.4   Stage 3: the TCA cycle

The 2C acetyl group (carried by CoA) is now dealt with by the TCA cycle (Figure 6.14). Like the link reaction, this circular sequence of enzyme-catalysed reactions occurs in the fluid-filled matrix of the mitochondrion. The overall change brought about by this cycle is the breaking of the C−C bond in the acetyl group, thus producing two molecules of carbon dioxide for each acetyl group entering the cycle.

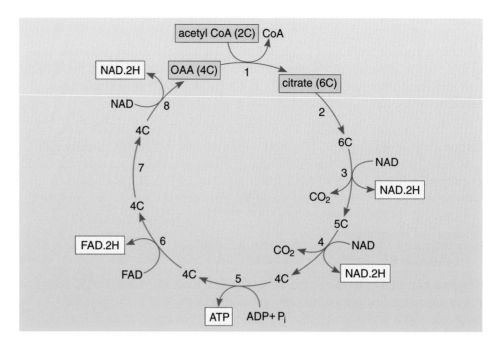

**Figure 6.14**   Details of the TCA cycle. The numbers 1–8 refer to the reactions that make up the cycle. OAA is the abbreviation for oxaloacetate.

This pathway is a cycle because one of the two compounds that take part in the first reaction (1) is regenerated at the end of the cycle, as shown in Figure 6.14.

■ From Figure 6.14, what are the two compounds that react together in reaction 1, and which one of these is regenerated at the end of the cycle?

☐ The two compounds that take part in reaction 1 are acetyl CoA (whose acetyl group is removed, releasing CoA again) and the 4C intermediate, oxaloacetate (OAA). Oxaloacetate is regenerated in the last reaction (reaction 8) of the cycle.

You can see from Figure 6.14 that the product of reaction 1 of the TCA cycle is citrate, a 6C compound. This is the result of combining 4C oxaloacetate with a 2C acetyl group. The 6C citrate is converted to another 6C intermediate, which is then converted via a 5C intermediate to a series of 4C intermediates, the last one of these being oxaloacetate (produced in reaction 8).

■ What happens to the two carbon atoms that are lost between 6C and 4C?

☐ They are converted to carbon dioxide (in reactions 3 and 4 of Figure 6.14).

During the TCA cycle hydrogen atoms are also 'lost'.

■ Where have these hydrogen atoms gone?

☐ They have been picked up by coenzymes, mainly NAD, forming the reduced coenzymes, mainly NAD.2H, that are so important for making ATP in the final stage of glucose oxidation. Another coenzyme shown in Figure 6.14 is FAD that, like NAD, carries pairs of hydrogen atoms.

Some ATP is made directly during each turn of the TCA cycle (reaction 5 in Figure 6.14), like the ATP produced in glycolysis. But as you will see, most of the cell's ATP is synthesised while dealing with the reduced coenzymes produced in Stages 1–3.

For each turn of the cycle, acetyl CoA has to be fed in from outside, from pyruvate via the link reaction as just described. Because two molecules of acetyl CoA are produced from each glucose molecule, the cycle has to turn twice to deal with both of them. (Some people remember this by thinking of the TCA cycle as the TCA bicycle!)

The important points to remember about the TCA cycle are:

- the remaining carbon atoms of glucose are released as carbon dioxide
- a large quantity of reduced coenzyme molecules are formed. (These are oxidised in Stage 4)
- some ATP is produced
- useful 4C and 5C intermediates are formed (you will return to these later).

Question 6.10

Complete Table 6.3 to summarise the key inputs and outputs and processes involved in the TCA cycle. You should include the number of molecules of substrate, the number of carbon-containing products and the number of any other products produced for each molecule of glucose moving along the pathway.

**Table 6.3**  Summary of the TCA cycle.

| Reaction or metabolic pathway | Part of cell/ mitochondria located in | Begins with (principal substrate) | Carbon-containing end-products | Other products |
|---|---|---|---|---|
| TCA cycle | | | | |

Question 6.11

Where in the cell is the carbon dioxide produced that animals breathe out?

## 6.4.5    Stage 4: electron transport and oxidative phosphorylation

In the overall equation for glucose oxidation, the one substance that has not been considered so far is oxygen. We spend our lives extracting it from the atmosphere by breathing and, effectively, all of it is used in the mitochondria in the last stage of glucose respiration. This stage comprises two processes which are *coupled*: first, electron transport, which brings about the oxidation of NAD.2H to NAD by oxygen; and second, oxidative phosphorylation, which is the associated production of ATP from ADP and $P_i$. The overall reaction of Stage 4 can be summarised as:

$$NAD.2H + \tfrac{1}{2}O_2 + ADP + P_i \longrightarrow NAD + H_2O + ATP \qquad (6.10)$$

Just one molecule of NAD.2H is being considered, hence only *half* an oxygen molecule is required to balance the equation. This equation is however not accurate with respect to the amounts of ADP and ATP. The number of ATP molecules produced per molecule of NAD.2H is variable and can only be estimated.

■ Where have you met coupling of phosphorylation and electron transport before?

☐ In the light reactions of photosynthesis, where NADP is reduced to NADP.2H as ADP is phosphorylated to ATP.

Looking back at Figure 6.11 will reveal that NAD.2H is produced in all three of the preceding stages of glucose oxidation, in fact most of it is produced in Stage 3, the TCA cycle. NAD.2H is processed in Stage 4. The oxidation of reduced coenzymes inside the mitochondrion in Stage 4 does not occur in a single step, but just like the oxidation of water in photosynthesis, it is brought about by a series of steps involving membrane components known as electron carriers, which form the mitochondrial electron transport chain (ETC). As Figure 6.15 shows, the ETC is made up of five carriers, numbered 1–5. This figure also shows that at the beginning of the electron transport chain the hydrogen atoms are removed from NAD.2H, and at the end of the chain molecular oxygen comes in to oxidise the hydrogen atoms to water. The overall reaction is summarised in Equation 6.11:

$$NAD.2H + \tfrac{1}{2}O_2 \longrightarrow NAD + H_2O \qquad (6.11)$$

**Figure 6.15** The electron transport chain consists of five electron carriers, numbered 1–5 in order of increasing electron affinity. The carriers are alternately reduced and oxidised as electrons are transported down the chain. The relative size and shape of each carrier is shown, as determined by electron microscopy.

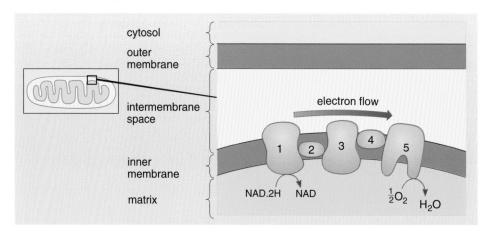

As in photosynthesis, the ETC relies on the increasing electron affinity of the carriers. In this way, they form a chain that can pass electrons from NAD.2H bound to the first carrier, to molecular oxygen bound to the last carrier, as illustrated in Figure 6.15. The electron affinity of the first carrier is high enough to remove a pair of electrons from the hydrogens in NAD.2H, leaving the two protons in the large pool of protons and other ions and molecules in the mitochondrial matrix. Carrier 2 removes the electrons from carrier 1, and so on down the chain. Eventually electrons reach the last carrier, carrier 5, an enzyme known as cytochrome oxidase. Cytochrome oxidase releases the electrons to molecular oxygen, which combines with the protons drawn from the surrounding matrix to form water (Figure 6.15).

So even though electrons do not appear in the overall equation for NAD.2H oxidation, their role is vital. Equation 6.11 can be broken down into two separate parts that show how the two components of the hydrogen atom are processed separately. At the beginning of the chain NAD.2H loses its 2H as two protons and two electrons:

$$NAD.2H \longrightarrow NAD + 2H^+ + 2e^- \tag{6.12}$$

and at the end molecular oxygen accepts the protons and electrons, so becoming water, as in Equation 6.13:

$$2H^+ + 2e^- + \tfrac{1}{2}O_2 \longrightarrow H_2O \tag{6.13}$$

So the oxidation of glucose is now complete – oxygen has entered the process at last and water has been produced. Look back to Equation 6.7 to remind yourself of the whole reaction. Once relieved of its 2H 'passenger group', the NAD can be recycled to pick up more 2H pairs.

Interestingly, the oxygen-binding site of the last carrier, cytochrome oxidase, can be irreversibly blocked by both cyanide and carbon monoxide, preventing it from binding oxygen, hence the disastrous effects of these poisons on aerobic organisms (such as ourselves).

■  What would happen at the biochemical level if potassium cyanide entered the mitochondrion?

☐  Electron transport would stop because the final electron carrier would no longer be able to bind oxygen. Consequently, NAD.2H could not be oxidised, so NAD would not be regenerated.

The vital consequence of the fact that NAD.2H could not be oxidised is that there would be no oxidative phosphorylation, so very little ATP would be produced and cell respiration would stop (resulting in death of the organism).

### Question 6.12

Which of the following biological transformations directly involves: (i) the breaking of a C–C bond; (ii) reduction of NAD to NAD.2H; (iii) electron transport within the inner mitochondrial membrane?

(a)  $NAD.2H + \tfrac{1}{2}O_2 \longrightarrow NAD + H_2O$

(b)  glucose $\longrightarrow$ 2 pyruvate

(c)  pyruvate $+ CoA \longrightarrow$ acetyl CoA $+ CO_2$

(d)  acetyl CoA $\longrightarrow CoA + 2CO_2$

You now need to consider how ATP is produced as electrons are transferred along the electron transport chain. A major outcome of glucose oxidation is the transfer of energy from glucose to ATP, but so far, mention has only been made of the few ATP molecules that are produced directly in glycolysis and the TCA cycle. As you have seen, the transfer of hydrogen atoms from NAD.2H to oxygen takes place in several steps. This is not surprising; if the NAD.2H were oxidised directly by oxygen, there would be unacceptably large amounts of energy released (as heat), which might damage the cell, as well as being wasteful. The small oxidation (electron transfer) steps ensure the controlled release of energy, which is tapped off into making ATP. However, as in photosynthesis, the energy released during electron transfer is not harnessed *directly* into the production of ATP but relies on the creation of a proton concentration gradient across a membrane, this time the inner mitochondrial membrane. There is, however, a slight difference: in the respiratory ETC, the flow of electrons leads to the pumping of protons from the mitochondrial matrix into the intermembrane space. This contrasts with photosynthesis, where the proton gradient is induced by the location of hydrogen-releasing (photolysis reactions and proton shuttling) and hydrogen-removing (reduction of NADP to NADP.2H) reactions on different sides of the thylakoid membrane. In both cases, however, it is the movement of protons along the concentration gradient that generates ATP.

The link between the electron transport in Stage 4 and ATP synthesis is described by the **chemiosmotic hypothesis**, which was proposed by the British biochemist, Peter Mitchell (Figure 6.16). For this work he was awarded the Nobel Prize for Medicine and Physiology in 1978. An important clue to the nature of this link came from experiments with mitochondria isolated from cells and suspended in a medium supplied with nutrients and oxygen. Such mitochondria can oxidise NAD.2H and simultaneously form ATP, but only if they are not damaged and, in particular, if the inner mitochondrial membrane is still intact.

The inner membrane is largely made up of electron carriers, as shown in Figure 6.15. Three of these carriers simultaneously act as **proton pumps**, as shown in Figure 6.17. The discovery of proton pumps in oxidative phosphorylation revolutionised scientists' way of thinking about energy transformations in the cell. Proton pumping provides a way of linking energy from electron transport to ATP synthesis in mitochondria.

**Figure 6.16**  Peter Mitchell (1920–1992), working in the UK, in 1961 proposed the chemiosmotic hypothesis, according to which electron transport and ATP synthesis are linked by a proton gradient across the inner mitochondrial membrane. He regarded experimental results as of prime importance and made predominant contributions towards establishing the validity of the hypothesis. As with many revolutionary hypotheses, it took a number of years to convince an initially hostile scientific community. Proton gradients have now been found to power a variety of energy-requiring processes in biology, including the synthesis of ATP in chloroplasts and bacteria.

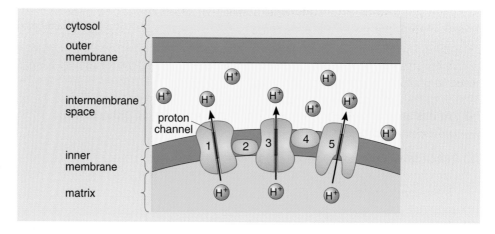

**Figure 6.17**  Three of the five electron carriers in the electron transport chain are also proton pumps, which transfer protons ($H^+$) from the matrix across the inner membrane and into the intermembrane space.

As electrons are transferred along the ETC, protons are moved out of the mitochondrial matrix, through the proton channels, and into the intermembrane space (Figure 6.17). Thus the concentration of protons in the intermembrane space becomes progressively greater than that in the mitochondrial matrix. Hence a proton concentration gradient is formed, with a low concentration in the matrix and a high concentration in the intermembrane space, as shown in Figure 6.17. This is exactly analogous to the proton concentration gradient between the thylakoid lumen and the stroma of the chloroplast.

Once again, the energy from electron transport is now effectively *stored*, because there is a proton concentration gradient between different compartments within an organelle. This energy can be released, simply by allowing protons to move in the reverse direction, i.e. *down* their concentration gradient, from high to low concentration. As in the chloroplast, protons are allowed to flood back down the concentration gradient through the channel protein, ATP synthase (Figure 6.18).

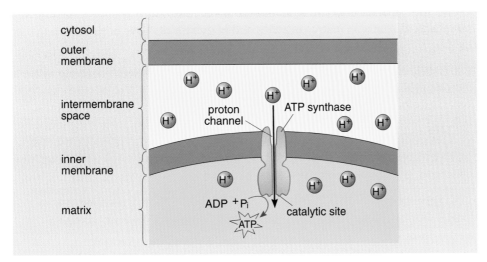

**Figure 6.18**  ATP synthase, a proton channel protein in the inner mitochondrial membrane, which allows protons to flow down their concentration gradient from the intermembrane space into the matrix and at the same time converts $ADP + P_i$ to ATP. (For clarity, only one ATP synthase molecule is shown here.)

In the discussion of photophosphorylation in Section 6.2.1, an analogy was used in comparing the production of a proton gradient across the thylakoid membrane with the pump-storage method of electricity generation. In the case of the mitochondria, the analogy is even more useful as protons are actually pumped out of the mitochondrial matrix by electron carriers 1, 3 and 5 when energy is made available from electron transport. This is analogous to off-peak electricity being used to pump water to a higher reservoir.

■  In this analogy, which reservoir, the higher or the lower, represents the mitochondrial matrix?

☐  The mitochondrial matrix is the lower reservoir as the protons (represented by water in the analogy) flow 'down' from the higher reservoir, the intermembrane space.

■  Why must the inner mitochondrial membrane be intact for ATP synthesis to occur?

☐  To produce the concentration gradient necessary for ATP synthesis, the protons must be pumped across the inner membrane and be stored within the intermembrane space. If the inner membrane is broken, protons will leak back into the matrix.

Thus if the inner mitochondrial membrane is damaged, it is impossible to maintain a proton concentration gradient, so the energy from electron transport can no longer be coupled to ATP synthesis. Large amounts of glucose would still be broken down to carbon dioxide and water, because electrons would still flow from NAD.2H to oxygen, but the energy would be lost as heat, and no ATP would be produced. An ideal slimming pill would be a drug that could alter the inner membrane temporarily, and disconnect, or *uncouple*, electron transport from ATP synthesis. Unfortunately, no such uncoupler drug has been found to do this safely. A highly unsafe uncoupler was used in World War I, quite by accident. This compound, an explosive called 2,4-dinitrophenol (2,4-DNP) was packed into shells by female munitions workers, many of whom became ill, suffering from severe and sometimes fatal weight loss and very high body temperatures. These women had absorbed 2,4-DNP through the skin, and some of the compound had entered the mitochondria and damaged the inner membrane. More recently, DNP is available illegally in many countries and bodybuilders have been known to use the drug to rapidly lose body fat.

A summary of Stages 2–4 of glucose breakdown (i.e. the stages occurring in the mitochondrion) is shown in Figure 6.19.

**Figure 6.19**   A summary of Stages 2–4 of the process of glucose breakdown, all of which take place in the mitochondrion. The starting point is pyruvate, the end-product of glycolysis, which occurs in the cytosol. (In reality, the electron carriers and ATP synthase occur along the whole of the inner mitochondrial membrane.)

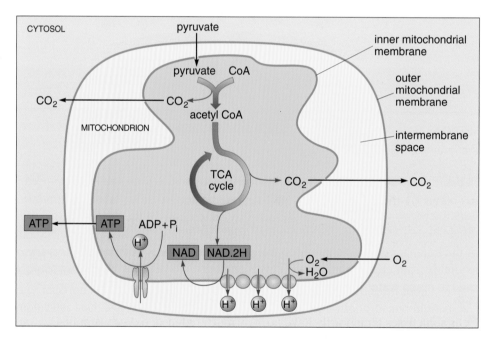

The net yield of ATP per glucose molecule completely oxidised to carbon dioxide and water is around 30 ATP molecules. The vast majority of this ATP is made by oxidative phosphorylation in the mitochondria. As you have seen, this process involves an energy-releasing reaction, the oxidation of NAD.2H, coupled to an energy-requiring reaction, the phosphorylation of ADP. This is a different mechanism from the direct production of ATP in glycolysis and the TCA cycle (Figures 6.13 and 6.14), which does not involve electron transport to oxygen. This second type of phosphorylation is called **substrate-level phosphorylation**. Here the intermediates contain phosphate groups that are transferred directly to ADP to produce ATP. In certain conditions, substrate-level phosphorylation can be crucially important to cells, as explained in the next section.

Question 6.13

Complete Table 6.4 to summarise the key inputs and outputs and processes involved in the electron transport chain and oxidative phosphorylation. On this occasion you should include the number of substrate molecules, the number of carbon-containing products and the number of other products for each molecule of glucose moving through the pathway.

**Table 6.4** Summary of electron transport chain/oxidative phosphorylation.

| Reaction or metabolic pathway | Part of cell/ mitochondria located in | Begins with (principal substrate) | Carbon-containing end-products | Other products |
|---|---|---|---|---|
| electron transport chain/oxidative phosphorylation | | | | |

Question 6.14

Stage 4 of glucose oxidation includes oxidative phosphorylation. What is oxidised and what is phosphorylated in this process?

Question 6.15

What changes, if any, take place in the distribution of protons on either side of the inner mitochondrial membrane during electron transport:

(a)  when the membrane is intact?

(b)  when 2,4-dinitrophenol (2,4-DNP) is present?

(c)  when the oxygen-binding site of cytochrome oxidase is blocked by carbon monoxide?

## 6.4.6   Respiration without oxygen

Cells sometimes temporarily have no, or a much reduced, oxygen supply. One such example is muscle cells in mammals, including humans. Muscles can exhaust their supply of oxygen, for example, as a herbivore escapes from the attack of a carnivore, or a human runs for a bus, and under these conditions they resort to **anaerobic respiration** (meaning respiration in the absence of oxygen) instead of the usual aerobic respiration. Thus muscles can continue to contract in the absence of oxygen and ATP is produced entirely by substrate-level phosphorylation.

In anaerobic respiration in muscles, the only energy-producing process in operation is glycolysis. Figure 6.13 showed that during glycolysis some NAD.2H is produced. Because oxygen is not present, this reduced coenzyme cannot be oxidised via the ETC. Under anaerobic conditions, pyruvate – the end-product of glycolysis – serves as the oxidising agent (hydrogen acceptor). The pyruvate is reduced to lactate by the two hydrogen atoms from NAD.2H. The enzyme involved is one you have met already (Section 5.6.4), lactate dehydrogenase (LDH), which is present in the cytosol.

$$\underset{\text{pyruvate}}{C_3H_4O_3} + NAD.2H \xrightarrow{\text{LDH}} \underset{\text{lactate}}{C_3H_6O_3} + NAD \qquad (6.14)$$

Notice that this is the reverse of the forward reaction in Equation 5.4.

Figure 6.13 also showed that during glycolysis some ATP is produced. In fact, four molecules of ATP are formed but two molecules are used to activate the glucose, making a net gain of only two molecules of ATP per molecule of glucose. This is an extremely small yield compared with the 30 or so molecules produced by the complete oxidation of glucose (Section 6.3.2). Nevertheless, the production of this relatively small amount of ATP is sufficient for muscle contraction to continue and, since the NAD.2H is converted back to NAD, the process of glycolysis can continue – at least for a while.

■  Are mitochondria involved in anaerobic respiration?

☐  No, because glycolysis occurs in the cytosol.

Anaerobic respiration leads to a build-up of lactate in muscles. You may be aware of this during exercise, because it causes the muscles to feel stiff. When exercise is over, the large amount of lactate that has accumulated is oxidised back to pyruvate, and this reaction is catalysed by lactate dehydrogenase (Equation 5.4). This reaction requires large amounts of oxygen (to oxidise the NAD.2H produced), which is provided by the deep and rapid breathing that continues for some time after physical activity has ceased.

Many organisms can live without oxygen, for example the bacterium that causes tetanus is an anaerobic organism. Yeast can live with or without oxygen, depending upon the environment. In aerobic conditions, respiration in yeast is the same as that described earlier. However, under anaerobic conditions, the NAD required for the continuation of glycolysis is regenerated, not via lactate formation, but by the process of *fermentation*. Here, the pyruvate is converted, via two steps, to alcohol and carbon dioxide – hence the use of yeast in the brewing and bread-making industries.

## Activity 6.2   The 'powerhouse of the cell'

We expect this activity will take you approximately 20 minutes.

The stages of glucose oxidation that occur in the mitochondria are not straightforward, and Stage 4 in particular – electron transport coupled to oxidative phosphorylation – is quite complicated. In order to help your understanding of the reactions that occur in the mitochondria, including the coupling of the reactions that take place at the inner mitochondrial membrane, draw a flow diagram to summarise the steps by which the energy stored in pyruvate is transformed into energy stored in ATP. Your diagram should include the production of reduced coenzymes, and the steps by which the energy stored in these coenzymes is transferred to ATP.

Now look at the comments on this activity at the end of this book.

## 6.5    Integration of metabolism

Besides carbohydrates, most heterotrophs also consume substantial quantities of triacylglycerols (TAGs) and proteins. And in both animals and plants there is continuous synthesis and breakdown of TAGs and proteins as part of cellular turnover. Therefore, you would expect there to be effective biochemical systems for catabolising these substances – and indeed there are. In this section, these systems are examined, with the focus mainly on animals, particularly mammals.

Since this section will involve a discussion of TAGs and proteins, introduced in Chapter 5, it will help you first to revise the structures of these molecules. You will begin, however, by looking at glycogen, because this is the energy source that animals use first.

■    Describe the structure of glycogen.

☐    It comprises branched chains of glucose monomers (Section 5.3).

■    What are the breakdown products of TAGs?

☐    Fatty acids and glycerol (Section 5.1.2).

■    What are the monomer units of proteins and what is the name of the type of bond that links these monomers together in a polypeptide chain?

☐    Amino acids are linked by peptide bonds in a polypeptide chain (Section 5.5.2).

Fatty acids, glycerol and amino acids, produced by the hydrolysis of TAGs and proteins, are used by cells for both biosynthetic and catabolic processes. The points at which they feed into the glucose oxidation pathway are shown in Figure 6.20. This *central pathway* is shown by the thicker arrows in the figure. The other arrows indicate pathways that are linked to the central pathway. Thus the pathway of glucose breakdown is central to metabolism, and the information summarised in Figure 6.20 is the focus of Sections 6.5.1–6.5.3.

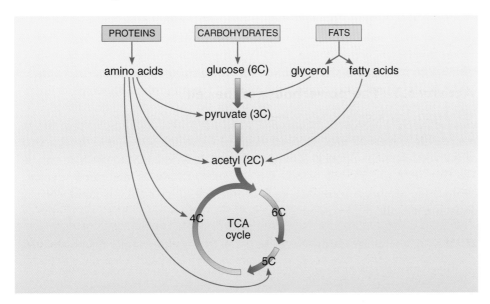

**Figure 6.20**   Links between the glucose oxidation pathway and the oxidation of other nutrients, which feed into this central pathway. For example, there are amino acids that join the central pathway at various points.

### 6.5.1　Blood sugar levels and glycogen

The control mechanisms that coordinate the breakdown of different energy sources in cells are complex. But in addition to these control mechanisms within individual cells, of crucial importance is regulation at the level of the whole organism. In mammals, including humans, one such vitally important mechanism keeps blood glucose level constant. This is particularly important for the brain, which has no energy reserves of its own and relies on glucose from the blood.

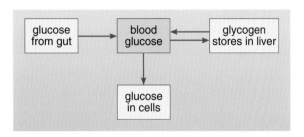

**Figure 6.21**　The balance between glycogen stores and blood glucose. The two full arrows between blood glucose and liver glycogen stores indicate that the glycogen synthesis pathway is not simply the reverse of the pathway that releases glucose from glycogen. Each pathway comprises a different set of reactions.

Immediately after a meal, glucose floods into the bloodstream, and most of it is converted into glycogen in the liver and muscles, where it is stored. As blood glucose level falls between meals, glycogen is hydrolysed to glucose. In the muscles, this glucose is used directly by the tissue, whereas in the liver it is released slowly back into the bloodstream. In this way, an adequate blood glucose concentration is maintained. Between meals, glucose is taken up from the bloodstream continuously by the cells of the body, so the blood glucose pool has to be continuously replenished by mobilisation of the glycogen stores. This process is summarised in Figure 6.21.

In order to appreciate the regulation of blood glucose level, consider the following data. The normal level of blood glucose in humans before breakfast is 4.5–5.5 millimoles per litre (mmol l$^{-1}$; the conventional style of expressing blood glucose level is using units of mmol l$^{-1}$ rather than mmol dm$^{-3}$). After a meal containing carbohydrates (for example, a breakfast of cereal with milk and sugar) the level will rise temporarily to around 7 mmol l$^{-1}$. Going without food for 24 hours will cause the level of blood glucose to fall to around 3.5 mmol l$^{-1}$, but the level will not normally fall further even if fasting is prolonged. This minimum level is maintained by the release of glucose from glycogen stores. So constant topping-up from glycogen stores ensures that the blood glucose level is kept within narrow limits. How is this level maintained? In fact, the balance between blood glucose level and glycogen stores is regulated by hormones which are secreted into the bloodstream. A hormone is a 'chemical messenger', which is produced in very small quantities in one part of an organism and transported, via the bloodstream, to a target tissue, where it exerts an effect. You met the hormone adrenalin in Book 4 (Section 16.2.2). One of the hormones that regulates blood sugar level is a protein called insulin. Food intake triggers the release of insulin from an abdominal organ called the pancreas. The main effects of insulin are to promote the transfer of glucose from the bloodstream into cells, particularly liver and muscle cells, and to promote its conversion into glycogen. Hence the rise in blood glucose level after a carbohydrate-containing meal is only temporary. Individuals who produce only a low level of insulin in their blood have one form of diabetes, and can be treated by injecting insulin. A constant supply is essential, since insulin is rapidly broken down in the body.

■　Why do you think insulin has to be given by injection, rather than by mouth?

☐　Since insulin is a protein, if taken by mouth, it would be broken down by digestive enzymes in the gut before it could reach the bloodstream.

As blood glucose level falls between meals, or during bouts of exercise when the muscles use large quantities of glucose, insulin secretion is greatly reduced and another hormone, glucagon ('glue-ka-gon'), is released into the blood. Glucagon stimulates the breakdown of glycogen stores in the liver and muscles and the release of glucose from the liver into the bloodstream. Thus the effects of glucagon on liver and muscle cells are opposite to those of insulin.

So stored glycogen can be used to provide glucose to fuel the metabolism of body cells. However, glycogen stores are limited, even in a well-fed animal. During prolonged exercise, or if there is a long period without food intake, the body must turn to its alternative energy stores – TAGs (fats).

## 6.5.2    Energy from triacylglycerols

As well as sugars, both fatty acids and glycerol (released by the hydrolysis of TAGs) can be used by cells to provide energy. The hormone glucagon not only stimulates the release of glucose from the liver but also promotes the mobilisation of fat reserves from adipose tissue. (The terms TAGs and fat are used interchangeably here.) Quantitatively, fat is usually more important as an energy store than glycogen. On average, an adult human stores enough glycogen to last for only about a day of typical activities, but enough fat to last at least a month. This is partly because the body stores a much greater quantity of fat than glycogen and partly because the oxidation of fatty acids generates about six times as much energy as the oxidation of the same mass of glycogen.

When TAGs are broken down to generate energy, they are first hydrolysed to fatty acids and glycerol. The glycerol is eventually converted to a 3C intermediate of glycolysis, as shown in Figure 6.20. The fatty acids are converted via another catabolic pathway into acetyl groups, which are carried by CoA (Figure 6.19). This acetyl CoA then feeds into the TCA cycle.

CoA can accept acetyl groups from either fatty acids or pyruvate (in the link reaction). However, whether the acetyl groups come from fatty acids or from glucose depends on the availability of these fuels. As long as there is sufficient glucose, the oxidation of fats is suppressed. A high-energy diet, rich in both carbohydrates and fats (as is common in the western world) may eventually lead to obesity, because the carbohydrates meet most of the energy needs of the body and so the excess fat consumed gets stored in adipose tissue. (Carbohydrate consumed in excess of requirements can also be converted into fat and stored.)

■ Imagine a person on a low-energy diet. What will be happening to their TAG stores?

☐ They will be slowly broken down, via fatty acids to acetyl CoA, which will be catabolised in the TCA cycle, thereby making up the shortfall in energy provision from the diet.

Such a diet would lead to weight loss over time as more and more of the stored TAGs would be mobilised to provide energy for the rest of the body.

### 6.5.3   Catabolism of proteins

Protein breakdown happens all the time as part of body maintenance. But proteins can also serve as an energy source. When amino acids from protein digestion in the gut are in excess of the body's requirements for growth and maintenance, they are broken down to provide energy, and during periods of inadequate food intake body proteins, particularly muscle proteins, can be catabolised to provide energy.

When proteins are broken down, they are first split into the individual amino acid monomers. Since there are 20 of these (Section 5.5.2), there are 20 different starting points to their catabolic routes. However, you will focus only on the general principles of amino acid catabolism. In all cases, the amino group ($NH_2$) is first removed, and the remaining non-nitrogenous acids, either directly or after further catabolism, feed into the central pathway at one of a number of points: to pyruvate (at the end of glycolysis), to acetyl CoA (after the link reaction) or to one of several TCA cycle intermediates (see Figure 6.20). A proportion of the amino groups are recycled in the process of amino acid biosynthesis and the rest are ultimately excreted; for example, as urea, in the urine of humans.

In conclusion, the key point is that energy stores of all types are catabolised via the central pathway of glucose catabolism.

## 6.6   Metabolic pathways revisited

Growth and survival depend on a well-ordered system of cell biochemistry, involving an adjustable balance of interrelated catabolism and biosynthesis.

You now know that processes of biosynthesis and catabolism take place in stages. Thus, there are biosynthetic pathways for building (synthesising) compounds and catabolic pathways for breaking them down. Figure 6.22 shows the catabolic glucose oxidation pathway linked to a biosynthetic metabolic pathway. You know that biosynthesis requires energy in the form of ATP and so in this example of two linked pathways the oxidation of glucose to carbon dioxide and water is synthesising the ATP, which allows the biosynthesis pathway to take place. However, the two pathways are more intimately linked than merely by the supply of ATP. During glucose oxidation, numerous intermediates – the partial breakdown products of each reaction in the sequence, such as A, B, Q and R – are formed. The cell can use these intermediates by putting them together again in different ways to form different molecules. In this way, the early products of a catabolic pathway, such as intermediate B, may participate in a biosynthetic pathway. Here the intermediate B from one pathway is being combined with another intermediate, Y, from a different pathway, to form a new compound Y–B. These intermediates are called precursor molecules: for example, the acetyl group is a precursor of cholesterol (a type of lipid) in mammals and vitamin A in plants. Because of the links between different pathways, the routes of catabolism and biosynthesis are all interconnected, forming a complex network of chemical reactions.

Oxidation and reduction reactions are central to energy metabolism. You have seen that the chemical energy in food molecules is *released* in catabolic oxidative reactions. However, the synthesis of biological molecules like glucose in photosynthesis involves reduction reactions and *requires* energy. Because of

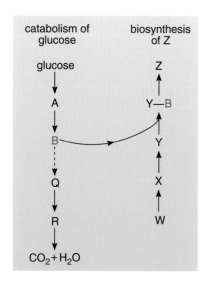

**Figure 6.22**   Two metabolic pathways: a catabolic pathway involving the breakdown of glucose to carbon dioxide, and a biosynthetic pathway that produces substance Z. Note that some of the intermediates from one pathway can be used in other pathways.

the energy requirements, biosynthetic pathways (e.g. glycogen synthesis, fatty acid synthesis) are not simply the reverse of the corresponding catabolic routes, although there may be some reactions that are common to both (such as the interconversion of pyruvate and lactate; Section 5.6.4).

Protein synthesis is a typical biosynthetic process, which in most cells requires more energy than any other biosynthetic activity. The production of proteins must be highly regulated within the cell, because each cell type has its own characteristic set of proteins and each protein has a specific sequence of amino acids. The synthesis of proteins in the cell is achieved by a complex sequence of steps. Recall that ribosomes, studded in the endoplasmic reticulum which pervades the cytosol, are the sites of protein synthesis. How the cell synthesises proteins, each with its own specific sequence of amino acids, is the subject of Chapter 8.

## Question 6.16

Which of the following statements about metabolism in mammals are true?

(a) Biosynthetic pathways involve the conversion of ATP to $ADP + P_i$.

(b) The breakdown of amino acids involves first removing the carboxylic acid (COOH) group.

(c) Insulin helps to control the blood glucose level by stimulating the uptake of glucose by cells that can synthesise and store glycogen.

(d) The pathways of fat and protein catabolism both merge with the glucose oxidation pathway.

## 6.7    Energy in cells: a review

The two processes of respiration and photosynthesis are biologically very important. You have seen that, in overall chemical terms, respiration is the exact reverse of photosynthesis and that they both involve a sequence of chemical reactions that occur in a number of cellular compartments.

There are striking similarities and differences in structure and function between the two organelles that are involved in these two processes: mitochondria and chloroplasts.

Mitochondria, which are present in all eukaryotic cells, and chloroplasts, which occur only in plants, are membrane-bound organelles with a large amount of internal membranes. The internal membranes of these organelles carry key components, for example the electron transport chain and ATP synthase. Functionally, both organelles convert energy to forms that can be used to drive chemical reactions. Large amounts of ATP are produced by the same fundamental mechanism: the energy derived from sugar and fats (in mitochondria) or from light (in chloroplasts) is used to establish a proton concentration gradient. In both organelles, the movement of protons across membranes provides a way of linking the energy released from electron transport to ATP synthesis.

Although the similarities between the two organelles are striking, there are significant differences between them. Mitochondria are involved in the oxidation of sugars and fats to carbon dioxide and water, and enable much of the energy stored in these metabolic fuels to be temporarily stored in ATP before it is used to drive a variety of energy-requiring reactions in the cell. In contrast, chloroplasts convert carbon dioxide and water to sugars and oxygen, and in the process they store some of the energy trapped from sunlight. The differences between the two organelles are thought to be a consequence of their different origins from different bacterial ancestors, as described in Section 4.3.

### Activity 6.3   Similarities and differences between the processes of oxidative phosphorylation and photophosphorylation

We expect this activity will take you approximately 15 minutes.

This activity will help you draw together the most important aspects of the processes of photophosphorylation (ATP production in photosynthesis) and oxidative phosphorylation (ATP synthesis in respiration). Complete Table 6.5 to list the features of these two types of phosphorylation. Some of the entries have been completed in order to help you. Then highlight in some way which features are common to the two processes (the similarities) and which features are different.

**Table 6.5** For use with Activity 6.3.

| Feature | Oxidative phosphorylation | Photophosphorylation |
|---|---|---|
| type of cell found in | | plant cells containing chlorophyll |
| location of process in cell | | |
| location of ETC | inner mitochondrial membrane | |
| energy source | carbohydrates/lipids/amino acids | |
| source of electrons for ETC | NAD.2H/FAD.2H | |
| electron acceptor | | NADP |
| proton gradient established across a membrane | | |
| ATP synthase is site for ATP synthesis | | yes |
| ATP produced from ADP and $P_i$ | | |
| end-products of process | | ATP and NADP.2H and $O_2$ |

Now look at the comments on this activity at the end of this book.

Despite the complex biochemistry you have covered in this chapter there is a simple take-home message and one that will serve you well in Chapter 7 where the flow of energy through ecological systems is examined in greater depth. Energy and resources flow through ecosystems. All ecosystems are ultimately dependent on solar energy; this energy is made available to autotrophs through the process of photosynthesis. Heterotrophs obtain chemical energy by consuming autotrophs and they release the energy in their food by metabolic pathways such as glucose oxidation. It is possible to measure the flow of energy through ecosystems and this is the subject of the next chapter.

## 6.8  Summary of Chapter 6

Energy for almost all living organisms is ultimately derived from the Sun by photosynthesis.

Energy-requiring reactions are coupled to the conversion of ATP to ADP + $P_i$, while the reverse reaction, the conversion of ADP + $P_i$ to ATP, is coupled to energy-releasing reactions.

The essential feature of photosynthesis is that solar energy is converted by means of the pigment chlorophyll into chemical energy in sugar.

Photosynthesis consists of two sets of reactions; the light reactions harness energy from the Sun (absorbed by chlorophyll) and use it to produce ATP and reducing power in the form of reduced coenzymes, NADP.2H. The dark reactions use the products of the light reactions to fix atmospheric $CO_2$ and convert it to glucose. Oxygen is released as a by-product.

The glucose manufactured by photosynthesis can be used for further biosynthesis of more complex molecules or in catabolism to release energy stored in the fuel molecule for other uses in the cell. This process is called respiration and is the oxidation of glucose to release energy.

Respiration (glucose oxidation) occurs in all cells; it proceeds via a large number of small steps, releasing small quantities of energy at a time.

Metabolism is the sum of all chemical reactions in the cell and comprises catabolic (breaking down) and biosynthetic (building up) reactions.

Glucose is oxidised in the cell in four consecutive stages: glycolysis, which takes place in the cytosol; the link reaction and the tricarboxylic acid (TCA) cycle, both of which take place in the mitochondrial matrix; and electron transport coupled to oxidative phosphorylation, which occurs in the inner mitochondrial membrane.

Anaerobic respiration occurs in mammals in the absence of oxygen.

In mammals, glucose is stored as glycogen in muscle and liver. Between meals, glycogen is hydrolysed to release glucose. Blood glucose level is regulated by hormones, including insulin and glucagon.

Activity 6.1 gave you an opportunity to practise the important skill of integrating diagrams into short pieces of writing. Communicating effectively with diagrams is an essential skill to develop. Written accounts are enhanced by the use of diagrams, which should be given suitable titles, fully labelled and referred to explicitly in the text of the written account.

# Chapter 7
# Ecosystems and energy flow

So far, Book 5 has been chiefly concerned with the individual organism; with what makes it an organism (as opposed to, say, a rock), what distinguishes one organism from another and how many different kinds there might be. Real organisms, though, are parts of communities and populations in which there are complex interactions. You are already aware of the complex predator and prey relationships exhibited by certain species (Section 2.4 and Activity 2.2). The relationship between the snowshoe hare and the lynx is relatively straightforward compared with the relationships between the huge numbers of different species inhabiting an oak woodland. In this section, the oak tree is explored as a habitat upon (and in) which many organisms of many species live. The oak tree is also part of an ecological system, or **ecosystem**, through which resources, including energy, flow. A large proportion of the study material for this chapter is provided in the computer-based activity *Ecological Chains: Finding the Links*. You should begin by reading this chapter and tackle the various sections of the computer-based activity when directed in the text. It is important that you study each section in the given order. The activity introduces you to the study of an oak woodland ecosystem. You will investigate a number of interactions between species in this ecosystem. In doing so, you will learn about the interdependence of communities of organisms, sometimes referred to as the balance of nature.

## 7.1   An introduction to ecology

This introduction to **ecology** begins with a first look at the ecosystem that will be the focus of your investigations, oak woodland. This ecosystem is in turn made up of a variety of **habitats**. In simple terms, a habitat is the specific place where an organism lives. You will start Activity 7.1 with a look around the woodland, discovering some of the species living there and investigating some of their important characteristics.

The oak woodland does not just provide habitats for individual organisms but rather is a place that supports a huge range of different species, a distinct **community** of organisms. A community is made up of several different populations. You were introduced to the idea of populations when you studied the interaction between predators and prey (Section 2.4). In ecology, the term population refers to all the organisms of a certain species living in the same place at the same time. The greater the number of different populations found in an ecosystem, the richer its species diversity. An ecosystem has two vital components, the biological community of organisms and the physical environment it occupies and ecology is primarily a study of the interactions of organisms with each other and with their environment. Taking the oak woodland example, of particular interest is the way the various species you have identified interact with each other. However, time does not permit you to investigate the rich complexity of all the interactions in the ecosystem so instead you will take a few examples. The most obvious (and final) way an organism can interact with another is to eat it and, in Activity 7.1 Section 2, you will investigate feeding relationships between four of the oak woodland species. You will learn some basic principles of feeding relationships before turning to this specific example. From Chapter 6, you know that all organisms need constant supplies of energy and carbon to support life. For heterotrophic organisms, these requirements come from the food they eat. The breakdown of food molecules during respiration releases the energy they require for movement, keeping their bodies warm, and via biosynthesis (the manufacture of new cellular materials) for growth and reproduction. The feeding relationships between specific organisms are called food chains; these sequences identify the fixed order in which organisms feed on each other.

Organisms can sustain life only if they consume sufficient food from the species below them in the food chain. By making careful observations of an ecosystem, it is possible to quantify how much food each organism in the food chain requires for its energy needs and you will undertake some calculations using field data to establish how many organisms are consumed in a specific food chain. Activity 7.1 Section 3 will demonstrate how these complex calculations are made in the field.

---

### Activity 7.1 Ecological chains, Sections 1–3

We expect these sections of the activity will take you approximately 2 hours.

As the name 'Ecological chains' suggests, this activity is an introduction to key ecological ideas and techniques, based on the ecology of temperate woodland that is dominated by oak trees. The activity introduces the ideas of producers and consumers within an ecosystem, and examines the links between different organisms in food chains and more complex food webs. These links can be viewed in terms of the flow of energy through an ecosystem.

For this activity you should study Sections 1, 2 and 3 of the computer-based activity *Ecological Chains*. The estimated study time for each of these sections is as follows:

| | | | |
|---|---|---|---|
| Section 1 | 'Introduction to an oak woodland' | 30 min | DVD screens 1–3 |
| Section 2 | 'A sparrowhawk's eye view' | 30 min | DVD screens 4–11 |
| Section 3 | 'How much food to raise a brood?' | 1 hour | DVD screens 12–17 |

Now look at the comments on Sections 1–3 of this activity at the end of this book.

---

## 7.2 Feeding relationships

You have now established a simple food chain containing four different species: oak tree, winter moth caterpillar, great tit and sparrowhawk.

Like all food chains, this one begins with an autotroph (Section 2.3), the oak tree, an organism that can capture energy from the Sun and use it to convert simple inorganic molecules into organic molecules by photosynthesis. Autotrophs are known as **primary producers** since they produce living matter from carbon dioxide and water. You will return to the role of autotrophs at the base of food chains in Section 7.3 when energy flow through the oak woodland ecosystem is considered. For the moment, consider the heterotrophic organisms in this food chain.

■ Which of the other members of the food chain are heterotrophic?

☐ All of them. Winter moth caterpillars, great tits and sparrowhawks are all heterotrophs.

Heterotrophs can be subdivided into consumers and decomposers; the difference between these groups is quite subtle. Consumers (animals) ingest organic matter and digest it inside their bodies, whereas decomposers (fungi and bacteria) digest organic matter externally and absorb it into their cells. The group of consumers can be further subdivided into herbivores (animals that eat plants), carnivores (animals that eat other animals) and detritivores (animals that consume dead organic matter).

■ Which members of the food chain are herbivores and which are carnivores?

☐ Winter moth caterpillars are herbivores; great tits and sparrowhawks are carnivores.

In Activity 7.1 Section 3, you quantified the number of members of a species required to sustain the organisms above it in the food chain and the information was displayed as a pyramid of numbers. Like all ecosystems, the animals near the base of the food chain are relatively abundant; however, as one progresses along the food chain, the numbers progressively decrease. To construct a pyramid, the base of the pyramid is assigned to the autotroph and the relative size of the base indicates the number of organisms present. The total number of consumers (herbivores) occupies the next box up and again is sized relative to the abundance of that particular organism. As these organisms consume autotrophs, they are referred to as **primary consumers**. Next up in the pyramid are the **secondary consumers**, by definition carnivores since they eat other animals. Boxes for other consumers (usually called higher consumers) can be added until the top predator is reached.

■ In the case of the oak woodland food chain, which species is the primary consumer?

☐ The winter moth caterpillar is the first consumer in the food chain as it eats oak tree leaves.

■ Which species is the tertiary consumer?

☐ The sparrowhawk is the third consumer in the sequence (Figure 7.1).

**Figure 7.1**   Pyramid of numbers for the oak–winter moth caterpillar–great tit–sparrowhawk food chain. You will notice that the base of the pyramid is very small; this reflects the small number of individual oak trees required to sustain the food chain. In the computer-based activity, the base of the pyramid has been drawn to represent the number of oak leaves and not the number of oak trees; this gives a broad-based pyramid. In both cases, the numbers of consumers decrease with each successive level.

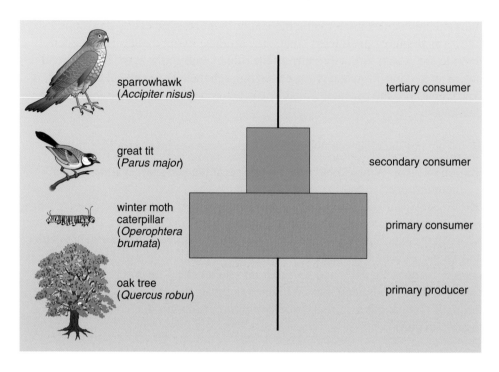

Each successive layer in the pyramid is described as a **trophic** (feeding) level. Ecologists often want to compare pyramids of numbers from different ecosystems, but pyramids of numbers for ecosystems based on trees such as this one can be quite misleading as there are few individual autotrophs sustaining the food chains. If you drew a pyramid for a grassland ecosystem, the number of grass plants would be enormous and this would be reflected in a pyramid with a very broad base (Figure 7.2).

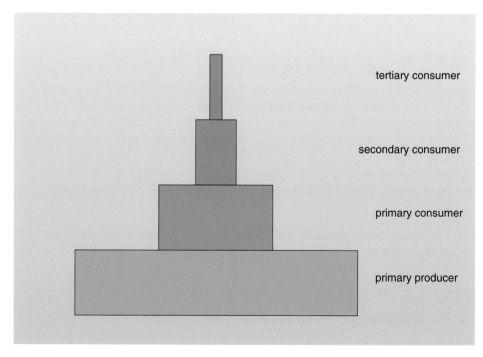

**Figure 7.2**   Pyramid of numbers for a grassland ecosystem; this time, the broad base reflects the large number of grass plants that are primary producers.

Clearly the difference here is the size of the autotrophic organisms at the base of the pyramid. The oak trees are massive and consequently few are needed to sustain the consumers above them in the food chain. A pyramid of numbers does not always accurately represent the feeding relationships between the species in an ecosystem; sometimes it is better to use alternative methods to quantify each trophic level.

One such method requires taking samples of organisms at each trophic level over a fixed area, drying them and weighing them to give an estimate of the **biomass** (kg m$^{-2}$), the amount of dry biological material per unit area.

■ Sketch the shape of the pyramid of biomass for the oak–winter moth caterpillar–great tit– sparrowhawk food chain.

☐ Figure 7.3 shows a sketch of this pyramid, which is similar in shape to Figure 7.2, but here the base of the pyramid reflects the huge amount of living material in the oak trees.

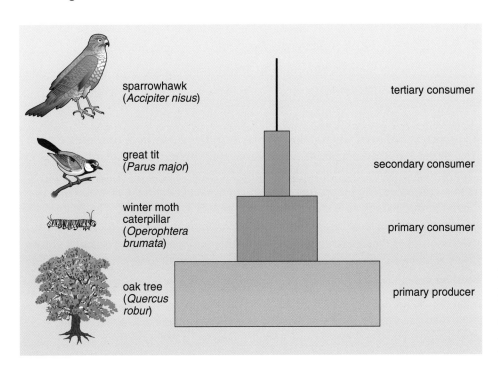

sparrowhawk
(*Accipiter nisus*) — tertiary consumer

great tit
(*Parus major*) — secondary consumer

winter moth caterpillar
(*Operophtera brumata*) — primary consumer

oak tree
(*Quercus robur*) — primary producer

**Figure 7.3** The woodland food chain illustrated as a pyramid of biomass, the broad base reflects the enormous quantity of biomass in oak trees and gives a clearer indication of the importance of the producer.

In fact, the most useful way of representing ecosystems is by constructing a pyramid of energy and this is the next part on the computer-based activity for you to try.

## Activity 7.1 (continued)  Ecological chains – Section 4

We expect this section of the activity will take you approximately 1 hour.

For this activity you should study Section 4 'Energy flow' DVD screens 18–32 of the computer-based activity *Ecological Chains*.

Now look at the comments on Section 4 of this activity at the end of this book.

## 7.3    Primary production

You know that all food chains begin with autotrophs but you now need to investigate how the process of photosynthesis makes energy available for all the consumers in the food chain. **Gross primary productivity (GPP)** is a measure of the amount of solar energy trapped by photosynthesis and therefore converted into food molecules over a specified time and in a specified area or volume or in a specified food chain, food web or ecosystem. In the computer-based activity, you calculated the GPP for immature oak leaves on a typical day and found that the efficiency of photosynthesis is surprisingly low. Given that the total solar energy reaching the Earth from the Sun is so high, it is interesting to investigate why more of this energy does not get converted to GPP. Recall from Book 1 that a large proportion of the intercepted solar radiation is absorbed by the atmosphere or reflected from the Earth's surface or the atmosphere. Only around one-tenth of this energy actually reaches the surface of the land and, of this, a large proportion is made up of ultraviolet and infrared wavelengths, which cannot be absorbed by plants.

■    Which part of the electromagnetic spectrum can plants absorb?

☐    Plants (via the pigment chlorophyll) absorb light energy from specific regions of the visible spectrum.

Obviously, a large proportion of the solar energy reaching the ground does not fall on plants and even when it does it may be reflected from or transmitted through the leaf. Consequently, only a very small proportion of solar energy is actually absorbed by the chlorophyll molecules and used to manufacture glucose. As you calculated, the proportion of light energy reaching the oak wood that is converted into energy stored in carbon compounds is around 1%. The first step in your food chain, converting solar energy into chemical energy is therefore very inefficient. These inefficiencies continue with significant energy losses as you progress along the food chain. Your first step is therefore to determine where and how this energy is lost.

What then is the fate of the GPP? The carbon compounds produced during photosynthesis can be used to provide energy for maintenance, growth and reproduction. As you know from Chapter 6, energy is released from food molecules such as glucose via the process of plant respiration (R) and ultimately this energy is dissipated as heat. Alternatively, a proportion of the GPP can be stored in the cells of the plant contributing to additional biomass; this is called the **net primary production (NPP)**. The relationship between GPP, R and NPP can therefore be summarised as:

$$GPP = NPP + R \tag{7.1}$$

You will notice that this simple equation demonstrates the principle of the conservation of energy very well (Book 3, Chapter 2). All the energy 'fixed' by the ecosystem as GPP during photosynthesis is either converted into energy and stored as biomass (NPP) or 'lost' from the ecosystem as a result of respiration (R); indeed the energy used for respiration really is lost, as it is no longer available to other organisms in the food chain to utilise. GPP and NPP are expressed in units of energy per unit area and per unit time ($kJ\ ha^{-1}\ y^{-1}$) where the unit area is usually the hectare (unit equal to 10 000 m²) and the unit time is the year. Biomass is often expressed in terms of its chemical energy content rather than in units of mass and so the terms biomass and energy can be used interchangeably.

## 7.4 Secondary production

Once the energy losses due to plant respiration are taken into account, the next species in the food chain has only the NPP (energy captured in oak tree biomass) left to feed on. In fact, the winter moth caterpillar only eats the leaves of the oak tree so any energy in the biomass of bark, twigs or roots is not available to it. Hence only a small proportion of the oak's biomass is actually consumed and, even more significantly, a large proportion of the biomass consumed will be lost as faeces without being absorbed by the caterpillar.

This can be expressed as:

$$\text{biomass consumption}_W = \text{energy assimilated}_W + \text{energy lost in faeces}_W \quad (7.2)$$

where w represents the winter moth caterpillar.

Once the energy lost from faeces is taken into account, you are left with the energy in the food that is actually absorbed in the gut of the winter moth caterpillar. This is known as assimilation because the food has become incorporated into the consumer.

Of this available food energy, a proportion will be used in the respiratory process (R) to release energy for movement and biosynthesis (and ultimately be lost from the ecosystem in the form of heat). The remainder will be stored in the cells of the caterpillar as additional biomass, so-called **secondary production**. It is this biomass that is available to the organisms in the next trophic level when they feed:

$$\text{energy assimilated}_W = \text{increase in biomass}_W + \text{energy lost in respiration}_W \quad (7.3)$$

As there are two more consumers in this food chain, these steps will be repeated twice more, for great tits and for sparrowhawks. It is clear that very little of the biomass of one trophic level ends up as biomass in the next trophic level.

To summarise, consider the flow of energy through the oak woodland ecosystem. It is apparent that energy flows in one direction, from solar energy to chemical energy (in organisms) to heat as a final product of respiration. Once energy is lost as heat it is no longer available to the ecosystem. Consequently, the oak woodland is totally dependent on a constant supply of solar energy for primary production. This is in contrast to various chemical elements, which can be said to cycle through ecosystems.

■ Recall from Book 1 and Chapter 6 of this book, a chemical element that cycles.

☐ Carbon. The carbon dioxide given off during respiration may be reabsorbed by plants during photosynthesis and used to manufacture glucose.

Now that you have fully explored the feeding relationships and the flow of energy along the oak woodland food chain, you need to consider how food chains 'fit together' into more complex food webs.

**Activity 7.1 (continued)    Ecological chains – Section 5**

We expect this section of the activity will take you approximately 30 minutes.

For this activity you should study Section 5 'Food webs' DVD screens 33–46 of the computer-based activity *Ecological Chains*.

Now look at the comments on Section 5 of this activity at the end of this book.

## 7.5    Food webs

Food chains consist of a linear relationship in which energy from plants is consumed by a herbivore, which is consumed by a carnivore, and so on. In reality, the nature of feeding relationships is much more complicated than this. Food chains are, in fact, often interconnected. Indeed, some organisms can feed at more than one trophic level in several different food chains. This complex set of interrelated food chains is called a **food web** and this is a much more accurate representation of the feeding relationships between species and an indication of possible competition between species for certain foods.

In the case of the oak wood food web, there is **interspecific competition** between the sparrowhawk, the weasel and the greater spotted woodpecker for the same food supply, the great tit. As these three species are sharing this one resource, the availability of this food may be limiting the growth of their populations. However, species usually have differing requirements for their particular food and this limits the extent of their competition. As the oak woodland food web shows, weasels will take small rodents in preference to great tits and only seek out small birds when rodents are in short supply. Similarly, greater spotted woodpeckers prefer grubs and larvae and only certain woodpeckers seem to 'learn' to take small birds by drilling through nesting boxes.

Where species share the same food resource, their **ecological niches** are said to overlap. The term niche describes the relationship a species has with its habitat, other species in the community and its method of obtaining food. A full description of all these characteristics would describe the particular niche the species occupies. For example, the niche of a bird species might include the range of temperatures that it can tolerate and the availability of appropriate food and nesting sites. The total environmental conditions that are suitable for the existence of a species describe its **fundamental niche**; however, competition between species for food (like the sparrowhawk and the woodpecker in the oak wood) or by predation (like the hare and the lynx) may result in a species being forced into a less extensive **realised niche**. This will be the part of the fundamental niche to which that species is most highly adapted, i.e. most suited. If species only partially share a niche, say they compete for one food organism but are both also able to consume other types of food, like woodpeckers and sparrowhawks then both species can coexist. If, however, species compete directly with each other for every factor (all food, nesting sites) in the same niche it is likely that one species may not survive. In Chapter 14, you will investigate further the effect on competition for niches on species and touch on the important concept of extinction.

There are two important groups of organisms not yet included in the discussions of the oak woodland ecosystem: detritivores and decomposers. A significant proportion of biomass from one trophic level can remain unassimilated by the next trophic level because of the feeding behaviour of the organisms concerned: for example, sparrowhawks pluck the feathers and remove the feet from their great tit prey before feeding them to their nestlings. In addition, the large quantities of faecal matter produced by all the heterotrophs in the food chain represent chemical energy not available to the organism, often because it is difficult to digest. Decomposers and detritivores process unassimilated material, faeces and dead plant and animal material and use the biomass it contains for their own respiration and to increase their biomass. This means that all the energy captured by photosynthesis in an ecosystem is ultimately released through respiration by one organism or another. The flow of energy through the oak wood ecosystem can be represented as a flow chart. Figure 7.4 illustrates the flow of energy through the various trophic levels in an ecosystem, with the thickness of the lines between levels crudely representing the amount of energy flow. In the next activity, you will try to quantify the energy flowing between the trophic levels of the oak woodland ecosystem.

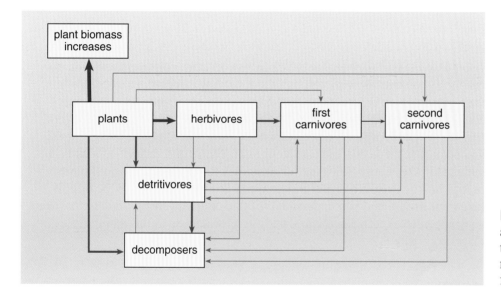

**Figure 7.4**   Food web for a typical ecosystem – the thickness of the lines represents roughly the amount of energy flowing between trophic levels.

## Activity 7.2   Ecological chains: energy flow

We expect this part of the activity will take you approximately 1 hour.

This activity pulls together the first five sections of Activity 7.1 (you will return to Section 6 of the activity later). It allows you to assign numerical values to the flow of energy through a hectare of oak woodland for a whole year and try to quantify the amount of discarded/unassimilated material at each trophic level and the amount of energy lost in respiration. You will be using the information about the oak woodland ecosystem from the computer-based activity to complete an energy flow diagram (Figure 7.5). You will calculate a number of these energy values for yourself, making use of the word equations introduced in Sections 7.3 and 7.4. These values will then be used to complete an energy flow diagram for the oak woodland ecosystem. Finally, the completed diagram will be used to summarise the fundamental concepts concerning energy flow through ecosystems.

Figure 7.5 is a simplification of the real world. The assumption is made that photosynthetic efficiency is the same for all plants as it is for the oak leaf. Detritivores and decomposers have been lumped together into one category and it has been assumed that nothing eats them. Parasites are also ignored. The energy content of animals that have died of natural causes and not been consumed by carnivores has been combined with energy in discarded/unassimilated plant material and shown as one value.

The units used throughout this activity are $kJ\ ha^{-1}\ y^{-1}$ expressed to 2 significant figures throughout. You will begin by considering the amount of solar energy that is incident on one hectare of oak woodland in one year. This is $1.0 \times 10^{10}\ kJ\ ha^{-1}\ y^{-1}$. We cannot assume however, that the entire solar energy incident on the hectare of oak woodland is all used for photosynthesis. From Activity 7.1 Section 4, you know that the efficiency of the photosynthetic process is actually only about 1%.

So, assume the amount of solar energy absorbed by plants is 1.0% of the amount of solar energy that is incident on one hectare of oak woodland in one year, i.e.

$$0.010 \times 1.0 \times 10^{10}\ kJ\ ha^{-1}\ y^{-1} = 1.0 \times 10^{8}\ kJ\ ha^{-1}\ y^{-1}$$

Recall from Activity 7.1 Section 4 that this value is the gross primary production (GPP).

Using this value of GPP ($1.0 \times 10^{8}\ kJ\ ha^{-1}\ y^{-1}$) for the oak woodland, you now need to systematically work through the following calculations to establish the various energy inputs and outputs at the different trophic levels. In this ecosystem, four trophic levels, plants (autotrophs), herbivores, first carnivores and second carnivores, have been identified. You will calculate energy inputs and outputs as far as the first carnivores; data for second carnivores is already included in the energy flow diagram. You may find these calculations rather repetitive; however, it is a useful exercise to go stepwise through the trophic levels and ensure that you understand the fate of all the energy in the ecosystem. As you complete each calculation, add the relevant data to the energy flow diagram (Figure 7.5).

1   Given that only 20% of the energy assimilated from solar energy is used in respiration, calculate the amount of energy lost to respiration by plants (R) in $kJ\ ha^{-1}\ y^{-1}$.

2   Use Equation 7.1 to calculate the NPP for the oak woodland per hectare per year.

3   You can now move up to the next trophic level, the herbivores. Given that 10% of the energy in plant material is available to herbivores, calculate the amount of biomass consumed by herbivores when they eat the plants.

4   Using your answer to Question 3 and, given that 60% of the energy consumed by herbivores is unassimilated, i.e. lost in faeces, calculate the energy assimilated by the herbivores using the equation:

biomass consumption = energy assimilated + energy lost in faeces     (7.4)

You may find an alternative way to reach the required value for energy assimilated by herbivores here – this is not incorrect, but it is advisable to use the equation provided to demonstrate your understanding of the energy flow through the ecosystem.

5   Using your answer to Question 4 and, given that 15% of the energy consumed by the herbivores is converted into biomass, calculate the energy lost to respiration using the equation:

energy assimilated = increase in biomass + energy lost in respiration     (7.5)

6   Now you move up to the next trophic level in the ecosystem, the first carnivores. Given that 25% of herbivore biomass is consumed by carnivores, calculate the amount of energy consumed by the carnivores by eating plant biomass.

7   Using your answer to Question 6 and, given that 25% of the energy consumed by the first carnivore is unassimilated, i.e. lost in faeces, calculate the energy assimilated by the carnivore using the equation:

biomass consumption = energy assimilated + energy lost in faeces     (7.6)

8   Using your answer to Question 7 and, given that 5% of the energy consumed by first carnivores is converted into biomass, calculate the energy lost to respiration using the equation:

energy assimilated = increase in biomass + energy lost in respiration     (7.7)

9   The energy flow diagram shows that the total amount of discarded and unassimilated energy for all the trophic levels is $2.9 \times 10^7$ kJ ha$^{-1}$ y$^{-1}$.

   (a)   What type of material does this include?

   (b)   50% of this material is consumed by detritivores and decomposers and they are able to assimilate 25% of this material. Calculate the energy value of this assimilated material in kJ ha$^{-1}$ y$^{-1}$.

   (c)   Use your answer to part (b) to calculate the amount of energy lost to respiration if 5% of the energy consumed is used to increase detritivore and decomposer biomass.

Remember to add all your calculated data to the appropriate spaces in Figure 7.5.

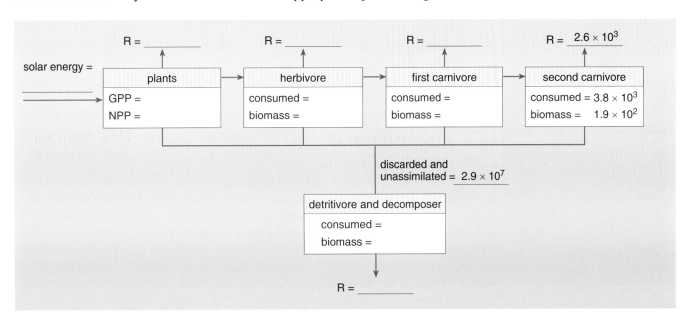

**Figure 7.5**   Energy flow through an oak woodland ecosystem.

Use Figure 7.5 to answer the following questions.

10   Calculate the percentage of energy entering the ecosystem from the Sun that ends up as biomass in the highest carnivore. Explain where most of the energy has 'gone'.

11   Why are there progressively fewer organisms as you move from herbivore level to highest carnivore level in an ecosystem?

12   The energy values in the flow diagram show that organisms in the different trophic levels of this ecosystem differ in their efficiency to assimilate energy from their food. Plants assimilate only 1% of the energy available from the Sun, herbivores assimilate 40% and carnivores 75%. Explain why carnivores assimilate a much higher proportion of the food they consume compared with herbivores.

Now look at the comments on this activity at the end of this book.

## 7.6   Steady state

From your detailed look at the fates of energy absorbed by the various trophic levels in the oak woodland ecosystem, you now need to consider the overall energy inputs and outputs to the system. In Book 1, Section 4.2.2, the idea of the leaky tank to model energy inputs and outputs from the Earth's surface was introduced and the term steady state was used to describe situations where energy inputs and outputs are completely balanced. In any ecosystem, if all the energy captured by photosynthesis is ultimately released as heat as a consequence of respiration by one organism or another, then the ecosystem is said to be in a steady state.

■   Is this the case, for the oak woodland ecosystem? *Hint*: you need to add up all the values for energy lost via respiration at each trophic level from your energy flow diagram.

☐   From the data, it appears that $2.2 \times 10^7$ kJ ha$^{-1}$ y$^{-1}$ (energy output) are lost via respiration, while $1.0 \times 10^8$ kJ ha$^{-1}$ y$^{-1}$ are absorbed by the system (energy input) by photosynthesis. This suggests that outputs are significantly less than inputs and so the ecosystem is not in steady state.

One possible reason for energy input being higher than energy output may be the age of the woodland. If the producers, the oak trees, are still rapidly growing, then a greater proportion of the energy inputs are stored as tree biomass or wood and not respired. In comparision, in a mature woodland, the trees are larger, not actively growing and the increased biomass requires more respiration to sustain it. Any production of new wood/leaf is balanced by decomposition of old material and, ultimately, the steady state where energy input equals output is reached. From your observations of the oak woodland in the computer-based activity, can you tell if this is an old established woodland or an actively growing young one? Although only a small section of the wood can be seen in the activity, it seems that the trees are relatively young and therefore could be still actively storing energy as biomass. It would be interesting to revisit the site in the future to see if a steady state has been reached.

## Activity 7.3 The correct use of terminology

We expect this activity will take you approximately 30 minutes.

Write an account (of about 350 words) describing the flow of energy through an ecosystem. Your account should include and show a good understanding of the following terms (some of which you may want to use more than once and some of which you may want to use in different forms, e.g. autotrophic rather that autotroph):

| | | |
|---|---|---|
| assimilation | autotroph | biomass |
| carnivore | decomposer | detritivores |
| ecosystem | faeces | food chain |
| food web | gross primary productivity | herbivore |
| heterotrophs | net primary productivity | photosynthesis |
| respiration | solar energy | trophic level |

As you study this course, you will have realised that many scientific words and phrases have a very precise meaning. In this activity, you are asked to demonstrate your understanding of some scientific terms by using new words and phrases introduced in Chapter 7 in a piece of writing. We suggest that you follow the five steps outlined below.

1   Plan your piece of writing. You may need to look back at your notes from Chapter 7. Put your ideas into a logical order.

2   Make sure that you understand the meaning of the terms that you are expected to use. Look them up in the course Glossary. Where in your account do you think that each term will fit? Remember that you can use each word or phrase more than once. Do any of the required terms not fit comfortably into your plan? This could be because you've missed something from your plan or because you've not properly understood the term.

3   Write out the answer. Remember to be as precise as possible in your use of words.

4   Include a brief introductory statement that explains the overarching theme of your account and a final concluding sentence that summarises the main points without introducing any new information.

5   Read your answer again. Does the overall meaning seem clear? Do you think that you have used each of the new terms in the correct way? Does your answer have a clear structure?

Now compare your answer with the one given in the comments on this activity at the end of this book and also read the general advice for writing scientific accounts given there.

Before leaving the oak woodland you need to consider one last problem for food chain organisms – you know what they eat and how much they need, but the remaining question is: how do they get the timing right? How do species make sure that they breed at the same time that appropriate food supplies will be available for their offspring? In the final part of Activity 7.1, you will investigate this interesting problem and consider how changes to the climate may endanger breeding success for some species.

### Activity 7.1 (continued)  Ecological chains – Section 6

We expect this section of the activity will take you approximately 30 minutes.

Study Section 6 'Getting the timing right' DVD screens 47–66 of the computer-based activity *Ecological Chains*. This is the final computer-based activity in this series and it concludes your exploration of the oak woodland ecosystem. Now you have fully explored the feeding relationships and the flow of energy along your food chain, you need to consider how important it is that the various species in the chain synchronise their breeding period with the availability of their food.

Now look at the comments on Section 6 of this activity at the end of this book.

## 7.7  Summary of Chapter 7

All the principles applicable to the oak woodland ecosystem also apply to any other ecosystem.

Food chains begin with autotrophs.

All organisms are part of several food chains, which combine to form a food web.

Species occupy distinct ecological niches within an ecosystem.

Food chains can vary with the time of year, but always consist of several trophic levels separated by the consumption (in whole or in part) of one organism by another.

Different organisms have different life cycles that vary in the number of stages, their duration and their location. Each of these stages is a potential food source for other organisms; each of the stages may have different food requirements from other stages.

It is possible to calculate the energy flow through food chains and hence through an ecosystem. This can be done by measuring the amount of energy captured by photosynthesis, accumulated in biomass and lost through respiration in plants, and by measuring the consumption, biomass accumulation and energy lost through respiration and faeces in animals.

When an ecosystem is in steady state, all the energy captured by photosynthesis is ultimately released by respiration.

An organism's success depends on getting the timing right in terms of when it reproduces with respect to the availability of a suitable food resource.

In your study of this chapter, you had the opportunity to observe a specific ecosystem at close hand in a qualitative way (description and explanation) and in a quantitative way where you were able to assign numerical values to determine the energy flow through the ecosystem. In Activities 7.1 and 7.2 you have presented data in a variety of ways including constructing a complex flow diagram of energy inputs and outputs. You have then used this numerical data to draw some general conclusions about energy flow in ecosystems.

Activity 7.3 allowed you to further develop your writing skills, this time with a focus on the correct use of scientific terminology. Here you were able to practise the vital processes of planning your writing, arranging concepts into a logical order, and writing brief introductions and conclusions.

# Chapter 8
# Meiosis and the genetic lottery

Earlier chapters in this book have demonstrated how living organisms use the components of the world around them and convert these into their own living material. An acorn grows into an oak tree using only water, oxygen, carbon dioxide, some inorganic materials from the soil, and light energy. Similarly, a human baby grows into an adult by digesting and metabolising food and drink. The parents in each case pass to their progeny, or offspring, the information and specification for building cells from materials around them. This information lies in the genetic material, or DNA, which is found in the chromosomes within the nucleus, and which is transmitted from generation to generation. Chromosomes can be regarded as strings of genes, the units of inheritance. It is to the study of chromosomes and genes that this chapter turns.

The idea of passing on information from parents to offspring raises an important question: *how* are the units of inheritance transmitted from one generation to the next? This section takes two approaches to answering this question. First, it looks at what happens to the chromosomes of animals and plants during the process of sexual reproduction. Second, it examines how genes are transmitted in particular patterns from generation to generation. These two approaches are then combined to show how the patterns of inheritance can be explained by the behaviour of chromosomes during sexual reproduction. Since genes are an integral part of chromosomes, following the behaviour of chromosomes allows the movement of genes to be traced. Thus the focus of this chapter will be at both the gene and chromosomal levels of explanation.

The majority of the study time will be dedicated to learning about genes and chromosomes and their patterns of inheritance. Your study of inheritance will involve the computer-based activity *Mitosis, Meiosis and Recombination*, which explores the relationship between division of the nucleus and the inheritance of genes. You will practise some basic maths skills, particularly the use of ratios and you will learn about the mathematical idea of probability.

## 8.1    Meiosis and the life cycle

The type of nuclear division called meiosis is intimately linked to the life cycle of organisms that reproduce sexually. You were introduced to the essential features of life cycles in Section 4.5. Try to recall the essential stage of a life cycle, such as the human life cycle, by answering Question 8.1.

Question 8.1

Complete Figure 8.1 using the following terms: fertilisation, haploid, mitosis, diploid and meiosis. Each term may be used more than once.

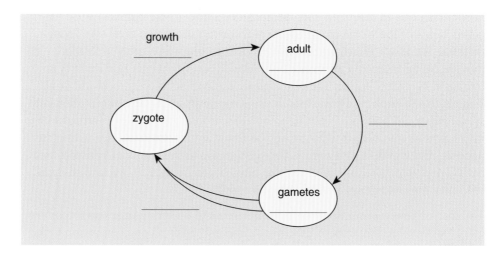

**Figure 8.1**   Diagram to summarise the human life cycle and the changes in chromosome number at each stage. For completion in Question 8.1.

The answer to Question 8.1 shows that haploid gametes contain one set of chromosomes, and diploid cells contain two sets (with each chromosome (usually) having a morphologically identical partner). Chromosomes are present in the cells of all eukaryotes. Their number varies enormously and is characteristic for each species. The parasitic worm *Ascaris lumbricoides* has only four chromosomes whereas some ferns, such as the adder's tongue fern (*Ophioglossum vulgatum*), have more than 1000 chromosomes. Most eukaryotes have between 10 and 50 chromosomes; for example, humans have 46. However, there is no obvious relationship between chromosome number and an organism's complexity of organisation.

When the chromosomes are aligned along the centre of the cell during metaphase of mitosis (Figure 4.19b), they are in their most condensed state so their number, size and shape can be most easily studied. Figure 8.2 shows the metaphase chromosomes of a human female. These have been stained and spread out so that they are readily distinguishable. The array of chromosomes that a particular species possesses is called the **karyotype**. For any one species, the male and female karyotypes may differ slightly because of the sex chromosomes. By cutting out the chromosomes from photographs taken down the microscope and lining them up according to their size and shape, the distinctive features of the karyotype can be revealed (Figure 8.3).

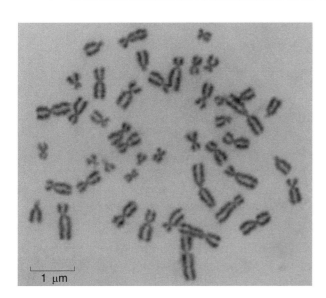

**Figure 8.2**   Metaphase chromosomes of a human female. These chromosomes were prepared from a cell in the blood. Each chromosome is made up of a pair of identical chromatids, joined at the centromere (Section 4.4.1).

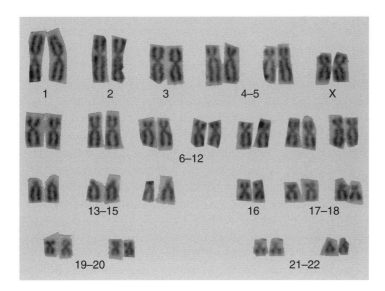

**Figure 8.3**   Chromosomes of a human female arranged as a karyotype. The pairs of autosomes (chromosomes that are not sex chromosomes) are numbered 1–22, and the pair of sex chromosomes is labelled X. Pairs of chromosomes that are difficult to separate from each other are grouped together, e.g. pairs 6–12.

■   What is the most striking feature of the karyotype shown in Figure 8.3?

☐   All the chromosomes are present in pairs; each member of a pair has the same structure and appearance.

Each member of a pair of chromosomes is said to be **homologous** to its partner, that is, to have the same size, shape and function. Another feature of the karyotype in Figure 8.3 is the different appearances of the chromosomes; non-homologous chromosomes can be distinguished from each other by their length and the position of the centromere and, although many look very similar, to the trained eye and using more sophisticated staining techniques, each pair is different.

■  How can you tell that the karyotype in Figure 8.3 is of a diploid cell?

☐  The chromosomes are present in pairs – homologous pairs – hence they must be from a diploid cell.

Sexual reproduction includes two distinctive processes:

1  The production of haploid gametes, such as sperm and ova (Section 4.5.2), which involves the specialised nuclear division called meiosis. (Later, in Section 8.5, you will learn how this is brought about.)

2  The fusion of gametes at *fertilisation*, which results in the restoration of the diploid number of chromosomes.

The relationship between these two processes, and the changes in chromosome number that each process brings about, are shown in outline in Figure 8.4. This figure represents a hypothetical organism with only four chromosomes, that is, two pairs of homologous chromosomes – one long pair and one short pair – as shown for each of the parents in row 1 of the figure. For simplicity, each chromosome is shown as a single strand, rather than as a pair of chromatids as shown in Figures 8.2 and 8.3. The chromosomes of the female parent (*maternal* chromosomes) are shown in red (lighter shade) and those of the male parent (*paternal* chromosomes) are shown in blue (darker shade). As a result of meiosis, the chromosome number is halved in the gametes, each of which contains two chromosomes, as shown in row 2 of Figure 8.4. Notice that the

**Figure 8.4**   Changes in number of chromosomes at gamete production (meiosis) and at fertilisation in a hypothetical organism with only two pairs of homologous chromosomes. For simplicity, each chromosome is shown as a single strand, rather than as a pair of chromatids (Figures 8.2 and 8.3).

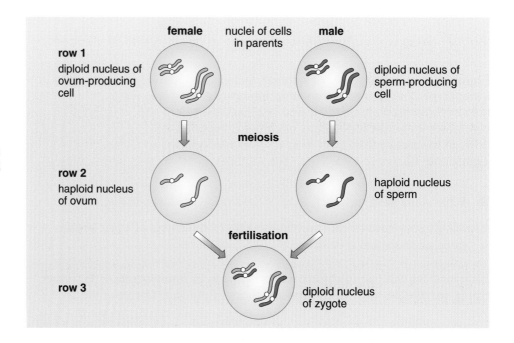

set of chromosomes in the gametes is not a random collection; it is made up of one member of each homologous pair – one long chromosome and one short chromosome. Row 3 shows that fertilisation restores the original number of four chromosomes in the zygote, which contains a pair of the long homologous chromosomes and a pair of the short homologous chromosomes. Note that in the zygote, half the chromosomes are shown in red (lighter shade) and half in blue (darker shade), since one member of each homologous pair comes from the female parent and its partner comes from the male parent.

■ What would happen to the chromosome number in future generations if gamete production did not involve the halving of the diploid chromosome number?

☐ If the chromosome number were not reduced by half during gamete formation, to produce the gametes containing the haploid number, a zygote would have twice the diploid number and the chromosome number would double in each subsequent generation.

Question 8.2

Insert the missing term in each of the following sentences.

(a) _____ chromosomes are pairs of chromosomes that are present in diploid cells and have the same appearance and function.

(b) The number, size and shape of all the chromosomes in a cell is called the _____ and is characteristic for a species.

(c) The process of _____ is involved in the production of gametes, which have the haploid number of chromosomes.

(d) The process of combining two gametes to produce a zygote is called

_____ .

The distribution of one member of each homologous pair of chromosomes to each gamete is a consequence of the precision of the process of meiosis. An understanding of the distribution of chromosomes, both during the production of gametes and at fertilisation, is important for exploring the inheritance of genes.

## 8.2   Like begets like

It is possible to follow a character, such as eye colour or hair colour in humans, that is handed down from generation to generation. Such characters are said to be **inherited characters** (or heritable characters) and are determined by genes. A **gene** can be considered as a unit of inheritance that determines a particular character and which is passed on from parent to offspring.

Genes maintain the differences between species, such as oak and human, but they also contribute to differences between individuals within a species. For example, consider hair colour or eye colour within a family. Brothers and sisters may share features, such as brown hair, that they also share with their biological parents, but in addition they have their own particular combination of characters that make them recognisable as individuals. For example, one sister may have blue eyes whilst her siblings have brown eyes; a brother may have curly hair whilst his siblings have straight hair, and so on. To understand the differences and similarities in characters between individuals, you need to look at how copies of genes are transmitted from parent to offspring. In so doing, you will discover the rules that govern inheritance.

While at one level there is continuity from one generation to the next, at another level a degree of variation occurs. In fact, there is so much variation that every human alive today is different from all others – we are all genetically unique (with the exception of identical twins, who have identical genes). Some of this variation can be seen with the unaided eye, whereas other variation, such as blood groups or the activity of a particular enzyme, is revealed only by more sophisticated molecular biological techniques. The sum of all the characters that an individual organism possesses, not only structural features but also biochemical, behavioural and physiological features, is described as the **phenotype**. All aspects of an organism's phenotype depend ultimately on that organism's chemical composition and on the biochemical reactions that go on inside it.

The full complement of an individual's genes is called the **genotype**. The phenotype of each individual is the result of the combined action of their genes (their genotype) and their environment, some characters being influenced more by the environment than are others.

- From your own experience, suggest a human character that might be influenced by environmental factors.

□ One example is body mass, which is greatly influenced by the amount and type of food that people eat and the amount of exercise they take.

Phenotype, as well as meaning the sum total of *all* an individual's characters, also has a more restricted meaning; it is used as a shorthand way of referring to the expression of just *one* character, for example, 'blue-eyed phenotype'. Similarly, genotype is also used to refer to the specific genes associated with a particular character, for example, 'blue-eyed genotype'.

Question 8.3

Which of the following is the same for every individual of a species:
(a) karyotype; (b) genotype; (c) phenotype? Explain your answer.

## 8.3   Patterns of inheritance

The inheritance of characters in animals and plants can be traced by following the phenotype from generation to generation, in breeding experiments. We will describe work with the garden pea (*Pisum sativum*), which occurs throughout the world as an important commercial crop plant, and which is used in genetic research. The breeding experiments described here are the famous experiments carried out by an Austrian monk called Gregor Mendel (Figure 8.5). These

**Figure 8.5**   Gregor Mendel (1822–1884), who laid the foundation of the modern science of genetics. The results of his experiments, carried out in the monastery gardens in Brno, Moravia (subsequently incorporated in Czechoslovakia and now the Czech Republic), were published in 1865. His work was largely ignored or unnoticed until 1900 when it was 'rediscovered' by other workers after they had come to similar conclusions from their own work. Mendel had died 16 years before his work was recognised.

experiments were published in 1865, and laid the foundation of the modern science of genetics.

As well as following the phenotype, the inheritance of characters at the level of the genotype can also be studied. In this section, you will jump between these two levels, and in so doing you will be jumping from the fundamental work of 19th century biologists such as Mendel, who could only trace phenotypes, to that of present-day geneticists, who work at the level of the gene.

This section begins with one of the simplest known examples of inheritance – that of flower colour in the garden pea. The two possible colours, purple and white, will be considered. A plant in which all the flowers are purple has the 'purple phenotype'; a plant with white flowers has the 'white phenotype' (Figure 8.6a and b). The two plants are said to have **contrasting characters**.

(a)                                          (b)                                          (c)

**Figure 8.6**   (a) The purple flower of the garden pea; (b) the white flower of the garden pea; (c) cutaway view of the reproductive parts of a pea flower.

Mendel chose his experimental plant very carefully, and found the garden pea admirably suited to his purpose. There were pure-breeding lines of plants that had constant contrasting characters, for example, a variety of purple-flowering plants and a variety of white-flowering plants. A variety is said to be **pure-breeding** for a character if all its members have the same character, such as purple flowers, and all breeding within that variety leads to offspring that have the same character.

The enclosed floral structure of the pea, which produces both ovules and pollen grains (Figure 8.6c), ensured that **self-fertilisation** occurred, whereby pollen fertilises the female gametes of the same plant, without the risk of contamination by pollen from another plant. However, **cross-fertilisation**, whereby the pollen from one plant fertilises the female gametes of another plant, was also possible (Figure 8.7, row 1). The terms 'ovule' and 'pollen grain' are used as shorthand for the female and the male gametes, respectively (Section 4.5.2), although these structures are not actually the gametes of plants but *contain* the gametes.

But why should flower colour be different in the two varieties of pea? And if plants of these two varieties were cross-fertilised, what would be the flower colour of the offspring? In order to answer these questions, we will look at a breeding experiment, carried out in two stages and using these two pea varieties.

### 8.3.1   A breeding experiment: stage one

In the first stage of the breeding experiment, shown in Figure 8.7, plants from the pure-breeding purple-flowered variety are crossed with (fertilised by) plants from the pure-breeding white-flowered variety. This can be done artificially by dabbing pollen grains from one plant onto the flowers of another plant. These plants are the **parental generation** (abbreviated to **P**), and the peas in the pods resulting from the cross are the seeds which produce the first offspring generation or **first filial** (pronounced 'phil-ee-al') **generation** (abbreviated to $F_1$). The subsequent generations in such an experiment are called $F_2$, $F_3$, and so on. Incidentally, if you read information on seed packets, you may well be familiar with $F_1$ hybrid seeds, which are the product of crossing two pure-breeding parental varieties.

Returning to the pea cross (Figure 8.7), the most striking observation is that these cross-fertilisations result in $F_1$ plants all of which have purple flowers. Two important features of the results of this cross should be noted:

1   No $F_1$ plants have any white flowers. This is true even if large numbers of $F_1$ plants are examined. Hence, one of the two characters present in the parental generation, white flower colour, has vanished in the $F_1$ offspring generation.

2   It does not matter which way round the cross is carried out; that is, the result is the same whether the pollen comes from the purple-flowered variety and the ovules from the white-flowered variety, or vice versa. This rules out the possibility that flower colour is determined by the plant on which the flower has grown.

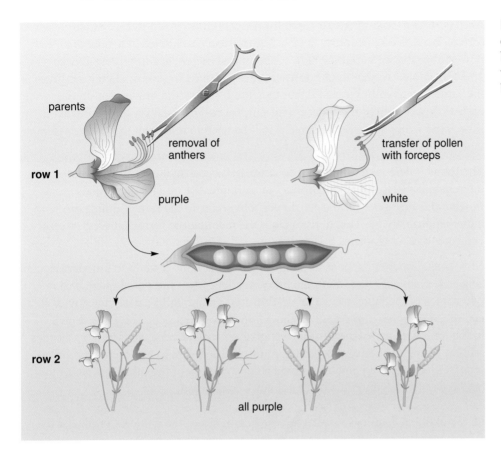

**Figure 8.7**   The result of crossing pea plants of a pure-breeding purple-flowered variety with those of a pure-breeding white-flowered variety.

Now that we have examined the phenotype of the flowers in the breeding experiment, we will explore what is happening at the level of the gene. A gene can be considered as a small section of the DNA in a chromosome, which issues instructions for a specific phenotypic character such that a pea flower is either purple (presence of purple pigment) or white (absence of purple pigment); for brevity it can be called the gene for flower colour. Most importantly for understanding the patterns of inheritance of genes, it is known that a gene has a particular location on a chromosome, such as band A in Figure 8.8. As this figure shows, a diploid cell contains two copies of a gene for a particular character situated at corresponding locations on the two homologous chromosomes. The technical term for the location of a gene on a chromosome is **locus** (pronounced 'lock–us', plural loci, pronounced 'low-sigh').

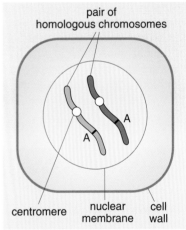

**Figure 8.8**   A gene, labelled A, is a small section of a chromosome at a particular locus. For simplicity, only one pair of homologous chromosomes is shown in this hypothetical plant cell. The length of the gene relative to length of the chromosome is very much smaller than shown here.

■   Where do each of these two copies of a gene in a diploid cell come from?

☐   One comes from the female gamete and the other from the male gamete. (Fertilisation restores the chromosomes as homologous pairs, as shown in Figure 8.4.)

■   Why is the outcome of the breeding experiment described above the same regardless of which of the parental phenotypes provides the ovules and which provides the pollen?

☐   The simplest explanation is that the instructions that a gene issues are the same, irrespective of whether the gene is from the male or female parent.

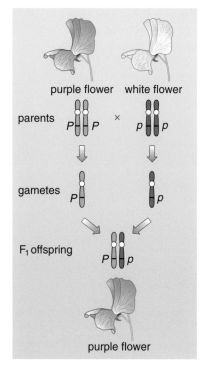

**Figure 8.9** The cross between pure-breeding purple-flowered peas (genotype *P P*) and pure-breeding white-flowered peas (genotype *p p*). The diagram shows the fate of the flower-colour genes and of the chromosomes on which they are carried during gamete production and fertilisation.

(labels in figure: purple flower; white flower; parents; *P P* × *p p*; gametes; *P*; *p*; F₁ offspring; *P p*; purple flower)

Each gene can exist in one or more forms; each form is a different **allele** (pronounced 'a', as in apple, 'leel'). The existence of alleles of a gene is a powerful source of variation. It is conventional in genetics to represent each allele by a letter (either upper or lower case), printed in italics; alleles are given the same letter symbol to show that they are forms of the same gene. In the case of flower colour, the letter *P* (for purple) will be used for the allele that is associated with purple flowers and *p* will be used to represent the different allele that is associated with white flowers.

The terms 'allele' and 'gene' can be confusing because the terms are used interchangeably in some situations. For example, the 'allele for purple flower' and the 'gene for purple flower' both refer to the same thing in an interchangeable way. This derives from the fact that the forms (alleles) of any gene are, of course, genes themselves.

Now consider what happens at the gene level when the pure-breeding purple-flowered plant is crossed with the pure-breeding white-flowered plant. The two copies of the gene in the purple-flowered parent will be designated as *P P* and the two copies of the gene in the white-flowered parent as *p p*, as shown in Figure 8.9. (The reason for this designation will become clear later in the section.) Note the convention of the multiplication sign to represent a breeding cross. Of course, the gametes contain a copy of each of the other pea genes too, but here only the gene for flower colour is considered.

■ Looking at Figure 8.9, what are the genotypes of the gametes produced by each parent?

□ *P* and *p*. Gametes from the purple-flowered parent all contain the *P* allele and those from the white-flowered parent all contain the *p* allele.

Recall from Figure 8.4 that meiosis ensures that each gamete contains one member of each homologous pair of chromosomes and hence only one copy of each gene.

■ What would be the possible genotypes of the offspring of such a cross?

□ They would all be *P p* or *p P*, and these are the *same* genotype.

The convention is to write the allele with the capital letter first, so the genotype of all the F₁ offspring would be written as *P p*. Notice that not only do all the F₁ offspring have the same genotype, *P p*, but that this genotype is different from that of either parent. Where the two copies of a gene are different, as in the offspring of this cross, they are said to be **heterozygous** (pronounced 'het-er-oh-zye-guss') and the individual is referred to as a **heterozygote** (pronounced 'het-er-oh-zye-goat') for that particular gene. When the two copies of the gene are the same (as in the case of each parent), they are said to be **homozygous** and the individual is a **homozygote** for the gene for flower colour.

But what is the phenotype of the F₁ offspring with the heterozygous genotype *P p*? You should recall (Figure 8.7) that the phenotype of all the F₁ offspring of this cross was purple. The character that is expressed, or manifest, in the heterozygote, purple flowers in this case, is said to be the **dominant** character because it masks the presence of the alternative character, white flowers. The character that is not expressed in the heterozygote is said to be **recessive**. In this case, white flowers are recessive to, or masked by, the dominant character, purple flowers. Strictly speaking, it is the phenotype – rather than the allele – that is dominant or recessive; however, alleles are usually referred to as being dominant or recessive on the basis of the associated phenotype.

### 8.3.2   A breeding experiment: stage two

We are now going to move on to the second stage of the breeding experiment, but this time you will follow the phenotypes and genotypes simultaneously. The seeds of the $F_1$ generation are sown and when these have developed into mature $F_1$ plants they produce flowers. Mendel allowed the $F_1$ plants to self-fertilise. This is the same as crossing one $F_1$ plant with another $F_1$ plant, as shown in Figure 8.10. The fertilised ovules develop into pea seeds borne in peapods, and these seeds are the beginning of the **second filial generation ($F_2$)**.

The mating diagram and the outcome of the fertilisations of this cross are shown in Figure 8.10. First consider the gametes produced by the $F_1$ generation, shown in Figure 8.10.

■   What are the genotypes of the gametes produced by the $F_1$ purple-flowered plants?

☐   The gametes are either $P$ or $p$, since all $F_1$ plants are $Pp$.

In fact, half the gametes would be $P$ and half would be $p$ because the pair of homologous chromosomes on which they are located separate into different gametes in equal proportions. However, geneticists use ratios to show the relationship between the sizes of two (or more) similar quantities. For example, if there are 200 $P$ gametes and 200 $p$ gametes, then the ratio of $P$ to $p$ is 200 : 200 or, given as the lowest numbers, 1:1.

Now consider the possible fertilisations between the gametes produced by the $F_1$ generation, as shown in Figure 8.10, and the genotypes and phenotypes of the $F_2$ generation that arises from these fertilisations.

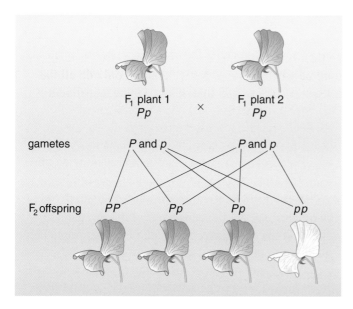

**Figure 8.10**   Crossing $F_1$ plants with $F_1$ plants (or self-fertilisation) gives $F_2$ plants, bearing $F_2$ flowers. Drawings of the $F_2$ offspring flowers are included, to show the phenotypes. The recessive phenotype reappears in the $F_2$ generation. Unlike Figure 8.9, the chromosomes bearing the flower-colour alleles are not shown; it is conventional to simplify mating diagrams in this way.

Looking at Figure 8.10, you can see that the allele $P$ of plant 1 might combine with either the $P$ or the $p$ allele of plant 2 at fertilisation. Over a large number of fertilisations a $P$-bearing ovule of plant 1 would combine with a $P$-bearing pollen grain of plant 2 in half of the fertilisations and combine with a $p$-bearing pollen grain of plant 2 in the other half. Similarly, the $p$-bearing ovule of plant 1 might combine with either the $P$- or $p$-bearing pollen grain of plant 2. Hence, in the $F_2$ generation, three different genotypes are produced: $PP$, $Pp$ and $pp$.

■   What is the expected ratio of the three genotypes in the $F_2$ generation?

□   The expected ratio is $1\ PP : 2\ Pp : 1\ pp$ (see Figure 8.10).

This ratio follows for two reasons. First, the two different gametes, $P$ and $p$, are produced in equal numbers. Second, which ovule is fertilised by which pollen occurs at random; that is, a $P$ ovule is equally likely to be fertilised by either a $P$ pollen flower or $p$ pollen flower.

The phenotype of each of these genotypes in the $F_2$ generation can be determined since you know that the allele $P$ (purple flower) is dominant to $p$.

■   What are the phenotypes corresponding to each of the genotypes $PP$, $Pp$ and $pp$ of the $F_2$ generation?

□   $PP$ and $Pp$ plants are purple-flowered and $pp$ plants are white-flowered.

■   In what ratio would flowers with the purple phenotype and flowers with the white phenotype be expected to occur in the $F_2$ generation?

□   The expected ratio is three purple (the dominant phenotype) : one white (the recessive phenotype), since three of the four possible fertilisations have at least one dominant $P$ allele (see Figure 8.10).

The phenotypic ratio of $3 : 1$ (three of the dominant phenotype : one of the recessive phenotype) and the genotypic ratio of $1 : 2 : 1$ (one homozygous dominant : two heterozygous : one homozygous recessive) are of fundamental importance in genetics.

Figure 8.11 presents the same information about the breeding experiment as shown in Figure 8.10, but the information is laid out in a different way. Either way of presenting the details of a cross can be used, and when producing your own diagrams you can use whichever is easier for you (although you are not expected to draw the phenotypes).

In Figure 8.11, the fertilisations between the various combinations of gametes from the $F_1$ generation are shown in boxes at the bottom. Along the top, you can see the two types of gamete produced by plant 1 of the $F_1$ generation; down the left-hand side you can see the two types of gamete produced by plant 2 of the $F_1$ generation. Inside the other boxes are the genotypes of the products of fertilisation between the various kinds of gamete, that is, the $F_2$ generation. Thus, for example, the top left-hand box records the outcome of fertilisation between a $P$ ovule and a $P$ pollen nucleus. An examination of the contents of the four boxes should convince you that the expected ratio of genotypes of the $F_2$ generation is $1\ PP : 2\ Pp : 1\ pp$ (one homozygous dominant : two heterozygous : one

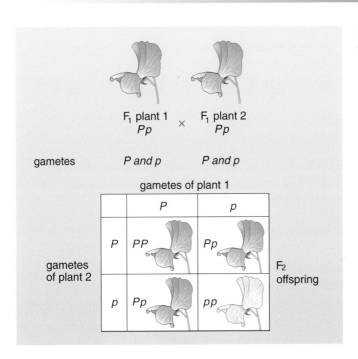

homozygous recessive) and that the expected phenotypic ratio is therefore three purple : one white (three of the dominant phenotype : one of the recessive phenotype).

Why was Mendel so successful at determining the pattern of inheritance of characters?

Mendel introduced the scientific approach to breeding experiments by:

- following a single pair of contrasting characters in each investigation
- breeding beyond one generation
- counting the individuals showing each of the phenotypes
- working with large numbers of offspring.

Although the existence of genes and chromosomes was not known in Mendel's time, he predicted the separation or **segregation** of units (now called genes and alleles) during gamete formation. You now know that meiosis ensures that each gamete contains only one copy of a gene, because the pairs of chromosomes on which the genes are located separate into different gametes (Figure 8.9). This segregation of genes (units) has been given formal recognition as Mendel's **law of segregation**.

The breeding experiment in peas shows that characters due to dominant or recessive alleles, such as flower colour, show a particular pattern of inheritance from generation to generation: the $F_1$ offspring all resemble one of the parents (Figure 8.9), and the $F_2$ offspring have the phenotypic ratio of 3 : 1 and the genotypic ratio of 1 : 2 : 1 (Figures 8.10 and 8.11). The action of dominant alleles explains why the recessive character 'disappears' in the $F_1$ generation and why this character reappears in the $F_2$ generation. Most importantly, this pattern of inheritance is a consequence of two events:

1    The two copies of a gene separate into different gametes in equal numbers.

2    The combining of a female gamete and a male gamete at fertilisation occurs at random.

These conclusions you have drawn from the breeding experiment in pea apply to all sexually reproducing eukaryotes, including humans. The main features of the experiment described so far, and that can be explained by the theory of inheritance, are summarised in Table 8.1.

**Table 8.1**  A summary of features of the pea-breeding experiment.

| | |
|---|---|
| 1 | The phenotype of pure-breeding varieties for a particular character is constant when crossed with members of the same variety. |
| 2 | One parental character disappears in the $F_1$ generation when parents differ in the character for which each is pure-breeding (the recessive character is masked by the dominant character). |
| 3 | The outcome of a cross is independent of which parent provides the ovules and which parent provides the pollen. |
| 4 | The vanished (recessive) character reappears in about one-quarter of the $F_2$ generation. |
| 5 | The two copies of a gene segregate to different gametes at meiosis and in equal numbers. |
| 6 | Gametes combine at random at fertilisation. |

Question 8.4

Note down your answers to each of the following breeding experiments, which use the same species of plant. Assume that the patterns of inheritance follow the same as those of Mendel's garden peas.

**Experiment 1**

100 pure-breeding red-flowered plants (genotype $R R$) are crossed with 100 pure-breeding white-flowered plants (genotype $r r$). All of the offspring have red flowers. These offspring are then crossed with each other. What is the expected ratio of red flowers to white flowers in the $F_2$?

**Experiment 2**

100 pure-breeding red-flowered plants (genotype $R R$) are crossed with 100 pure-breeding white-flowered plants (genotype $r r$). How many of the offspring would have pink flowers?

**Experiment 3**

Would you expect the colour of the offspring of the following two crosses to be the same or different, and why? Cross 1: the pollen from 100 pure-breeding red-flowered plants fertilises the ovules of 100 pure-breeding white-flowered plants. Cross 2: the pollen from 100 pure-breeding white-flowered plants fertilises the ovules of 100 pure-breeding red-flowered plants.

### 8.3.3   Predicting the outcome of crosses

By knowing the pattern of inheritance of genes as described in Section 8.3.2, it is possible to make some predictions about the phenotypes and genotypes of each generation in breeding experiments. This section considers some examples of such predictions.

First consider whether it is possible to determine the genotype for certain characters, such as flower colour, from observing an organism's phenotype.

■   Is it possible to determine the genotype of all white-flowered pea plants just by observing their phenotype?

☐   Yes, it is possible; since white flower colour is recessive, white-flowered plants must be *p p*.

■   Is it possible to determine the genotype of all purple-flowered flowers just by observing their colour?

☐   No, it is not possible, because purple-flowered plants may be either *P P* or *P p*. It is possible to say that one copy of the gene must be *P* but it is not possible to predict the identity of the second copy without further information.

Think back to the original pure-breeding parents (Figure 8.9). The white-flowered parent was *p p* and any crosses between individuals of that variety would involve only *p* gametes. All offspring, therefore, must also be *p p*. Hence this is a pure-breeding variety because all breeding within the variety would lead to offspring that have the same character. Similarly, all the white-flowered plants in the $F_2$ generation (Figures 8.10 and 8.11) would also be pure-breeding for flower colour when crossed with each other.

Now consider the parental pure-breeding purple-flowered variety (Figure 8.9).

■   Why must this variety be *P P* and not *P p?*

☐   To be pure-breeding, all the offspring must have the same phenotype as the parents – this is the definition of pure-breeding. If the parent variety had the genotype *P p*, then a cross between individuals of this variety would produce offspring some of which would be purple-flowered and some of which would be white-flowered (similar to the cross shown in Figures 8.10 and 8.11). Hence it would not be pure-breeding.

Therefore, all members of a pure-breeding variety not only have the same phenotype, but they also have the same genotype. One of the important things that can be learned from the study of genetics, particularly in the case of humans and agricultural breeding, is that many of the outcomes of inheritance are statistical ones; that is, they are to do with probability. What is meant by the term probability?

**Probability** is a way of providing a quantitative measure of the 'chance' or 'likelihood' of a given event under given circumstances. For instance, suppose you have a 'fair' coin that can always be relied upon to have an equal likelihood of coming down heads or tails when given a fair toss. Then you could say that, as a result of a fair toss, the probability of obtaining heads is 0.5 and the probability of obtaining tails is 0.5. The fact that these two probabilities are equal indicates the 'fairness' of the coin, and the fact that they are both equal to 0.5 ensures that the total probability of obtaining either a head or a tail as the result of a fair toss is 1. It is a convention that a probability of 1 represents a certainty. In other words, by assigning probabilities of 0.5 to both heads *and* tails we are saying that there are only two possible outcomes, and they are equally likely.

■  When rolling a fair dice (or die, as one is more properly called) there are six equally likely outcomes (1, 2, 3, 4, 5 or 6). What is the probability of any one of those outcomes?

☐  The probability of any one of the six outcomes is $\frac{1}{6}$.

In general, the probability of a particular outcome, such as throwing heads with a coin, is defined mathematically as:

$$\text{probability of outcome} = \frac{\text{number of ways to get that particular outcome}}{\text{total number of possible outcomes}}$$

In the case of throwing a six-sided die and getting a 4, there is only *one* way of getting that outcome, but there are *six* possible outcomes, so the probability is $\frac{1}{6}$.

■  What would be the probability of throwing an even number with the die?

☐  $\frac{3}{6}$ or $\frac{1}{2}$, since three of the six possible different outcomes are even numbers.

■  What is the probability that a gamete produced by a $Pp$ plant will have the white-flowered allele?

☐  The probability is $\frac{1}{2}$, since there are two possible outcomes and each one is equally likely. Only one of these corresponds to the white-flowered allele.

■  Recall the reason why each of these two possibilities is equally likely.

☐  It is because the two copies of a chromosome separate from each other into different gametes at meiosis, and in equal numbers.

■  What is the probability that an offspring of a cross between two pea plants that are heterozygous for flower colour ($Pp$) will have the white-flowered genotype? (*Hint*: you might find it helpful to draw out such a cross, or to look at the one drawn in Figures 8.10 and 8.11.)

☐  The probability is $\frac{1}{4}$, since there are four possible outcomes ($PP$, two $Pp$, and $pp$), and only one of these corresponds to the white-flowered genotype.

Again, recall that this probability is based on two events: first on an equal number of $P$ and $p$ gametes being produced by each $Pp$ plant; and second, on male and female gametes combining at random at fertilisation.

Question 8.5

What is the probability that an $F_2$ pea flower, as shown in Figures 8.10 and 8.11, will contain at least one $p$ allele?

So far in Section 8.3 you have looked at only two types of cross, one between two pure-breeding varieties, which gives rise to the $F_1$ generation, and one between $F_1$ individuals which gives rise to the $F_2$ generation. However, other crosses can be carried out and they show that inheritance of the copies of a gene follows the same basic rules. An understanding of probability, the relationship between dominant and recessive alleles, and the way that the two copies of a gene segregate at meiosis, enables the outcome of many breeding experiments to be predicted.

Consider the following example. Suppose a breeding experiment was carried out in which plants from a pure-breeding white-flowered variety of pea ($p\,p$) were crossed with heterozygous pea plants of genotype $P\,p$. What are the expected genotypes and phenotypes of the offspring arising from this cross, and in what ratio would they occur? You can begin to answer this question by first determining the genotypes of the gametes produced by each of the parents. The pure-breeding white-flowered plants ($p\,p$) will produce gametes that all carry the $p$ allele, as shown in Figure 8.12. The heterozygous $P\,p$ plants will produce gametes, half of which carry the $P$ allele and half the $p$ allele (Figure 8.12).

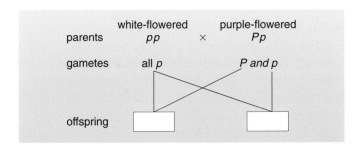

**Figure 8.12**   A cross between a pure-breeding white-flowered variety of pea and a heterozygous purple-flowered variety. Unlike Figures 8.8 and 8.9, drawings to show the phenotypes are not included; it is conventional to simplify mating diagrams in this way. To be completed in Question 8.6.

Question 8.6

Complete Figure 8.12 and hence determine the ratios of the genotypes and phenotypes of the offspring.

The expected outcome of the cross reveals a further important genetic ratio of $1 : 1$. This ratio confirms that during meiosis alleles $P$ and $p$ in a $P\,p$ plant segregate from each other into *equal* numbers of gametes containing $P$ and $p$ alleles, and that fertilisations between these gametes and those of the other parent occurs at random and therefore both possible combinations are equally likely.

You have seen that the phenotypes of members of each generation in a breeding experiment can be understood by using a model of inheritance. This model involves representing alleles by letters. The relative proportions of the possible combinations of letters then account for the ratio of the phenotypes. In fact, this is an example of *mathematical modelling*; the mechanism of inheritance is regarded as equivalent to a mathematical process whose consequence can be calculated by the well established laws of chance and probability.

To help you solve problems in genetics, some general hints for tackling problems have been provided in Box 8.1.

---

### Box 8.1   General hints for tackling problems in genetics

In Book 3 you were encouraged to develop strategies for solving different sorts of problems. Here you are offered some guidelines on how to set about solving genetics problems, and you will then tackle a couple of questions using these guidelines. You need to bear in mind that genetics problems cannot be solved by rote learning; each one has to be tackled afresh using your understanding of genetic principles, common sense, and sometimes trial and error. Here is a list of guidelines, which should help you to tackle a wide range of genetics problems; you may need to adjust the order in which you work through the steps according to the information given in the question.

1  Read the question and make sure that you understand all of the terms that are used (e.g. pure-breeding, heterozygous, etc.).

2  Draw out the crosses as mating diagrams, using one of the two alternative layouts shown in Figures 8.10 and 8.11 in this book, and include all the information that is given in the question. For example pure-breeding tells you that a variety is homozygous. This will help you to think about the problem logically, and show what information you need to deduce, e.g. the genotypes of one or more of the generations involved.

3  Assign letters to the alleles of the genes, or the copies of genes, that are involved, if they are not specified in the question. You may need to use information provided in the question to deduce which phenotype is dominant and which is recessive; for example, if a particular phenotype disappears in the progeny of one generation and reappears in the next generation, you can infer that this phenotype is recessive to the phenotype that is masking its presence.

4  Complete the mating diagram; for example, use the genotypes of each generation to deduce the genotypes of the gametes, and use the genotypes of the gametes to determine the genotypes of the offspring. (With some problems you may be working from genotypes of offspring back to the genotypes of the parents.)

5  Use information about the dominant allele or character to determine the phenotypes of each generation. (In some problems you will start by using phenotypes to determine genotypes.)

6  Calculate the ratios of the genotypes and of the phenotypes from the mating diagram.

7  Ask yourself whether the results are consistent with what you have learned about genetics and probability.

---

In Questions 8.7 and 8.8 you are asked to predict the results of some different sorts of crosses using the rules of dominant/recessive alleles, the segregation of the two copies of a gene and the combining of gametes at random at fertilisation.

## Question 8.7

A breeding experiment was carried out in which plants from a pure-breeding purple-flowered variety of pea were crossed with plants that were heterozygous for flower colour. Draw the mating diagram for this cross and then predict the genotypic and phenotypic ratios of the offspring.

## Question 8.8

The common fruit-fly *Drosophila melanogaster* (Figure 8.13) is widely used by geneticists for breeding experiments in the laboratory because it is easy and inexpensive to rear and each female produces hundreds of eggs. Suppose that you carry out a breeding experiment using two pure-breeding varieties of *D. melanogaster*, one with normal-shaped eyes and one with eyes reduced to about half the normal size, called 'eye-less'. The first cross is between these two varieties. The $F_1$ offspring all have normal eyes. The second cross is between an $F_1$ normal-eyed fruit-fly and a pure-breeding eye-less variety. What is the expected ratio of genotypes, and the expected ratio of phenotypes of the offspring of the second cross?

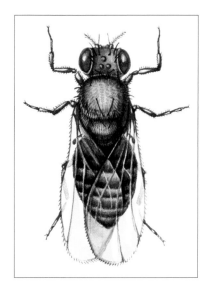

**Figure 8.13**   The common fruit-fly, *Drosophila melanogaster* (about 12 times actual size).

## 8.4   Why not an exact 3 : 1 ratio?

Returning to the pea-breeding experiments, you will now look more closely at some actual values obtained for the $F_2$ generation and how closely they fit the expected phenotypic ratio of 3 : 1. Mendel worked with seven different pairs of contrasting characters, which are listed in column two of Table 8.2. He carried out a separate set of breeding experiments for each pair of contrasting characters. In one experiment, for example, he cross-fertilised pure-breeding plants that grew from round seeds with pure-breeding plants with wrinkled seeds. All of the first generation offspring had round seeds. When he allowed these first generation offspring ($F_1$) to self-fertilise and produce the second generation of offspring ($F_2$), he found that the latter contained nearly three times as many plants with round seeds as those with wrinkled seeds. Table 8.2 gives the exact numbers of phenotypes of the $F_2$ of Mendel's experiments.

**Table 8.2**   The numbers of $F_2$ offspring possessing particular phenotypic characters in seven breeding experiments carried out by Mendel. The character in *italics* is the one that is found in all of the $F_1$ generation of offspring.

| Experiment number | Character | Numbers | Ratio |
|---|---|---|---|
| 1 | seed shape: *round* or wrinkled | 5474 : 1850 | 2.96 : 1 |
| 2 | seed colour: *yellow* or green | 6022 : 2001 | 3.01 : 1 |
| 3 | pod shape: *inflated* or constricted | 822 : 299 | 2.95 : 1 |
| 4 | pod colour: *green* or yellow | 428 : 152 | 2.82 : 1 |
| 5 | flower colour: *purple* or white | 705 : 224 | 3.15 : 1 |
| 6 | flower position: *along stem* or at tip | 651 : 207 | 3.14 : 1 |
| 7 | stem length: *long* or short | 787 : 277 | 2.84 : 1 |

Look at the characters in Table 8.2 and note that for the phenotype for seed colour (Experiment 2), yellow is dominant to green, but in the phenotype for pod colour (Experiment 4), green is dominant to yellow! So one cannot make assumptions about which phenotype is likely to be dominant and which might be recessive.

Now examine the ratios in Table 8.2. All the ratios that Mendel found in the $F_2$ generation were close to, but not exactly equal to 3 : 1. As with the experiment described above involving purple- and white-flowered plants, the character found in approximately three-quarters of the second-generation plants was the one that occurred in all of the first-generation plants (that is, it is dominant), and the character found in approximately one-quarter of the second-generation plants was the one that had vanished in the first generation of offspring (that is, it is recessive). It is clear then that the results of the experiments involving purple and white flowers discussed in Section 8.3 are not an isolated phenomenon.

Consider the variation around the 3 : 1 ratio in Table 8.2. Why is there a variation in this ratio and why is this ratio not exactly the expected ratio of 3 : 1? The short answer is 'chance'. The *predicted* or *expected* ratio does not tell you the *actual* ratio of purple- to white-flowered plants in a particular flower, but rather the most probable ratio. In order to understand this, consider chance and probability again.

The observed deviations in genetics experiments from predicted ratios like 3 : 1 are similar, in principle, to what you observe when you toss a coin. The *expected* ratio of heads to tails is 1 : 1 because each is equally likely. If you were to toss a coin a million times, the result would be a ratio very close to 1 : 1. If you tossed it only ten times, however, the result *might* be quite a marked deviation from a 1 : 1 ratio (e.g. six heads and four tails – a ratio of 3 : 2, or 1.5 : 1 – instead of five heads and five tails).

In an experiment with peas, suppose that exactly half of the ovules on a plant contained the allele $P$ and the other half contained $p$. Imagine also that of the millions of pollen grains that are artificially dabbed onto the flowers in a breeding experiment, exactly half contain $P$ and the other half contain $p$. It does not matter whether the pollen grain contains a $P$- or a $p$-bearing gamete; both types of male gamete have an equal chance of winning the race to fertilise the female gamete in each ovule. Purely by chance, the proportion of $P$-bearing gametes that succeed in this way may be rather higher than one-half for one plant. The plant would then develop rather more than the 3 : 1 ratio of purple- to white-flowered offspring. On another plant the opposite might occur, with a disproportionately higher number of $p$-bearing pollen grains fertilising the ovules. Similarly, the proportion of $p$-bearing ovules fertilised may be more (or less) than one-half. If a sufficiently large number of plants are investigated, giving a very large total of the number of offspring counted, then the ratio will be very close to 3 : 1, but for any one plant it may deviate quite markedly from 3 : 1.

### Question 8.9

Examine the data in Table 8.2 more closely. In the seed colour experiment (Experiment 2) Mendel counted more $F_2$ progeny than in any of his other experiments while in the pod colour experiment (Experiment 4) he counted the smallest number of $F_2$ progeny. Comment on the ratios in these two experiments.

## 8.5    Genetic variation between gametes of an individual

It was noted at the beginning of Section 8.2 that there is so much genetic variation between individuals that, for example, every human alive today is different from all others. But so far observations in this chapter have been limited to the inheritance of one pair of contrasting characters that involves the segregation of the two copies of one gene in peas.

However, a single chromosome carries many genes, hundreds on smaller chromosomes and thousands on larger chromosomes, each gene carrying its own information, and each with its specific location, its own locus, on the chromosome. In a pair of homologous chromosomes, there will be many pairs of genes strung along their length. These observations raise some intriguing questions. Are genes that are present on the same chromosome inherited together, that is, do they always travel together and remain on the same chromosome during meiosis? In addition, what happens when you consider a cross involving two, or more, different contrasting characters that are carried on different homologous pairs of chromosomes?

In order to answer these questions, the process of meiosis is examined in more detail. The behaviour of chromosomes at meiosis leads to a great deal of genetic variation between gametes and thus between individuals of a species such as the garden pea or humans, and this variation is examined in the next section.

### 8.5.1    More about meiosis

In order to understand how the behaviour of chromosomes at meiosis leads to the production of genetic variation between gametes, you need to examine the process in a little more detail. An understanding of the sequence of nuclear events and the physical structures involved in mitosis (see Figure 4.19) is a necessary background for this section, in which you will study the nuclear division of meiosis and the production of haploid gamete cells in more detail. Try to recall the essential features of mitosis by answering Question 8.10.

Question 8.10

Try to complete each of the following sentences.

(a) At the start of mitosis, the chromosomes become visible and each can be seen to be replicated along its length; that is, each consists of two _____.

(b) During mitosis, the two _____ of each chromosome separate, one to one end of the _____ and the other to the other end.

(c) The movement of the _____ is facilitated by delicate threads.

(d) At the end of mitosis, the number of chromosomes in each progeny cell is the _____ as in the original parent cell.

(e) At metaphase, the chromosomes line up across the _____ of the cell.

The process of meiosis is shown in more detail in Figure 8.14 for four chromosomes, i.e. two pairs of homologous chromosomes. One pair of chromosomes is short and the other pair is long (as shown in Figure 8.4). In the gamete-producing cell shown in Figure 8.14, row 1, one member of each pair of chromosomes is shown red (maternal origin, lighter shade) and the other is shown blue (paternal origin, darker shade) so you can readily follow the movement of each chromosome. Now follow row by row the important stages of the process of meiosis illustrated in Figure 8.14, which shows only those features that are important for understanding the transmission of genes and alleles (a full description of all the stages of meiosis will be given in Activity 4.3). The most striking feature of meiosis is that it consists of two divisions: meiosis I and meiosis II.

At the beginning of the first division, the chromosomes appear divided into chromatids, i.e. they each appear double along their length (Figure 8.14, row 1). (This was omitted from the figures in Sections 8.2 and 8.3 for simplicity, and the chromosomes were drawn as single strands.) Early in meiosis, the homologous chromosomes pair along their lengths in very close juxtaposition – so that each homologous pair consists of four chromatids, i.e. four strands (Figure 8.14, row 2). The *chromosomes* separate, one member of each homologous pair moving to one end of the cell and the other member of the pair moving to the other end of the cell (Figure 8.14, row 3). Hence the pairing of homologous chromosomes is the prelude to the members of the pair separating or segregating. Meiosis I reduces the number of chromosomes to a half of that of the original parent cell. The result of meiosis I is two cells each containing half the number of chromosomes (Figure 8.14, row 4), i.e. the haploid number, although each chromosome is still double along its length.

Meiosis II begins with two haploid cells (Figure 8.14, row 4). In the second division, in both haploid cells the *chromatids* separate, one chromatid of each chromosome moving to one end of the cell and the other chromatid moving to the other end (Figure 8.14, row 5). Both haploid cells now divide into two cells. Thus the result of meiosis is a total of four cells, because there are two cell divisions, $2 \times 2 = 4$ cells representing the four products of meiosis. Each of the four cells contains half the number of chromosomes and each chromosome appears as a single strand (Figure 8.14, row 6).

Note again that the set of chromosomes in the gametes is not a random collection; it is made up of one member of each homologous pair – one long chromosome and one short chromosome.

■  This collection is a result of two events at meiosis. What are the two events?

☐  The collection is a consequence of the pairing of homologous chromosomes, followed by the separation of each member of the pair to opposite ends of the cell at meiosis I, and the separation of one chromatid of each chromosome to opposite ends of the cell at meiosis II.

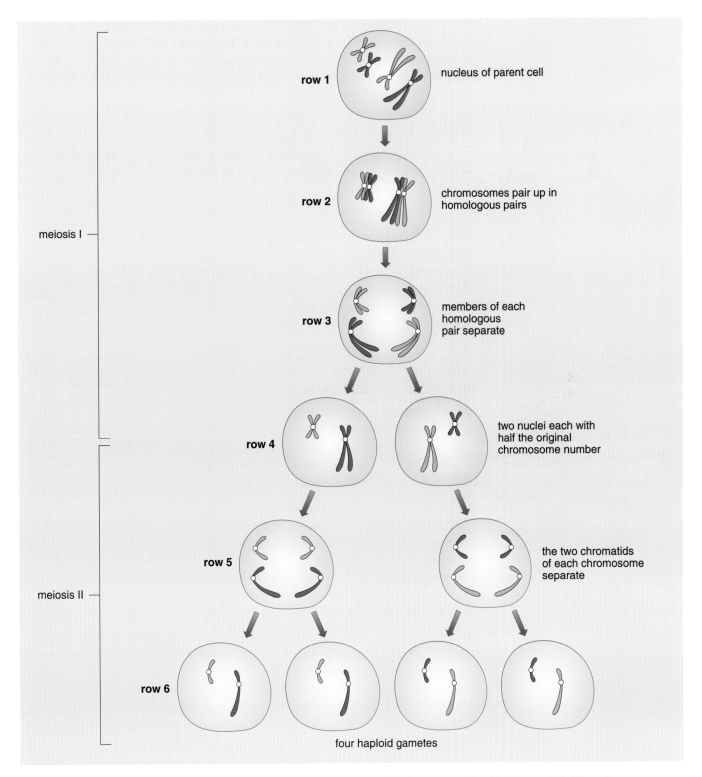

**Figure 8.14** A more detailed examination of the process of meiosis compared with Figure 8.4. Here the chromatids are shown. Note that meiosis consists of two separate divisions: meiosis I where members of each homologous pair of chromosomes separate, and meiosis II where the two chromatids of each chromosome separate. Only the cell membrane is shown, the nuclear membrane is omitted.

The sum total of meiosis is four haploid cells, each containing one member of each homologous pair of chromosomes. The garden pea has seven pairs of homologous chromosomes, so the diploid number is 14. Hence a gamete of the garden pea contains one chromosome 1, one chromosome 2, one chromosome 3, etc., giving a total of seven chromosomes.

Question 8.11

In order to ensure that you understand the major stages of the process of meiosis and how these differ from those of mitosis, complete Table 8.3 by ticking the appropriate box(es) in each row.

**Table 8.3** Similarities and differences between mitosis and meiosis. For use with Question 8.11.

| **Feature** | **Mitosis** | **Meiosis I** | **Meiosis II** |
|---|---|---|---|
| Members of a homologous chromosome separate | | | |
| The two chromatids of a chromosome separate | | | |
| The product of this division is two cells | | | |
| The product of this division is four cells | | | |
| The chromosomes are single-stranded at the end of this division | | | |

## 8.5.2    Recombination of chromosomes

This section examines the behaviour of chromosomes at meiosis, shown in Figure 8.14, in even more detail in order to understand how the large amount of genetic variation between gametes from one individual is generated. The **recombination** of chromosomes at meiosis, which generates new combinations of genetic material, is brought about in two ways: the *random assortment* of chromosomes and *crossing over*. What is important here is an understanding of these two processes and the products of meiosis.

When the paired homologous chromosomes separate at meiosis I, as in Figure 8.14, it is a matter of chance whether the red chromosome (maternal origin, lighter shade) is orientated on the 'left' and the blue chromosome (darker shade) on the 'right' as shown for the short chromosome in Figure 8.14. The arrangement could equally be the blue chromosome of a pair on the 'left' and the red on the 'right'. When the chromosome number is halved, one member of a pair will enter one cell and the other member the other cell. Hence it is a matter of chance as to which chromosome of a pair eventually enters a particular gamete, the blue one or the red one of each pair. Thus each gamete receives a *random assortment* or an **independent assortment** of the chromosomes, but always one of each pair.

In order to understand this, consider the two pairs of homologous chromosomes in the gamete-producing cell in Figure 8.14. Two combinations of these chromosomes are shown in the gametes: one short red and long blue, and one short blue and long red (Figure 8.14, row 6). Figure 8.15 shows the alternative arrangement. Here, when the homologues pair, the short red chromosome is on the 'right' and the short blue chromosome is on the 'left' as shown in Figure 8.15, rows 1 and 2.

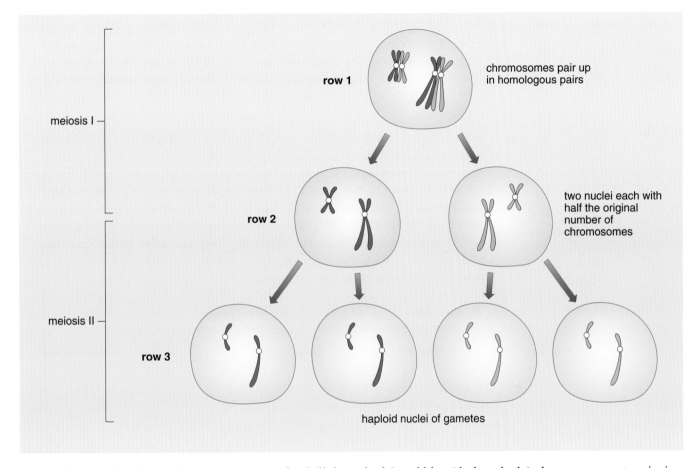

**Figure 8.15**   The alternative arrangements of red (lighter shade) and blue (darker shade) chromosomes at meiosis compared with that shown in Figure 8.14. Most stages of the process have been omitted for ease of reference. Compare the chromosome content of the gametes in row 3 of this figure with that of row 6 in Figure 8.14.

■   What is the possible combination of chromosomes in the resulting gametes of meiosis shown in Figure 8.15?

☐   A short red chromosome combined with a long red chromosome and a short blue chromosome combined with a long blue chromosome.

Note that this combination of chromosomes in the products of meiosis in Figure 8.15, row 3 is different from the outcome of meiosis shown in Figure 8.14, row 6. It is a matter of chance whether the red chromosome of a given pair enters a particular gamete or whether a blue one enters it. This is like tossing a coin, it is a matter of chance whether you get a head or a tail. In some meioses, the gametes will contain the combination of red and blue chromosomes shown in Figure 8.14 and in others, the combinations will be as shown in Figure 8.15. Thus the independent assortment of chromosomes in an organism with two pairs of chromosomes (as shown in Figures 8.14 and 8.15) results in four possible outcomes; the result is four different combinations of genetic material:

- one long red, one short blue (Figure 8.14)
- one long blue, one short red (Figure 8.14)
- one long red, one short red (Figure 8.15)
- one long blue, one short blue (Figure 8.15).

So far, the products of meiosis have only been considered from the point of view of the behaviour of chromosomes, but since genes and alleles are parts of chromosomes it follows that they too show independent assortment during gamete production. You will shortly explore this in the second part of Activity 4.3 (continued).

So far you have considered two pairs of homologous chromosomes. But most organisms contain more pairs than that. The number of maternal and paternal chromosome combinations produced by meiosis is equal to $2^n$, where 2 represents the chromosomes in each pair, and $n$ represents the number of chromosomes in a haploid set. Because the garden pea has 7 chromosomes in the haploid set, then $2^7$ or 128 different combinations of maternal and paternal chromosomes are possible, in haploid cells. The greater the haploid number of chromosomes in an organism, the higher the number of possible combinations of maternal and paternal chromosomes in haploid cells.

■ Humans have 23 chromosomes in a haploid set. How many different combinations of maternal and paternal chromosomes are possible?

☐ $2^{23}$ different combinations, i.e. 8 388 608.

Independent assortment of chromosomes during meiosis produces various combinations of red and blue chromosomes but it does not break up the set of genes arranged along the length of each individual chromosome. However, the process of **crossing over** does break up and rearrange the genetic material on individual chromosomes. When homologous chromosomes come into physical contact with each other along their lengths, as shown in Figure 8.14, row 2, the chromatids of different members of the homologous pair can exchange genetic material. Homologous chromatids break at identical points along their length, and rejoin with their homologous partner, as shown in Figure 8.16. In other words, the chromatids of a homologous pair physically exchange segments and the genes they contain.

**Figure 8.16**   The process of crossing over between chromatids of two chromosomes of a homologous pair, which breaks up and rearranges the combination of alleles (gene variants) on individual chromosomes.

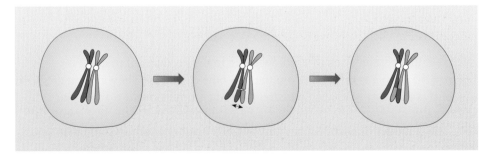

The genetic difference between red and blue members of a homologous pair lies not in the order of genes, which is identical between all individuals of a species, but in the variants, or alleles, of each gene. Thus through the process of crossing over, new combinations of variants are produced, here represented by the rearrangement of segments of the red and blue chromosomes (Figure 8.16).

Look back at Figures 8.14 and 8.15 and note that crossing over is not shown here. If it had been, then each of the products of meiosis would show more genetic variation. Without crossing over, the combination of gene variants on a particular chromosome would remain **linked**, i.e. joined together indefinitely (as shown in Figures 8.14 and 8.15). Crossing over produces new combinations of gene variants along a chromosome (as shown in Figure 8.16) that might be advantageous to a species.

The points at which breakage and rejoining occurs is essentially random, but always at the same distance from the ends of both partners of a homologous pair. In most organisms (with some exceptions) crossing over typically occurs between one and three times along the length of each pair of homologous chromosomes, depending on their lengths. Hence the chromosomes in each gamete are not an exact copy of either member of a homologous pair present in the parent cell.

When the genetic variability generated by crossing over is added to that generated by independent assortment, an infinite number of combinations of variation is possible. Recombination helps to explain the enormous range of variation between gametes and hence between individuals.

In summary, it can be seen that new combinations of genetic material produced by any one individual organism is the result of recombination: independent assortment of homologous chromosomes (Figures 8.14 and 8.15) and crossing over between chromatids of a homologous pair (Figure 8.16).

---

### Activity 4.3 (continued)   Mitosis, meiosis and recombination – Part 2

We expect this part of the activity will take you approximately 1 hour.

Begin by revisiting Part 1 of this activity (at the end of Section 4.4 DVD, screens 1–5) where you investigated the nuclear division of mitosis, which results in the production of two identical progeny cells. An understanding of the sequence of the nuclear events and the physical structures involved in mitosis will now help you to study Part 2 of this activity (DVD screens 6–16), in which you will study the nuclear division of meiosis and the production of haploid gametes. In this part of the activity you will revise the segregation of genes/alleles, which follows the behaviour of chromosomes at meiosis. This behaviour of chromosomes is also important for understanding the patterns of inheritance when more than one pair of contrasting characters are observed simultaneously.

There are no additional comments for this activity.

---

Your study of Activity 4.3 should have given you a better understanding of both the separation of two copies of a gene and the recombination of genes during meiosis. Test your understanding by answering the following questions.

Question 8.12

A heterozygous plant with the genotype *E e T t* produces four kinds of gametes. What are these? Explain how these would be produced when (a) the gene *T t* is on a separate pair of homologous chromosomes from that of the gene *E e* and (b) the two genes are linked, *E T* on one chromosome and *e t* on the other member of the homologous pair.

Question 8.13

In no more than 50 words, describe the two processes that lead to the recombination of alleles during meiosis.

## 8.6    Summary of Chapter 8

The number of chromosomes is characteristic of each species and can vary enormously between species.

Sexual reproduction always includes two distinctive processes: the production of gametes, which involves meiosis, and fertilisation. The two processes are accompanied by changes in the chromosome number, from diploid to haploid and from haploid to diploid, respectively.

Genetics is based on the concept of the gene as the unit of inheritance. A particular phenotypic character is determined by the two copies of a gene that an organism possesses and these two copies are identical in a pure-breeding variety.

When organisms with contrasting characters for which they are pure-breeding are crossed, the dominant character appears in the $F_1$ generation and the recessive character is masked. Crossing the $F_1$ offspring gives rise to the $F_2$ offspring with a phenotypic ratio of 3 : 1 (three with the dominant phenotype : one with the recessive phenotype) and a corresponding genotypic ratio of 1 : 2 : 1 (one homozygous dominant : two heterozygous : one homozygous recessive). A cross of a heterozygote with a homozygous recessive individual produces offspring with a 1 : 1 phenotypic and genotypic ratio (one heterozygous : one homozygous recessive).

The genotypic ratios of a cross result from the separation of the two copies of a gene to different gametes in equal numbers, and because gametes combine at random at fertilisation. The expected ratios in genetics do not tell us the actual ratios observed, but rather the most probable ratios.

The behaviour of chromosomes at meiosis explains the segregation of the two copies of a gene and the independent assortment of genes. The linkage of genes on a chromosome can be broken by means of crossing over.

Recombination – the production of new combinations of alleles – arises during meiosis from independent assortment of chromosomes and crossing over between homologous chromosomes.

In your study of this chapter you have further developed strategies for problem solving, this time in the context of genetic problems by the use of probability to predict the possible numerical outcomes of genetic crosses.

# Chapter 9
# Variations on a gene

The range of phenotypes and patterns of inheritance associated with some genes is more complex than for the examples considered so far. You have looked at examples of the inheritance of one or two pairs of contrasting characters where one allele of each gene is dominant to the other allele of the gene, and you have seen how the segregation and recombination of genes and alleles can be correlated with the behaviour of chromosomes at meiosis. These are the basic principles of genetics. However, these are only a base for understanding inheritance and, in this chapter, a number of extensions to these basic rules will be considered. Rather than creating a bewildering situation, these examples reveal a unifying set of principles. The examples include widely different situations – from sex-linkage to the inheritance of characters that show continuous variation, such as height in humans. In addition, you will look at the process of *mutation* – the ultimate source of new variation.

## 9.1 Sex and X-linked inheritance

All the genes that have been considered so far have been on autosomes. This section looks at the patterns of inheritance of genes on the sex chromosomes. Since the same rule of segregation applies to the sex chromosomes and the copies of genes present on them, this section will help you review your understanding of the behaviour of chromosomes at meiosis and the segregation of the two copies of a gene.

In humans, males and females can be distinguished by a particular pair of chromosomes, the sex chromosomes, which direct the development of the sex of the individual. The sex chromosomes (introduced in Section 4.4) are of two types, called X and Y, the Y chromosome being much smaller than the X. Females have two X chromosomes; these are clearly visible in the human female karyotype that you saw in Figure 8.3. Males have one X chromosome and one Y chromosome, as shown in Figure 9.1. Hence, females are said to be XX and males are said to be XY.

The sex chromosomes segregate from each other at meiosis in the same way as the pairs of autosomes, with the consequence that in females all the ova contain 22 autosomes and an X chromosome.

■ With respect to the sex chromosomes of a human male, what do the gametes (i.e. the sperm) contain?

□ Half the sperm contain an X chromosome and the other half contain a Y chromosome.

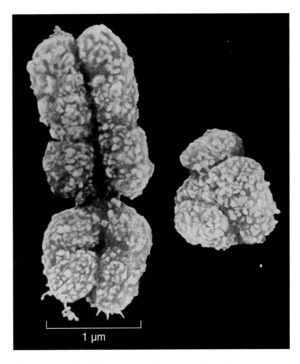

**Figure 9.1** Electron micrograph of a pair of human male sex chromosomes: the X chromosome (on the left) and the Y chromosome (on the right).

Question 9.1

To determine the distribution of sex chromosomes during gamete formation, and the expected ratio of male to female offspring, complete the mating diagram in Figure 9.2.

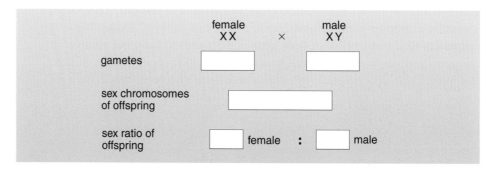

**Figure 9.2**    Mating diagram for use with Question 9.1.

The answer to this question (see Figure 9.8 in the answers at the end of this book) shows that it is the presence of the Y chromosome that determines maleness in humans.

■    From your completed Figure 9.2, what is the notable feature of the expected progeny?

☐    Equal numbers of males and females are expected.

Hence, the segregation of sex chromosomes into the gametes results in the maintenance of approximately equal numbers of male and female individuals.

The small Y chromosome carries very few genes, by far the majority of which are involved in directing the embryo to develop male characters. However, the larger X chromosome carries a number of other genes not involved in sex determination, called **X-linked genes**. Consequently females carry two copies of each X-linked gene, one on each X chromosome, but males carry only one copy of each X-linked gene on the single X chromosome, there being no counterpart on the Y chromosome. This difference between the sex chromosomes results in genes on the X chromosome having a pattern of inheritance that is different from genes on the autosomes, a pattern that is described as **X-linked inheritance**.

The XX/XY system of sex determination is not universal but is found in all mammals and also in some insects, including the common fruit-fly (*Drosophila melanogaster*).

## Activity 9.1    Applying genetic principles to X-linked genes

We expect this activity will take you approximately 30 minutes.

In this activity, you will follow the inheritance of an X-linked gene. T. H. Morgan, working in New York, USA, carried out investigations on *D. melanogaster* for which he was awarded a Nobel Prize in 1934. He noticed a white-eyed male fly in his stock of normal red-eyed flies. He mated this white-eyed male with a red-eyed female and all the $F_1$ offspring had red eyes. From this it can be concluded that red eye is dominant to white eye, so the normal allele can be represented as $R$ (red-eyed) and the recessive allele as $r$ (white-eyed). These observations in themselves are not unusual. When red-eyed $F_1$ males were mated with red-eyed $F_1$ females, the $F_2$ generation contained about 3000 red-eyed flies and about 1000 white-eyed flies. This result again may not appear to be striking since the ratio is 3 : 1, and this is consistent with breeding experiments in which the original parents were both pure-breeding for eye colour. However, Morgan made a crucial discovery: all the $F_2$ white-eyed flies were males!

(a)  To understand these results, complete the diagram in Figure 9.3, which is a summary of Morgan's observations. To help you with this, use the guidelines for tackling problems in genetics given in Box 8.1. The mating diagram has already been drawn for you and letters have been assigned to alleles. Note that each of the gene copies for eye colour is shown on the appropriate sex chromosome, denoted by the letter X or Y; you will find it helpful to use this notation when completing the diagram.

(b)  What are the possible phenotypes, for both sex and eye colour, of the $F_2$ flies, and what are their expected ratios?

(c)  Explain, in one sentence, why the incidence of phenotypes for recessive X-linked characters is much higher in males than in females.

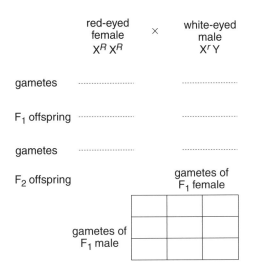

**Figure 9.3**  The breeding experiment that led to the identification of a linkage between eye colour and the sex of the fruit-fly, *Drosophila melanogaster*.

Now check your answers with those given in the comments at the end of this book.

The comments on Activity 9.1 show that the genetic results are consistent with the segregation of the X and Y chromosomes at meiosis and with the absence of X-linked genes on the Y chromosome. It also shows why males are more likely to manifest a recessive X-linked character than are females.

Note how the inheritance of X-linked genes follows the same basic principles of Mendel's law of segregation. The modification of the pattern of inheritance is a consequence of the absence of X-linked genes on the Y chromosome.

Question 9.2

With respect to humans, why does a son not inherit an X-linked character from his father?

## 9.2   Multiple alleles

When considering alleles of a gene, all the examples discussed so far have involved two different alleles, one of which is dominant to the other, such as purple and white flower colour in pea. However, early in the history of genetics, it became clear that many genes have more than two alleles; these are called **multiple alleles**.

One such example is the ABO blood group system in humans, of which there are four different phenotypes, A, B, AB and O. If you have to be given a blood transfusion, first a sample of your blood has to be taken to match your blood to that of potential donors. If this is not done, the results can be disastrous because some of the blood groups are incompatible with each other, resulting in the clumping together of red blood cells.

The genetic basis of the ABO system is well known and is based on three alleles at a single locus, denoted by the symbols $A$, $B$ and $O$. Note that, for historical reasons, the nomenclature of these alleles is different from the standard convention. Any individual carries only two copies of the gene, which might be the same or different alleles.

■   Why can an individual not carry all three alleles of the gene?

☐   Each gene has a fixed locus, one on each member of a homologous *pair* of chromosomes. For three alleles to be carried by one individual, three homologous chromosomes, instead of two, would have to be present in each cell.

Human ABO blood groups can be assigned to one of four phenotypes, which are determined by pair-wise combinations of three alleles A, B and O. The relationship between the phenotypes and the six possible genotypes is shown in Table 9.1.

**Table 9.1**  The genetic basis of ABO blood groups in humans.

| Genotype | Phenotype (blood group) | Genotype | Phenotype (blood group) |
|---|---|---|---|
| $A\,A$ | A | $B\,B$ | B |
| $A\,O$ | A | $B\,O$ | B |
| $A\,B$ | AB | $O\,O$ | O |

■ Referring to Table 9.1, what is the dominance relationship between allele $O$ and each of alleles $A$ and $B$?

☐ Since the genotypes $A\,A$ and $A\,O$ produce the same phenotype (A), allele $O$ must be recessive to allele $A$; similarly, the genotypes $B\,B$ and $B\,O$ have the same phenotype (B), so allele $O$ must be recessive to allele $B$.

It is interesting to note that the genotype $A\,B$ manifests the phenotype of both the $A$ and the $B$ alleles, i.e. the corresponding phenotype is AB. This phenomenon is called **codominance**. In a sense, codominance is no dominance at all, since the presence of one allele does not mask the presence of the other allele but rather the effects of both alleles are manifested! The ABO system also shows that alleles of a gene can show different dominance relationships with one another, for the A and B phenotypes are both dominant to the O phenotype but not to each other.

This example reveals an important feature of inheritance: the phenotype of a particular character is a result of the relationship between the two alleles of a gene and this relationship varies between different combinations of alleles. Recall that, although the term 'dominant alleles' is commonly used (see Section 8.3.1), it is the phenotype that is dominant, not the alleles.

Note the extensions of genetic analysis discussed in Sections 9.1 and 9.2 do not involve new laws of inheritance; the basic rules of inheritance described in Chapter 8 still apply.

### Question 9.3

Using the guidelines for solving problems in genetics given in Box 8.1, determine the possible phenotypes and genotypes of the children produced by two individuals, one of blood group AB and the other of blood group O. By drawing a mating diagram, compare the phenotypes of the children with those of the parents.

## 9.3  Effect of environment on phenotype

You have seen that an organism's genotype contributes to the development of its phenotype. However, the environment also plays a crucial role in the development of the phenotype and is another source of variation between individuals. The environment is never the same for any two individuals. Two plants growing side by side in a field do not receive precisely the same amount of light, water and minerals; no two animals, even in the same litter, receive exactly the same type and/or amount of food at the same stage of growth.

Breeders of agricultural plants and animals are always on the lookout for genotypic variants that, when raised under farm conditions, give greater yields of, for example, flour, oil from seeds, meat and milk. However, yields are influenced also by environmental factors, such as the quality of the soil, and the amount of moisture, heat and light.

One striking example of the effect of the environment on the phenotype is seen in the coat colour of Siamese cats. In these cats (Figure 9.4), the pattern of brown extremities – feet, face, ears and tail – and cream-coloured body are transmitted to their descendants. The kittens are all cream-coloured at birth and, some days later, pigment appears in their new fur, first along the margins of their ears and gradually over their extremities. If the kittens grow and develop in a warm environment, the amount of brown fur is smaller than if they develop at cold temperatures. Although it appears that the brown and cream pattern is itself inherited, in fact what is really inherited is the capacity of the fur to form brown pigment or not to form it, depending on the particular temperature at the time of growth. So a single genotype may produce different phenotypes, depending on the environment in which the organism develops.

**Figure 9.4** Siamese cats showing the variation in the distribution of brown colour on the body. The cat in (a) grew and developed in a colder environment than the cat in (b) and hence has more brown fur.

(a)                                                                                    (b)

This example illustrates that no character is inherited ready-made; the phenotype arises during the growth and development of the individual in a particular environment. This leads on to the important point that what is biologically inherited is not a character in itself (for example, you do not actually inherit your father's nose) but the *information* to produce that character.

## 9.4   Characters that show continuous variation

All the characters that were considered in Chapter 8 and Sections 9.1 and 9.2 have one of a number of contrasting phenotypes which can be classified into discrete classes. Such *qualitative* characters that vary in this way show **discontinuous variation**. However, not all differences between individuals are of this kind. Characters such as weight in humans and economically important traits in domestic animals and cultivated plants, such as amount of milk produced and yield of fruit, do not fall into distinct classes. Such characters that can be measured in some way to give a number with a unit attached to it are described as *quantitative* characters. They show **continuous variation** in the population. This section examines the differences in inheritance between characters showing discontinuous variation and those showing continuous variation.

A good example of a character that shows continuous variation is height in humans, as shown in Figure 9.5. This figure shows data on height for 1164 adult British men in 1946. The symmetrical distribution with the appearance of a bell-shaped curve shows that the majority of individuals have a height that is close to the mean value for the population, with numbers of individuals decreasing on either side of this mean value. Very few individuals – very tall and very short – are found at the two extremes. Such a pattern is described as a **normal distribution**.

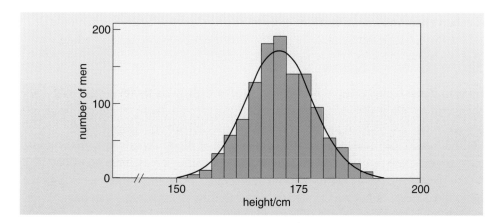

**Figure 9.5**   A normal distribution curve for a quantitative character: height for 1164 adult British men in 1946. The original measurements are presented as a histogram with 2.5 cm height intervals and interpreted as a smooth curve. (The mean height of adult British men nowadays is considerably greater than it was in the 1940s.)

The fact that the phenotype varies continuously does not mean that the variation is the result of some genetic mechanism different from that of the genes discussed so far. The development of the phenotype of continuously varying characters is due to the joint action of several genes, each of which has, individually, a very small effect on the phenotype. So height, for example, is the cumulative effect of a number of genes located at different loci. However, genes are not the only determinants of continuously varying characters; as with those that vary discontinuously, a major role is also played by environmental factors.

■  Suggest some environmental factors that might affect a person's height.

☐  Diet, and bouts of infections and disease during childhood. (The latter is particularly important in developing countries.)

The critical difference between characters that vary continuously and those that vary discontinuously is not the number of segregating genes but the range of the phenotypic differences between genotypes. In the case of characters that show discontinuous variation, there is a small number of clearly defined phenotypes, as in the case of flower colour in pea plants. In contrast, for characters that show continuous variation (such as height) there is a potentially infinite number of slightly different phenotypes.

## 9.5   Mutation

Genetic analysis, as you have seen, must start with parental differences, such as purple versus white flowers. Without variation, no genetic analysis is possible. Where do these variants come from? The answer is that the genetic material has an inherent tendency to undergo change in a spontaneous process called *mutation*. Geneticists recognise two different levels at which mutation takes place. In **gene mutation**, an allele of a gene changes and gives rise to a different allele. A different kind of mutation involves parts of or whole chromosomes and is called **chromosome mutation**.

### 9.5.1   Gene mutation

Gene mutations may bring about a change of one allele to another, such as a change in an allele for white flowers in pea plants to an allele for purple flowers, or vice versa. All present variation in organisms that are considered to be 'normal' variation, such as blue and brown eyes or blood groups in humans, must have arisen some time ago by mutation. Some mutations may have no effect on the phenotype, some are useful and some, such as haemophilia – a recessive X-linked disease in humans in which blood clotting is impaired – can have harmful consequences, whilst others are lethal.

Most importantly, only mutations in the cells that give rise to the gametes can be perpetuated from one generation to the next. Some gene changes transmitted in gametes are new, and arose very recently as new gametes were formed. In fact, it is highly probable that each of us has received at least one new mutation from one of our parents. Other gene changes transmitted in gametes, however, are descended from mutations that happened many generations ago, and these mutations have been copied and passed on from parent to offspring. One famous example is a mutation for haemophilia in the generations of interrelated royal families in Europe. The original haemophilia allele arose as a mutation in the reproductive cells of either Queen Victoria or one of her parents. One of Queen Victoria's sons, Leopold, Duke of Albany, suffered from the disease, as did many of her grandsons and great grandsons. For example, the son of the last czar of Russia, Alexis, inherited the allele from his mother, Alexandra, granddaughter of Queen Victoria.

### 9.5.2   Chromosome mutations

Meiosis is a well-ordered sequence of events that involves a large number of interdependent processes, including the separation of homologous chromosomes and the separation of chromatids into different gametes. However, occasionally things go wrong.

Sometimes errors occur during the separation and distribution of chromosomes during nuclear division. The commonest example of such an error in humans leads to Down's syndrome (Figure 9.6a). A typical karyotype of a person with Down's syndrome is shown in Figure 9.6b.

(a)

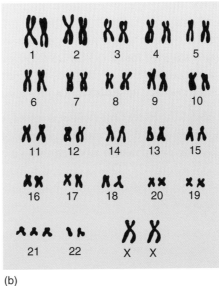

(b)

**Figure 9.6** (a) A girl with Down's syndrome blowing a bubble. (b) The karyotype of a female with Down's syndrome.

■ Compare the karyotype of a person with Down's syndrome (Figure 9.6b) with a typical human karyotype (Figure 8.3). How do these karyotypes differ?

☐ The Down's syndrome karyotype has 47 chromosomes instead of 46; there are three copies of chromosome 21, instead of the usual two copies.

The presence of an extra chromosome has a profound effect on the phenotype; Down's syndrome individuals usually have a particularly loving nature, short stature, poor muscle tone, a small round head, as well as showing varying degrees of learning disability. Why the presence of an extra chromosome 21 has these effects on the phenotype is an area of current intensive research.

The presence of an additional chromosome in an individual's cells is an example of a chromosome mutation. The reason for its occurrence is that occasionally a pair of chromosomes fails to separate during meiosis (in division I). Instead, both chromosomes move to the same end of the cell and this results in a gamete with *two* copies of the same chromosome. When this gamete combines with a normal gamete at fertilisation, the result is a zygote with *three* copies of this chromosome.

Intriguingly, the presence of an extra chromosome in a gamete is more frequent in women than in men and occurs more frequently in older than in younger women. Why should this be so? The main clue comes from the difference in the duration of meiosis in men and women. In men, meiosis begins at puberty and is maintained throughout life. The process takes about three hours, and the production of fully motile mature sperm is complete within three weeks. In contrast, meiosis begins in a developing female embryo whilst still inside her mother's womb, but the process is arrested at an early stage (the beginning of meiosis I) before the baby is born and is completed at some time between puberty and the menopause. During a woman's reproductive life, one cell completes the meiotic division and gives rise to one ovum during each menstrual cycle.

A cell that completes meiosis shortly after puberty has thus been arrested at an early stage of meiosis I for about 10–15 years. By contrast, a cell that completes meiosis late in a woman's reproductive life will have been arrested at an early stage of meiosis I for up to 50 years or more. As the duration of meiosis increases, the risk of chromosome mutations, such as the failure of homologous chromosomes to separate, also increases.

Hence, the longer meiosis is arrested, the greater the chance that chromosomal abnormalities will occur. Thus the older a woman is, the greater the likelihood that she will produce an ovum with a chromosome mutation such as an extra chromosome 21. This is clearly demonstrated by comparing the proportion of Down's syndrome babies born to mothers of different ages, as shown in Figure 9.7.

**Figure 9.7**  Graph showing the increase in frequency of Down's syndrome with maternal age.

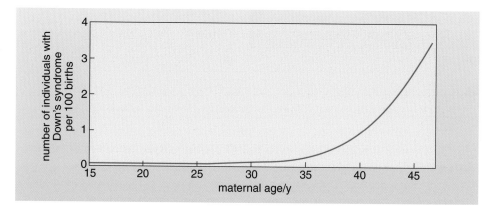

■ Looking at the graph in Figure 9.7, what is the frequency (as number per 100 births) of individuals born with Down's syndrome for mothers aged 20 years and those aged 45 years?

☐ The frequency of individuals born with Down's syndrome is very low (less than 0.1 per 100 births) in mothers aged 20 years but rises steeply to about three per 100 births in those aged 45 years.

Chromosome mutations in general play a prominent role in determining disability in humans. However, the number of individuals with chromosome mutations that are known about is a small fraction of the total number of zygotes produced that carry a chromosome mutation. The vast majority of human embryos with a major chromosome abnormality spontaneously abort. It is estimated that chromosome mutations account for about half of spontaneous abortions.

In conclusion, all the sources of variation considered in Chapters 8 and 9 contribute to the overall range of phenotypes in individuals of a species and help to explain why each individual is phenotypically unique.

In Chapters 8 and 9, the gene has been considered as a unit of inheritance with a specific location on a specific chromosome. Through genetic analysis, you have studied the inheritance of particular genes and chromosomes. But the physical nature of genes and chromosomes has not yet been considered, and it is the structure of genes and chromosomes that is the subject of Chapter 10.

Question 9.4

Match each of the situations found in pea plants and described in (a)–(d) with one of the explanations (i)–(v) in the list below.

**Situation**

(a) When two pea plants, each with round-shaped peas, were crossed, most of the progeny had round-shaped peas but about one-quarter of the progeny were found to have wrinkled peas.

(b) Stem length size in pea plants is very variable between varieties. Crosses between varieties revealed no predictable ratio of long to short plants, although there were relatively few of the extremely long and extremely short plants in the $F_2$ offspring and a relatively large number of intermediate stem length.

(c) Two pea plants, when crossed, produce white-flowered plants. However, one of the plants produced by crossing these two plants had purple flowers – the phenotype that is dominant to white.

(d) In pea plants, if a mutated recessive allele of any one of 15 particular genes is present, the leaves of the seedlings are virtually white instead of the normal green colour and are unable to photosynthesise and so die.

**Explanations**

(i) A new mutation occurred during gamete formation in the parents.

(ii) The affected offspring are homozygous for the recessive allele of the gene.

(iii) This character is a quantitative one, determined by the combined action of a number of genes.

(iv) This character is not genetically determined.

(v) This character shows discontinuous variation and is affected by the combined action of a number of genes.

# 9.6   Summary of Chapter 9

Genes present on the X chromosome (X-linked genes) with no counterpart on the Y chromosome have a modified pattern of inheritance compared with genes on the autosomes.

The phenotype of a particular character is a result of the relationship between the two copies of a gene that are present in an individual, and this relationship varies between different alleles (e.g. dominance, codominance). A gene can have more than two alleles but there are only two in any individual.

The phenotype is determined by the interaction of the genotype and the environment.

Characters that show continuous variation are influenced by several genes as well as by environmental factors.

Mutation is a source of heritable variation. Gene mutation involves the change of one allele of a gene to a different allele. Errors sometimes occur in the separation of homologous chromosomes at meiosis and this can result in chromosome mutations.

Activity 9.1 gave you the opportunity to apply your problem-solving skills in a new situation, that of X-linked genes.

# Chapter 10
# What are genes made of?

So far, genes have been considered as units of inheritance, and this chapter goes on to explore the chemical nature of genes. Genes are composed of DNA, and a knowledge of the structure of DNA is essential to understand how it can function as hereditary material. This biopolymer illustrates beautifully the precise relationship between chemical structure and biological function discussed in Chapter 5. DNA has three key properties: it is relatively stable and hence an appropriate store for vital information; its structure suggests an obvious way in which the molecule can be duplicated, or replicated; and it can convey information which is used continuously within a cell. This chapter examines the chemical nature of DNA, which accounts for both its stability and the way it can be replicated – the first two of these three key properties. The third property, how DNA functions as the genetic material, is the subject of Chapter 11.

## 10.1   The chemical structure of DNA

It was in 1953 that James Watson and Francis Crick deduced the three-dimensional structure of DNA. It was the year that might be described as the dawn of molecular biology, for their publication was to have far-reaching consequences in terms of our understanding of how cells function at the molecular level. So monumental was this work that they were awarded, together with Maurice Wilkins, the Nobel Prize for Medicine and Physiology in 1962. In this section, the structure of this biopolymer is examined in some detail. You were introduced to the essential features of the three classes of biopolymer – proteins, polysaccharides and nucleic acids – in Chapter 5. You should review your understanding of these by completing Question 10.1 and checking the answer before moving on.

Question 10.1

This question will help you to review the main features that proteins, polysaccharides and nucleic acids have in common.

Which of the following statements about biopolymers are correct and which are incorrect?

(a) Molecules of all three biopolymers, proteins, polysaccharides and nucleic acids are large.

(b) Each biopolymer is composed of repeat monomers: amino acids for proteins; monosaccharides, or sugars, for polysaccharides; and nucleotides for nucleic acids.

(c) Each monomer is linked to adjacent monomers by weak interactions.

(d) The higher-order structure is maintained by covalent bonds formed by condensation reactions, with loss of water.

(e) The structure of each biopolymer is closely related to the function it performs.

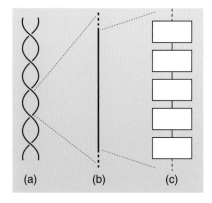

**Figure 10.1** A simplified sketch showing the structure of DNA. (a) The double helix – two intertwined strands. (b) A small section of one of the strands that has been straightened out and greatly magnified. (c) This same section, magnified further, showing how a strand is made up of monomers, each of which is represented as a rectangular box.

Watson and Crick showed that DNA has a *double helix* structure; it is this that accounts for the stability of DNA, one of the key features of the hereditary material. Its simplest representation is shown in Figure 10.1a and in this context 'double' means the *two* intertwined strands of this simplified sketch. You will first look at the composition of each separate strand as it is taken apart to reveal the monomers of this biopolymer. You will then look at how the two strands interact to form the characteristic double-helical molecule of DNA.

Figure 10.1b shows a small straightened-out section from one of the strands of the DNA molecule. Each strand is a polymer comprising a string of monomers, shown diagrammatically as rectangles in Figure 10.1c. Each monomer is a **nucleotide** and is more complicated in structure than the monomers of proteins and polysaccharides. Each nucleotide consists of three component parts: a phosphate group, a sugar molecule and a nitrogen-containing organic molecule called a *base*. (Here the term base is used as a general name for the nitrogen-containing organic group present in nucleic acids.) Figure 10.2a shows these separate parts and the relationship between them in a simplified structure of a nucleotide. The sugar is a 5-carbon molecule called *deoxyribose* (Figure 10.2b), and so these nucleotides are known as *deoxyribonucleotides*. From here on, this cumbersome term will be simplified to merely nucleotide. Note, though, that because of the presence of deoxyribose, the polymer of nucleotides described here is known as deoxyribonucleic acid, which is usually abbreviated to DNA.

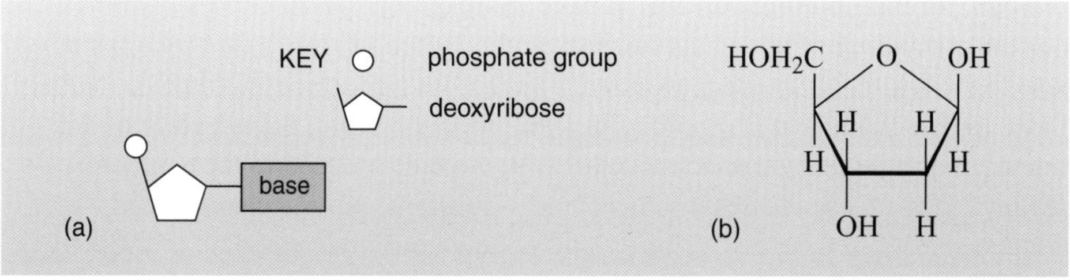

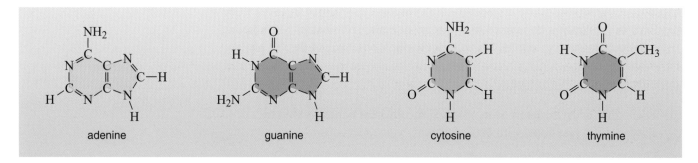

**Figure 10.2** (a) Simplified structure of a generalised nucleotide of DNA. (b) The full structure of the sugar deoxyribose. (As with the sugar structures given in Chapter 5, ring carbon atoms are not shown.)

In the nucleotide shown in Figure 10.2a the base is undefined. However, there are four different **bases** in DNA: adenine, guanine, cytosine and thymine. Their structures are shown in Figure 10.3. (You are not expected to memorise these structures, although you should remember the names of the bases.)

**Figure 10.3** The structures of the four DNA bases.

■ Look at the structure of each of the four bases shown in Figure 10.3. How might you distinguish, in simple terms, the structures of adenine and guanine from those of cytosine and thymine?

☐ Both adenine and guanine have *two* nitrogen-containing rings, whereas cytosine and thymine each have only *one* such ring. Consequently adenine and guanine are larger than cytosine and thymine.

The single strand of DNA separated from its pair (a portion of which is shown in Figure 10.1b and c) is a polymer of the nucleotides shown in Figure 10.2a. In each strand, the phosphate of one nucleotide forms a bond with the sugar of another nucleotide, and so on down the strand, as shown on the left (in white) in Figure 10.4. As with other biopolymers, the bonds joining the chain of monomers – in this case, nucleotides – are covalent bonds. The strand of alternating phosphate groups and sugars is known as the *sugar–phosphate backbone*, and the bases protrude out from this towards the other strand of the helix. A length of such a polymer with a number of nucleotides joined together, as shown in Figure 10.4, is described as a *polynucleotide*. The size differences between the bases are illustrated diagrammatically in this figure by the different-sized rectangles that denote the bases; the larger rectangles represent either an adenine or a guanine base and the smaller rectangles represent either a cytosine or a thymine base. When illustrating a polynucleotide, the name of each base can be simplified to a single capital letter, so that A = adenine, G = guanine, C = cytosine and T = thymine, as shown in Figure 10.4.

■ How many nucleotides are shown in the polynucleotide segment in Figure 10.4?

☐ The simplest way of answering this question is to count the number of rectangles that represent the bases; there are eight.

There is a simplified way of describing the structure of DNA in text, and that is to write out the sequence of bases in a single polynucleotide strand, representing each base by its initial letter A, G, C or T. This chemical shorthand will be used extensively from now on.

■ What is the base sequence in the portion of a DNA molecule shown in Figure 10.4, starting from the top?

☐ CTGACATA.

These sequences are usually written or printed in lines like the letters or characters on this page. This is a convention, like reading from left to right and from top to bottom of this page. There may be many hundreds of thousands of bases within a single DNA molecule, in a long linear sequence. Such a sequence might appear as follows (reading from left to right in successive lines):

…AACGCGCGTATATAAATCGCTAGCTTCAACGACTGCTGACGTAGTTCCCT

GCAAACACAAGTCACGAAGCAGTTTGCAGCAGCTGCAACATCTAGCAGCT…

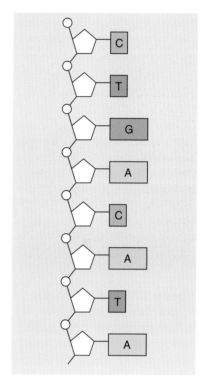

**Figure 10.4** A short segment of a polynucleotide, in which the bases adenine, guanine, cytosine and thymine are denoted simply as A, G, C and T, respectively. The sugar–phosphate backbone is shown in white. (This figure represents one strand of the DNA double helix.)

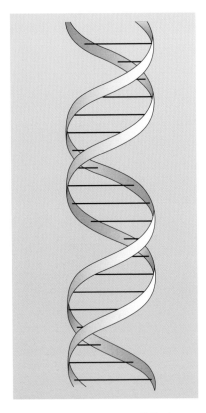

**Figure 10.5** A simplified model showing the double-helical structure of DNA. The bars represent base pairs, and the ribbons represent the sugar–phosphate backbones of the two polynucleotide chains that make up the DNA molecule.

DNA molecules are by far the largest known molecules in living organisms; some have relative molecular masses of many billions. If you consider the comparatively short sequence of 100 bases shown above, and think about how a simple coding language of just four letters could be rearranged in such a sequence, you will gain some appreciation of the huge variety of sequences that are possible. Take, for example, a short chain (i.e. a polynucleotide) of just eight nucleotides. Since there are four *different* bases, there are four options for each position, and therefore $4 \times 4 \times 4 \times 4 \times 4 \times 4 \times 4 \times 4 = 4^8 = 65\,536$ possible different sequences for a polynucleotide of this length. The much longer sequence shown above has 100 bases in it, so the number of different possibilities here is $4^{100}$ or $1.6 \times 10^{60}$. A DNA molecule consisting of thousands of bases therefore represents a vast store of potential information, the full consequences of which should become more apparent as you study subsequent sections.

So far only a single strand of DNA has been considered, but Figure 10.1a shows that DNA has a *double*-helical structure. The DNA double helix in fact consists of two polynucleotide chains spiralled around each other, as shown in Figure 10.5, which is an enlarged and more detailed version of Figure 10.1a. Here each of the two ribbons represents the sugar–phosphate backbone of Figure 10.4, whilst the horizontal bars represent the bases of the two strands and the bonds between them.

The key to understanding the structure of DNA and how it functions in the cell lies in the interaction between the bases at the core of the molecule. Along the length of a polynucleotide chain within the double helix, each base makes specific pairing and bonding with a corresponding base in the other polynucleotide chain. These interactions are known as **base-pairing**, for which there are very precise rules, as illustrated in Figure 10.6.

The base-pairing rules in DNA are as follows:

- T (thymine) pairs only with A (adenine)
- C (cytosine) pairs only with G (guanine).

Thus there are two pairs of **complementary bases**: T and A; C and G.

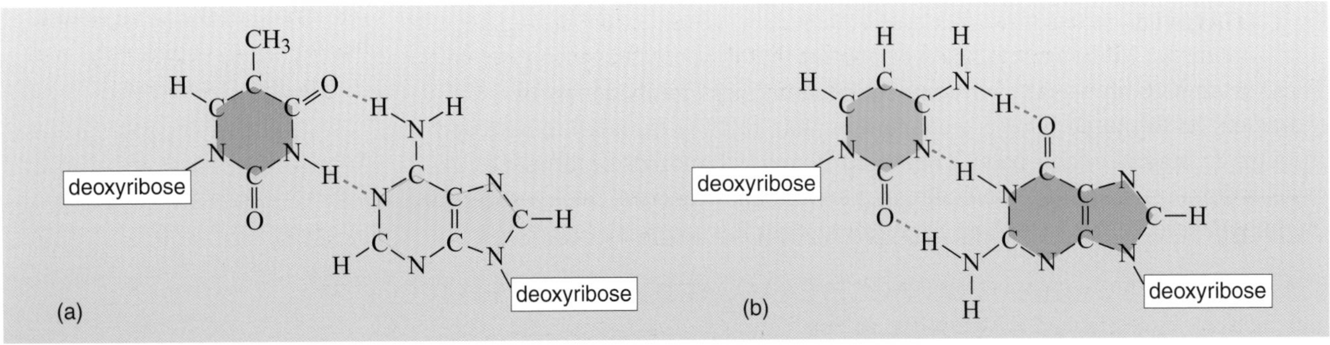

**Figure 10.6** Base-pairing between DNA bases: (a) thymine (T) pairs with adenine (A); (b) cytosine (C) pairs with guanine (G). The red dashed lines represent the hydrogen bonds between these two pairs of bases. The covalent linkage of each of the bases to deoxyribose in the sugar–phosphate backbone is also shown.

These pairs of complementary bases sit flat within the spiral of the DNA double helix, rather like the steps of a spiral staircase. The other important point to note about base-pairing is that T is bonded to A and C is bonded to G via weak interactions, shown as the red dashed lines in Figure 10.6. These weak interactions are hydrogen bonds, and you saw examples of situations where they are important for the higher-order structure of biopolymers in Sections 5.1 and 5.5. Figure 10.6 clearly illustrates the difference between the A–T base pair and the C–G base pair in terms of the number of hydrogen bonds: the A–T pair has only two hydrogen bonds, whereas the C–G pair has three.

The base composition of DNA is related to the base-pairing rules just outlined.

■ If you were to extract some DNA from cells, isolate and purify the four bases, how much adenine would you expect to find relative to thymine? Similarly, how much cytosine would you find relative to guanine?

☐ A consequence of the base-pairing rules is that the amount of adenine in a DNA molecule is always equal to the amount of thymine; the same applies to the amount of cytosine relative to that of guanine.

The alignment of base pairs within a DNA molecule is shown in Figure 10.7. Here the helix is shown unwound, with the two sugar–phosphate backbones now parallel but still on the outside; the complementary base pairs with their hydrogen bonds form the core of the molecule. Notice here the significance in the different sizes of the bases, even though Figure 10.7 shows them only in a diagrammatic form: a complementary A–T pair is a similar size to a complementary C–G pair, whereas in contrast a G–A pair would be too large to fit into the available space, and a C–T pair would be too small. Since the sequence of bases on one strand is complementary to the sequence of bases on the other strand, the two strands of the double helix are described as *complementary*.

The structure of DNA can be summarised as follows. The hydrogen-bonded complementary base pairs sit at the core of the molecule and are arranged flat – like the steps of a spiral staircase. The two sugar–phosphate backbones lie to the outside of the helix, each spiralled around the other.

Watson and Crick, in their famous 1953 paper published in the journal *Nature*, wrote:

> We wish to suggest a structure for … deoxyribose nucleic acid (DNA). This structure has novel features which are of considerable biological interest … It has not escaped our notice that the specific pairing we have postulated immediately suggests a possible copying mechanism for the genetic material.
>
> (Watson and Crick, 1953)

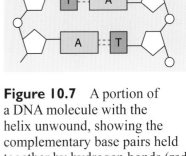

**Figure 10.7** A portion of a DNA molecule with the helix unwound, showing the complementary base pairs held together by hydrogen bonds (red dashed lines) between the two polynucleotide chains.

## Activity 10.1   Where does scientific information come from?

We expect this activity will take you approximately 1 hour.

This activity is composed of two parts. In Part 1, you will investigate the way in which new scientific information flows from the scientists working at the cutting edge of their field to the wider science community and eventually to the general public and OU course materials. In Part 2, you will consider the issue of information quality and critically evaluate two different websites with reference to specific criteria.

Most of the information that you will use during your studies will have started as laboratory results from research carried out in a university or in industry, or by a learned society. It is important to understand how information from this original research is made available more widely through the scientific community and beyond. Knowledge of this process will help you appreciate the different types of scientific information that are available, when to use them, and where to look for them. As the information moves from original research to formal publication (the so-called 'research supply chain'), it appears in many formats, for example as a report, a journal article or a book.

As an example of this, you will follow the discovery of the double helix structure of DNA by Watson and Crick and see where information about their discovery was published over time and how this developed. You will then concentrate on two resources in detail and consider the quality of information they contain.

Now go to Activity 10.1 on the course website.

There are no comments on this activity.

---

The following section considers how new DNA molecules are synthesised, and shows how true Watson and Crick's prediction was.

### Question 10.2

In a fragment of double-stranded DNA, there is a total of 100 bases, of which 30 are cytosine (C). Calculate the total number of each of the following items in the DNA fragment: (a) complementary base pairs; (b) nucleotides; (c) deoxyribose groups; (d) guanine (G) bases; (e) thymine (T) bases; (f) adenine (A) bases; (g) hydrogen bonds.

## 10.2   DNA replication

You know from Chapters 4 and 8 that eukaryotic cells divide by means of mitosis to produce two progeny cells that contain identical genetic material, which is also identical to that of the original parent cell. This is how unicellular organisms form large populations of individual cells, and how a zygote grows into an adult multicellular organism. Prokaryotic cells also undergo cell division, whereby one cell divides completely to become two. Recall from Section 4.1 that these cells do not contain nuclei, so the process of cell division is somewhat simpler. Whatever the cell type, for one cell to become two new ones the DNA within it must undergo a process in which an identical copy is made, otherwise the two new cells would not be genetically identical to the original parent cell.

This section begins at the molecular level by examining how DNA is replicated and then turns to the level of the chromosome to explore the relationship between DNA molecules and chromosome structure.

### 10.2.1   How DNA is replicated

As noted above, Watson and Crick postulated that DNA base-pairing provides a mechanism by which the DNA might be copied. This DNA copying mechanism, usually referred to as **DNA replication**, is the process considered here.

■ Recall the significant feature of the bonding between the two bases of a base pair, and compare this with the bonding in the sugar–phosphate backbone.

☐ The hydrogen bonds between a C–G pair and between an A–T pair are *weak* interactions, implying that these could be readily broken. The stronger covalent bonds of the sugar–phosphate backbone are very much more difficult to break.

Indeed, the breaking of the hydrogen bonds between base pairs and the separation of the two polynucleotide strands of DNA is an early event in the process of DNA replication. Once the strands have been separated, new DNA strands are synthesised; the enzyme that catalyses this process is called *DNA polymerase.*

Figure 10.8 shows the principal stages of DNA replication. The two strands of the double helix shown in Figure 10.8a unwind, starting at one end, to expose the bases on each strand. The two complementary single strands are shown separated in Figure 10.8b. Each of these strands now acts as a *template* (i.e. a mould) for DNA replication. The base-pairing rules are the basis of this process; that is, the nucleotides are added in a complementary manner – C always opposite G and A always opposite T – with the hydrogen bonds being formed in the process. At the same time, the two new sugar–phosphate backbones are synthesised by the formation of covalent bonds between alternating phosphate and deoxyribose molecules. The result is the production of two identical double-stranded DNA molecules (Figure 10.8c). Initially the DNA is unwound, as shown

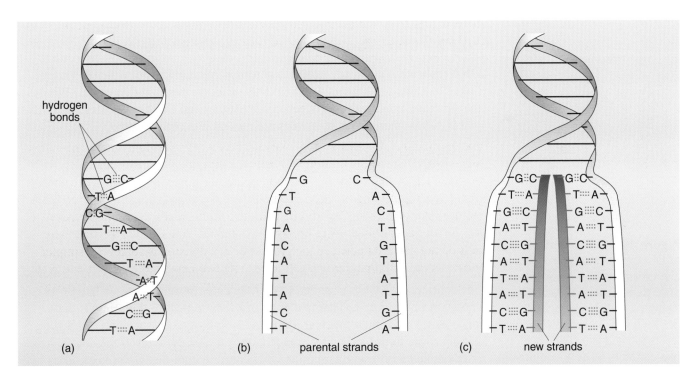

**Figure 10.8** The process of DNA replication. (a) A portion of a DNA double helix showing 10 labelled complementary base pairs. (b) Part of the double helix has unwound and come apart at one end, revealing two single-stranded polynucleotide chains. (c) Part of each polynucleotide chain has been replicated, but the two paired chains have not yet wound into double helices. The new DNA strands are shown in purple and the hydrogen bonds are shown as red dashed lines. The process continues until all of the parent DNA molecule has been replicated.

in Figure 10.8c; later the paired strands wind around each other to form the characteristic double-helical structure.

This process has been termed **semiconservative replication**, meaning 'half-conserved' replication. This is because in each new daughter DNA molecule, *one* of the two original polynucleotide strands is unchanged from the original parent molecule; these are labelled as the parental strands in Figure 10.8b. The second polynucleotide strand has been newly synthesised in its entirety; these are labelled as the new strands in Figure 10.8c. To put it crudely, each daughter double helix is only 'half new'; each has one parental strand and one new strand.

Figure 10.8 shows just a small portion of DNA being replicated. The process continues until the whole of the DNA molecule has been replicated, and the two daughter DNA molecules form the characteristic double-helical structures, as opposed to the unwound products of replication shown in Figure 10.8c. Before the cell can divide to produce identical progeny cells, *all* the DNA molecules in the cell have to replicate to produce two identical copies.

This, in outline, is how DNA is copied during cycles of cell division. If you compare Figures 10.8a and c, you will see that both DNA molecules in 10.8c are a faithful copy of the sequences of bases of the parent molecule in 10.8a, although in 10.8c they have not yet formed helices.

> An important feature of DNA structure is that the genetic information it contains is copied into more DNA with the same genetic information.

### 10.2.2   Chromosome structure and DNA replication

DNA replication is closely linked to chromosome replication, which in turn is linked to mitosis (Chapters 4 and 8). This raises an intriguing question, 'What is the structural relationship between chromosomes and DNA molecules?' In other words, 'How many DNA molecules are present in a chromosome?'

Chromosomes are composed of DNA intimately associated with protein. The DNA of the chromosomes is replicated during interphase, and when the chromosomes first become visible at prophase of mitosis they are double structures; that is, they are each composed of two chromatids. (The chromosomes in Figures 8.2 and 8.3 are clearly visible as paired chromatids.) During mitosis, the two chromatids of each pair separate to opposite poles (ends) of the cell so that at the end of mitosis each chromosome is a single unit. Evidence suggests that such a single (unreplicated) chromosome contains one continuous double-stranded DNA molecule running along its length, as shown in Figure 10.9a. That makes a very long molecule. This shows that since genes are linked together along the length of a chromosome, each gene is a short section of a double-stranded DNA molecule. Each DNA double helix is associated with protein, and the DNA–protein complex coils, loops and supercoils to form a chromosome.

Before the next round of cell division begins, each chromosome duplicates longitudinally to form two paired chromatids, as shown in Figure 10.9b. At the molecular level, the original DNA double helix has formed two identical daughter

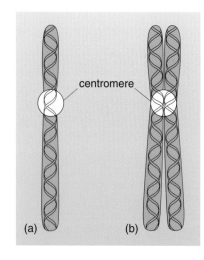

**Figure 10.9**   The number of DNA molecules in a chromosome: (a) a chromosome prior to replication contains a single DNA double helix molecule; (b) a chromosome that has replicated and consists of two chromatids, each comprising a single double-helical DNA molecule. In reality, each DNA double helix would be associated with protein, forming a DNA–protein complex.

centromere

(a)          (b)

DNA double helices and the total mass of DNA in the cell has doubled. Each chromatid contains one DNA double helix along its length (Figure 10.9b). Since the double helix in each chromatid has a base sequence identical to that in its partner chromatid (Figure 10.8c), the gene copies carried by pairs of chromatids are also identical.

The faithful replication of DNA is remarkable, considering that the copying of millions of bases is involved. However, as you will see in the following section, such accurate replication does not always occur.

### Question 10.3

Figure 10.10 shows part of a double-stranded DNA molecule during the process of replication. Each square represents a base.

(a) Identify the missing bases and write the correct letter (A, G, C or T) in each of the blank squares.

(b) At what stage of the cell cycle would DNA be undergoing replication?

## 10.3   Errors in replication and damage to DNA

The structure of DNA accounts for its stability over generations of replication. Nevertheless, errors can arise during the process of DNA replication, leading to mutations. Gene mutation as a fundamental source of heritable variation was considered in Section 9.5. This section examines these mutations at the level of DNA and shows that a gene mutation is an error in DNA sequence.

The machinery of DNA replication is generally remarkably efficient and accurate, so that a parent DNA molecule is faithfully reproduced as two new, identical helices. However, this process is not always perfect and mistakes sometimes occur, with the result that 'wrong' bases are inserted into the growing polynucleotide chain. For example, the replication machinery may add a T into the growing polynucleotide chain where a C should have been, or it may add a G instead of an A. Alternatively, slightly larger errors might be made, such as when a short sequence of the parental template strand is skipped over, or a few extra bases are inserted. Such errors in replication bring about changes in the DNA sequence. The 'wrong' sequence would be copied as faithfully in future cell divisions as would the 'correct' sequence, so the mutation would be perpetuated.

Not all these mistakes go undetected by the cell, however. There are 'surveillance' processes in cells that detect most of these replication errors. For example, there are DNA repair pathways containing enzymes that can identify a wrongly placed base in the growing polynucleotide chain, remove it, and replace it with the correct base. These DNA repair mechanisms can be viewed as being analogous to quality control systems in an industrial production line, such that 'faulty' products are removed before they leave the 'factory'. Hence the mutation is usually short-lived, since the incorrect base(s) are removed and replaced by the correct one(s).

In addition to errors brought about by mistakes made by the DNA replication machinery, environmental agents can produce mutations. Many of these

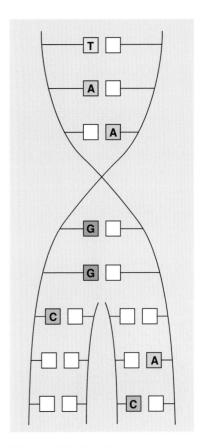

**Figure 10.10**   Part of a double-stranded DNA molecule during replication.

environmental agents are chemicals, some of which are used experimentally in the laboratory to produce mutants that are useful in identifying and finding genes. Others are physical agents, such as various forms of radiation, including ultraviolet radiation from the Sun.

As with mistakes made by the replication machinery, many mutations brought about by chemical or physical means can be detected by DNA repair mechanisms. For example, in the much studied bacterium *Escherichia coli*, one such repair mechanism has been termed the SOS system. As its name implies, it responds to a 'distress signal' produced as a result of damage to DNA caused by ultraviolet radiation.

However, if errors pass undetected by the repair mechanisms – an event that must happen relatively rarely, considering the total number of DNA bases replicated – they result in mutations. You will return to a consideration of mutation after you have considered how DNA functions as the genetic material, which is the major topic of the following chapter.

## 10.4   Summary of Chapter 10

DNA (deoxyribonucleic acid) is composed of two polynucleotide chains linked together by hydrogen bonds and wound around each other to form a double helix.

Four bases, adenine (A), guanine (G), cytosine (C) and thymine (T) make up the core of the DNA double helix. These form complementary base pairs, so that an A of one polynucleotide chain always pairs with a T of the other chain, whilst C and G always pair with each other. The outer part of the double helix consists of the two sugar–phosphate backbones.

The information carried by DNA is in a simple coding language of just the four bases: A, G, C and T. Using just these four letters, a DNA molecule represents a vast store of information.

The process of DNA replication is semiconservative. During replication, the DNA double helix unwinds, and each of the two parental polynucleotide strands forms a template on which a new strand is synthesised. DNA polymerase adds DNA nucleotides according to the base-pairing rules. Two identical double helices are thereby produced, each consisting of a parental strand and a newly synthesised strand.

An unduplicated chromosome consists of a long double-helical DNA molecule and proteins. The two chromatids of a duplicated chromosome each have a DNA double helix in which the base sequences and hence the gene copies are identical.

Although the structure of DNA is relatively stable, errors sometimes occur in DNA replication and, if they are not identified and rectified by the cell, are perpetuated as mutations. Changes to DNA sequence are also brought about by environmental factors, such as certain chemicals and radiation.

During Activity 10.1 you had an opportunity to examine how scientific information is disseminated to the scientific community and in time to the wider public. This activity also allowed you to critically evaluate different sources of scientific information available on the web.

# Chapter 11
# Using genetic information

One important property of DNA is that it carries genetic information. The simple coding language of just four letters (bases), which can be arranged in a huge variety of sequences, represents a vast potential store of information. This chapter examines how this information is accessed and used by the cell. You have seen in Chapter 10 that DNA's double-helical structure both gives rise to its stability and permits its faithful replication to produce two identical daughter double helices. The key structural features of complementary base pairs joined by hydrogen bonds that play an important role both in stability and replication are also the basis for how DNA functions as genetic material.

How does the simple coding language of DNA relate to the nature of the gene; that is, how do genes function and how do they control phenotype? For example, how can one allele of a gene result in white flower colour in the garden pea and another allele lead to purple flower colour, as you saw in Section 8.3? The focus of this chapter is, therefore, on the gene as a unit of function.

The phenotype of an organism largely depends on its chemical composition and on the biochemical reactions that go on inside it. So, for example, the different colour forms of pea flowers will have slightly different biochemical processes, causing different colours to be produced. All the biochemical reactions of a cell are catalysed by enzymes, which are proteins (Section 5.5). The enzymes present in a cell, and structural proteins too, are determined by that cell's genotype. Genes specify polypeptides. *How* genes do this is the topic of this chapter and the essence is that the structure of the DNA can be related to the structure of proteins. As you saw in Chapter 5, proteins come in a huge range of sizes and shapes, and this diversity arises from different combinations of just 20 amino acids. You will examine how the simple coding language of DNA of just four letters contains information for thousands of different proteins, each with its own unique sequence of amino acids.

The synthesis of proteins is a far more complex process than the more straightforward process of DNA replication, partly because many other molecules are involved. This chapter begins by viewing the overall scheme in barest outline and then goes on to examine each step in turn. The computer-based video sequence (Activity 11.2) at the end of the chapter provides an animation of the flow of information from DNA to polypeptide. This will enable you to consolidate your understanding of the processes involved and help to bring them 'alive'.

## 11.1    One gene – one polypeptide

The concept that genes contain hereditary information leads inevitably to the question, 'Information for what?' Most genes contain the information for the production of a specific polypeptide or protein. Recall that these terms are used interchangeably. However, in the context of protein synthesis, it is actually the polypeptide chain that is being made; it becomes a fully functional protein molecule later.

You have seen that a gene is part of a long DNA molecule, which comprises a linear sequence of base pairs (Section 10.1). So, a gene is divisible into a specific sequence of DNA base pairs.

■  What can you recall about the monomers in a polypeptide?

☐  A polypeptide has a linear sequence of amino acids. (Recall that by convention this is written with the N-terminal amino acid on the left and the C-terminal one on the right, Section 5.5.2.)

There is a direct and specific relationship between the linear sequence of base pairs in a DNA molecule that goes to make up a gene and the linear sequence of amino acids in a polypeptide molecule. This relationship is presented in a very simplistic manner in Figure 11.1, which shows (in particular in Figure 11.1b) that the *base sequence* of the DNA in a gene can be related precisely to the *amino acid sequence* of the polypeptide. This collinearity of sequence between a gene and a polypeptide is known as the **one gene–one polypeptide hypothesis**.

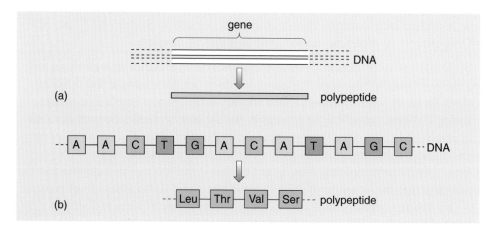

**Figure 11.1**  (a) The linear relationship between a gene and the polypeptide for which it codes. (b) More detail of this relationship: the linear sequence of base pairs corresponds directly to the linear sequence of amino acids in the polypeptide. (Leu, Thr, Val and Ser are the abbreviations for four consecutive amino acids in this polypeptide: leucine, threonine, valine and serine.)

> The one gene–one polypeptide hypothesis states that a given gene has a very precise linear sequence that codes for the linear sequence of amino acids in one polypeptide molecule.

This linear relationship has been a remarkably useful working hypothesis which holds true for many polypeptides in many organisms, but with some modification in the case of others, as you will see in Chapter 12. However, for the moment it is convenient to view the base sequence of a DNA molecule as having a direct relationship to the amino acid sequence, or primary structure, of a polypeptide. How the DNA base sequence gives rise to the polypeptide molecule is the subject of the rest of Chapter 11.

## 11.2   The flow of information from DNA to RNA to polypeptide

The genetic information encoded within a gene is carried via an intermediary class of molecules, **ribonucleic acid (RNA)**. Information within a cell can therefore be seen as passing from DNA, via RNA, to a polypeptide. This flow of information is often called the *central dogma* (a dogma is a widely held belief) of molecular biology and can be expressed in another way:

DNA makes RNA makes polypeptide.

The central dogma implies that there are two separate steps in this information flow: from DNA to RNA and from RNA to polypeptide; these are called, respectively, *transcription* and *translation*. **Transcription** of DNA produces RNA (Section 11.3) and the subsequent **translation** of this RNA produces polypeptides (Section 11.4). These steps are summarised in Figure 11.2.

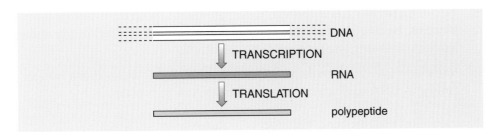

**Figure 11.2**   Information flow from DNA to RNA to polypeptide.

## 11.3   From DNA to RNA: transcription

In the process of transcription, the information in a gene, i.e. the DNA base sequence, is transcribed, or copied, to form an RNA molecule. RNA is therefore an intermediate in the flow of information from DNA to polypeptide. Before considering the details of transcription, first look at the structure of RNA.

### 11.3.1   The structure of RNA

The name ribonucleic acid suggests that chemically it is related to DNA, deoxyribonucleic acid. Like DNA, RNA is a polymer of nucleotides, a polynucleotide, and each nucleotide consists of three parts covalently joined together: a sugar, a phosphate group and a base (Figure 11.3a). However, there are some important differences between DNA and RNA.

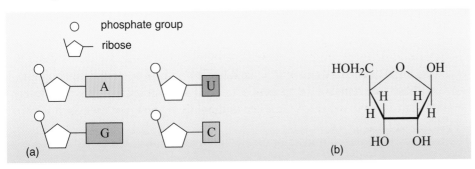

**Figure 11.3**   (a) The simplified structures of the four nucleotides of RNA. (b) The structure of the sugar ribose. (As for sugar structures given in earlier chapters, ring carbon atoms are not shown.)

207

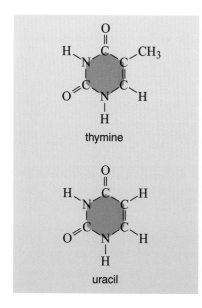

**Figure 11.4**   The structures of the bases thymine (T) and uracil (U). Note that T occurs only in DNA, whereas U occurs only in RNA. You do not need to memorise these structures.

One way in which RNA and DNA differ is in the sugar component; RNA has ribose, not deoxyribose as in DNA (compare Figures 11.3b and 10.2b). A second difference is in the constituent nucleotide bases. RNA has four bases: adenine (A), guanine (G), cytosine (C) and uracil (U), whereas the DNA bases are adenine, guanine, cytosine and thymine (T). Figure 11.4 compares the structures of thymine and uracil. Why one of the four bases in RNA is different from the equivalent base in DNA is not understood.

There is another important structural difference between DNA and RNA. Recall that DNA is a double helix of two spiralled polynucleotide chains, i.e. it is double-stranded. In contrast, RNA is usually a single-stranded polynucleotide chain.

## 11.3.2   DNA makes RNA

Having considered the structure of RNA and contrasted it with DNA, you will now move on to examine how RNA molecules are synthesised – the process of transcription.

■   Before transcription is described, you might like to speculate in outline how it occurs, bearing in mind what you now know of DNA replication and of the similarities in structure between DNA and RNA.

☐   You might have come to the conclusion that RNA is synthesised in a manner similar to DNA replication, i.e. using the DNA as a template.

This is indeed what happens. The process of transcription is illustrated diagrammatically in Figure 11.5. As in DNA replication, the starting point is a double-helical molecule of DNA (Figure 11.5a). The hydrogen bonds between the complementary base pairs are broken, the DNA unwinds and the two polynucleotide strands separate (Figure 11.5b). Here the process of transcription diverges from the familiar one of DNA replication because synthesis of RNA molecules occurs on only *one* of the two strands: only one DNA strand is the template for RNA synthesis, and this is termed the **template strand**. The other DNA strand, which is not used as a template in RNA synthesis, is termed the **non-template strand** (Figure 11.5b). Apart from this important difference, the basic mechanism of RNA synthesis is the same as that for DNA, in that pairing of complementary bases is the key to the process.

■   Which bases are paired together in DNA?

☐   C pairs with G, and A pairs with T.

■   Considering these base-pairing rules in DNA, together with the information in Figures 11.3–11.5, what base-pairing rules would you expect to apply to transcription?

☐   The T of DNA is replaced with U in RNA, so A–U is a 'new' base pair. The C–G base pair remains the same. T–A is still a possible base pair, but clearly the T has to be in the DNA template and not in the newly synthesised RNA.

The base-pairing rules in transcription are summarised in Table 11.1.

**Table 11.1**   Base-pairing rules in transcription.

| DNA base | RNA base |
|----------|----------|
| A | U |
| G | C |
| C | G |
| T | A |

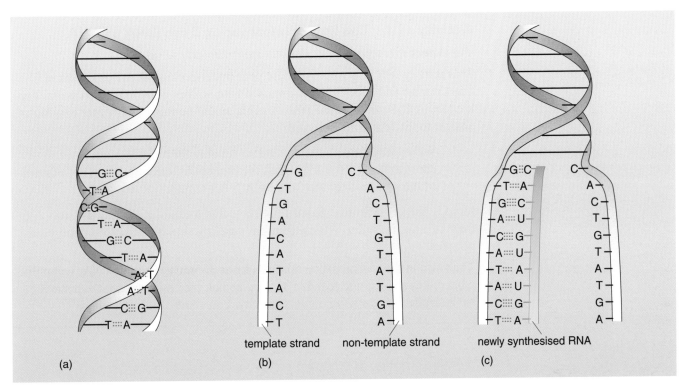

(a)                (b)                (c)

template strand    non-template strand        newly synthesised RNA

**Figure 11.5**   The synthesis of RNA on a DNA template. (a) The DNA double helix with 10 labelled base pairs. (b) The hydrogen bonds between the base pairs have been broken and the two strands have separated; note that only one of the strands is used as the template for RNA synthesis. (c) A short length of RNA (labelled, and shown in orange) has been synthesised. In reality, the RNA molecule would be much longer than the chain of 10 nucleotides shown here.

Thus, the template strand of DNA forms the template on which an RNA molecule is synthesised, according to the base-pairing rules shown in Table 11.1. The enzyme *RNA polymerase* binds to the DNA template strand and moves along it, extending the growing RNA chain by the successive addition of nucleotides containing bases complementary to those in the template strand. The formation of the covalent links between phosphate groups and the ribose sugar molecules produces the sugar–phosphate backbone of the RNA, as shown in Figure 11.5c.

Another important difference between DNA replication and transcription is that, in transcription, only relatively short regions of the DNA molecule, corresponding to genes, are transcribed into RNA molecules. This raises the intriguing questions of where on the DNA molecule does RNA synthesis begin, and where does it end? RNA polymerase binds to the template strand of DNA at a particular sequence of bases at one end of the gene, called a transcriptional start site. Transcription comes to an end at a termination sequence, a specific sequence of bases in the DNA at the other end of the gene. At this point, the RNA polymerase leaves the DNA, as does the newly synthesised RNA molecule. The DNA double helix reforms and transcription has been completed.

Question 11.1

In what ways do the structures of DNA and RNA differ?

## Activity 11.1   The flow of information from DNA to RNA

We expect this activity will take you approximately 15 minutes.

This activity will help to consolidate your understanding of the processes of transcription and is designed to improve your written communication skills. You are required to *carry out the planning* that would be required in order to write an answer to the following question:

> Write an account, which would be suitable for revision purposes, that summarises in 100–150 words the process of transcription. A description of the structure of DNA and RNA is not required.

Identify the key scientific points relating to this molecular process and put them in a logical order. Which diagrams would you plan to use to support your account?

Then turn to the comments on this activity at the end of this book. These include a list of key points, one possible answer, and an indication of what you should have achieved in carrying out this activity. You should look at these now.

## 11.4   From RNA to polypeptide: translation

The second process in the production of polypeptides is translation. Here the base sequence of an RNA molecule is converted into the amino acid sequence of a polypeptide chain. This is a more complex process than transcription. As you have seen, the base sequence of a gene is transcribed into an RNA base sequence, the language of which consists of a mere four characters. Translation is the conversion from the four-character language of RNA into the corresponding 20-character language of a polypeptide. In any language, not all characters are used in every word, and in the same way not all 20 amino acids are used in every polypeptide.

### 11.4.1   Different forms of RNA

The term RNA covers a collection of somewhat different molecules, which can be classed together under three main headings: *messenger RNA* (*mRNA*), *transfer RNA* (*tRNA*) and *ribosomal RNA* (*rRNA*). All three types of RNA are produced on a DNA template, and in a similar way. Their respective roles are outlined here, but details will follow in Sections 11.4.2–11.4.4.

**Messenger RNA (mRNA)** has preserved within it the sequence of DNA bases, although now in an RNA code, which determines the precise amino acid sequence of a particular polypeptide. The code in mRNA consists of consecutive three-base sequences, or triplets (e.g. AUG, CCU). Each triplet is termed a **codon**, and there are many different ones. Each codon contains the information for a particular amino acid, and this relationship between codon and amino acid forms the basis of the *genetic code*. For example, the mRNA codon AUG codes for the amino acid methionine (abbreviated to Met), and CCU codes for the amino acid proline (Pro). Examination of the sequence of codons within a molecule of mRNA enables the sequence of amino acids in the polypeptide for which it codes to be determined, since there is a collinear relationship between the two sequences. The details of the genetic code will be examined in detail in Section 11.5. In the context of translation, all you need to appreciate for now is that an mRNA molecule consists of a very specific sequence of consecutive codons.

The other significant feature of the genetic code is that, because the sequence of bases in an mRNA molecule is determined by the base sequence of the DNA, the genetic code in the RNA is a copy of the code present in the DNA on which the mRNA was synthesised during transcription.

The consequence of the genetic code being carried in an mRNA molecule is that a given polypeptide has a particular mRNA molecule coding for it. Since there are thousands of different proteins, there are thousands of different mRNA molecules, each transcribed from a different section of DNA, that is, from a different gene.

There are two other types of RNA, neither of which code for polypeptides, but which have important roles to play in the process of polypeptide synthesis.

**Transfer RNA (tRNA)** molecules carry individual amino acids, which join together to form polypeptides.

**Ribosomal RNA (rRNA)** molecules, together with proteins, make up the ribosomes (Section 4.1). These large macromolecular aggregates are the sites of polypeptide synthesis.

Both these types of RNA are produced on DNA in the same way as mRNA, and for both types, RNA is their final product.

Ribosomes, mRNA, tRNAs with their associated amino acids, and several different enzymes, together form the protein-synthesising machinery, the functioning of which will now be described.

## 11.4.2   Recognition of the codon by tRNA

Transfer RNA (tRNA) is the molecule that brings an individual amino acid to the mRNA where it will be incorporated into a growing polypeptide molecule. The generalised structure of a tRNA molecule is shown in Figure 11.6a, and a stylised version is shown in Figure 11.6b.

■ Look at Figure 11.6a. Follow the ribbon, which represents the sugar–phosphate backbone. Is tRNA a single-stranded or a double-stranded molecule?

☐ There is just one ribbon of a sugar–phosphate backbone, so tRNA is single-stranded.

Note, however, that parts of the molecule are folded up around itself, allowing some base-pairing. Figure 11.6a shows more than 20 such base pairs.

Figure 11.6a shows two other significant features of tRNA, which demonstrate the relationship between the structure and function of the molecule. First, there is a 'loose' arm, which is available to bind an amino acid. Second, there is a region

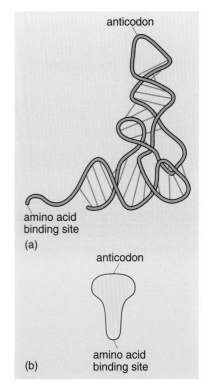

**Figure 11.6**   (a) The generalised structure of a tRNA molecule showing its three-dimensional shape and functional regions. The straight lines represent the paired bases. (b) A stylised version of (a), which is used in subsequent figures.

at the other end of the molecule where there are *three* free, or unpaired, RNA bases; these constitute the **anticodon**.

■ Assuming that each tRNA can bind specifically to only one kind of amino acid, what can you predict about the number of different tRNA molecules present in a cell?

☐ There must be at least 20 different tRNA molecules, one for each amino acid.

This is indeed what is found; for each amino acid there is a different tRNA molecule. Enzymes are involved in joining each amino acid to its specific tRNA to produce a specific tRNA–amino acid complex (i.e. a tRNA and an amino acid covalently linked together).

### 11.4.3   mRNA and its codons

A crucially important molecule involved in translation is mRNA. This has a linear sequence of RNA bases which is translated into the amino acid sequence of a polypeptide, a process that depends on the interaction between mRNA and tRNA, as shown in Figure 11.7.

The three bases that make up the tRNA anticodon pair with the three bases of the corresponding mRNA codon. The amino acids are inserted at the correct position because the tRNA molecule recognises the mRNA codon; the tRNA molecules are the link between the mRNA codon and amino acid recognition. Thus tRNA allows the mRNA code to be interpreted as (i.e. translated into) a sequence of amino acids.

■ What base-pairing rules must apply to the interaction between the codon and the anticodon?

☐ Here RNA is base-pairing with another RNA molecule, so the base-pairing rules would be C–G (and vice versa) and A–U (and vice versa).

■ Some RNA base pairs are shown in Figure 11.7. What is the nature of the interactions within these base pairs?

☐ The base pairs are held together by hydrogen bonds (shown in the figure as red dashed lines).

■ What is the significance of the interaction between the mRNA codon and tRNA anticodon being via weak interactions?

☐ These bonds can be readily formed and are easily broken.

There is another important feature to be emphasised about the relationship between the binding of tRNA to mRNA, as illustrated in Figure 11.7. The relationship between the mRNA codon and the amino acid that is bound to the specific tRNA is *precise* because complementary base-pairing occurs between the codon of the mRNA and the anticodon of the tRNA.

Thus, the interaction between mRNA and tRNA forms the basis of translation, as shown in Figure 11.8. The first tRNA to bind at the mRNA does so at a very

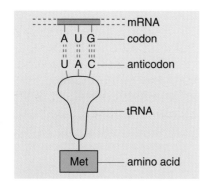

**Figure 11.7**   The interaction between one tRNA molecule attached to the amino acid methionine (Met) and a short mRNA sequence.

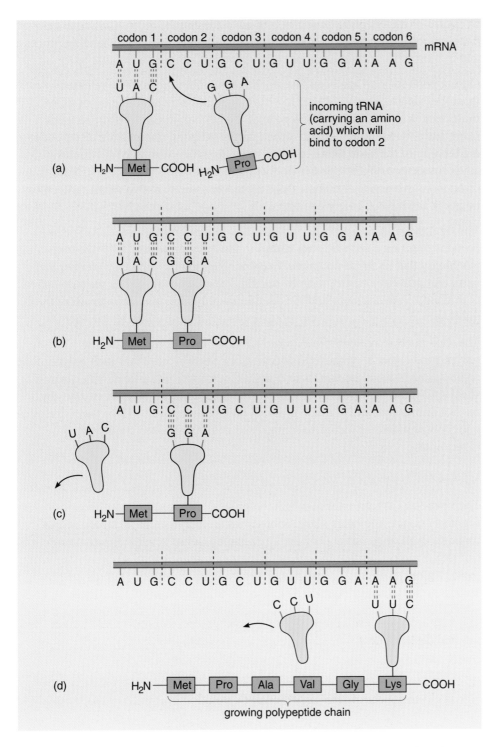

**Figure 11.8** Simplified scheme for translation. (a) One tRNA molecule is already bound to mRNA and a second is about to bind. (b) Two tRNA molecules are now bound to mRNA, and a peptide bond has formed between the first two amino acids of the polypeptide chain. (c) The first tRNA molecule is released. (d) A few steps further on in the process – the growing polypeptide chain now consists of six amino acids; the sixth amino acid corresponds to codon 6. As in earlier figures, the hydrogen bonds between the bases are shown as red dashed lines. (Met, Pro, Ala, Val, Gly and Lys are the abbreviations for the first six amino acids in this polypeptide: methionine, proline, alanine, valine, glycine and lysine.) Note that the different components shown are not drawn to scale.

particular **start codon** (labelled codon 1 in this figure), which always has the base sequence AUG and codes for methionine. Once this first tRNA has bound, a second follows suit (Figure 11.8a).

■ To synthesise a polypeptide chain from individual amino acids, what type of bonds must be formed? (If you're not sure, look back at Section 5.5.2.)

☐ Peptide bonds link the constituent amino acid units together in a polypeptide chain.

In Figure 11.8b a peptide bond has formed between the first two amino acids that have arrived at the mRNA. Protein synthesis is a very energy-demanding process, and in most cells consumes more energy than any other biosynthetic process.

Once a peptide bond has been formed, the first tRNA molecule is released from the mRNA (Figure 11.8c). The binding and subsequent release of tRNA molecules is repeated along the length of the mRNA chain, with amino acids being added sequentially, one at a time, to the growing polypeptide chain. After the binding of the sixth tRNA, the polypeptide chain consists of six amino acids covalently linked together by five peptide bonds (Figure 11.8d). Note that throughout this series of events, there are never more than two tRNA molecules bound to the mRNA at any one time.

The final event in polypeptide synthesis is termination of translation. This is brought about by a specific **stop codon** in the mRNA, which 'tells' the translation machinery that its job is complete. Each polypeptide has a precise number and particular sequence of amino acids in its primary structure. When the stop codon is reached, synthesis stops and the completed polypeptide dissociates from the mRNA.

The final point to notice from Figure 11.8 is the direction in which the polypeptide chain is synthesised. Recall from Section 5.5.2 that each polypeptide chain has an N-terminal amino acid and a C-terminal amino acid. You can now see from Figure 11.8 that the first amino acid added is the N-terminal one, and the last amino acid added to the growing polypeptide chain will be the C-terminal one. Polypeptides are therefore synthesised from their N-terminus to their C-terminus.

### 11.4.4   The role of ribosomes in translation

The ribosomes are the sites at which the process of translation, outlined in Figure 11.8, actually takes place. Ribosomes are very similar in structure and function in all organisms. They are large aggregates of several different protein and rRNA molecules that fit together to form a complex with a relative molecular mass of many millions. The ribosome has three binding sites; it binds mRNA and up to two tRNA molecules. The stage of translation shown in Figure 11.9 is the same as that shown in Figure 11.8b. Here two tRNA molecules plus their attached amino acids have bound to the mRNA at a ribosome, and a peptide bond has formed between the two amino acids (methionine (Met) and proline (Pro)).

**Figure 11.9**   Binding of mRNA and tRNA at a ribosome. Each ribosome binds up to two tRNA molecules at a time. Here two tRNA molecules have bound, and a peptide bond has just formed between the two amino acids they carry.

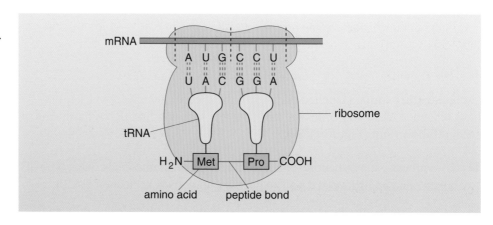

The two tRNA molecules remain at the ribosome for the short time necessary for a peptide bond to form between the two amino acids that they carry.

The next stage in the process (as shown in Figure 11.8c) would be the departure of the left-hand tRNA from the ribosome. Since only two tRNA molecules can be bound at a ribosome at any one time, a vacant 'slot' has now been created. The ribosome then moves one codon along the mRNA, so that this vacant 'slot' is shifted to the right of the remaining bound tRNA. Another tRNA can now bind to the mRNA in this vacant slot.

In this way, the ribosome moves stepwise along the mRNA chain, moving from left to right of the mRNA molecule in Figure 11.8 until it reaches the 'stop' codon. However, a number of ribosomes can bind simultaneously to the same mRNA molecule. Figure 11.10 shows this; a string of ribosomes is synthesising molecules of the same polypeptide and each one is at a different stage in the process. This string of ribosomes on an mRNA chain is termed a polyribosome – more usually abbreviated to **polysome**; each polysome is a string of ribosomes with growing polypeptide chains at different stages of completion. The polypeptide folds up as it is being synthesised to give the protein product with its own characteristic shape (Figure 11.10). When a protein chain is complete, both it and the ribosome are released from the mRNA. The ribosome can bind to either the same or a different mRNA molecule, and so begin the synthesis of another molecule of polypeptide.

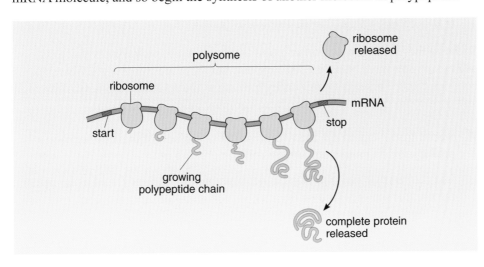

**Figure 11.10** Synthesis of a polypeptide by ribosomes attached to an mRNA chain. A ribosome binds first at a precise 'start' codon and shifts along the mRNA until it reaches the 'stop' codon when polypeptide synthesis terminates. On the mRNA there is a string of ribosomes with growing polypeptide chains at different stages of completion. This string of ribosomes is called a polysome.

Question 11.2

Fill in the blanks in each of the following sentences about RNA and protein synthesis. (In some cases more than one word is required to fill a blank.)

(a) The enzyme _____ copies a stretch of DNA into RNA in a process known as _____ .

(b) Only the _____ strand of DNA is 'read' in the process of RNA synthesis; the other DNA strand is known as the _____ strand.

(c) There are three different types of RNA molecule: _____ , _____ and _____ .

(d)  The transfer of information from the mRNA base sequence to the amino acid sequence of a polypeptide is known as _____ .

(e)  The mRNA sequence has a triplet code, and each triplet is known as a _____ .

(f)  Reading of the mRNA base sequence begins at a _____ and finishes at a _____ .

(g)  _____ binds both an amino acid and mRNA; it attaches to the latter via its three-base _____ .

(h)  A ribosome has three RNA binding sites: one for _____ and two for tRNA.

(i)  A ribosome moves along an mRNA chain, and there are several ribosomes attached to a particular mRNA at any one time; such a string of ribosomes along an mRNA chain is termed a _____ .

## 11.4.5   Where does translation occur?

So far in the discussion of transcription and translation, prokaryotes (bacteria) and eukaryotes have been lumped together, but there are important differences between them. This section begins by looking at the relative simplicity of bacteria and then compares them with the more complex eukaryotic cells.

■  Recall from Section 4.1 the two principal structural differences between a prokaryotic cell and a eukaryotic cell.

☐  In a prokaryotic cell, the DNA is not separated from the cytosol by a nuclear membrane and there are no organelles such as mitochondria and chloroplasts.

Compared with eukaryotic cells, therefore, bacterial cells are relatively simple; they are the simplest of known cells. The absence of a nuclear membrane in a bacterial cell has an important consequence for the location of transcription and translation. It means that the synthesis of RNA and protein occur together in the cytosol. In fact, a newly synthesised mRNA molecule is translated into polypeptide molecules whilst being transcribed. Thus the two processes of transcription and translation occur more or less simultaneously and in close proximity to each other in the cell. This is shown in a diagrammatic way in Figure 11.11. This shows that whilst the mRNA is being synthesised on the DNA template, the 'older' part of this molecule has been released from the DNA. Ribosomes have attached themselves and polypeptide synthesis has started on the mRNA molecule (from the left-hand end of Figure 11.11). Several such ribosomes are attached, so forming a polysome. Moving from left to right, the growing polypeptide chains are getting increasingly longer and more complete.

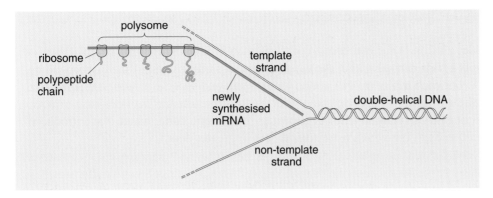

**Figure 11.11**    The synthesis of mRNA and protein in a bacterial cell. The dashed lines indicate that the DNA strands are longer than shown here.

However, in cells of eukaryotes, mRNA is produced in the nucleus; it then leaves the cell nucleus and passes into the cytosol where translation occurs. This represents a significant difference between eukaryote and bacterial protein synthesis.

■ Once in the cytosol, on which structures does translation occur?

☐ mRNA binds to the ribosomes (Section 4.1), where it is translated into a polypeptide chain.

From Figure 11.11 you can see that, in bacteria, transcription and translation occur in close proximity to the DNA. In contrast, in eukaryotes, transcription and translation are separated both in space within the cell and in time, in that one happens after the other, as summarised in Figure 11.12.

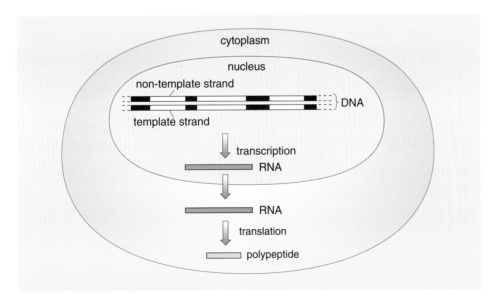

**Figure 11.12**    Summary of transcription and translation in eukaryotic cells; these two processes are separated in space and time.

## 11.5   The genetic code

The description of the mechanism of translation in Section 11.4 has revealed that there is a code carried within the base sequence of mRNA and of the corresponding DNA. For each triplet mRNA codon that is read, one specific amino acid is inserted into the growing polypeptide chain. The specific relationship between base triplets in DNA or RNA and amino acids is known as the **genetic code**, which was introduced in Section 11.4, but which is examined here in greater detail.

> The DNA and corresponding mRNA codons form the basis of the genetic code, whereby each triplet of three bases specifies a particular amino acid.

■ Look back at Figure 11.8b and write down the sequence of bases in the mRNA that codes for the amino acid methionine (Met), i.e. the codon for Met.

□ AUG.

■ Similarly, look at Figure 11.8d and find the codon for lysine (Lys).

□ AAG.

Note that these are the sequences of the three bases – the codons – in the mRNA (shown at the top of the diagrams). These codons are complementary to the sequences of three bases – the anticodons – of the tRNA molecules.

Figure 11.8 shows the codons for a mere six amino acids, but as you know there are 20 commonly occurring amino acids in proteins. There are also four different bases in RNA, but only three are included in any one codon. These four bases can be arranged in 64 different combinations of a three-letter codon, i.e. $4 \times 4 \times 4 = 4^3 = 64$, since there are four possibilities for the first base of a triplet, four possibilities for the second, and four for the third.

■ There are 64 possible mRNA codons but only 20 amino acids. What does this tell you?

□ One possible conclusion is that there are several codons for each amino acid. An alternative possibility is that many codons do not code for amino acids.

Both answers are in fact correct to a certain extent. Actually, 61 codons code for particular amino acids, and the other three are stop codons.

■ What is the role of a stop codon?

□ It signals termination of translation and the release of the completed polypeptide and the ribosome from the mRNA molecule (look back at Figure 11.10).

A considerable amount of work from the mid-1950s until the mid-1960s was required before the full genetic code was deciphered. It is shown in Figure 11.13. Here the 64 different codons are arranged in terms of the order of the three bases. Consider one example: the codon UUU, in the top left-hand corner of the figure. This is the sequence coding for the amino acid phenylalanine, abbreviated to Phe. (The abbreviations for all the amino acids are given in the figure caption.) The figure shows that for most of the 20 amino acids found in proteins there are several codons.

| first base | second base: U | second base: C | second base: A | second base: G | third base |
|---|---|---|---|---|---|
| U | UUU Phe | UCU Ser | UAU Tyr | UGU Cys | U |
| U | UUC Phe | UCC Ser | UAC Tyr | UGC Cys | C |
| U | UUA Leu | UCA Ser | UAA stop | UGA stop | A |
| U | UUG Leu | UCG Ser | UAG stop | UGG Trp | G |
| C | CUU Leu | CCU Pro | CAU His | CGU Arg | U |
| C | CUC Leu | CCC Pro | CAC His | CGC Arg | C |
| C | CUA Leu | CCA Pro | CAA Gln | CGA Arg | A |
| C | CUG Leu | CCG Pro | CAG Gln | CGG Arg | G |
| A | AUU Ile | ACU Thr | AAU Asn | AGU Ser | U |
| A | AUC Ile | ACC Thr | AAC Asn | AGC Ser | C |
| A | AUA Ile | ACA Thr | AAA Lys | AGA Arg | A |
| A | AUG Met | ACG Thr | AAG Lys | AGG Arg | G |
| G | GUU Val | GCU Ala | GAU Asp | GGU Gly | U |
| G | GUC Val | GCC Ala | GAC Asp | GGC Gly | C |
| G | GUA Val | GCA Ala | GAA Glu | GGA Gly | A |
| G | GUG Val | GCG Ala | GAG Glu | GGG Gly | G |

**Figure 11.13** mRNA codons. (Note that AUG, the codon for Met, is also the start codon.) The abbreviated names of the 20 amino acids are as follows:
Ala = alanine
Arg = arginine
Asn = asparagine
Asp = aspartate
Cys = cysteine
Gln = glutamine
Glu = glutamate
Gly = glycine
His = histidine
Ile = isoleucine
Leu = leucine
Lys = lysine
Met = methionine
Phe = phenylalanine
Pro = proline
Ser = serine
Thr = threonine
Trp = tryptophan
Tyr = tyrosine
Val = valine.
You do not need to remember these abbreviations, nor which codons correspond to which amino acids.

■ Looking at Figure 11.13, which amino acids have the largest number of codons?

□ Leu (leucine), Ser (serine) and Arg (arginine) each have six codons.

■ Which amino acids have the fewest codons?

□ Both Met (methionine) and Trp (tryptophan) have only one each. [Interestingly, methionine and tryptophan are the least abundant amino acids found in proteins.]

The other amino acids each have a number of codons somewhere between these extremes. The fact that most amino acids have several codons has led to the description of the code as being a *degenerate* genetic code. A consequence of this is that it is not as precise as might be expected, as explained in the following discussion.

■ Figure 11.13 shows that 61 mRNA codons code for the 20 amino acids. How many different tRNA molecules would you expect to find as a consequence of this?

□ If there are 61 mRNA codons, you would expect 61 complementary tRNA anticodons and hence 61 different tRNA molecules.

In fact, far fewer than 61 different tRNA molecules are found in a given cell. This is because, in many (but not all) cases, accurate base-pairing between codon and anticodon occurs at only the first two of the three bases and a mismatch (or *wobble*) can be tolerated at the third base.

■ Look at Figure 11.13 and identify the codons for alanine (Ala). How do these codons compare?

□ There are four codons: GCU, GCC, GCA and GCG, and the first two bases are identical for each of them.

This wobble makes it possible to fit 20 amino acids to the 61 mRNA codons with fewer than 61 tRNA molecules. For Ala, for example, there is usually a single tRNA in a cell, with an anticodon that can bind to the mRNA codon GC–, where the third base can be any one of U, C, A or G. Although this wobble is tolerated for many codons, it is not tolerated for all; for example, as noted above, methionine (Met) and tryptophan (Trp) each have just one codon.

Figure 11.13 shows that the codon AUG codes for the amino acid methionine. As described in Section 11.4.3, the codon AUG is also the start codon for initiating the translation of all polypeptides. Methionine can therefore appear both at the beginning and within a polypeptide. Every newly completed polypeptide chain released from polysomes has methionine at the N-terminal position. However, this methionine is removed after the polypeptide chain leaves the ribosome.

The final aspect of the genetic code to be considered is its *universal* nature. What this means is that the mRNA codons shown in Figure 11.13 apply in virtually all organisms where the code has been examined. This observation provides strong evidence that all cells, or at least the nuclear component of them (leaving the mitochondria and chloroplasts aside), have evolved from a common ancestor.

In fact, the processes of information storage in DNA, replication, transcription and translation are fundamentally similar in all organisms. This demonstrates, most powerfully, the evolutionary continuity between organisms.

### Question 11.3

In this question you will examine the relationship between base sequences of DNA and mRNA, and the amino acid sequence coded for by these polynucleotides.

Below is the start of the base sequence in the template strand of a section of a DNA molecule isolated from a particular population of cells:

TACCTCGGTCATCCCT…

Use the information given in Table 11.1 and Figure 11.13 to answer the following questions:

(a) If the above sequence is transcribed, what will be the corresponding mRNA base sequence?

(b) If the mRNA sequence is translated, what will be the amino acid sequence of the product?

(c) Write down the corresponding DNA sequence of the non-template strand.

---

### Activity 11.2   Information flow in cells

We expect this activity will take you approximately 35 minutes.

This computer-based video sequence *Information Flow in Cells* illustrates the key points of Chapters 10 and 11. It concentrates on the flow of information from DNA to RNA to polypeptide, showing the relationship between the sequence of bases in DNA and the sequence of amino acids in a polypeptide chain. This activity will help you revise and consolidate your understanding of DNA structure, DNA replication and polypeptide synthesis.

You will find it helpful to have the summary given in Table 11.2 to hand whilst watching the video sequence, pausing after each point to check that you have understood the key points and to add details in the 'Comments' column of Table 11.2, making your revision active. To get you started, comments to the Introduction have been added.

**Table 11.2** Summary of computer-based video sequence *Information Flow in Cells.*

| Summary | Comments |
|---|---|
| (1) *Introduction* <br> The three key features of DNA | DNA is stable, can be accurately copied, and contains information that can be used to direct the synthesis of polypeptides. |
| (2) *DNA structure* <br> The basic building blocks of DNA, the nucleotides, are linked to form polynucleotide chains. There are two strands. | |
| (3) *DNA replication* <br> A DNA double helix unwinds and each polynucleotide chain forms a template for DNA replication. Two daughter DNA double helices are produced, each identical to the original. | |
| (4) *The information in DNA* <br> This is coded within the base sequence and composed of the four-letter language of A, G, C and T. One particular sequence of bases is equivalent to one gene. | |
| (5) *Gene to polypeptide* <br> In the flow of information from DNA to polypeptide, first an mRNA strand is synthesised with a base sequence complementary to the template strand of the appropriate gene – a process called transcription. The information in mRNA is translated into the sequence of amino acids in a polypeptide chain. | |
| (6) *RNA structure* <br> (Compare it with DNA.) | |
| (7) *Transcription – writing the message* <br> A section of DNA unwinds and the message, mRNA, is produced by transcription on the template stand. | |
| (8) *Translation – reading the message* <br> A tRNA molecule, carrying its specific amino acid, binds to the mRNA codon via the anticodon. A second tRNA molecule binds to the mRNA and the two amino acids become joined by a peptide bond. The process repeats, elongating the polypeptide chain until the stop codon is reached. | |
| (9) *At the ribosome* <br> Translation begins when mRNA binds to a ribosome. The process continues as the ribosome moves along the mRNA one codon at a time, until a stop codon is reached. The completed polypeptide chain is released to form the ribosome. | |

Now read the comments on this activity at the end of this book.

## 11.6    Summary of Chapter 11

The collinearity of sequences between a gene and a polypeptide is known as the 'one gene–one polypeptide' hypothesis. The flow of information is: DNA makes RNA makes polypeptide.

Transcription is the process of RNA synthesis, in which information coded in one of the strands of DNA becomes coded in mRNA. RNA polymerase adds RNA nucleotides one at a time and the base-pairing rules apply: G of DNA binds C of RNA, and vice versa; T of DNA binds A of RNA, but A of DNA binds U of RNA.

In the process of translation, the four-character language of mRNA is translated into the 20-character language of proteins. A triplet codon of mRNA binds a triplet anticodon of a tRNA molecule, to which is attached a specific amino acid.

The ribosome binds mRNA and up to two tRNA molecules. The first tRNA binds to a particular sequence known as the start codon, which codes for methionine. A second tRNA also binds to the ribosome, and a peptide bond forms between the two amino acids. The first tRNA molecule then leaves the ribosome. The ribosome moves, so that a vacant site is available for another tRNA molecule. In this way, the ribosome moves along the mRNA and the polypeptide chain gets longer. Once the ribosome reaches the stop codon, translation comes to an end. A string of ribosomes attached to a single mRNA molecule is known as a polysome.

In both prokaryotes and eukaryotes, there are sequences that are transcribed into tRNA and rRNA.

In bacteria, transcription and translation occur in close proximity to the DNA. In contrast, in eukaryotes, transcription and translation are separated both in space within the cell and in time.

The genetic code is degenerate in that some amino acids are specified by more than one codon. It consists of 64 triplet codons, each of which codes for a specific amino acid or is a stop codon. This is a universal genetic code, which applies to virtually all organisms. The processes of information storage in DNA, replication, transcription and translation are fundamentally similar in all organisms.

# Chapter 12
# Gene structure and function in eukaryotes

In this chapter, you will explore the structure and function of genes with particular reference to eukaryotes using the specific example of the cystic fibrosis gene in humans. This example has been chosen because a lot is known about the gene involved and the protein for which it codes. It is a relatively common genetic disease, affecting 1 in 2500 babies born in the UK.

Chapter 8 was primarily concerned with the inheritance of normal variation such as purple and white flowers in pea plants. The present chapter moves on to look at disease phenotypes that are considered to be outside the normal range. Many diseases are described as genetic diseases because they have a genetic origin, unlike mumps for example, which is caused by a virus. Thousands of genetic diseases or genetic disorders, many of them rare, have been shown to be due to defective copies of genes.

The defective, or disease, alleles involved are variants of genes that we all contain in our genotypes. However, most of us contain non-disease alleles or normal alleles of these genes. Some genetic disorders occur when the individual inherits only one defective allele (dominant disorder); others require both copies of the gene to be defective (recessive disorder) and some genetic diseases are X-linked. Disease alleles follow exactly the same patterns of inheritance as non-disease alleles, so the rules already described in Chapter 8 also apply to their inheritance.

This chapter looks at the relationship between the structure and function of the cystic fibrosis gene, and then examines the organisation of the gene. In cystic fibrosis, individuals are usually affected by lung disease, although other tissues and organs, such as the pancreas (which produces digestive enzymes that are released into the intestine), may be affected too. In order to understand the origin of the cystic fibrosis disease, the next section explores mutation in more detail.

## 12.1    Mutation revisited

You saw in Chapter 11 that genes are composed of DNA, and that the DNA base sequence of these genes determines the structure of polypeptides via mRNA as the intermediary. The genetic code is the key to understanding this information flow from DNA to RNA to polypeptide. Sequences of three bases (codons) in DNA relate directly to mRNA codons, which in turn provide the template on which a precise sequence of amino acids is joined together to form a polypeptide.

In Section 10.3, however, you saw that the machinery of DNA replication does not always produce an accurate copy of the template strand. In other words, mistakes can occur, in which incorrect bases are inserted into the growing polynucleotide chain. If the errors are not detected and removed, then these become mutations. These errors will then be copied each time the DNA molecule is replicated.

■ If the DNA replication machinery makes such an error so that a base is 'misread' and the 'wrong' base inserted, consider what will happen at transcription. How will the mRNA be affected?

☐ The error in the template strand of DNA is transferred to the mRNA, so that a 'faulty' message will be produced.

■ What effect will this 'faulty' message have on the amino acid sequence of the polypeptide produced at translation?

☐ An incorrect codon could result in a completely different amino acid being inserted into the growing polypeptide chain.

So, modifications to a DNA sequence can lead ultimately to changes in the amino acid sequence of a polypeptide. It requires only a very small change in a DNA sequence to produce a change at the level of the functional protein.

Consider the following straightforward example:

■ Look back at Figure 11.8. What is the second codon in the short mRNA sequence shown there and for which amino acid does it code?

☐ The codon is CCU and the corresponding amino acid is proline (Pro).

Consider an error in DNA replication that resulted in this mRNA codon being CAU instead of CCU, i.e. the second base, C, has been replaced by A.

■ From Figure 11.13, which amino acid would then be inserted into the polypeptide chain?

☐ CAU is a codon for the amino acid histidine (His).

As you learned in Chapter 10, there are different types of mutations; as well as producing changes in individual bases, sometimes bases can be deleted or additional bases inserted, as demonstrated in the following question.

## Question 12.1

In this question, you will look at the consequences of (a) the deletion of a base and (b) the addition of an extra base starting with the same DNA sequence as in Question 11.3.

(a) A population of cells has been treated with a chemical agent that has brought about a change in the DNA sequence. This is very specific, such that the sixth base in that sequence is deleted, shown here underlined in the sequence of the template strand:

TACCT<u>C</u>GGTCATCCCT…

The new template sequence is as follows:

TACCTGGTCATCCCT…

Use Table 11.1 and Figure 11.13 to work out the effect this change will have on the amino acid sequence if this DNA sequence is transcribed and the RNA product is translated. What is the significance of this result?

(b)  Another population of the same type of cells as used in (a) has been treated with a different chemical agent, which results in a different kind of mutation. This time an extra base is added to the DNA, such that the template sequence, with the inserted base shown underlined, now reads as follows:

   TAC<u>C</u>CTCGGTCATCCCT…

What effect will this have on the corresponding amino acid sequence? What is the significance of the result you have obtained?

The answer to this question shows that if a base is deleted or an additional base inserted, all subsequent codons in the mRNA following this error would be changed. In turn, the sequence of amino acids in the polypeptide would also be changed.

The effect of a mutation on the function of the protein will depend on the position and number of the changed amino acid in the polypeptide chain. For example, in an enzyme some positions can be filled by alternative amino acids, and at least partial function is maintained. But at other positions in the chain the normal amino acid must be present for the enzyme to be fully active.

■  Thinking back to the structure and function of enzymes (Chapter 5), which parts of an enzyme are most likely to be affected by a change of amino acid sequence?

☐  The parts of the enzyme molecule that contribute to the active site, either directly, or indirectly by helping to maintain the precise shape of the active site.

Where the mutation results in a large number of amino acids being changed (as in the answer to Question 12.1), the enzyme is unlikely to have any activity.

Very rarely, mutations can be advantageous, producing a protein with 'enhanced' qualities, conferring advantages on the host organism in a particular environment. Such mutations may be replicated and spread throughout the population. (Examples of these mutations are discussed in Chapter 14.) Other mutations are deleterious and the next section turns to one such mutation – that associated with the cystic fibrosis phenotype in humans.

## 12.2   The relationship between genotype and phenotype

Chapter 8 introduced the idea of alleles for alternative forms of a character, e.g. flower colour in the garden pea. But sometimes a gene can only be identified when it is associated with a disease phenotype, as in the case of cystic fibrosis. This section examines the 'cystic fibrosis gene' and the alleles are referred to as the cystic fibrosis, or mutant, allele and the normal allele of the cystic fibrosis gene.

The disease results from a mutation on chromosome 7 (see Figure 8.3) in which three consecutive base pairs are lost from the cystic fibrosis gene. Consequently, there are two alleles of this gene: the normal allele that includes these three base

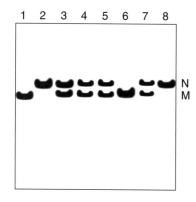

**Figure 12.1** Visualising pieces of DNA that contain a specific gene – in this example, the cystic fibrosis gene. Here the DNA has been extracted from cells of eight individuals (numbered 1–8) and two bands have been identified: band N corresponds to the normal allele and band M corresponds to the mutant (cystic fibrosis) allele.

pairs, and the mutant allele that lacks them. This description reveals how the two alleles differ from each other at the level of the DNA. The exact position of the gene on chromosome 7 was located in 1989. Using sophisticated molecular techniques, it is possible to extract and identify the DNA of this gene, as shown in Figure 12.1. In this procedure, DNA is extracted from cells (usually white blood cells in the case of humans) and it is cut into fragments using enzymes that recognise and cut within particular sequences. These fragments are loaded at one end of a gel (jelly-like substance) and separated according to their size. Since the DNA fragments have a negative charge, when an electric voltage is applied they move across the gel towards the positive electrode; large fragments move with difficulty, but smaller pieces move more easily. Once separated, specific sequences of DNA (i.e. genes or parts of genes) can then be visualised in the gel. Mutations can create or destroy a cutting site for an enzyme, thus altering the pattern of cuts in the DNA. Hence it is possible to tell whether a gene is present and whether it is normal in structure.

What can you learn from the image shown in Figure 12.1? The first point is that there is gene variation amongst the eight individuals. For each person, there are either one or two bands. There are two band types, one corresponding to the normal allele (N) and the other corresponding to the mutant (cystic fibrosis) allele (M). The individuals can be grouped into three categories in terms of the bands each has. Look at the bands for individuals 1, 2 and 3. Person 1 has just a single band, which corresponds to the mutant allele. So, person 1 has only the mutant allele for this gene. Person 2 has also just a single band, but here it corresponds to the normal allele. In contrast, person 3 has both bands and hence has both alleles.

■ Using Figure 12.1, group the eight people into three groups (I–III) in terms of the bands and hence alleles that each has: group I, mutant allele only; group II, normal allele only; group III, both alleles.

☐ Group I: individuals 1 and 6 have only the band for the mutant allele.

  Group II: individuals 2 and 8 have only the band for the normal allele.

  Group III: individuals 3, 4, 5 and 7 have both bands, and hence both alleles.

The people in group III have been identified as having two different alleles of the cystic fibrosis gene.

■ What is the term used to describe this genotype, in contrast to that of individuals in groups I and II?

☐ Group III individuals are said to be heterozygous, in contrast to members of groups I and II, who are homozygous.

A further significant point is that the mutant allele is recessive.

■ Which individuals will exhibit the disease symptoms, and why?

☐ Individuals 1 and 6 would be expected to exhibit disease symptoms because they have only the mutant allele.

The question of which individuals will exhibit the disease, and why, can be explored further by relating the genetics of cystic fibrosis to events at the level of the polypeptide coded for by the gene and considering how the normal and mutant alleles of the gene and their protein products are operating. The cystic fibrosis gene codes for a protein that is involved in the transport of chloride ions across cellular membranes. The normal allele codes for a fully functional protein, whereas the mutant allele codes for a defective protein with greatly reduced chloride transport activity.

Individuals 1 and 6 have only the mutant allele and consequently their cells are able to synthesise only the defective protein. The transport function of the protein in their cells is significantly impaired. In contrast, individuals in group II have just the normal allele, and hence synthesise the non-mutant protein, which functions normally.

Individuals in group III, however, have both alleles, normal and mutant. In these individuals both forms of the protein are synthesised, and yet these people do not exhibit the disease symptoms. The key to understanding this is that the cells of these individuals synthesise sufficient normally functioning protein to ensure the transport of chloride ions, so that disease symptoms are not expressed in the phenotype.

This example shows that the terms 'dominant' and 'recessive' can be better understood at the level of the functioning protein, rather than at the level of the gene. In the cystic fibrosis example, the dominant normal phenotype represents the presence of a fully-functioning protein and the recessive phenotype represents the protein with significantly reduced chloride transport activity. The heterozygote makes both proteins, yet the individual has the phenotype associated with the fully-functioning protein; the mutant protein is not expressed at the level of the whole organism.

Finally, examples like cystic fibrosis tell the story of how information in genes becomes realised in the phenotype. This is illustrated in Figure 12.2. This figure summarises the sequence of events from the normal allele of the cystic fibrosis gene to the development of the normal phenotype, and, for comparison, shows the sequence of events from the mutation in the cystic fibrosis gene to the development of the disease phenotype.

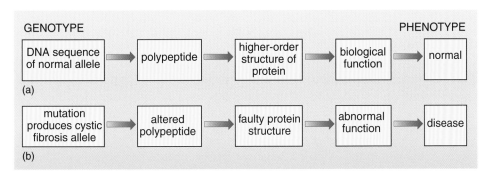

**Figure 12.2** The sequence of events from genotype to phenotype, illustrated for the cystic fibrosis gene: (a) from the normal allele to the normal phenotype; (b) from the mutant allele to the disease phenotype.

So far the precise linear relationship between DNA base sequence and polypeptide structure in the non-disease and the disease allele of the cystic fibrosis gene has been considered. However, the relationship is not quite so straightforward, as you will discover in the next section.

## 12.3   Gene organisation in eukaryotes

Although the simple story of the flow of information from DNA to polypeptide is largely true for bacteria, important complexities exist in eukaryotes. In fact, the structure of genes in eukaryotes is far more complicated. The information for making polypeptides in most genes is *not* an uninterrupted sequence of bases. Rather, most eukaryote genes are 'split' into separate parts along the length of a DNA molecule by intervening non-coding sequences.

■ Consider a protein with a sequence of 300 amino acids. Approximately how many mRNA bases and hence how many DNA base pairs would you expect to code for this protein?

☐ Each mRNA codon is a triplet of three bases, so 900 mRNA bases and hence 900 DNA base pairs would be expected to code for this protein.

You may be surprised to learn that for many proteins of average length of around 300–400 amino acids, each gene contains a staggering 100 000 base pairs – about 100 times the number that is apparently needed. Some eukaryote genes coding for proteins of this size even contain as many as two million base pairs. What then is the relationship between all these extra DNA base pairs and the final protein sequence? The rules you have learnt so far apply in that, for example, 900 DNA bases would be needed to code for a sequence of 300 amino acids. However, only a relatively small number of DNA bases within such a gene actually code for amino acids in the protein product: such protein-coding DNA sequences are termed **exons**. Within the DNA sequence of a gene, the exons are interspersed with non-protein-coding regions termed **introns**. For a gene of 100 000 base pairs, a large proportion of the base pairs of the gene comprises introns, the sequences of which do not 'appear' in the final protein product of the gene. Such a gene, with exons and introns is described as a **split gene**, a simple sketch of which is shown in Figure 12.3. As this figure shows, usually there are relatively long intron regions interspersed with relatively short exon regions.

**Figure 12.3**   A sketch of a hypothetical split gene, consisting of four short exons (protein-coding regions) and three larger, intervening introns (non-protein-coding regions).

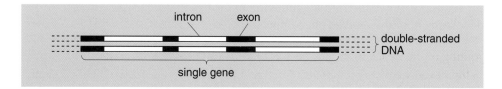

The split gene shown in Figure 12.3 is a very simple, indeed hypothetical, example with only four exons. Many genes that have actually been identified and characterised are much more complicated than this. For example, the cystic fibrosis gene is large, comprising 250 000 base pairs including 26 introns.

If a large amount of the DNA in a gene comprises introns, then somehow there must be a series of events between transcription of DNA and protein synthesis (translation), in which these intervening sequences are removed. This series of events is called *RNA processing* and is illustrated in Figure 12.4.

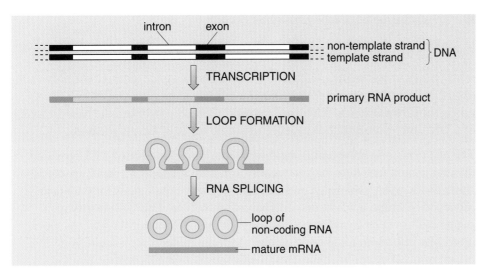

**Figure 12.4**   A hypothetical example of RNA processing. DNA is first transcribed into a long molecule including exons (protein-coding regions) and introns (non-protein-coding regions), and called the primary RNA product. RNA splicing reactions remove the introns and join the exons to produce the mature mRNA.

As Figure 12.4 shows, the DNA sequence of the entire split gene is transcribed, and the **primary RNA product** includes the non-protein-coding introns as well as the protein-coding exons.

■ How many bases would you expect to find in the primary RNA product?

☐ Since this contains both exons and introns, the primary RNA product should have the same number of bases as there are base pairs in the DNA template on which it was produced. This follows from the base-pairing rules of transcription.

Indeed, the primary product of transcription is a very large RNA molecule.

■ What must happen to this primary RNA product, in terms of its length, before protein synthesis takes place?

☐ After transcription, this RNA must be shortened in some way.

The existence of introns means that the primary RNA product must be processed before translation can occur. This processing involves removal of the introns and joining of the exons to produce a continuous mRNA ready for translation. This is the **mature mRNA** molecule. As shown in Figure 12.4, the RNA regions that do not code for amino acid sequences of the protein form loops that are cut out of the molecule.

■ What is the relationship, in terms of size, between the primary RNA product and the mature mRNA?

☐ The mature mRNA is much smaller than the primary RNA product. Its length corresponds to the total length of all of the exon sequences.

■ What would be the next step in the sequence of polypeptide production?

☐ The mature mRNA would leave the nucleus and pass into the cytosol where it would be translated.

■   On what structures does translation occur?

☐   mRNA binds to the ribosomes, where it is translated into a polypeptide chain.

Many genes in eukaryotes, such as the cystic fibrosis gene, consist of introns and exons, with the sequences comprising the introns being removed during RNA processing. Thus there is not a continuous relationship between the base sequence of a DNA molecule and the sequence of amino acids in the polypeptide.

The one gene–one polypeptide hypothesis introduced in Section 11.1 provided the first insight into how the gene works as a unit of function. This hypothesis states that a given gene has a precise linear sequence that codes for the linear sequence of amino acids in one polypeptide molecule. This collinearity of sequences has been found to be true for prokaryotes (Section 11.4.5). As more molecular information has been gained about the molecular structure and organisation of genes in eukaryotes, the one gene–one polypeptide hypothesis has been found to be no longer true. The discovery of split genes which are not collinear with the corresponding mature mRNA contributed to the shattering of this hypothesis.

### Question 12.2

It was stated above that the cystic fibrosis gene has 250 000 base pairs, including 26 introns. Its mRNA, however, is only about 6500 bases.

(a)  How many bases are there in the primary RNA product of the cystic fibrosis gene?

(b)  What percentage of this primary RNA product consists of non-protein-coding sequences?

(c)  What is the mean size of an intron in the cystic fibrosis gene?

A great deal is now known about the structure and function of individual genes, and scientists are uncovering information about how genes are organised along chromosomes. This is one of the topics of the next chapter.

## 12.4   Summary of Chapter 12

A mutation in the DNA code can be transcribed into mRNA and subsequently translated into a protein. For example, a single base change in DNA can result in a faulty protein product. Such defects can result in heritable diseases, such as cystic fibrosis in humans.

Many eukaryote genes are split genes, containing non-protein-coding introns and protein-coding exons.

The primary RNA product, resulting from transcription, is spliced to remove the introns; the resultant mature mRNA molecule is therefore much smaller. After processing, the mRNA leaves the nucleus and moves to the cytosol where translation occurs.

# Chapter 13
# Looking at genomes

The previous chapter showed that not all DNA codes for polypeptides. Genes have both coding and non-coding sequences of DNA, the latter of which are transcribed into RNA but are not translated into polypeptides. However surprisingly large amounts of DNA in most eukaryotes is non-coding and is not even transcribed into RNA. What is the role of such DNA sequences? This chapter broadens to examine a cell's total complement of genetic material, which is called the **genome**.

Genomes usually consist of only DNA, but some viruses have RNA instead of DNA as their genetic material, as in the case of the human immunodeficiency virus (HIV, the virus responsible for the acquired immune deficiency syndrome, AIDS). For eukaryotes, the term genome can also be applied to the genetic material of an organelle, as distinct from that in the nucleus: for example, the mitochondrial or chloroplast genome. You should recall from Section 4.3 that both these organelles also contain DNA, as a consequence of their bacterial ancestry.

In the discussion of DNA replication and polypeptide synthesis (Sections 10.2 and 11.4.1–11.4.4), prokaryotes (bacteria), and eukaryotes were, implicitly, lumped together, but there are important differences between them as far as their genomes are concerned. This chapter begins by looking at the relative simplicity of bacteria, where most of the DNA codes for protein. Then it moves on to look at the more complex eukaryotes where a lot of the DNA is non-coding. Some of these non-protein-coding sequences have well defined roles, whereas others do not. The chapter then looks at current projects that are aimed at investigating the complete DNA sequence of the genomes of certain organisms. Genome studies consider the molecular organisation and structure of the genetic material, and have given rise to the very new science of genomics. Genomics often involves comparing the genomes of organisms from widely different taxonomic groups, in a search for similar sequences and gene structures, and this chapter compares the genomes of yeast (*Saccharomyces cerevisiae*), fruit-fly (*Drosophila melanogaster*) and humans (*Homo sapiens*). Finally the chapter explores some of the ethical considerations that arise from our knowledge of the human genome.

## 13.1    Bacterial genomes

Bacterial genomes are relatively small – just a few million base pairs – as against, for example, the few billion base pairs of the human genome. There are three important features of the bacterial genome to appreciate. First, the genome consists of a single DNA molecule, and hence, the bacterial cell is haploid. Second, unlike eukaryote chromosomes, bacterial DNA is essentially naked, in that it is not associated with proteins that help condense the DNA into chromosomes. Third, there is great 'gene density' in the bacterial genome, such that virtually all the DNA codes for protein products (apart from those genes that code for rRNA and tRNA).

■ Recall from Chapter 4 the two principal structural differences between a prokaryotic cell and a eukaryotic cell.

☐ In a prokaryotic cell, the DNA is not separated from the cytosol by a nuclear membrane, and there are no organelles such as mitochondria and chloroplasts.

Compared with eukaryotic cells, therefore, bacterial cells are relatively simple; they are the simplest of known cells.

## 13.2   Eukaryote genomes

Although the simple picture of DNA consisting of a collection of consecutive genes, like beads on a string, is largely true for bacteria, important complexities exist in eukaryotes. In order to understand the degree of complexity, consider the human genome. Here, the base sequence of DNA in the 23 pairs of human chromosomes – some three billion base pairs in total – is equivalent to the number of letters in about two hundred large phone directories. Most intriguingly, eukaryotes have far more DNA than is apparently needed to code for all their proteins (and for transcription into tRNA and rRNA). This section looks at this 'extra' DNA, some of which has identifiable roles, but there are other DNA sequences that have no known roles.

For a long time, biologists have been puzzled by the large amount of DNA in eukaryote genomes, but what kind of amounts are being referred to here? For example, a typical mammalian cell such as from a human, has around 800 times the amount of DNA present in the bacterium *E. coli*; here it should be emphasised that such comparisons relate to haploid amounts, so as to compare like with like. A human cell is far more complex than a bacterium, but there is not a direct relationship between the complexity of the organism and the (haploid) amount of DNA contained within its cells. The mammalian genome has, in theory, enough DNA to code for perhaps three million average-sized proteins and yet estimates suggest that a typical mammal is constructed from 20 000–30 000 different proteins. Many plant genomes are even larger than mammalian ones.

In the case of split genes, you have already met DNA sequences (introns) that do not code for protein. In the human genome, only 3% of the entire genome represents genes. If you look back at Figure 12.3, you will see that there a split gene is considered to be the sum of the exons and introns it contains. In addition to the introns, which occur within split genes, there are other non-protein-coding sequences that lie between genes. Many of these have no known function.

However, some non-protein-coding DNA sequences between genes have a vital function in controlling the activity of genes. These supporting sequences are called control sequences, which are stretches of the DNA that facilitate the operation of the protein-coding genes in eukaryotes. These sequences may be located far away from the transcription start site and a number of these may be involved in the control of just one gene. Their function relates to the 'switching on and off' of genes in different tissues. As you learned in Chapter 4, the cells of different tissues of multicellular organisms such as humans are not all the same; there are nerve, muscle and bone cells, to give just three examples. However, the different cell types of an organism all have the same genome. All of these specialised cells have some proteins in common, but each has other proteins that are unique to that particular cell type. Clearly, therefore, in any particular cell only a certain number of genes are active, that is, they are 'switched on', and transcribed into RNA and subsequently translated into protein. The vast majority of other genes are inactive or 'switched off' and are not transcribed, so that the polypeptides for which they code are not being produced. This control of gene activity in eukaryotes is brought about by the control sequences and these ensure that only the right genes are transcribed in a given cell type. The total percentage of the human genome that corresponds to genes and their supporting sequences is around 30%.

Hence, one of the most striking features of the genome is the relatively small amount of space taken up by the genes and their control sequences – the majority of the genome appears to be nothing to do with genes. In fact it is unclear what the roles of the remaining DNA might be. Examination shows that it falls into different categories according to its structure. One category of DNA is made up of stretches of non repetitive, single-copy DNA of unknown function.

The remaining DNA is called repetitive DNA, because each DNA sequence is repeated a number of times. Repetitive DNA falls into one of two classes according to its distribution along the chromosomes. One class of repetitive DNA is dispersed throughout the genome; that is, it occurs at many different sites. Each repeat varies in length from hundreds to thousands of base pairs long. The other class of repeats are short sequences of DNA such as:

CAAA

GTTT

repeated about 10–25 times and grouped together consecutively; that is, they sit next to one another (Figure 13.1). This type of DNA has proved very useful to geneticists as described later in Section 13.3.1.

So, in eukaryotes, protein-coding genes are embedded in a complex array of repetitive DNA sequences and single-copy DNA, which have no known function. So far, the various categories of DNA have been described, but the variation between individuals of a species and differences between species have yet to be examined. The next section considers the DNA variations within the genome of a species – humans – before moving on to review the differences in the organisation of the genome of different species.

**Figure 13.1** A simple repeat sequence. This consists of many serially arranged repeats of a sequence of four base pairs.

Question 13.1

Table 13.1 is for you to record information about the genomes and gene function in prokaryotes and eukaryotes. Complete the table by writing an appropriate single word, such as 'present' or 'absent', or the name of a site, such as 'cytosol' or 'nucleus', in the blank space in each column opposite each feature.

**Table 13.1** Record of information to allow comparison of genomes and gene function in prokaryotes and eukaryotes.

| Feature | Prokaryotes | Eukaryotes |
|---|---|---|
| genome complexity | | |
| site of DNA replication | | |
| site of transcription | | |
| site of translation (ribosomes) | | |
| introns | | |
| exons | | |
| split genes | | |
| repeat sequences | | |
| mRNA splicing | | |

## 13.3   Genome diversity

Although humans all have the same genome, differences between individuals do exist. As a starting point, this section considers genetic variation within a population by returning briefly to the example of the cystic fibrosis gene in Chapter 12. There you considered one gene with two different alleles, for which there are three genotypes:

• homozygous for the normal allele

• homozygous for the mutant allele

• heterozygous, where an individual has both alleles.

Imagine for a moment how much genetic variation there is within a human population with different alleles for many, many different genes. The number of possible different combinations is really quite staggering. In order to appreciate this, consider approximately 25 000 genes, each with one of three possible genotypes (homozygous recessive, homozygous dominant and heterozygous). The possible combinations for an individual are then $3^{25000}$. It is easier to appreciate how big this number is by converting it to powers of ten: approximately $10^{12000}$. So within a population, the chance of any two individuals having the same genotype is infinitesimally small. However, in reality, many genes have *more* than two known alleles, for example the ABO system (Section 9.2). Hence the number of different possible combinations is much greater than this. Furthermore, the variation in base sequences found outside of the protein-coding regions, especially in the repetitive sequences, is even greater – so much so, that every individual, apart from identical twins, has a unique DNA profile, which can be identified using the technique of DNA fingerprinting.

## 13.3.1 DNA fingerprinting

The theoretical basis of DNA fingerprinting is that each individual in a species (apart from identical twins and clones), whether human or oak tree, has a unique DNA profile. This profile is as unique as the familiar human fingerprint itself, hence the name applied to the technique used in visualising DNA profiles, six of which are shown in Figure 13.2. The procedure used here is similar to that described earlier for visualising the cystic fibrosis gene (Figure 12.1). Much detectable variation results from differences between individuals in terms of repeat sequences. You saw in Section 13.2 that short base sequences within a genome can be serially or consecutively repeated. The number of times they are repeated at a given location, however, can vary between individuals of the same species and it is this variation, rather than the variation in protein-coding genes, that contributes most to unique, individual DNA fingerprints. For example, in one of these regions of repeats a person might inherit five repeats from their mother and six repeats from their father at the same location. Another person might inherit four copies from their mother and eight repeats from their father. So far, only the variation in the number of repeats at one location has been considered, but many hundreds of locations are involved, giving rise to a unique genetic profile for every individual in the world. Thus members of a given population can be compared in an attempt to quantify their relatedness. When two DNA samples match completely in a large number of locations throughout the genome, the probability that they could have come from two unrelated individuals is infinitesimally small. Hence DNA identification is extremely reliable.

DNA fingerprinting – sometimes called DNA testing – is a remarkable example of the spin-off to society from scientific research. It has revolutionised the fields of paternity/maternity disputes, criminal investigations and identification of military personnel and disaster victims. To appreciate this revolution, consider the following two case studies. First, consider a maternity case, which is illustrated by the data shown in Figure 13.2. This figure shows DNA fingerprints of six individuals (A–F), five of whom belong to the same family, whereas one does not. The first impression you should get from Figure 13.2 is that there is a fair amount of variation in the band pattern of the six individuals, even though five are closely related. If you look closely at the patterns of bands, you should see that A is somewhat different from the other five. Consider just the patterns of bands in the four rows marked by the red arrows. These bands are common to the DNA fingerprints of individuals B–F, but are missing for individual A.

In fact, these fingerprints were produced to test the relatedness of one of the offspring (C) to the mother (B) and to siblings D–F; in this case, the father's DNA was not available for comparison. The question was, 'Did individual C have the same mother (B) as individuals D, E and F?' The degree of sharing of bands by relatives depends on their degree of relatedness: closer relatives have more bands in common than do more distant relatives. In this particular case, close examination showed that C shared enough bands with B, D, E and F to vindicate the claimed family relatedness. Some of the bands, such as the top one present in individuals D and F only, must have been inherited from the father. In reality, a superficial, visual comparison like this would be insufficient for an accurate analysis of relatedness, and quantitative methods of comparison are generally used.

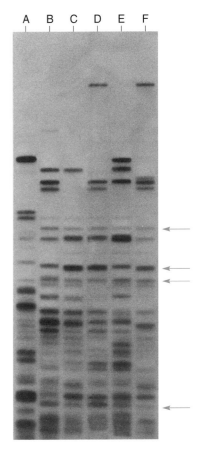

**Figure 13.2** DNA fingerprints of six individuals, A–F. The red arrows point to shared bands in individuals B–F that are missing for individual A. Note that only a portion of the complete fingerprint is shown.

The second case study that demonstrates the usefulness of DNA relates to how DNA fingerprints can be used in forensic science, such as in cases of sexual assault or murder. For example, the DNA from very small samples of blood or semen found at sites of crime can be compared with that of potential suspects. The first forensic case to use the technique occurred in 1986 and was quite dramatic. It involved the assault and murder of a schoolgirl called Dawn Ashworth in Narborough, Leicestershire. A hospital porter, Richard Buckland, confessed to the murder. Dawn Ashworth's murder had many similarities to an unresolved murder three years previously. The question was, 'Did the DNA fingerprint of Buckland's blood match that of the semen found at the scene of both of these crimes?' Genetic fingerprinting showed that the two semen fingerprints were identical but neither matched the fingerprint of Buckland's blood. Buckland was not the murderer!

Five months after Dawn Ashworth's death, the police tested the blood of 5500 men who lived in the area of Narborough. There was no DNA match with the semen found at the scene of the crime. It happened that one of the men tested, called Ian Kelly, mentioned to a colleague that he had stood in for a friend – Colin Pitchfork – at the blood test. Pitchfork had asked him to do this because he was concerned that the police were trying to frame him. However, the police got to hear of this tale and arrested Pitchfork. He confessed to both murders and, importantly, his blood was found to have the same DNA fingerprint as the two sets of semen found at the scenes of the crimes. Proving Buckland's innocence and Pitchfork's guilt were a direct result of evidence provided by tiny samples of DNA extracted from suspects' cells and the technique of DNA fingerprinting.

## 13.4    Genome projects

Genome projects are revealing much information about how genes are organised in genomes of various organisms. Towards the end of the last century, a number of research projects were initiated to elucidate the entire DNA sequence of selected eukaryote genomes and thereby determine their organisation. The most notable one is that of humans. The ultimate goal of the Human Genome Project (HGP) was to discover all the genes and determine the entire sequence and understand every detail of our genome. This started in 1990 with the goal to sequence all three billion DNA base pairs by the year 2005. Sequencing the human genome was a mammoth task. The HGP involved hundreds of laboratories in six different countries, the main centres being in the USA, Europe and Japan.

In 2000, 85% of the three billion base pairs were published, and by 2005 the sequence was virtually complete. However, fully interpreting the sequence will take much longer. The completed genome sequence is being analysed in order to determine gene function, how genes are controlled and how their function is coordinated, and this is done with the help of computerised data banks.

In parallel with the study of the human genome, scientists have been sequencing the genomes of many other organisms. Here the genetic features of the eukaryote genome are examined, by comparing three organisms, *Saccharomyces cerevisiae* (the unicellular bakers' or brewers' yeast, which you met in Chapter 4), *Drosophila melanogaster* (the fruit-fly, which you met in Section 8.3.3), as well as that of *Homo sapiens* (humans). The features you will consider and the relevant data are given in Table 13.2.

**Table 13.2** A comparison of the genomes of yeast, fruit-fly and humans (all figures have been rounded).

| Feature | Yeast | Fruit-fly | Humans |
| --- | --- | --- | --- |
| size of genome ($10^6$ bases ) | 12 | 180 | 3200 |
| number of genes (estimated) | 6100 | 13 000 | 25 000 |
| gene density (average number per $10^6$ bases) | 496 | 76 | 7 |
| number of introns per gene (average) | <1 | 3 | 9 |

The first feature to note is that there are very substantial differences in the size of the genomes of these three organisms. An important point to realise is that the yeast genome is about 15 times smaller than the fruit-fly genome and 250 times smaller than the human one. Given the relatively small size of the yeast genome it is not surprising that this was the first eukaryote genome to be completely sequenced (in 1996). The size range for the three species coincides with the complexity of the organism, which might be expected since more complex organisms require more genes. But an examination of the genome size of other organisms reveals that the correlation is far from precise. Organisms with a similar number of genes can have genomes of very different sizes.

The second feature to note in Table 13.2 is the total number of genes within the genome of the three species. The yeast genome includes about 6000 protein-coding genes representing about 64% of the genome. Expressed another way, 6000 genes are needed to 'construct' this unicellular eukaryote organism. Given the relative complexity of humans compared with yeast, it was somewhat a surprise to learn that humans have only about 25 000 genes (this number had still to be confirmed in 2007), and that humans require only about twice the number of genes needed to build and maintain a fruit-fly.

■   What role(s) might the remaining 36% of the yeast genome play?

☐   Such non-protein-coding regions might be control sequences, repeat sequences or single-copy DNA of no known function.

The repetitive sequences play an important role in determining the compactness of a genome: yeast has about 4% repetitive sequences compared with 50% in humans. The result is that the spaces between genes are much shorter in yeast. Remarkably some genomes appear to be dominated by repetitive sequences, as in the case of maize (*Zea mays*).

A further feature of the data in Table 13.2 show is that the genetic organisation of yeast is much more economical than that of fruit-fly and humans. In order to appreciate the compactness of the yeast genome compared with that of fruit-fly and humans, consider the data for gene density and the average number of introns per gene. The gene density, or distribution of genes, is given as the average number of genes along the DNA double helix per million bases.

■   Compare the gene density in the three organisms in Table 13.2.

☐   A glance at the data reveals that the genes in yeast have a greater density than in the fruit-fly and in turn the genes in fruit-fly have a greater density than in humans.

■ Compare the number of introns in the three organisms in Table 13.2.

☐ The data shows that the genes in yeast have fewer introns than in the fruit-fly and in turn the genes in fruit-fly have fewer introns than in humans.

In fact, a striking feature of all eukaryote genomes is that the genes are not evenly spread along the chromosomes. The distribution of genes varies from region to region within any one genome, so that it is hard to define a typical arrangement of genes for any one species.

Genome projects of organisms other than humans are important for a number of reasons, such as revealing that gene sequences of one species are similar but not identical with those of another species as well as giving clues about biological processes that are common to all living organisms. But why is the Human Genome Project itself important? Many human diseases, such as cystic fibrosis discussed in Chapter 12, are inherited; others at least have a heritable component, such as some forms of diabetes. For cystic fibrosis, we are in the fortunate position of knowing precisely where the gene is located on the chromosome, how big it is, and what its protein product is. Arguably, such knowledge of genes opens the way to cure or prevent diseases. Having determined where these genes are on the chromosomes, and what their precise base sequences are, the function of each gene can be determined. Therefore, the Human Genome Project will provide the basic information required for the development of improved therapies for – at least some – genetically based diseases.

However, the scientific knowledge surrounding such endeavours along with modern scientific technologies raise a number of ethical considerations. One of these is explored in the next section.

Question 13.2

Which one of the following statements (a)–(d) about the distribution of genes in the eukaryote genome is correct?

(a)  Genes are evenly distributed throughout eukaryote genomes.

(b)  There are always at least 7 genes per 100 000 bases in eukaryote genomes.

(c)  Genes are distributed at specific locations on each chromosome and their density is similar on each chromosome.

(d)  Genes appear to be randomly distributed throughout genomes and their density varies greatly.

# 13.5   Ethical considerations

The development of technologies that not only enable individual genes to be identified but can also be used to establish whether or not a particular mutation is present makes it possible to predict an inherited disorder in children. Such procedures when combined with reproductive technologies raise ethical concerns that we all need to engage with and which require regulation. In order to appreciate these concerns, consider one example that often reaches the headlines of news articles – that of the selection of embryos for implanting into the uterus (womb). This procedure uses the technique of *in vitro* fertilisation (IVF), which brings eggs and sperm together to form an embryo outside the prospective mother's body.

■ What is the name for the nuclear division that brings about the production of gametes?

☐ Meiosis (which results in haploid cells).

IVF was originally developed for the purpose of overcoming some kinds of infertility. On 25 July 1978, the world's first test-tube (IVF) baby, Louise Brown, was born in Oldham, England. She was described in the press as 'a miracle of medicine'. From this single birth, the use of IVF as a method of reproduction has exploded throughout the world.

Fertility treatment and embryo research are regulated in the UK by the Human Fertilisation and Embryology Authority. They engage with public opinion to provide confidence about the work researchers are doing. Consider for a moment some of the ethical implications surrounding the technique of IVF alone. This technique has opened up the possibility of moving embryos from one maternal womb to another with implications for the meaning of motherhood. In other words, it is possible for one woman to donate eggs and another to carry the embryo and fetus to term (Figure 13.3). Whose baby is it? If you were offered to participate in such a procedure, would your decision be based on emotional considerations or ethical ones? There are no easy answers here.

**Figure 13.3**   The procedure of *in vitro* fertilisation.

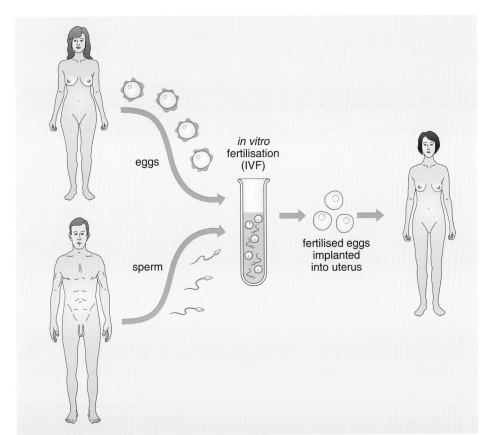

eggs

*in vitro* fertilisation (IVF)

sperm

fertilised eggs implanted into uterus

But IVF also provides access to the eggs, sperm and embryos. With this access comes the possibility of reading the sequence of DNA and manipulating the genetic material and the embryo before it is implanted in the uterus. It is possible to remove one or two cells from individual embryos at an early development stage and then use sophisticated molecular techniques to determine whether particular genes/alleles are present or not. Removal of one or two cells for analysis following IVF before implanting into the uterus does not affect the development of the embryo. Hence by combining our ability to identify individual genes with the procedure of IVF, embryos can be tested for the presence of mutations, and only those free of particular alleles implanted. For example, those embryos with two, or even one, damaged cystic fibrosis genes can be selected out. Similarly those embryos produced by means of IVF with genetic diseases such as haemophilia (defects in blood clotting), Huntington's disease (a degenerative disease of the nervous system) and muscular dystrophy (a muscle-wasting disease) are currently discarded in the UK.

Some couples require IVF treatment because they are unable to conceive naturally, but there is a question as to whether a woman who can have children naturally should go through the IVF process. For example, should couples known to be carriers of the cystic fibrosis mutation be offered IVF? Some individuals consider selecting an embryo that does not carry mutations is a more acceptable option than having to make a decision about terminating a pregnancy of an affected embryo. This is particularly so since the test for an affected embryo occurs whilst it is in the uterus, at a later stage of development than tests *in vitro* prior to IVF. The choice of giving birth to an affected child or terminating the pregnancy is not an easy one to confront.

## 13.6    Summary of Chapter 13

Bacterial genomes are relatively simple, consisting mainly of protein-coding sequences. In contrast, eukaryote genomes are larger and much more complex.

In both prokaryotes and eukaryotes there are sequences that are transcribed into tRNA and rRNA.

Eukaryotes have several types of other non-protein-coding sequences such as single-copy DNA, long repeated sequences dispersed throughout the genome and short, serially repeated sequences of a small number of bases that have, as yet, no known function. Protein-coding genes are embedded within these repeat sequences and non-coding single-copy DNA. Eukaryotes have control sequences, which regulate the 'switching on' and 'switching off' of genes.

The technique of DNA fingerprinting enables genetic variation to be visualised and genetic relatedness to be measured.

The DNA sequences of selected eukaryote genomes, notably those of yeast and human, are being investigated in genome projects.

Ethical considerations emerge with the development of reproductive technologies and as knowledge of our genome expands.

# Chapter 14
# Evolution, selection, species and populations

So far in this book, you have become aware of the very large number of very diverse species on the planet, which are nevertheless clearly related to one another (Chapter 3). Also you have seen that organisms are generally well adapted to their particular way of life, within a specific environment. However, until now you have not studied the mechanisms underlying such diversity. Diversity and adaptation are important observations linked together by the concept of evolution. In this chapter, you will look at the processes that contribute to evolution and their impact at the level of both the individual and the population. The visible characters of individuals – their phenotypic characters – are influenced by their genes – their genotypic characters. So, in investigating evolutionary processes, both phenotype and genotype must be considered. Observations and experiments all provide evidence for evolutionary processes and there are examples of both in this chapter. When you have finished the chapter, you should be able to formulate questions about the natural world, from an evolutionary standpoint.

## 14.1   Adaptation and evolution through natural selection

The word 'evolution' means 'change over time' and it can be used in relation to anything that has a history; thus, it could refer, for example, to the evolution of the motor car or of parliamentary democracy. Biological **evolution** refers to the fact that the many organisms that inhabit the Earth today are different from those that existed in the past, and changes can be observed now that represent continuing evolution. The processes that have brought about changes among living organisms are many and varied and one of them is natural selection.

This section describes the theory of evolution by natural selection as proposed by Charles Darwin (Figure 14.1) in his book *On The Origin of Species by Means of Natural Selection, or The Preservation of Favoured Races in the Struggle for Life*, first published in 1859. Incidentally, the title of this book, which is generally abbreviated to *The Origin of Species*, is somewhat misleading, as Darwin wrote rather little about how new species are formed, but did write a great deal about adaptation. It is important to note that, at the time when Darwin was writing, there was no knowledge of the mechanism for a crucial aspect of his theory – the passing of characters from parents to offspring. Research by Gregor Mendel on the inheritance of characters in peas was published in 1865, only six years after the first edition of *The Origin of Species*, but it did not get disseminated widely and remained generally unknown until 1900. However, Darwin was aware that inheritance is a fundamental feature of living things, but he had no knowledge of DNA or chromosomes. This section looks at natural selection as Darwin did, taking inheritance for granted, but ignoring the mechanisms underlying it.

**Figure 14.1**   Charles Darwin (1809–1882) briefly studied medicine in Edinburgh before going to Cambridge intending to become an Anglican clergyman. Soon after the voyage of the *Beagle* (1831–1836), during which he was gentleman companion to Captain Fitzroy, Darwin became convinced that biological evolution had occurred *and* saw how it could have been brought about by natural selection. Despite having gathered massive amounts of supporting evidence, Darwin refrained from publishing his revolutionary ideas on evolution for about 20 years until he was almost 'scooped' in 1858 by Alfred Russel Wallace (1823–1913). Darwin continued to live quietly in the country and although plagued by ill health, worked on a wide variety of biological problems, as the rest of the world struggled to come to terms with the implications of evolution.

You have almost certainly heard of natural selection before and probably have an idea of what it means, but the way that the term 'natural selection' is often used in newspapers, for example, can be misleading. To clarify the scientific meaning, first the theory of natural selection as set out by Darwin is described, and then follows a specific example that illustrates evolution by natural selection.

### 14.1.1    Darwin and natural selection

While Darwin knew nothing about the mechanism of inheritance, he was very aware of many other aspects of living organisms. Among these, three are particularly emphasised in his theory:

- The species that inhabit the Earth today are not the same species that existed in the past, although they do resemble them. This aspect of evolution was very apparent to Darwin from the fossil record.

- Each species possesses a number of characters that adapt individuals within that species to their way of life and their particular environment. Much of *The Origin of Species* is devoted to detailed descriptions of the adaptations of individual species, for example the various beak shapes of finches on the Galápagos Islands (Section 14.4).

- Selective breeding of domestic species can produce characters in a diversity of forms. For example, dog breeders have produced numerous breeds that differ in characters such as ear length, stature and behaviour: different breeds have different forms of a character.

Darwin's theory of **natural selection** can be expressed as four propositions. These propositions are so important to an understanding of evolution through natural selection that you should try to remember them, although not necessarily word-for-word.

Darwin's four propositions are:

1   Within a given species, more individuals are produced by reproduction than can survive within the constraints (e.g. food supply) imposed by the species' environment.

2   Consequently, there is a **struggle for existence**, because of the disparity between the number of individuals produced by reproduction and the number that can survive.

3   Individuals within a species show **variation**; no two individuals are exactly alike (not even those referred to as 'identical' twins). Those with advantageous characters have a greater probability of survival, and therefore of reproducing, in the struggle for existence.

4   Individuals produce offspring that tend to resemble their parents (the principle of **inheritance**). Provided that the advantageous characters that promote survival are inherited by offspring, individuals possessing those characters will become more common in the population over successive generations because they are more likely than individuals not possessing those characters to survive and produce offspring in the next generation.

The essence of Darwin's theory is that natural selection will occur if three conditions are met. These conditions, highlighted in bold above, are a struggle for existence, variation and inheritance. These are said to be the *necessary and sufficient* conditions for natural selection to occur. To say that the three conditions are *necessary* means that, unless all three conditions are met, natural selection will not occur. Thus, it will not occur if reproduction does not produce more progeny than can survive, it will not occur if a character does not show variation, and it will not occur if variation does not have a heritable basis. To say that the three conditions are *sufficient* means that, if all three conditions are met, natural selection will inevitably occur and this *can* lead to change in the characters of a population from one generation to the next.

Darwin was concerned with evolution, i.e. change over time, and he proposed a process, natural selection, that could bring about such change. Evolution through natural selection is the main focus here. However, it is important to bear in mind that natural selection is also a process that can *prevent* change, i.e. promote stability. In other words, natural selection can occur *without* evolution. Furthermore, there are factors other than natural selection that affect evolution (some of which are considered in Section 14.1.3). The three conditions listed above are necessary and sufficient for natural selection to occur, rather than for evolution to occur. Nevertheless, the vast majority of biologists accept that *natural selection is the most important process by which evolution is brought about*.

Here we will look a little more closely at the three necessary and sufficient conditions and consider how likely it is that they will be met. The first, a struggle for existence, is probably almost always met, because living organisms produce more progeny than are required to replace their parents when they die. The second condition, variation, is often but not always met. Some characters show virtually no variation between members of a species, whilst other characters show considerable variation. The third condition, inheritance, is only sometimes met; not all variation has a heritable basis.

■ Before reading on, take a few moments to think about variable characters of animals that might *not* be entirely heritable.

☐ You might have thought of size, or strength of muscles.

For example, toads vary in size. The two factors that make the largest contribution to variation in the body size of toads are variation in age (toads continue to grow throughout their lives) and variation in their environment (e.g. a good food supply). These are both external causes (i.e. body size is not a result of particular characters possessed by the toad). So body size in toads is not primarily an inherited character.

This last point leads on to an important aspect of natural selection, which was much discussed when Darwin first proposed his theory. This debate concerns the possible *inheritance of acquired characters*. As well as growing, individual organisms may develop particular skills or physical characters during the course of their lives as a result of differences in the way they live. Consider the human practices of body piercing, circumcision and decorative body scars. These characters, which are acquired deliberately during the course of an individual's life, are not inherited by that individual's offspring even though the practice may have been carried out for hundreds of generations. Likewise, a plant that has grown particularly large in a patch of good ground, or a toad that has grown very big because it lives in a garden full of food, will not pass their large size on to their progeny. So, inheritance of *acquired* characters does not occur.

Inheritance of a character occurs only if that character is passed from one generation to the next during reproduction. In other words, it is reproduction that is the crucial factor in natural selection. In a nutshell, natural selection is about the reproduction – rather than the survival – of the fittest. The term 'fitness' has a very particular meaning in biology, which is discussed below.

### The concept of fitness

Biologists often use familiar words in special and unfamiliar ways. One such word is 'fitness', a very important concept in the study of natural selection. In everyday language, fitness is something that is acquired by taking exercise; in biology, it is a measure of an individual organism's biological *success*.

■ How would you rate the success of an individual organism?

☐ A successful individual is one that leaves many descendants.

To say that fitness is a *measure* of individual success means that it is not just an abstract concept but something to which can be assigned a specific numerical value. Here you will first explore the meaning and definition of fitness and later, in Section 14.2.1, using the example of clutch size in birds, learn how it can be measured in nature.

The second part of Darwin's third proposition says that 'Those [individuals] with advantageous characters have a greater probability of survival, and therefore of reproducing, in the struggle for existence'. The concept of fitness relates to the 'greater probability' referred to in this sentence. Individuals certainly vary in their probabilities of survival. Although Darwin emphasised the importance of variation in those characters that enhance survival, he also recognised that, for such variations to evolve, they must be passed on in reproduction. The modern view of fitness emphasises the reproductive success of individuals, defined as the number of an individual's progeny that survive to adulthood, relative to that of other individuals. However, an individual might produce many offspring that survive to reproductive age but which themselves fail to reproduce, perhaps because they are less robust than other individuals or because they are the sterile progeny of a hybrid mating. The full definition of fitness, therefore, incorporates the reproductive success of the progeny:

> **Fitness** is defined as the *relative* ability of an organism to survive and leave offspring that themselves survive and leave offspring.

This definition is simple and concise, but it is not a convenient one for an evolutionary biologist who seeks to measure fitness in a natural population.

Consider the example of great tits that you studied in Chapter 7. Suppose, for example, that you wanted to measure fitness in a population of great tits. It is obvious that you would have to record the fledging success of many pairs of great tits, not just for one year, but for as long as the longest-lived bird. Great tits can live for up to six years. You would also have to follow the survival and breeding success of all those birds' progeny, some of which might also live for six years. Thus, to measure accurately the fitness of a single cohort of great tits (i.e. all the birds born in a given year) would take something like 13 years. A succession of biologists in Oxford has effectively done this over 50 years. Great tits lay easily counted numbers of eggs in convenient nest boxes. However, not all animal species can be as easily studied.

■ Suggest examples of animals where such a study would be difficult.

☐ Animals with very long lifespans would not be easy – some tortoises live for a hundred or more years. In other species, the number of progeny produced might be too huge to count – some fishes shed millions of eggs into the ocean. Accurate measurements of fitness for such animals are clearly impossible.

Because it is often so difficult to measure fitness accurately, in most studies of animals and plants researchers measure one or more **components of fitness**. Examples include survival to reproductive age, number of fertilised eggs produced, and number of surviving young. What these components have in common is that they are to some extent inherited. The ability of an individual to lay a large clutch or produce offspring that survive is partly determined by what that individual inherits from its parents. Many other factors affect the survival of offspring (e.g. the abundance of predators) but, because these other factors are not inherited, they are not components of fitness.

There is one final, but extremely important, point about fitness in the context of natural selection. What matters is not the actual value of an individual's fitness in terms of the number of its progeny that survive to reproduce, but which individuals have *higher* fitness than others. Fitness is thus a *relative* measure, with the most fit individual in a population being assigned the value 1. All other individuals have their fitness expressed as fractions or proportions of 1. Thus, if the fittest bird in a population of great tits leaves ten offspring that survive to reproduce, a bird that leaves five offspring has a fitness of $\frac{5}{10} \times 1 = 0.5$.

Up to this point, evolution and natural selection have been considered from a theoretical viewpoint. For any theory to be of value, it has to be both testable experimentally and predictive, in the sense that you can erect a hypothesis to test. Lots of experiments have been designed to test natural selection. One of these will be used to explore Darwin's propositions in an experimental situation.

### 14.1.2   Natural selection in the guppy

The guppy (*Poecilia reticulata*) is a small fish whose natural habitat is small streams in northern Trinidad, but it is also a popular aquarium fish. Male and female guppies are very different in appearance (Figure 14.2); they are said to show sexual dimorphism (Section 3.1) as male guppies are very much more brightly coloured than females. This section considers how natural selection influences bright coloration in male guppies, and will do so by considering each of Darwin's four propositions in turn.

**Figure 14.2**   A variety of guppies produced by selective breeding by aquarists. The two females in the foreground are relatively plain. The four brightly coloured males show variation in the number, size and colour of the spots on their bodies.

#### 1   Number of progeny

Female guppies begin to breed as soon as they become mature at about three months old; they then produce clutches of eggs, most of which become fertilised, at roughly one-month intervals until they die or become too old. Clutches vary in size from one to 40 eggs; the average clutch contains about ten eggs. Thus, female guppies produce a large number of offspring during their lives, far more than can survive to maturity.

#### Question 14.1

Suppose that, in a particular stream, the size of a population of guppies stays more or less stable over several years. How many of a given female's offspring, on average, must survive to reproductive age in such a population?

Given the large number of fertilised eggs produced by female guppies, and the fact that, on average, only two survive to reproduce, it is clear that there is very high mortality among young organisms in this species. This obviously meets the first of Darwin's propositions. Guppies are fairly typical organisms and illustrate that mortality in nature is typically very high. This mortality provides the background against which natural selection acts.

## 2 The struggle for existence

During their lives, guppies face a variety of environmental hazards which cause mortality. They must find food and, if food supply is limited, some will die through starvation. Heavy rain periodically causes floods that may wash a large part of a population out to sea; occasional droughts cause populations to perish when streams dry out. Like all organisms, guppies are attacked by a rich variety of parasites and diseases. Of most interest in this discussion is that guppies are preyed upon by larger, predatory fishes. Of importance to what follows is the fact that, in their natural habitat, some streams contain many predatory fish, others contain few or none. There is thus variation in the level of predation to which wild populations of guppies are subjected.

## 3 Variation

Guppies vary in a number of characters; in particular, male guppies vary in the number, size and brightness of the coloured spots that decorate their bodies (Figure 14.2). This variation can be detected within a single population in a given stretch of stream, but is much more obvious when different populations, from different streams, are compared. Biologists working in Trinidad have shown that this variation is related to the presence of predatory fish. Male guppies from streams where predators are absent are much more brightly coloured than those from streams that contain predators. The underlying variation that results in the colour varieties in the guppy is random.

### Question 14.2

Suggest an explanation, in terms of adaptation, for the relationship between the presence or absence of predatory fish in streams and the brightness of male guppies.

As you will see shortly, the explanation given in the answer to Question 14.2 is supported by other observations. But it does beg an important question, 'Why are male guppies brightly coloured at all?' It is quite common among animals that males are more brightly coloured than females. The explanation for this is quite complex, but can be summarised briefly. In the majority of animal species, males are the more active partner in initiating mating behaviour and they perform a variety of behaviour patterns to attract the attention of, and stimulate, females. Commonly, females are more effectively attracted and stimulated by the most brightly coloured males, giving such males an advantage in terms of enjoying a higher mating success. For example, peacocks with the greatest number of 'eyespots' in their tails mate with more females than those with fewer eyespots. Likewise, male guppies with more brightly coloured spots are more attractive to females than are those with fewer spots.

The possibility that bright coloration makes male guppies more conspicuous to predators, and the observation that such males are more attractive to females, suggests that the evolution of coloration in male guppies must be seen as an example of a **trade-off**, that is the balance of advantage lies with being attractive and hence conspicuous to females despite the risk of being more conspicuous to predators. Moreover, the point of balance in this trade-off is likely to differ between streams or to shift over time in any one stream, depending on the presence or absence of predators. This example illustrates an important point about trying to explain specific characters of organisms in terms of adaptation. It is not sufficient to explain adaptations just in terms of their apparent advantages. Characters typically also involve costs of some kind and so the actual form of a particular character is the result of a trade-off between costs and benefits.

### 4  Inheritance

The adaptive explanation for bright coloration in male guppies given above can only be correct, and can only have evolved by natural selection, if male coloration has a heritable basis. Direct evidence that it is a heritable character is of two kinds. First, a wide variety of decorative guppies have been bred for sale on the aquarium market (Figure 14.2). Such forms could not have been produced if male coloration were not heritable. Second, if samples of guppies are taken from different Trinidadian streams and bred in the laboratory, they yield male offspring that resemble their fathers; stocks derived from predator-free streams are more brightly coloured than those from predator-rich streams.

The discussion so far of the biology of guppies has concentrated on whether the necessary and sufficient conditions for natural selection exist in this species. The fact that they do exist strongly supports the hypothesis that male coloration has evolved by natural selection. However, this does not constitute a direct, rigorous test of the hypothesis. A series of experiments carried out during the late 1970s by the American zoologist John Endler did put the hypothesis to such a test.

In one of his experiments, Endler built several artificial ponds and stocked each with a population of guppies derived from several different localities in Trinidad. At this stage, guppies were the only fish in the ponds. There was considerable variation among males in the number of their spots, but the mean number of spots per male across all the populations at the start of the experiment (time = 0 months) was 10 (Figure 14.3). He left the ponds alone for six months, then sampled the populations in each of the ponds and counted the number of spots on the male guppies. He found that the mean number of spots per male had increased to 11.8 (Figure 14.3).

■ What adaptive explanation can you suggest for this increase in male spot number?

☐ In the absence of any predatory fish, natural selection had favoured an increase in spot number. The more heavily spotted males had more offspring because they were more attractive to females.

Six months may well seem a remarkably short period of time for such a change to have come about. Indeed it is, although it is not the actual time that is important. A guppy breeds several times during its life, known as **iteroparity** (or, alternatively, the guppy is iteroparous), and over the course of six months, Endler's artificial populations were able to reproduce several times.

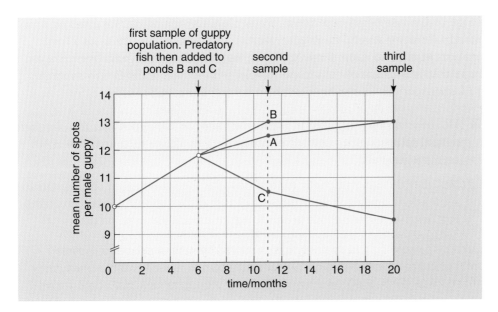

**Figure 14.3** Results of Endler's experiment with artificial populations of guppies (for description, see text).

■ Why is the number of breeding episodes more significant than the time in months?

☐ Because, at each breeding episode, females choose the most attractive males with which to mate. The more attractive males, i.e. those that have more spots, father more offspring and as spots are inherited, those offspring have more spots.

Having sampled his populations at six months, Endler divided them into three groups (A, B and C).

1 To each group C pond, he added one individual of a fish called *Crenicichla alta*, which is a particularly voracious predator of guppies.

2 To each group B pond, he added six individuals of another predatory fish called *Rivulus hartii*, which does not prey on guppies.

3 No additional fish were added to the group A ponds.

The ponds were then left alone for a further five months (time for guppies to breed several more times), at which point he sampled them again and counted the number of spots on the male guppies.

■ From Figure 14.3, how did the mean number of spots per male differ between the time of the second sample (at 11 months) and the time of the first sample (at six months) for the three groups of ponds?

☐ The values for groups A and B had increased slightly from 11.8 to 12.5 and 13.0 spots, respectively. However, the value for group C had declined, from 11.8 to 10.5. The populations had therefore diverged in terms of mean male spot number.

In the final phase of his experiment, Endler left his populations for a further nine months (time for several more generations), after which he carried out a final analysis of male spot numbers. At 20 months, the populations had diverged even more than at the time of the second sample, with groups A and B now averaging 13.0 spots per fish and group C averaging 9.5 (Figure 14.3).

■ Do the results summarised in Figure 14.3 support the hypothesis that, through natural selection, the presence of predatory fish affects the number of spots on male guppies?

☐ Yes, they do. Several guppy generations after the introduction of predators to some ponds, male guppies in those ponds that contained voracious predators had fewer spots than those in ponds that contained either no predators or predators that are innocuous to guppies.

## Question 14.3

The purpose of the group C ponds was to see what the effect would be on the guppy populations of adding a voracious predator after several generations in which there had been no predation. What do you think was the purpose of the group A and B ponds?

This example has illustrated four important points about natural selection. First, provided the three necessary and sufficient conditions (struggle for existence, variation and inheritance) are met, the form of a character can change from generation to generation. Second, the form of the character that results from natural selection represents a trade-off between the various ways in which that character affects the survival and reproduction of individuals. Third, natural selection can lead to a quite marked change in the form of a character in only a few generations. Finally, and perhaps most crucially, it shows that the theory of natural selection can be tested by carrying out experiments.

### 14.1.3   Other influences on evolution

One of the key requirements for natural selection to occur is that there is variation upon which selection can act. However, it is extremely important to appreciate that natural selection does not itself *cause* that variation; it simply acts on existing variation. The processes that do bring about variation are therefore major components of evolution.

■ Using information from Chapter 9, what process might be a source of variation in individuals?

☐ The most important of the processes is really the ultimate source of all variation: mutation.

As you read in Section 9.5, a mutation is an alteration in the genetic material that is copied from parent to offspring – the DNA in the cells of an organism. Such an alteration may be associated with a change in the appearance or behaviour of an individual carrying it. For example, there might be a mutant male guppy that has no spots at all, or one that has an unusually large number of spots. You should also remember that sexual reproduction brings about further variation by 'shuffling' the genes and chromosomes between generations Section 8.5.2). Mutations are chance events and you should realise that underlying evolution as a whole are a series of processes that are dependent upon chance. As a consequence, evolution cannot have a predetermined direction. Another element of chance is introduced by genetic drift.

**Genetic drift** is defined as chance variation in the genetic make-up of a *population* between one generation and the next. If, for a few years and purely by chance, the red-haired residents of Liverpool happened to have more children on average than the other residents did, then (as red hair is a heritable character) the proportion of red-haired people in the population of that city would increase. The change would be due to chance and not because red-haired people were better adapted than other people. Genetic drift would be responsible, not natural selection. In a large population, however, genetic drift is unlikely to have a great effect because chance differences in reproductive success between individuals will tend to even themselves out when a large number of individuals are involved. But in very small populations (say, fewer than 20 individuals) genetic drift can have a strong effect because if only one individual happens, purely by chance, to produce more offspring than the others, its characters will become more common in the next generation. Similarly, a particular character can easily disappear from a small population as a consequence of genetic drift.

A somewhat different cause of variation between populations can be illustrated by the case of the Dunker sect. A number of small religious sects emigrated from Germany to the USA in the 18th century and have since married almost exclusively among their own numbers. The Dunkers are a sect that settled in Pennsylvania. The frequency of blood group A in the general population of Pennsylvania is 42%, and in Germany it is 45%. However, 60% of Dunkers are of blood group A.

■ How would you account for the unusually high frequency of blood group A among the Dunkers?

☐ The small number of emigrants who established the Pennsylvania population in the 18th century must have included an unrepresentatively high number of people with blood group A. Marrying almost exclusively amongst themselves has preserved the high frequency of the A blood group.

For obvious reasons, this phenomenon is known as the **founder effect**. The frequency of a particular character in a particular population, in this case the frequency of blood group A in the Dunker population of Pennsylvania, may be due more to chance (the frequency of the character in the small founding population being different from that in the population from which it was derived) than to natural selection.

You will have cause to think about the founder effect again when you take a virtual field trip to the Galápagos Islands as part of Activity 14.1, for early colonisers of islands may bring with them a subset of genetic characters from their population that is not representative of the population as a whole.

## 14.2   Interactions

Short-term fluctuations and long-term changes in the environment mean that organisms have to adapt continually to new conditions. Even if the Earth were not subject to physical and climatic changes, the environment in which organisms live would not be constant. This is because species live and interact with each other. There is probably no species on Earth that suffers neither predation nor parasitism. Top predators of food chains may suffer only the problem of parasites, but individuals of most species are probably affected by both. Thus any evolutionary change in one species alters the environment for other species, which in turn have to adapt. Such interactions between an organism and its physical environment, and between one species and another, *drive* adaptation and maintain much of the genetic variation on which selection acts.

These continual evolutionary battles are commonly referred to as the **Red Queen effect**. In Lewis Carroll's *Through the Looking Glass*, the Red Queen was famous for telling Alice, 'Now here, you see, it takes all the running you can do, to keep in the same place'. In other words, it is necessary for organisms to constantly change if they are to survive. The forces that drive change are known as **selection pressures** and they may be constant or changing. The overall balance of a multitude of different selection pressures upon a single organism often shifts and there is a change of evolutionary direction.

In this section, you will read about the Red Queen effect and consider how fluctuations in the physical environment and interactions between species drive evolutionary change.

### 14.2.1   Interaction with the environment

If the environment in which organisms live were stable, one could envisage that natural selection could produce organisms that were perfectly adapted and so did not become extinct. However, the physical environment is far from stable, and changes in two principal ways:

*Short-term fluctuations*

We know from personal experience that the weather changes from year to year: there may be a warm, sunny summer one year, a wet one the next. Climatic fluctuations are the cause of numerous biological fluctuations; for example, changes can occur in the time of the year that plants flower, which will affect any organisms that are dependent on them for food, such as insects that feed on the nectar and herbivores that consume the fruits and seeds they bear.

*Long-term trends*

The Earth's climate keeps changing in the long term. Over geological time, the Earth has gone through a succession of glacial periods separated by warmer interglacial periods. There is substantial evidence that the effects of human activities on the Earth's atmosphere are raising surface temperatures on the planet, which may result in major changes in both the abundance and geographical distribution of numerous species. Both short-term fluctuations and relatively long-term trends are shown in Figure 14.4 (which you should recall from Book 1, Chapter 3).

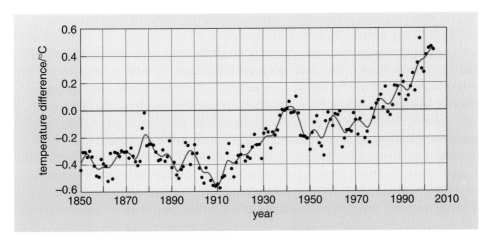

**Figure 14.4**    Variations in the global mean surface temperature (GMST) of the Earth over the period 1850 to 2004. Note that temperature fluctuates from year to year and that there is an underlying upward trend. (The 1961–1990 GMST is indicated by the horizontal line at a temperature difference of 0 °C and represents about 15 °C.)

If natural selection is viewed as a process that causes animals to approach perfect adaptation, it is as if the goalposts keep moving, so that perfect adaptation can never be achieved. This is where the Red Queen effect comes into play. This effect is well illustrated by the size of clutches of birds' eggs. In any given year, there is an optimal clutch size, determined by the food supply available during the nestling stage. Only some birds will lay a clutch of that size. In years of very unusual conditions, the optimal clutch size may be very different from the mean clutch size, so that only a few birds get even close to it. Natural selection will favour those individuals whose clutch size is closest to the optimum, so that alleles for clutch sizes near the optimum value will increase in frequency in the next generation. The next year, however, will typically bring different conditions; there will be a different optimal clutch size and different alleles will be favoured.

It is important to appreciate that, while natural selection favours an increase in the frequency of alleles that confer fitness advantages, at the same time it reduces the frequency, and may eliminate altogether, alleles that do not. In many organisms there can be very high mortality. This mortality involves the loss of a huge amount of the genetic variation that exists in natural populations. Suppose that a population of great tits (*Parus major*) experiences, alternately, a succession of warm springs and a succession of cold springs. During the mild years, alleles for larger clutch size will increase in frequency and those for smaller clutches will decline. When cold springs return, selection favouring an increase in alleles for smaller clutches will only be effective if natural selection has failed to eliminate all the 'small-clutch' alleles in the population. If natural selection has eliminated them during warmer years, clutch size will remain high and the great tit population may go into sharp decline as a result. Reduced population size exacerbates this effect and makes extinction more likely, because there is obviously less genetic variation in a small population than there is in a large one.

The effect of small population size is illustrated by the recent history of the northern elephant seal (*Mirounga angustirostris*), a species that lives in the Pacific Ocean and breeds on the west coast of North America (Figure 3.3a).

At one time, elephant seals were ruthlessly hunted (for the oil they contained) and very nearly became extinct. Hunting has now been banned and their numbers are increasing rapidly. Genetic studies of elephant seals have revealed that they show very little genetic variation between individuals; in other words, the gene pool of the species is very small. Elephant seals are said to have gone through a **genetic bottleneck**. When their population was reduced to a very small size, it also reduced the amount of genetic variation in the population. Even though the population is now increasing again, the amount of genetic variation has not yet increased to previous levels. In Africa, the cheetah (*Acinonyx jubatus*) seems also to have gone through a genetic bottleneck and, in this instance, the resultant loss of genetic variation has had a harmful effect. Cheetahs are very susceptible to a leukaemia-like disease and it is thought that a reduction in their numbers has eliminated alleles that previously conferred some resistance to this disease.

■   In which other context have you come across a link between small population size and reduced genetic variation?

☐   In the founder effect, where a small population that is formed from a large one contains less genetic variation than the larger population (Section 14.1.3).

Thus, the Red Queen effect means that organisms can never be optimally adapted to their environment because it is constantly changing. As a result of natural selection, a species may keep up with environmental fluctuations for a time but, eventually, changes may be such that a population becomes greatly reduced in size. Small populations are especially likely to become extinct, in part because of their reduced levels of genetic variation.

### 14.2.2   Interactions among species

Even if the Earth were not subject to physical and climatic changes, the environment in which organisms evolve would not be constant. Species do not live and evolve in isolation but interact with one another in many different ways, so that any evolutionary change in one species alters the environment for other species. Consider a predator and its prey, for example. The most important cause of mortality in African lions (*Panthera leo*) is starvation among their cubs; many prides of lions cannot catch enough prey to keep their cubs adequately fed. Consequently, natural selection will favour any adaptation in lions that makes them more effective hunters. Such adaptations would, however, impose selection on wildebeest (*Connochaetes taurinus*) and other species on which lions prey, favouring the evolution of better defences against predators. Thus any relationship between species in which one species exploits the other is inherently unstable and contributes to the overall environmental instability that creates the Red Queen effect.

Even more important than predator–prey relationships as a cause of environmental instability are *pathogens* (disease-causing organisms), which include parasites of all sizes, such as tapeworms, and microscopic pathogens, such as bacteria and viruses. Such is the specificity and intimacy of the relationship between pathogens and their hosts that it is clear that each has become adapted in many ways to the other – an example of what is called coevolution. Coevolution refers to specific, reciprocal adaptations between two, or a few, species that have evolved through prolonged, intricate interaction with one another and is not just confined to host and pathogens.

- ■ Recall, from earlier in the course, an example of coevolution.

- ☐ The relationship between the Arum lily and the beetle, which you read about in Chapter 1, is a good example of coevolution.

In the coevolution of a host and a pathogen, the pathogen has a huge advantage. Pathogens typically have a very short generation time and a very high reproductive rate; a bacterium in the human gut can generate several dozen generations in a single day. Although pathogens typically reproduce asexually, their genotypes are subject to mutation, so there is some genetic variation on which natural selection can act. Some viruses, such as HIV and the influenza virus, have very high mutation rates and so generate many, slightly different varieties. As a result, pathogens can evolve, becoming better adapted to the defences of their host, within the host's lifetime.

Any new mutation arising either in the host and causing it to be more resistant to a pathogen, or in the pathogen and causing it to be more damaging to its host, alters the relationship between them and leads to evolutionary changes in the partner. If the pathogen becomes more damaging, the host species will die out if greater resistance does not evolve. If a more effective immune response evolves in the host, the parasite will only survive if more effective countermeasures evolve. For this reason, pathogen–host relationships are evolutionarily unstable and are subject to change over time, favouring one partner or the other at different times.

Coevolution between host and pathogen, one or both of which has a harmful effect on the other, is often likened, incorrectly, to the human arms race, because any adaptation by one side that increases its effectiveness tends to lead to counter-adaptations by the other side. This analogy fails because, in the natural world, coevolution commonly leads to adaptations by each organism that reduce, rather than increase, its harmful effects on the other. This means that pathogen–host relationships tend to evolve towards a situation in which both organisms can coexist without the host being affected as severely as it once was. Is this due to evolutionary changes in the host, the pathogen or both? The history of the disease myxomatosis provides some answers to this question.

The *Myxoma* virus is indigenous to South America. Rabbits (*Oryctolagus cuniculus*) there are prone to myxomatosis (a form of fibrous skin cancer) but do not usually die from the disease. The virus was unknown in other parts of the world until it was deliberately introduced into Australia in 1950 in an attempt to control the rabbit population, which threatened the livelihood of sheep farmers. Rabbits had themselves been introduced to Australia from Europe in the 19th century and had undergone a population explosion. Carried by mosquitoes, the *Myxoma* virus caused an epidemic that killed 99.8% of all rabbits; a second epidemic killed 90% of the generation that resulted from those that survived the first. A third epidemic, however, killed only 50% of the remaining rabbits. This rapid decline in the virulence of myxomatosis was due to two evolutionary trends. The rabbits became more resistant to the virus and the virulence of the evolving virus reduced. The rapid speed of evolution here is striking.

- Why do you suppose that reduced virulence might be adaptive for the *Myxoma* virus?

☐ A pathogen that does not kill its host has a greater opportunity to survive, reproduce and infect new hosts than one that kills its host quickly. At the point when it had reduced the host population by 99.8%, the *Myxoma* virus must itself have been at some risk of becoming extinct.

- At the point when the rabbit population was reduced to 0.2% of its original size, what process do you suppose the gene pool of rabbits went through?

☐ A genetic bottleneck.

- A further – and very important – feature played a role in this evolutionary story. What is it? You need to cast your mind back to the discussion of Darwin's four propositions in Section 14.1.

☐ The important point is variation. There must have been variation in the virulence of the virus, upon which natural selection could act. Similarly, there must have been variation in the rabbits. For example, there could have been a mutation that conferred resistance to infection. This mutation would have had no selective advantage when the virus was absent, but a huge selective advantage when the virus appeared.

The myxomatosis story illustrates the potentially devastating effect that pathogens can have on other organisms. It also illustrates the power of natural selection. Evolutionary biologists have come to regard pathogens as one of the most potent forces in the course of evolution.

The above examples of interactions between species not only reveal how complex these can be, but also show that evolution can occur even in the absence of changes in the physical environment. Both types of interaction, between organism and environment and between species and species, drive change over time within individual species.

Question 14.4

Which of the factors (a)–(f) below would tend to promote genetic diversity and which would lead to its reduction?

(a) Founder effect; (b) Red Queen effect; (c) a constant environment; (d) recombination; (e) a genetic bottleneck; (f) mutations.

## 14.2.3   The language of evolution

In writing about evolution it is very easy to slip into a rather journalistic style that ends up as implying more than you meant to say. Evolution is not directed from outside, depending as it does upon chance events, nor is it influenced by animals and plants themselves. So any statement that implies that an animal or plant evolved a particular character *in order to* do something is clearly wrong. However, such looseness of language is widespread in the mass media and can be misleading. Consider the following photo caption from a book published in 2005. The picture is of a scene in Siberia, with huts built in the snow and two men walking towards the camera in their full polar gear and with two dogs. The caption is:

> Evidence from DNA suggests that humans adapted to the harsh, cold climate of Siberia by evolving the ability to produce more heat from the food they eat.

The way in which the caption is worded is misleading because it implies that humans evolved the ability in order to adapt to the cold, which you will appreciate is not a possibility. No animal or plant can consciously adapt. The wording implies positive action whereas in reality natural selection has been operating. The caption can be easily rewritten without losing any meaning:

> Evidence from DNA suggests that humans who are adapted to the harsh, cold climate of Siberia are able to convert more of the energy from the food they eat into heat.

Knowing that energy can be neither created nor destroyed (Book 3, Chapter 2, the law of conservation of energy) the end of the caption has also been rewritten as the original version implies that heat is produced, which is not correct. Accuracy of language is important in science.

## 14.3  Adaptation and evolution in real time

Up to this point, you have considered examples of evolution and experimentation that support the idea of natural selection. Armed with this knowledge, you are now going to explore the concepts of adaptation and evolution in a natural setting.

---

### Activity 14.1  Galápagos, Sections 1–3

We expect this section of the activity will take you approximately 2 hours.

You will follow in Darwin's footsteps and explore the Galápagos Islands by taking a virtual field trip. Much of what you see will be as he saw it and you will visit a crater lake, just as he did, and search for animals there.

Your base is a ship, with a cabin containing different sources of information to help you – books, videos, maps, etc. After studying the geological and biological history of the islands, you will explore two different environments, observing the diversity of life there. Then, using this information, you will complete some guided exercises on adaptation before moving on to study an example of evolution in real time.

For this activity you should study Sections 1 'Galápagos Past and Present', 2 'Adaptation' and 3 'Evolution in Real Time' of the computer-based activity *Galápagos*.

There are no comments on this activity.

---

## 14.4   From variation to species

There is more to evolution than the changes that take place over time within a single species; evolution can also lead to the splitting of one species into two or more different species. (The definition of a species was discussed in Section 3.1.) This section examines the process of splitting that gives rise to new species.

In your study of the animals on the Galápagos, you have seen how species evolve as both their physical environment and their interaction with other species change over time. However, throughout the history of life, new species have continually emerged, while existing ones have continually become extinct. Even if the figure of 30 million species living today seems a huge one, it is but a tiny proportion of the thousands of millions that have probably existed over the whole of evolutionary time. Extinction is the rule and the vast majority of all the species that have ever existed are now extinct. Extinction is considered in more detail in Chapter 15.

How can the emergence of a new species be explained? It can only happen by the splitting of one species into two or more different species, a process called **speciation**. Without speciation, the world would contain just one species of living organism, descended from the first form of life that ever existed. Some of the species living today have diverged from each other only recently, but others have followed separate evolutionary pathways for millions of years or more.

Many mechanisms have been proposed to account for how speciation might occur, but argument still rages among evolutionary biologists as to which mechanisms could and could not work, and which are likely to be the most common. You have seen how speciation might have taken place in the Galápagos finches after the original population of birds became separated on different islands. In such geographically separated populations, interbreeding is reduced because of the distance between them. If interbreeding is reduced sufficiently, and for long enough, genetic recombination between the two populations will be at such a low level that each population will be able to evolve in a different direction without being swamped by alleles from the other population. When interbreeding between two groups of organisms is reduced sufficiently to allow them to diverge, they are said to be in reproductive isolation from each other (this does not mean necessarily that no interbreeding takes place at all, just that it is reduced to a very low level). Speciation that results from geographical separation is called **allopatric speciation** (literally 'other country' speciation).

It is generally accepted that allopatric speciation, the divergence of two or more populations into separate species after they have become separated geographically, has occurred commonly. However, most suggested mechanisms for **sympatric speciation** ('same country' speciation), the formation of two or more species without any geographical separation between the diverging populations, remain controversial. These two types of speciation are now considered in more detail.

## 14.4.1   Allopatric speciation

In the Galápagos Islands, the finches on different islands are separated by sea, but populations can be separated geographically by all kinds of barriers.

Geographical barriers need not be on a grand scale – a tiny stream can be just as great a barrier for a land snail as the English Channel is for a land mammal. Differences in habitat can also be important – a woodland species may be unable to cross a grassy field to reach the next wood, and a population of fish adapted to living by a rocky coastline may be separated from another population by a stretch of sandy seabed. During evolutionary history, new geographical barriers have arisen constantly, separating populations and creating conditions suitable for allopatric speciation to take place. Land masses have moved apart as a result of plate tectonic motion; mountain ranges have been formed; large lakes have divided into a collection of smaller pools as water levels declined, and have reformed millennia later as water levels rose again; rivers have changed their course; and lava flows from volcanic eruptions or ice flows during glacial periods have cut off one population from another.

### Question 14.5

Make a list of possible geographical barriers that could separate populations. In addition to the ideas already introduced to you, try to think of some of your own.

## 14.4.2   Sympatric speciation

For sympatric speciation to occur, two groups of organisms within the same species must diverge from each other without there being any geographical barrier to separate them. Divergence can take place between two sympatric forms (the ancestral type and a novel type) without total geographical separation, as long as they are reproductively isolated.

■ Recall the term used to describe two or more distinct forms of the same species that occur sympatrically (i.e. in the same geographical area).

☐ Polymorphic species (Section 3.1).

There are a number of ways in which sympatric forms can be reproductively isolated. The two forms may fail to interbreed because, for example, they occupy different habitats within the same area and so do not meet, or they show differences in sexual behaviour, or they become sexually active at different times of year.

The American haw-fly (*Rhagoletis pomonella*), for example, has very specific host-plant preferences. Females lay their eggs only inside fallen fruit from either the hawthorn (*Crataegus* spp., i.e. several species within the genus *Crataegus*) or the apple tree (*Malus pumila*). The larvae develop in the fruit and, when the adult insects emerge, they normally mate on the same food plant and usually lay their eggs on the same food plant. There are thus two sympatric forms of this fly: one that lives and breeds only on hawthorn and one that lives and breeds only on apple trees.

■ What will be the likelihood of interbreeding between individuals of the hawthorn form and the apple form?

☐ The two forms will very rarely interbreed because mating usually takes place on the food plant.

Haw-flies prefer the plant in which they hatched and their offspring are adapted to it. Analysis of proteins in the two sympatric forms has also shown that there are marked genetic differences between them. However, apple trees were introduced into the USA only in the late 18th century and, previous to that, only the hawthorn form of the fly existed. Thus, within the last 100 years or so, a single species of fly has split into two sympatric forms with very little interbreeding between them. Eventually the two forms may become completely separate species.

Insects frequently have very specific habitat preferences, e.g. parasites that have only a single host species, herbivores that feed on only one species of plant, and predators that have only one type of prey. Insects also often show a tendency to mate and lay their eggs in their preferred habitat. So it is not surprising that some biologists think that many insect species evolved by this kind of sympatric speciation. Others believe that **gene flow** (the spread of alleles from one population to another) will usually remain too high to allow speciation to occur in this way.

### 14.4.3   Genetic and phenotypic differences between species

Non-interbreeding populations, whether separated allopatrically or sympatrically, are affected by natural selection in different ways, experience different chance fluctuations in allele frequencies, and are unlikely to develop exactly the same mutations as each other. As a result, the longer two populations are reproductively separated, the more different they are likely to become, both genetically and phenotypically. Differences in allele frequencies between populations or between species can therefore be used to estimate the length of time they have been separated. Closely related species have not been separated as long as less closely related species and the number of genetic differences between them should be smaller. By analysing DNA from different populations or different species, and comparing allele frequencies, taxonomists can work out the *phylogeny*, or evolutionary history, of a group of organisms. This method has allowed taxonomists to work out the phylogenies of many groups of organisms that have traditionally been difficult to classify on morphological grounds alone.

However, there is not always a strict relationship between the amount of difference between genotypes and the amount of difference between the corresponding phenotypes. Some species may look almost identical but be very different genetically, while others may look very different yet be very similar genetically.

■   Think about frogs compared with mammals. Which group shows the greater variation in morphology?

☐   Mammals.

There are thousands of species of frog living today but they all look very similar, even though their genomes may differ substantially. Mammals, on the other hand, show enormous variation in morphology – just think about bats, whales, horses and cats. Yet the genomes of two mammalian species, e.g. a bat and a whale, or a chimp and a human, may show relatively few differences.

## 14.4.4   Speciation past and present

Speciation is not something that just happened in the past. It is going on all around us. We just do not notice it, because the process is generally very slow. There is often quite a lot of variation between populations within a single species, both in genotype and phenotype. A species in a particular geographical area may be polymorphic, like the peppered moth with its light and dark forms, which we are going to look at in Section 14.5.1. Where polymorphisms exist, the different sympatric forms may interbreed freely or be reproductively isolated to a greater or lesser extent. If a particular species has a wide range, it is also quite common for individuals in one part of the range to differ in one or more characteristics from those in another part of the range – they might be larger, for example, or have different coloration.

■   What familiar animal species varies in coloration in different parts of its range?

☐   Humans (*Homo sapiens*) vary in eye colour, hair colour and skin colour in different parts of the world.

Depending on the degree of difference between them, distinct forms of a species in different geographical areas are designated as *races* (slight differences) or *subspecies* (greater differences). Subspecies are recognised by adding a third part to the Latin name for the species. Many of the species of Darwin's finch are divided into a number of subspecies, each found on a different island or island group within the Galápagos. Another example is the crow (*Corvus corone*), which is divided into two subspecies: the carrion crow (*C. corone corone*) and the hooded crow (*C. corone cornix*). The all-black carrion crow is found in Western Europe, including southern Scotland. The hooded crow is grey with a black head, wings and tail, and is found in central and Eastern Europe, northern Scotland

and Ireland. Figure 14.5 shows the area of overlap, where the two subspecies interbreed.

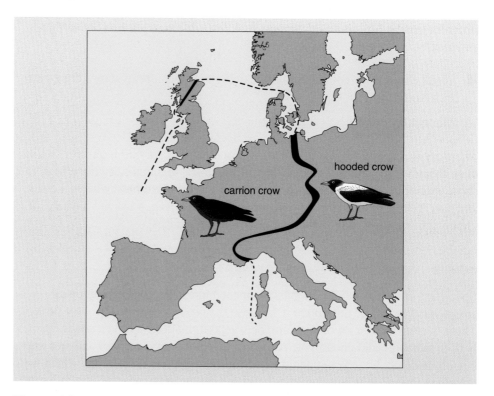

**Figure 14.5**   Map of part of Europe to show the range of the hooded crow and of the carrion crow. The solid black band denotes the area of overlap between the two subspecies, and it runs from the south of Ireland northwards across Scotland, across the North Sea and then down from the Baltic across Germany and Austria to the Mediterranean coast between France and Italy. The hooded crow is found to the east and north of this line and the carrion crow to the west and south. The Isle of Man has only hooded crows.

The various degrees of difference between geographically separated populations or between sympatric forms can be thought of as a 'snapshot' of the speciation process. The process takes place over many generations as differences accumulate. As long as there is little or no interbreeding between diverging populations or between sympatric forms, they will continue to evolve in different directions and will eventually become so different that they are recognisable as completely separate species. The two populations or two forms may become reproductively incompatible at some stage because of a specific change in one of them, or the accumulated differences between them may cause a gradual increase in the degree of reproductive isolation. However, the evolution of reproductive incompatibility is not inevitable. Different species of frogs, for example, with very different genotypes (as determined by analysis of DNA base sequences or of amino acid sequences of proteins) often can and do hybridise easily.

At any one point in time, some geographically separated populations will be just starting to diverge from each other; some will have diverged further into different races, while others will have become subspecies so different that they are almost separate species. Sympatric forms will go through a similar process of gradual divergence, as long as interbreeding between them is sufficiently reduced. The populations or forms that have completed the process are the separate species we recognise today. The ones that have not are seen as examples of within-species variation. This is why is it not always easy for biologists to decide whether a particular group of organisms should be classified as one species or as several.

This does not mean to say that speciation is inevitable. If gene flow between two races or subspecies, or between two sympatric forms, remains high enough, the speciation process will never be completed. Depending on the amount of gene flow and the different selection pressures operating on the two types, either the two types will merge and the species will become uniform throughout its range, or a 'balance' will be maintained with each type occupying a different area or a different habitat but hybridising relatively freely with the other.

If conditions are stable, speciation may not take place. Some species may be relatively stable over long periods of geological time. Recall from Chapter 1 the brachiopod *Lingulella*, which appeared in the Cambrian Period and is still with us today, largely unchanged. Another good example of little or no change over a long period is the coelacanth *Latimeria chalumnae*, which was thought to have been extinct for 70 million years, for it disappeared completely from the fossil record in the Cretaceous Period. A live specimen was caught off the mouth of the Chalumna River in South Africa in December 1938 and subsequently others have been found off the Comoros Islands (off the eastern coast of Africa) and in the Celebes Sea (in the western Pacific Ocean, near Borneo). A third example, which you met in Chapter 1, is *Nautilus*, a shelled mollusc which is very similar to species found in the Cretaceous Period, and also very similar to the ammonites, which were so common in Jurassic and Cretaceous seas and whose fossils can be found in large numbers on parts of the Dorset coast.

■ Suggest a possible explanation for the longevity of these animals.

☐ One thing that they all have in common is that they live in the sea.

The sea provides a much more stable environment than the land. The oceans of the world are all linked, so it is comparatively easy for marine animals to move as sea temperatures change. A word of caution, though: all the ammonites became extinct just after the end of the Cretaceous Period, so being marine is not a guarantee of exceptional longevity in the geological record.

*Molecules and the rate of evolution*

During evolution, one species may be transformed over time into another or a species may split into two or more new species. You read about these two processes in Sections 14.4.1 and 14.4.2. Speciation involves changes in the genotypes of the species and analysing the extent of the differences between two species can indicate how long ago they separated. Consider two species in which a particular sequence of bases in the DNA of a gene differs by four bases. Mutations that involve base substitutions are known to accumulate in DNA at a constant rate for any given gene, so if in the example, a substitution of a single base in that particular length of DNA is known to happen roughly every 1 million years, it is possible to estimate that the separation of the two species took place 2 million years ago. The sequence of DNA for each of the two present-day species is shown in Table 14.1 and there are four base differences between them. One million years ago there would have been only two base differences between the species and 2 million years ago was probably the time when a single species split into two species. The changed bases are underlined in the table.

**Table 14.1** DNA sequences from two hypothetical present-day species, with the four base differences underlined. Assuming that single base changes occur with a frequency of one per million years, the sequences of the two species 1 Ma ago would show only two base differences and 2 Ma ago there would have been no differences.

| 2 Ma ago | 1 Ma ago | Present |
|----------|----------|---------|
| ACTCGATTCCTA | ACTTGATTCCTA | ACTTGATTCCTT |
|  | ACTCCATTCCTA | ACTCCATACCTA |

In the hypothetical example a mutation rate was assumed. Calibration of the rate at which bases are substituted is necessary if the method is to be of any value. Research on human influenza virus has a long history. The virus mutates rapidly (and more rapidly than bird flu virus strains) and it is possible to look at changes that have occurred in the virus over time and calculate a mutation rate. This has been done for a 20-year period for the influenza A virus. The virus has a spherical lipid coat in which are embedded protein spikes. About 20% of these are a protein (neuraminidase) that is involved in the release of new virus particles from an infected cell and 80% are a protein (haemagglutinin) that attaches the virus to the host cell. Researchers sequenced the haemagglutinin gene from flu viruses isolated during the 20-year period and then plotted the number of base substitutions against the year in which the virus first appeared. The result was a straight line, indicating that the base substitutions in this gene accumulate at a steady rate. Knowing this rate, it will be possible to look at new viruses when they appear and work out when they diverged from a common ancestor.

There are different types of both neuraminidase and haemagglutinin. Viruses are categorised according to the types of each protein that they carry. For example, the virus that caused the 1918 flu pandemic was an H1N1 type.

The ability to sequence DNA from different species and then compare them has enabled taxonomists, who have constructed evolutionary trees for living organisms based on anatomical information, to attempt to validate their trees using molecular data. Although DNA data from fossils is rarely available, knowing the rate at which a 'molecular clock' ticks allows a researcher to work backwards and to say, for example, that the last common ancestor of chimps and humans must have lived about 7 million years ago, based on the differences between particular genes in the human and chimp genomes. Molecular data is now being used to study the relationships between the species of Darwin's finches and you will read about some of this after your second virtual field trip to the Galápagos.

*Speciation on Galápagos*

## Activity 14.1 (continued)    Galápagos, Section 4

We expect this activity will take you approximately 2 hours.

In this activity, you will be looking at the process of colonisation of the islands before deploying your knowledge of the processes of speciation in considering how new species of finch might have arisen on the islands.

For this activity you should study Section 4 'Species and Speciation' of the computer-based activity *Galápagos*.

There are no comments for this activity.

*Islands and finches*

There are 13 species of finch recognised in the Galápagos population and on Cocos Island, and some of these have a number of subspecies. For example, the warbler finch (*Certhidia olivacea*) is found on 15 islands but on 9 of these there are subspecies. The species of finch are not evenly distributed between the islands. What factors might explain the uneven distribution? Perhaps the most important factor is the ability of the birds to migrate between islands. They are not particularly strong fliers. Secondly, not all islands offer the same habitats and hence the same range of food sources. Thirdly, competition between species for available niches may prevent some species colonising some islands.

You can get a clearer idea of what might be happening by looking at the distribution of the species across the main islands. Table 14.2 shows the islands, in alphabetical order of modern names, and the species and subspecies that occur on each island. The third column shows the number of those species and subspecies on each island that are **endemic**; that is, they occur on no other island.

**Table 14.2** Distribution of species and subspecies of Darwin's finches on some of the islands of Galápagos and Cocos Island.

| Island (modern name) | Number of species and subspecies present | Number of species or subspecies that are endemic |
|---|---|---|
| Cocos | 1 | 1 |
| Darwin and Wolf | 4 | 3 |
| Española | 3 | 2 |
| Fernandina | 10 | 2 |
| Floreana | 8 | 2 |
| Genovesa | 4 | 2 |
| Isobela | 10 | 2 |
| Marchena | 9 | 2 |
| Pinta | 9 | 2 |
| San Cristóbal | 7 | 3 |
| Santa Cruz | 10 | 0 |
| Santa Fé | 7 | 1 |
| Santiago | 10 | 0 |

Figure 14.6 is a map of Galápagos. Write beside each island the number of species and subspecies found on that island and, in brackets after each number, the number of species and subspecies that are found *only* on that island. Write the numbers either directly on the map or on a copy (you can download a copy from the course website).

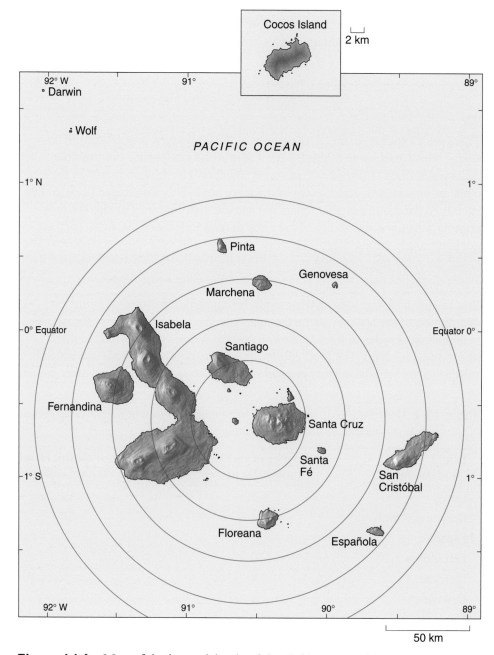

**Figure 14.6**  Map of the larger islands of the Galápagos archipelago.

(a)  Does any pattern emerge from your plotted data?

(b)  What would be a suitable way of expressing the data? The best way would be to work out the percentage of the total number of species and subspecies on each island that are endemic. Try working this out for yourself and add the percentages to Figure 14.6 (or a copy).

You can deduce from your calculations of percentages that the further away from the centre that an island is, the greater the percentage of endemic species that are present. As the birds are weak fliers, the amount of travel between islands is inversely proportional to their separation. Thus the further out the islands are, the greater their degree of genetic isolation and hence the greater the chance that they will develop, as a consequence of genetic drift, a subspecies or species that is endemic, occurring nowhere else.

Recently it has been possible to use a form of DNA fingerprinting technique (Section 13.3.1) to study the relationships between finch species. The technique is called 'microsatellite DNA analysis'. From the analysis, it has been possible to draw up phylogenetic trees (Section 3.3) and one of these is shown in Figure 14.7. The beaks, finch species and island names should be familiar to you after your virtual field trip to the Galápagos. Six islands have populations of *Geospiza difficilis*, the sharp-beaked ground finch. When their microsatellite DNA profiles are compared, two distinct groups are apparent and one population of *G. difficilis* falls outside the group that contains all the other populations.

■  What deductions can you make about the population of *G. difficilis* on Genovesa?

☐  As the population on Genovesa is more closely related to five other species of finch than it is to the other *G. difficilis* populations, it suggests that the Genovesa population is actually a different species.

There are other indications that it might be a different species, notably a difference in size when compared with the other *G. difficilis* populations and a difference in beak shape when compared with other species that group with it in the phylogenetic tree. So, on the basis of the phylogenetic tree, the Genovesa population should be a separate species (as at one time it was – *G. acutirostris*). However, at present, the evidence from the phylogenetic tree is not sufficient on its own to justify a separate species and further work is required on how far there is reproductive isolation between the populations. Recall from Section 3.1 the biological species definition and until it can be shown to apply to the Genovesa population, the population will not be elevated to species status. This example shows clearly the values and limitations of molecular analysis in evolutionary studies.

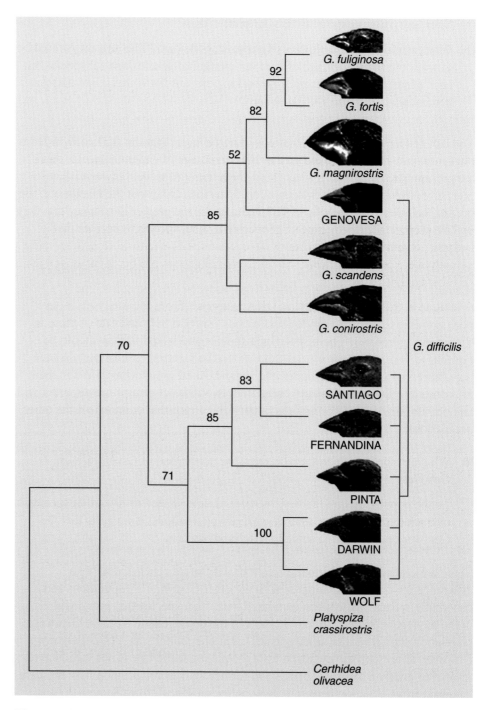

**Figure 14.7** A phylogenetic tree for some of Darwin's finches, drawn up on the basis of microsatellite DNA analysis. The tree shows two distinct groups of finches. Five of the six populations of *Geospiza difficilis* form one group, and five other species plus the population of *G. difficilis* from Genovesa form the other group. The number on each link gives the percentage support for that link – thus the link with 100 that separates the populations on Wolf and Darwin from the other three populations is very well supported. (*Note*: names in capital letters are islands; birds have been photographed in black and white.)

Question 14.7

Which of factors (a)–(g) would tend to hinder speciation and which would tend to promote it?

(a) Large numbers of individuals migrating between two diverging populations.

(b) A genetic bottleneck in which a geographically separate population is reduced to a very small size.

(c) The intense selection operating on a population in a newly colonised, novel environment.

(d) Hybridisation between two diverging populations.

(e) The presence of a polymorphism in a population, such that there are two types of female and two types of male; one type of female prefers to mate with one type of male while the other type of female prefers to mate with the other type of male.

(f) Reduced fertility of hybrids between two populations.

(g) A greater than average number of offspring produced by hybrids between two populations.

## 14.5 Genes, populations and evolution in action

In the oak woodland in Chapter 7, you looked at bird and insect populations and their interactions, as well as the relationships between predators and their prey. In your journey around the islands of the Galápagos archipelago, you studied the selection pressures on the populations of finches and the distribution of finch species between the islands. From your study, you were able to make deductions about the responses to selection pressures in finch populations.

The coloration of guppies and the experiments carried out by Endler (Section 14.1.2) show that during evolution, natural selection changes phenotypic characters in a population. This does not mean that the phenotypic character of every individual in the population is different from all individuals in the ancestral population, although this does happen in the course of large-scale evolutionary changes, such as the evolution of separate species. Instead, on a smaller scale, an evolutionary change in a population involves the change of *proportions* of phenotypes present in a population.

The phenotype of an organism is influenced by its genes. Evolutionary change, therefore, has to be considered at two levels. At one level, it consists of changes in phenotypes in populations over time. At another level, it consists of changes of proportions of alleles in the gene pool – that is, changes in genotype. This section examines an example in which genetic variation, and the associated phenotypic variation, within populations has been associated with natural selection, providing a good example of evolution in action. In this example, changes in the proportions of different forms in a population of a well-studied insect have been observed over long periods of time. It has been possible to relate the changing proportions observed to changes in the relative selection pressures on the different forms. Furthermore, it has been possible to make predictions about how a population might react to a change in selection pressure, predictions that are potentially testable.

### 14.5.1  The peppered moth in Britain

The peppered moth (*Biston betularia*) is quite common in Britain. It flies around at night and rests on the trunks of trees by day, and it is polymorphic, existing in two distinct forms, as shown in Figure 14.8. (There is a third form, called the *insularia* form, which was not studied in the experiments described here.) Prior to 1848, the peppered moth apparently occurred only in the pale, speckled grey

(a)

(b)

**Figure 14.8**  Photographs of the peppered moth, taken by the original researchers and published in a book by E. B. Ford, whose Oxford research group carried out the first experiments on natural selection in the peppered moth. (a) One typical and one *carbonaria* form placed on a blackened, lichen-free tree trunk in polluted Birmingham. (b) One typical and one *carbonaria* form placed on a lichen-covered tree trunk in unpolluted Dorset.

(typical) form, but in that year a completely black individual was reported from Manchester. This darker form, called the *carbonaria* form, rapidly increased in relative abundance until, by 1900, it formed 95% of populations in industrial areas of Britain, while it remained rare in most rural areas. The spread of the dark form, from almost zero to 95% in about 50 generations, illustrates how rapid evolutionary changes can be under certain circumstances.

■ Can you suggest what the scientific source was of the information about the peppered moth history?

☐ Moth collecting has been a popular pastime from early in the 19th century and museum collections – at least those that are well documented – provide specimens covering nearly 200 years.

Differences in the relative abundance of the two forms in different areas were attributed to how well they were camouflaged during the day. In industrial areas, sulfur dioxide pollution kills the pale lichens that grow on tree trunks, making them black in comparison with lichen-covered tree trunks in unpolluted rural areas. Viewed against a background of bark of a tree from a rural area, the pale form of the moth is rather difficult to see, whereas the dark form is very obvious. On the other hand, when viewed against the bark of a tree from an industrialised area, exactly the reverse is true; the pale form stands out, and the *carbonaria* form is nearly invisible. It was hypothesised that birds, hunting for food by day, would find the dark form much more easily than the pale form in rural areas, and the pale form more easily than the dark form in urban areas. This hypothesis was tested by the English entomologist H. Bernard Kettlewell, who caught, marked and released a large number of peppered moths and then recorded how many he recaptured alive in moth traps. Moths that were caught in traps were thus those that had escaped predation by birds. The results are shown in Table 14.3.

**Table 14.3** The proportions of dark (*carbonaria*) and pale (typical) peppered moths, marked and released into the wild, that were subsequently recaptured in moth traps in two localities, one urban, the other rural.

| Locality | Dark form/% | Pale form/% |
|---|---|---|
| Birmingham (urban area) | 53.2 | 25.0 |
| Dorset (rural area) | 6.3 | 12.5 |

■ Does the data presented in Table 14.3 support the hypothesis that there is differential survival of the two forms in the two localities?

☐ Yes, it does. A smaller proportion of the pale form was recaptured in the urban area, and a smaller proportion of the dark form in rural areas.

The results of Kettlewell's experiment are consistent with the hypothesis that birds selectively eat the more conspicuous form of peppered moth in each area, but do not confirm it, as his experiment did not include direct observations of the foraging behaviour of birds. Subsequent observations have confirmed the predation hypothesis, but have also suggested that it is not the only factor involved in maintaining high frequencies of the dark form in industrial areas. For instance, there are certain rural areas of Britain (for example, Norfolk) where the dark form is found at quite high frequencies, for reasons that are not understood.

In a recent book *Of Moths and Men* by the journalist Judith Hooper (2002), the story of the research carried out by Bernard Kettlewell is subjected to scrutiny, and ends with the clear imputation that Kettlewell committed fraud, after being put under pressure by his supervisor E. B. Ford. There is no hard evidence to support this proposition and scientists in a position to know both the work and the people involved have written articles firmly refuting any suggestion of fraud. That experiments conducted over 50 years ago could have been better designed, using today's standards, is obviously true. It is also true that the designs were not as good as they could have been by the standards of that time. But that is a long way from arousing suspicion of fraud. Eight separate field studies carried out between 1966 and 1987 provided tests of the repeatability of Kettlewell's observations – part of the scientific process that assesses the correctness of published work.

What does such a change in the proportions of phenotypic forms in a population involve genetically? Such changes reflect changes in the frequency of different alleles in the population. **Allele frequency** is a measure of the commonness of an allele in a population; it is the proportion of a specific type of allele among all the alleles of a particular gene in the population. The genetic basis of colour polymorphism in *Biston betularia* is simple and well understood. There are two alleles at a single locus ($T$ and $t$), with the allele for dark colour ($T$) being dominant to that for pale colour ($t$). In the first part of the 19th century, the peppered moth gene pool for body colour would have been relatively constant, generation by generation, containing an overwhelming proportion of the $t$ allele. The genotype of almost all individuals would have been $t\,t$. Here and there, mutation would have produced a $T$ allele, so a few moths would have been $T\,t$.

■   What colour would heterozygotes be?

☐   They would be dark, because the dark-colour allele is dominant.

At the phenotypic level, these dark moths would have been disadvantaged through bird predation; almost all peppered moths would have been the pale typical form. The dark form caught in Manchester would have been the result of a mutation.

However, as the Industrial Revolution proceeded and the environment became dirtier, the dark *carbonaria* form would have gained a survival advantage and the proportion of dark moths would have increased. This means that the proportion of alleles for the dark form in the population would also have increased, and the proportion of alleles for the light form would have decreased. Putting it another way, there would have been an increase in the frequency of alleles for the dark form.

At the genetic level, evolution is expressed as change over time in the frequencies of alleles in a population.

Such change cannot proceed without the presence of genetic variation; in this case, there are alleles for the dark form and alleles for the light form, and one or other allele is favoured as the environment (presence or absence of sulfur dioxide pollution) changes. Thus the gene pool of the peppered moths in 1900 would have been very different from that of the population in, say, 1840, because in 1900 it would have contained a high proportion of *T* alleles. What was important for the course of evolution was the existence, albeit at a very low level, of the *T* allele in the gene pool in the 1840s.

The dark *carbonaria* form of the peppered moth is fitter than the pale form in a polluted environment. This illustrates that natural selection acts upon phenotypes. If one phenotype is less fit than another, fewer of its descendants will survive to reproductive maturity, and hence the allele responsible for the less-fit phenotype will be less common in the offspring generation. This can be summarised:

> Differences in fitness among phenotypes lead to changes in the allele frequencies in the gene pool of a population.

In Britain, industrial pollution is now controlled by legislation and, by the early 1970s, levels of sulfur dioxide in the environment had fallen substantially. The impact of this change on peppered moths has been monitored by Open University students taking an earlier version of this course. By 1985, they had collected a total of 1825 peppered moths from 190 localities in Britain. This long-term survey revealed a steady decline in the frequency of the *carbonaria* form across much of Britain so that, by 1985, it existed at very high frequency only in the extreme northeast of England, having largely disappeared from the Midlands. The OU study looked at the whole of the UK; other studies looked in more detail at particular localities.

■ How would the gene pool of the peppered moth in the UK in 1960 have differed from the peppered moth gene pool of today?

☐ The proportion of *T* alleles would have been much higher in 1960 than it is today and the proportion of *t* alleles would have been much lower.

This example of change in allele frequencies in *Biston betularia* shows a number of important points about natural selection, though the full story is far more complicated than could be presented here. It is interesting that there is, as yet, no understanding of the link between the alleles involved in the industrial melanism of *B. betularia* and the expression of melanism in the phenotype.

However, the studies clearly demonstrate that natural selection is dependent on genetic variation. It also shows how, when a favourable allele arises in a population, it can spread very rapidly under the influence of natural selection. In less than 50 years, the *carbonaria* form had become the predominant form in polluted areas. However, natural selection did not favour the dark form throughout the *range* of the species (i.e. the area over which it is found) and the pale form remained predominant in rural areas. This illustrates how natural selection can have quite different effects on gene frequencies in different parts of a species' range. In other words, natural selection, as well as acting upon genetic variation within a population, can also *maintain* such variation, by acting differently on certain alleles in different parts of a species' range. Finally, the example of *B. betularia* shows that natural selection acts on *individuals* (not on the population), but that evolutionary changes that result from natural selection are seen in the *population* (and not in the individual).

### Question 14.8

Which of the following statements about *B. betularia* are true and which are false? Give reasons for your answers.

(a) The increase in the *carbonaria* form between 1850 and 1900 in the UK was due to an increase in mutation rate.

(b) The moths are adversely affected by sulfur dioxide pollution.

(c) The fitness of the *carbonaria* form in urban areas increased over the decades between 1850 and 1900.

(d) As the environment changed between 1970 and 1980, allele frequencies of the colour gene in the Midlands would have changed simply by chance.

(e) The differences in fitness among the two colour phenotypes in the Midlands between 1970 and 1980 would have led to changes in the gene pool.

## 14.5.2   Darwin's finches

Finally, this section returns to the finches to consider a further study that illustrates the increasing influence that molecular genetics has on evolutionary studies. There is a clear relationship between the food source and the beak size and shape in Darwin's finches. Finches with beaks most closely matched to the food source will be selected for over time. However, the genes that underlie the variation in beak dimensions are largely unknown. One that has been studied recently (2006) is a gene that controls the production of a molecule called calmodulin (CaM). CaM is associated with the role of calcium ions in cells. The production of CaM is higher in cactus finches with their long pointed beaks than it is in ground finches with their shorter more robust beaks. The suggestion is that a change in the regulation of this, and other genes involved with beak development, is the primary molecular change that selection brings about. This work is in the very early stages and more detail can be expected in the future.

## 14.6   Summary of Chapter 14

By biological evolution we mean that many of the organisms that inhabit the Earth today are different from those that inhabited it in the past. Natural selection is one of several processes that can bring about evolution, although it can also promote stability rather than change.

The four propositions underlying Darwin's theory of evolution through natural selection are: (1) more individuals are produced than can survive; (2) there is therefore a struggle for existence; (3) individuals within a species show variation; and (4) offspring tend to inherit their parents' characters. The three necessary and sufficient conditions for natural selection to occur are: a struggle for existence; variation; and inheritance.

The frequency of a particular character in a particular population may be due to chance events (e.g. the founder effect and/or genetic drift) rather than to natural selection.

Mutation is a continuous source of new alleles and the ultimate source of variation. Mutation and recombination together produce a huge range of unique genotypes.

Natural selection alters the characteristics of species over time as a consequence of different phenotypes having different fitness.

Studies of the changing frequency of the *carbonaria* (dark) form of the peppered moth in Britain show how the frequency of individual alleles in a population changes under the influence of natural selection. This example shows that natural selection acts on individuals but that evolutionary change resulting from natural selection occurs in the population.

Natural selection cannot always prevent extinctions occurring, because the alleles necessary for adaptation to new conditions may not be present in the gene pool.

Speciation occurs as the result of a reduction in gene flow between two populations, for example when separated by a geographical barrier, as in allopatric speciation, or occupying different habitats within the same area, as in sympatric speciation. Darwin's finches evolved from the birds that originally colonised the Galápagos Islands, mainly by a process of allopatric speciation.

The longer that two species have been separated from each other, the greater the number of genetic differences between them tends to be.

# Chapter 15
# The timeline of life

This final chapter of this book is about evolutionary history, but more importantly it illustrates how, in modern biology, there is an integration of information from a wide range of disciplines in studying a particular problem. There are two case studies that concern evolutionary history but actually draw on environmental, physiological, biochemical, genetic and molecular sciences. First, however, in considering changes over time, it is appropriate to revisit the problem set in Chapter 1 about providing an evolutionary explanation for the existence of unrelated moles. How is it that three animals that look alike and have the same name, at least in English, are not closely related? By this stage in the book you should have sufficient theoretical knowledge to provide an explanation.

■ Apart from their appearance, what other feature links these animals?

☐ The three moles all occupy the same niche in their respective habitats – a burrowing one.

Animals that occupy similar niches are subject to similar selection pressures and burrows are probably more stable habitats than surface ones. Adaptations arise by chance. A mutation that enhances a character related to burrowing will be selected for and the same or similar mutation occurring in two different populations will be selected for in the same way in each. Thus, over time, the burrowing niche will provide a selective advantage for a similar suite of characters in each population. This process is known as **convergent evolution**, because the characters of animals in the same niche but different geographical locations converge as a consequence of being subjected to similar selection pressures. We know that the marsupial and placental mammals diverged in the late Jurassic/early Cretaceous period and from molecular studies we know that the marsupial mole diverged from other marsupials at least 50 Ma ago. So, it might be possible in future to place tentative figures on the time taken for the astonishing convergence to take place.

The marsupial mole has an unusual adaptation not shared with the other two moles. A marsupial rears its young in a pouch – you will be familiar with the kangaroo's pouch. Marsupial moles have a pouch too, but the pouch opening is at the rear, rather than the front as in kangaroos, which means that the pouch does not fill up with earth during burrowing as the opening faces away from the direction of travel.

## 15.1  Adaptation – a case study of Antarctic fish

When carrying out comparative studies, the characteristics of related groups are only understandable if the underlying evolutionary history – the phylogeny – is known. Closely related species are likely to have diverged from a common ancestor only recently, which means that they have not had as much time in which to accumulate differences, when compared with more distantly related species. So, for example, in comparing the resting metabolic rates of different species of fish, mapping the data for metabolic rate onto a secure phylogenetic tree would reveal evolutionary trends.

There is a correlation between environmental temperature and resting metabolic rate. The resting metabolic rate of tropical fish is six times that of Antarctic fish and you can see that there is an energetic advantage in living in cold water in that the energy costs of maintenance are decreased. So you would imagine that natural selection would favour individuals with low metabolic rates. Now that you have studied the evolutionary process, you should immediately be alert to what question to ask: what is the selection pressure that is keeping the resting metabolic rates of tropical fish high?

Clearly the higher metabolic rate of the tropical fish must have a selective advantage. One likely advantage is that with a higher metabolic rate a fish can generate a greater power output, making available more energy per unit time. This might be the result of a selection pressure such as predation making high power outputs advantageous. Recall from Book 3 (Section 4.3) that power is measured in watts. The power output that a fish can generate above the resting level can be measured. For a 50 g polar fish, it is an extra 0.33 watts. For a tropical fish, the figure is 2.05 watts, which is quite a large difference.

■ Why should you expect a correlation between water temperature, metabolic rate and power output?

☐ The rate of chemical reactions is temperature dependent (Book 4, Chapter 10, and Section 5.6.3 of this book) with the rate increasing with increasing temperature.

If the difference in the rates of biochemical reactions in the polar and tropical fish is considered, the effect of the water temperature is even more marked. Rates of most biochemical and physiological processes increase by 2 to 3 times for a 10 °C rise in temperature. The rate of change of such processes is represented as $Q_x$ where $x$ is the temperature change, so $Q_{10}$ lies between 2 and 3.

For polar fish at a temperature of –2 °C, biological processes would proceed at rates between 16- and 91-fold *lower* than tropical fish. This comparison assumes that all the enzymes that catalyse reactions in the two groups of fish respond in the same way to temperature change. There is now evidence that this is not the case. You will know from Section 5.6.3 that enzymes have an optimum temperature for catalysing a reaction.

■ What can you say about the rate of reaction at the optimum temperature?

☐ The rate of reaction at the optimum temperature is at its maximum.

Either side of the optimum temperature, the rate of reaction falls off. Now consider the same enzyme from a polar and a tropical fish. The enzyme could not be at its optimum temperature in both fish, so in one, the rate would be substantially different from the other. Indeed, if you think of the shape of the curve for rate of reaction against temperature (Figure 5.20), if in the tropical fish the enzyme was at or near its optimum, in the polar fish the rate would be very low indeed. In a series of measurements, samples of the same enzyme – lactate dehydrogenase (LDH) (Section 6.4.6) were taken from a whole of range of animals from habitats with different temperatures. The rate of reaction at 0 °C was estimated for each animal. The results are shown in Figure 15.1 and they show that the rate of reaction decreases as the body temperature rises. As the enzyme is catalysing the same reaction in all these animals, the active site (Section 5.5.1) must be conserved, but it also suggests that there must be subtle differences between the enzymes found in the different animals, differences that somehow alter the properties of the enzyme in relation to temperature. Exploring the differences has required analysis of the structure of the enzyme.

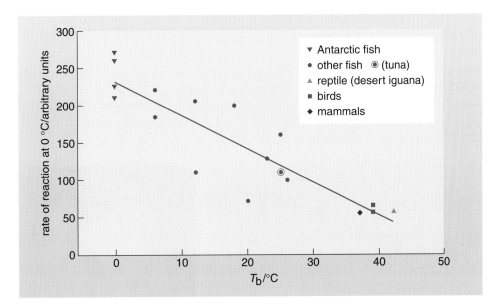

**Figure 15.1** Rate of reaction for the enzyme LDH from the white skeletal muscle of 18 different species, estimated at 0 °C, plotted against body temperature ($T_b$). The line drawn through the points has a negative slope – as the temperature increases, the rate of reaction decreases.

■ What type of molecule is an enzyme?

☐ An enzyme is a globular protein (Section 5.5.1).

■ What techniques might be used to study molecular structure?

☐ X-ray diffraction and sequencing of the amino acids that form the primary structure of the protein are two techniques that could be used.

The chain of amino acids that folds to form the globular protein has been sequenced and this has shown that there are just two amino acids that are different, when comparing the polar and tropical forms of LDH. This could mean that just two base pairs in the DNA have changed and a very small change at the gene level has given a wider range of habitats that fish can occupy.

Of course, the number of adaptations to temperature in fish is far greater than it is possible to describe here. One of particular evolutionary interest is the fact that some Antarctic fish have no haemoglobin in their blood. Cold waters are rich in oxygen and the fish have a relatively low metabolic rate so the loss of the protein that carries oxygen in the blood might not be too significant. What is significant in the present context is the fact that the loss of this particular protein in polar fish has occurred several times, independently, during evolution, an example of parallel evolution. The information about the distribution of protein loss amongst groups is valuable information when it comes to the construction of a phylogenetic tree for fish.

## 15.2    Unravelling evolution – a case study of human evolution

In 1998 in Portugal, archaeologists discovered the skeleton of a human child that had apparently been deliberately buried with some ceremony (Figure 15.2a). Carbon dating gave an age of 23 170 to 20 220 years ago. This date is of great interest to biologists because it is close to the period when the last member of another species of human, *Homo neanderthalensis*, died out, leaving only *H. sapiens* in Europe (although *H. floresiensis* was still present in Asia). The question raised by the find was, 'Which species of human did the skeleton represent?' The skull had been substantially damaged by a bulldozer before the identification of the site as an important archaeological one, but the remaining bones and the post-cranial skeleton were of great interest as they appeared to show characteristics of both species. Was the child a hybrid?

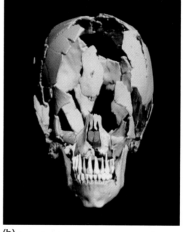

(a)                                                                                          (b)

**Figure 15.2**    (a) The skeleton of the Lapedo child as discovered. (b) Reconstruction of the skull fragments.

There are certain anatomical features of the skeleton that are interpreted as being a mixture of *H. sapiens* and *H. neanderthalensis* characters. When you have a single specimen – and an incomplete one – an identification of a possible hybrid is bound to be controversial, and it has been! From the remaining skull bones (shown in Figure 15.2b), it is clear that the child had a chin (a modern human feature) but a pit in the occipital bone of the skull (lower part of back of cranium) that is a definitive Neandertal feature. The body proportions, especially those of the legs, suggest a mixture between modern human and Neandertal. Overall, the Lapedo child is not a normal anatomically modern human, but nor is it clearly Neandertal. Can research take the identification any further?

Mitochondria have their own molecules of DNA (mtDNA) and there are normally several copies in each mitochondrion (Section 4.3, and introduction to Chapter 13). Unlike nuclear DNA, which is inherited from both parents, mtDNA is inherited from one parent only – the female. The mitochondria in the male sperm are destroyed in the early embryo. As a consequence, there is no recombination as there is in nuclear DNA and mtDNA sequences are inherited unchanged, except for random mutations. Mutations accumulate at a fairly standard rate and so the differences between mtDNA sequences of two individuals can be used to calculate how far back in time they had a common ancestor. A small amount of mtDNA was extracted from the right humerus of the first Neandertal to be discovered (in 1856 near Düsseldorf, Germany) and it was amplified before being sequenced. A sequence containing 379 bases was reconstructed. When the sequence was compared with the equivalent sequence from 994 modern humans, the mean number of differences between all the humans was only $8.0 \pm 3.1$ whereas the mean difference between all the humans and the Neandertal was $27 \pm 2.2$. This suggests that the Neandertal genome is outside the range for modern humans and therefore belongs genetically to a different population. From these differences, it would appear that the last common ancestor of humans and Neandertals lived well before the last common ancestor of all humans. So, it is unlikely that the Neandertal line gave rise to modern humans.

Analysis of nuclear DNA might provide more information, but with ancient bones there are problems with obtaining and analysing DNA.

■ Suggest some of the problems that researchers have to consider when extracting and analysing ancient DNA.

☐ Bones that have been lying in soil for many years will have been in contact with soil organisms and so there may be contamination from other DNA. Skin flakes from the anthropologists carrying out the excavation might also contaminate the specimen with foreign DNA. If the specimens are valuable as complete bones, removing a substantial section for analysis would be damaging.

To give you an idea of the difficulties of working with ancient DNA, of 70 specimens of Neandertal examined for a recent study, only six were suitable at all and only one had a low level of contamination with modern human DNA. Contamination is of very great importance since Neandertals are so closely related to modern humans that large sections of the two genomes will be identical. This one specimen (from the Vindija Cave in Croatia) has yielded sufficient DNA for a million base pairs to be sequenced and for the sequence to be compared with both modern humans and chimps. As we would like to establish whether or not hybridisation occurred between modern humans and Neandertals, the comparison between the three genomes is particularly interesting. In the human genome, there are several hundred places where single nucleotides vary – that is, a particular site is polymorphic, with two or more alleles that differ by just a single nucleotide. So, at each such site in the Neandertal genome there could be the ancestral allele, as found in the chimp, or a derived one, as found in modern humans. In fact, of the sites that have been examined in the Neandertal sequence, nearly 30% of them have a derived allele. This figure is high and has been interpreted as suggesting gene flow *from* modern humans.

So the limited evidence available suggests that Neandertals and modern humans may have interbred and thus the idea that the Lapedo child is a hybrid is at least possible. However, the anatomical evidence is certainly not convincing to everybody. To date, no DNA extraction has been attempted from the Lapedo child and it may well not be possible. Without DNA evidence, the Lapedo child will remain an enigma, but represents an example where anatomy and archaeology, on their own, could not provide a definitive answer but molecular genetics has the potential to do so. Once again, it is the integration of different techniques and disciplines that enables progress to be made.

### Question 15.1

What proportion of the total modern human genome would 1 million base pairs represent?

---

### Activity 15.1   Writing a short account

We expect this activity will take you approximately 30 minutes.

In this activity you will be writing a short piece about a subject that spans more than one chapter in this book. So, in addition to the information given to you in the question, you will need to draw on your knowledge of genetics from Chapters 8–13 and your knowledge of evolution from Chapter 14. This will test your understanding of the material in the chapters, your ability to integrate information from more than one source and your ability to communicate the results to another student.

In no more than 250 words, provide an explanation of the following observation for a fellow student who has read this book up until this point, but no further:

> A mutant allele for a human gene (*CCR5*), that prevents infection by the human immunodeficiency virus (HIV), is present at quite high frequencies in Northern European populations but is essentially absent from all other populations.

The reason that the name of the mutant of *CCR5* is *CCR5–Δ32* is that 32 base pairs have been lost from the DNA that codes for the *CCR5* gene.

To help you in this activity, here is some information from recent (2007) research on the *CCR5* gene and its allele *CCR5–Δ32*. Figure 15.3 shows the frequency of the mutant gene in the populations of Northern Europe. It is also found in Iceland. The frequencies of the mutant allele are high enough to show that it must be maintained by a selective advantage.

The gene codes for a protein that forms a receptor in the cell membrane of human cells that are part of the immune system. The receptor acts in the same way as an enzyme, with a site that a specific molecule can bind with (Section 5.5.1). HIV has a molecule on its surface that can bind to this receptor and so 'take over' the cell. The mutant allele of this gene prevents the receptor forming and so HIV cannot take over the cell and the person with this allele is immune to HIV. The mutant allele is recessive. The drug Maraviroc, which might be used to treat AIDS in the future, attaches to the receptor and prevents HIV from binding to it.

The mutation that produced the mutant allele is a very rare one, estimated to occur only once in 2000 years or so. It is possible to estimate, from genetic data, when the mutation first appeared and this estimate is approximately 2000 years ago. Thus we can be fairly sure that the allele in the Northern European populations only came from one original mutation. We can also suggest that the mutation originated in Scandinavia, on the basis of the frequency data. It probably occurred more than 1200 years ago, as it appears in countries that the Vikings invaded from about 1200–1000 years ago. However, HIV did not appear until after 1970 so there would have been no advantage for any individual who had the mutant gene, as far as infection by HIV was concerned, prior to 1970.

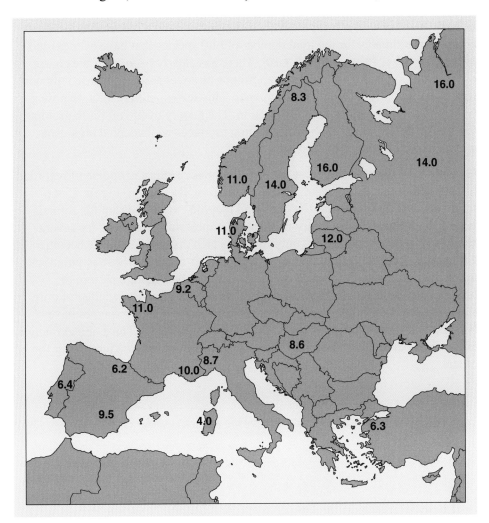

**Figure 15.3** A map of Europe showing the frequency of a mutant allele for a human gene known as *CCR5* in 18 European populations. The frequency is equivalent to the percentage of the population that carry it. The frequencies range from 16 in Finland to 4 in Sardinia and broadly there is a decrease in frequency moving south or west from Finland.

Now look at the comments on this activity at the end of this book.

# 15.3   Life through time – the pace of evolution

It is the fate of most species to become extinct. At some stage in their existence, their mortality rate exceeds their reproductive rate and then, inevitably, they die out. Estimating the total number of species living today is fraught with uncertainty (Section 3.5.1); estimating the total number of species that has ever existed is even more problematic. It is clear, however, that the species surviving today represent only a minute proportion of all the species that have ever existed on the Earth. For example, there are currently about 9000 species of birds, a group with a comparatively recent history and a reasonable fossil record, but estimates for the total number of bird species that have ever existed range from $1.5 \times 10^5$ to over $1.5 \times 10^6$. There has clearly been, over the course of the evolution of life on Earth, an enormous turnover among species, with new species continually replacing existing ones. This seems, at first sight, to pose a problem for the theory of natural selection. The history of life on Earth prompts the inevitable question, 'If natural selection produces well adapted organisms, why does the vast majority become extinct?'

Humans have witnessed a great many extinctions during the course of recorded history, many as a direct result of their activities. The data in Figure 15.4a might suggest that 'the worst is over' and that the extinction rate for animals is now declining. This is a very misleading impression, however, for several reasons. First, this data shows only those species that have actually become extinct and does not reflect the very much greater number whose populations are in decline. Second, the data is based on a very incomplete picture of biodiversity. As discussed in Section 3.5, we have a good knowledge of only a small proportion of the world's species and therefore many species have become extinct, and are now becoming extinct, *unnoticed*. Third, the extinction rate may apparently be declining for some groups, but may be increasing for others.

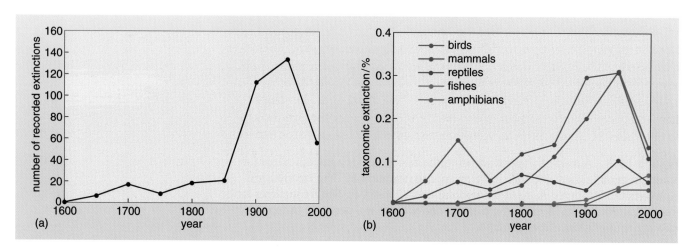

**Figure 15.4**   Graphs showing recorded animal extinctions. The data points correspond to the extinctions recorded in the previous 50 years. (a) *Number* of extinctions among all animals. (b) *Percentage* of species becoming extinct in each class of vertebrates.

■ Looking at the data in Figure 15.4b for the last 100 years, for which classes of vertebrates is the extinction rate apparently declining and for which classes is it apparently increasing?

☐ Extinction rate is declining for birds and mammals (and possibly reptiles), but is increasing for fishes and amphibians.

In recorded time, extinctions can often be attributed to specific causes. The great auk (*Alca impennis*, Figure 15.5), for example, was exterminated in about 1852 by a combination of hunting and egg collecting. The Stephens Island wren (*Xenicus lyalli*) lived only on one tiny island off New Zealand, and was totally exterminated in 1894 when a lighthouse keeper on the island acquired a cat. Examples such as these suggest that extinctions are just 'bad luck'. Certain species happened to be subjected to adverse conditions at particular times. However, most extinction cannot be explained in this way. Rather, it seems that natural selection does not always have the capacity to prevent extinction occurring because the appropriate alleles are not present in a species' gene pool. Underlying evolution is a whole series of chance events and so it is understandable that extinction can often be a random process.

**Figure 15.5**   Great auks diving for fish. The great auk (*Alca impennis*), extinct since the mid-19th century, was an inhabitant of the North Atlantic Ocean. It possessed many adaptations for life in the sea that are similar to those seen in living penguins, which inhabit the southern oceans.

In Chapter 1, you read about the ammonites and their living relative, a nautilus (Order Nautiloidea). Both have a similar structure and lifestyle and it is not clear why the ammonites were a substantially more successful order of molluscs, in terms of number of species, than the nautiloids, yet completely disappeared by the end of the Cretaceous. It is thought that the ammonites occupied a different niche, living in shallow, warm waters. Although the present-day *Nautilus* lives in tropical seas, it lives at depth during the day, in cooler waters around 600 m down and only comes closer to the surface at night. So, perhaps cooling of seawater led to the extinction of the ammonites but *Nautilus* was able to survive. It has also been suggested that ammonites could not dive deeper than 100 m as they could not survive the pressure changes. There is not sufficient evidence to support this assertion. During the final years of the ammonites, the shell chambers became more complex, particularly the lines joining the chambers to the outer shell (Figure 1.3c). The shells themselves became more ornate and some species had partially uncoiled shells. The significance of these changes is unclear.

Finding reasons for extinctions that occurred in the past is often very difficult. For example, the Irish elk, a giant deer that stood 2.1 m high at its shoulders and sported antlers over 3 m across, is often stated to have become extinct because there was a selective advantage for males in having large antlers and selection eventually went too far and the antlers became too big and heavy. Is there any evidence for this? Well, actually no, it is but a plausible hypothesis. The Irish elk (which, by the way, is neither Irish nor an elk) died out around 7000 years ago. There is evidence for a series of changes in the climate in what is now Siberia that would have reduced the availability of food plants. Neolithic humans were also at work establishing farms and so there may have been a combination of events that led to extinction. But getting hard evidence of causation is unlikely for most extinct animals and most species that have existed on this planet are now extinct. In Book 6 you will be studying the history of life on Earth, as revealed by fossils and the rocks they are found in.

## 15.4  Summary of Chapter 15

In this chapter you have seen how particular areas of biological study have benefited from an integrative approach in which different specialist areas are deployed to try and answer specific questions.

The evolutionary history of Antarctic fish, which show adaptations to a polar lifestyle, is being worked out using comparative studies of a widely occurring enzyme, LDH. Comparing the enzyme from polar fish with that found in tropical fish shows that there are slight differences in the structure of the molecules. While the structure of the active site of the enzyme is the same, small differences in the surrounding structure facilitate the functioning of the enzyme at a low temperature.

The Neandertals fascinate many of us and we would like to know if we are related to them. Analysis of both mtDNA and nuclear DNA is being used to define the extent to which we are directly related. The results so far indicate that the relationship is a distant one, although there is evidence for modern human genes having entered the Neandertal genome.

Extinction is the rule for all species and very few survive, as the evidence from the fossil record shows. The number of extinctions appears to be declining in modern times, but this is probably an illusory effect in that many populations are declining and face extinction in the near future, whilst there is also a large percentage of the total species on the planet that have yet to be described, so we have no knowledge of their progress towards extinction.

Activity 15.1 gave you another opportunity to improve your written communication skills, this time by writing a short account that integrates biological information from various chapters of Book 5.

# Chapter 16
# Summary of Book 5

This book has taken you on a journey of discovery through the biological world. You have met many important aspects of this vast subject, ranging from the biological molecules so vital for life, to whole populations of organisms and how they interact with each other. You have encountered some of the fundamental principles underpinning biology along your journey.

One such principle is the supposition that uniformity underlies diversity; the recurring observation that although living things show considerable variety, there is an underlying similarity in the way they function at a cellular and molecular level. In fact, in biology the living world can be considered at six different levels. We can look at life at the level of the ecosystem, the population, the whole organism, the individual cell or the biological molecules and chemical life processes contained within them. All these ways of looking at life are equally important and valid; indeed, you have met examples where modern biology relies on an understanding of life at all these levels. Without this integrative approach to biology many important questions would remain unanswered.

What follows is a review of the key concepts that you have encountered in this book. You have developed knowledge and understanding of the fundamental characteristics of living organisms and the classification and naming of species. You have studied the difference between cell types (prokaryotes and eukaryotes) and learnt something of their evolutionary history. The structure of cells and the organelles they contain prepared you for topics covering biosynthetic cellular reactions; protein synthesis on ribosomes and photosynthesis in chloroplasts and catabolic cellular reactions such as glucose oxidation in mitochondria. Book 5 has added to your considerable knowledge of organic molecules (from Book 4) and further developed your understanding of the structure and function of a whole range of biological molecules within living cells. You have encountered basic groups of chemicals such as proteins, nucleic acids, polysaccharides and TAGs and learnt about some of the specific roles they play in living organisms such as hormones, enzymes and structural components of cells.

You may have found the material in Chapter 6 rather daunting; metabolic pathways such as photosynthesis and glucose oxidation are complex to follow and time-consuming to master, but even a basic understanding of these pathways as a series of interlinked chemical reactions catalysed by enzymes will stand you in good stead if you decide to take your study of biology further than S104. Book 5 has also covered reproduction and genetics: from the simple ways in which unicellular organisms can reproduce themselves asexually by mitotic cell division through to the complex shuffling of genes during meiosis in sexual reproduction. You have considered how characters are inherited from one generation to the next and looked at Mendel's classic breeding experiments. You have learned about the structure of genetic material, DNA and a little about how this was originally elucidated and communicated to the scientific community. In addition, you now know the basic differences between genome organisation in different species and have a grasp of the sheer genetic diversity apparent in all species on Earth. Finally, you have been introduced to Darwin's big idea, the theory of natural selection as one process that can bring about evolution.

In addition to developing your knowledge and understanding of biology, this book has given you the opportunity to develop and practise some important skills. It largely concentrates on three skill areas: revision, communications skills and information literacy skills, although there are also additional activities that focus on practical work and working online with fellow students. You will have noticed that there is a fairly large overlap between the organic chemistry introduced in Book 4 and the material in Chapters 5 and 6 of this book. It is very difficult to follow the complex biochemistry in these chapters without a thorough understanding of functional groups. This was therefore an opportunity for you to revise and synthesise information; drawing on information from Book 4 and using it to help you make sense of related material in this book (several activities revisit Book 4 topics to help you consolidate and develop your understanding).

Communication skills have been developed consistently throughout S104 up to this point and the Book 5 activities have further extended these. You have practised skills such as drawing flow diagrams, planning short accounts, integrating diagrams appropriately into your writing, writing and referencing short accounts, and integrating complex information from more than one source. By completing these activities, you will be in a good position to write further extended pieces of scientific writing in assignment questions; you are advised to follow the advice given in the comments to these activities.

In addition to writing formal accounts, this book has enabled you to communicate your knowledge and understanding of biology in less-formal contexts. In Activity 2.1 you were able to discuss your experimental work with fellow students online and in Activity 3.1 you contributed to an online data-gathering activity related to biodiversity and conservation – a highly topical subject at present.

Finally, time has been devoted to investigating information literacy. Here the example of the elucidation of the structure of DNA by Watson and Crick was used as the subject of your trail through the 'research supply chain'. This also provided you with an opportunity to evaluate two related websites and critically assess the information they contained.

Like Book 4, the summary for this book has not required you to formally record your progress against the course learning outcomes. Once again, the summary has explored in a general way the skills and knowledge that you have developed in studying this book. It is recommended that you continue to record your progress against learning outcomes, even though this is not included as a formal activity here. You may now like to set aside a short time to note the skills from this summary in your study folder, so that you have an ongoing record.

## 16.1 Looking ahead to Book 6

You have now completed your study of Book 5, but you will find that the biology you have learned and the skills you have developed will be very useful as you progress through the remainder of the course. In Book 6, attention now turns to the Earth and the processes that shaped and are continuing to shape the biosphere. Here you will consider Earth history and geological time, examine the fossilised remnants of species long since extinct and consider the evolution of that most versatile and ubiquitous of species, *Homo sapiens.*

# Answers to questions

### Question 2.1

Duration of the life cycle and generation time are the same thing. The duration of the human life cycle/generation time is about 15 years. Since people can live about 80 years, the difference between the length of human life and the length of the life cycle/generation time is about 65 years. [This is in marked contrast with many other species; at the other extreme is the Atlantic salmon (*Salmo salar*), which dies immediately after it reproduces at the age of about seven years, i.e. there is no difference between the duration of its life cycle/generation time and the length of its life.]

### Question 2.2

You may have thought of two or three answers to this question. First, not all parts of a plant are exposed to the Sun. The roots, and those parts of the tree underneath the bark, receive no direct sunlight. So these unexposed parts have to rely on respiration for energy. Second, plants capture solar energy by photosynthesis and photosynthesis produces sugars, from which other organic molecules are subsequently made. Solar energy, therefore, cannot be used directly to 'drive' any other parts of metabolism. Once the energy has been stored in organic molecules, respiration is needed to release it for use in metabolism. Third, photosynthesis cannot occur in the dark. Respiration enables plants to have a source of energy at night.

### Question 2.3

(a) Yes, the adult mayfly metabolises. In order to be alive, an organism must obtain energy from organic molecules by respiration.

(b) Organisms have to grow at some stage in their life cycle, but not at every stage. The mayfly grew when it was young but does not need to grow as an adult.

(c) The mayfly is a heterotroph, although it feeds only when young. The mayfly is an animal and all animals are heterotrophs.

(d) There are many possibilities, such as most adult insects (e.g. flies, bees, wasps and ants), fungal spores, plant seeds and dried yeast. Do not forget adult humans, of course.

### Question 2.4

It does not matter whether you put the bread in a dark cupboard or leave it on a table in the light. Fungi are heterotrophs, so they grow just as well with or without light. [Do feel free to try this experiment if you would like to confirm the result for yourself.]

## Question 2.5

Metabolism in fungal spores must mean respiration is taking place (fungi are heterotrophs so they do not photosynthesise). Respiration is described by the chemical reaction:

$$\text{organic carbon} + \text{oxygen} \longrightarrow \text{carbon dioxide} + \text{water} \qquad (2.2)$$

To prove that respiration was occurring, it would be necessary to measure changes in one of these four substances. There would be a reduction in organic carbon and oxygen and an increase in carbon dioxide and water. [You have not been provided with any information to decide between these four, but it is generally easier to measure carbon dioxide production or oxygen removal.]

## Question 3.1

The first character is source of food: almost all plants are autotrophs (i.e. they make their own food by photosynthesis), while all fungi and animals are heterotrophs. The second character is mobility: most animals have the ability to move in search of food, while fungi and plants do not.

[The expression 'fairly reliably' had to be used in the question because, as so often in biology, there are exceptions. A few plant species have lost (or reduced) their ability to feed autotrophically and so live heterotrophically, feeding on other plants either while they are alive (i.e. as parasites) or after their death (i.e. as saprophytes). Insectivorous plants (e.g. Venus's flytrap) are autotrophs that derive *some* of their nutrients from the insects they trap. Some animals are not mobile (at least as adults) and rely on food being brought to them by, for example, water currents (e.g. certain corals).]

## Question 3.2

Figure 3.12 shows how *C. familiaris* can be 'nested' within successively broader, more inclusive, levels of classification.

## Question 3.3

Since 63% of the Indonesian bug species were new to science, 37% had previously been described. If you assume that the 80 000 species that have been described worldwide (Table 3.3) represent 37% of the total, then 1% of the total would be $\dfrac{80\,000}{37}$ and 100% of the total would be $\dfrac{80\,000}{37} \times 100\%$, which is about 220 000 bug species (to 2 significant figures). [This estimate depends on there being the same percentage of previously unknown bug species everywhere in the world. This is unlikely to be the case, so the estimate needs to be treated with caution.]

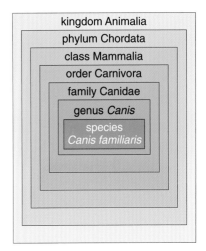

**Figure 3.12** Diagram to show how *Canis familiaris* can be 'nested' within successively broader levels of classification.

## Question 3.4

The six most important assumptions made by Erwin are the following:

- All the arthropods in the crowns of the trees would be collected using the insecticide fog method.
- The tree in which 163 species of beetle were found was typical of tropical trees in general.
- Beetles represent 40% of arthropod species (Table 3.3 data suggests 39%).
- There are about $5 \times 10^4$ species of tropical tree worldwide.
- Most arthropod species are confined to a single tree species.
- Half as many arthropod species live on the ground as in the crowns of tropical trees.

## Question 4.1

(a) See Table 4.2.

**Table 4.2** Completed version of Table 4.1, showing a comparison of three basic cell types.

| Cell feature | Cell type | | |
| --- | --- | --- | --- |
| | Animal | Plant | Prokaryote |
| cell membrane | ✓ | ✓ | ✓ |
| cell wall | ✗ | ✓ | ✓ |
| chloroplasts | ✗ | ✓ | ✗ |
| cytoplasm | ✓ | ✓ | ✓* |
| cytosol | ✓ | ✓ | ✓ |
| mitochondria | ✓ | ✓ | ✗ |
| nucleus | ✓ | ✓ | ✗ |
| nuclear membrane | ✓ | ✓ | ✗ |
| organelles | ✓ | ✓ | ✗ |
| ribosomes | ✓ | ✓ | ✓ |
| rough endoplasmic reticulum | ✓ | ✓ | ✗ |
| large vacuole | ✗ | ✓ | ✗ |

\* In the case of prokaryotes, the cytoplasm is everything contained within the cell membrane, i.e. cytosol and subcellular structures, including the DNA.

(b) From Table 2.2 you will see that all the cell features listed are found in plant cells, whereas some are absent from either animal or prokaryotic cells. Consequently, plant cells are the most varied in terms of the range of cell features present.

## Question 4.2

The following eukaryotic cell features are composed of, or are bounded by, membranes:

1   The *cell* itself has a cell membrane.

2   The *nucleus* has a nuclear membrane.

3   *Mitochondria* are bounded by a membrane, and have an internal membrane too.

4   *Chloroplasts* are bounded by a membrane, and have internal membranes too.

5   *Vacuoles* are bounded by a membrane.

6   *Rough endoplasmic reticulum* is composed of membranes.

## Question 4.3

(a) This is a eukaryotic cell because it contains a nucleus and other membrane-bound organelles.

(b) Structures labelled A are mitochondria; they resemble the mitochondria shown in Figure 4.3. There is an outer membrane and an internal convoluted membrane.

(c) Since this is a eukaryotic cell, the organism is *not* a bacterium. There is *no* evidence of chloroplasts, so it is unlikely to be a plant. Cell wall material is labelled in the figure, which precludes the organism from being an animal, since animal cells lack cell walls. It is probably not a protoctist for the same reason (although a few protoctists *do* have cell walls). By a process of elimination, therefore, the organism shown in Figure 4.11 is a fungus. [It is actually a unicellular yeast (*Saccharomyces cerevisiae*), which is producing a new progeny cell by the process of budding. Figure 4.11, which is an electron micrograph, shows more detail than does the drawing from a light micrograph of *S. cerevisiae* (Figure 4.8a).]

## Question 4.4

(a) (iv) Each DNA molecule forms one chromosome, so there is exactly the same number of chromosomes as there are molecules of DNA during growth phase I.

(b) (iv) The length of a DNA molecule is exactly the same during cell division as during interphase. [The DNA is coiled in mitosis, but the overall length of the molecule is the same.]

## Question 4.5

You would expect to see 92 chromosomes. The 46 chromosomes replicate to make 92 chromatids prior to mitosis. These 92 chromatids separate at anaphase to become 92 individual chromosomes. The cell has not yet divided so there are 92 chromosomes in the cell at anaphase.

## Question 4.6

(a) In a diploid cell, each autosome is one of a pair (and this is sometimes true also for the sex chromosomes). However, there may be *many* pairs of chromosomes in a cell. In a human cell there are either 22 or 23 pairs of chromosomes. [A few eukaryotic cells – for example human red blood cells – do not possess any chromosomes when mature.]

(b) This is only true after chromosomes have replicated themselves during interphase and before the chromatid pairs separate to become independent chromosomes at the start of anaphase.

(c) No chromosome has its own nucleus. Each nucleus may contain many chromosomes.

(d) Interphase begins when cell division ends and ends as mitosis starts (Figure 4.16), so is not part of mitosis.

(e) The cell could be eukaryotic, since a eukaryotic cell has no nucleus during mitosis. [Mature red blood cells have no nuclei at all.]

## Question 4.7

A clone is a genetically identical group of cells or organisms resulting from asexual reproduction or nuclear transplantation.

## Question 4.8

(a) A male *spermatozoon* fertilises a female *ovum* to produce a *diploid zygote*.

(b) Gametes are *haploid* and are produced by cell division that involves *meiosis*.

## Question 4.9

(a) A zygote is defined as the cell that results from a spermatozoon fertilising an ovum. Since asexual reproduction does not involve sperm or ova or fertilisation, there is no zygote in asexual reproduction. [Hence Dolly's first cell is described as 'the equivalent of a zygote'.]

(b) A spermatozoon contributes only half of the zygote's chromosomes. The other half come from the female. Thus, the zygote is not a clone of the male contributing the spermatozoon. [And neither is it a clone of the female contributing the ovum.]

## Question 5.1

The answer is shown in Figure 5.24.

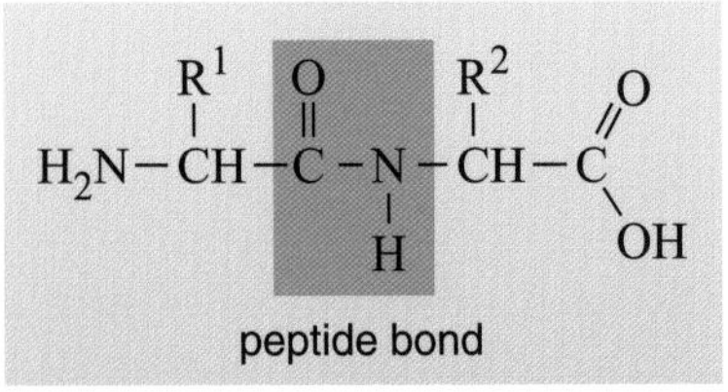

Remember that in a condensation reaction, a molecule of water is removed in the formation of a covalent bond between two molecules (an OH group is lost from one molecule and an H atom from the other).

## Question 5.2

(a) Two water molecules are released when a trisaccharide is formed. A trisaccharide consists of three monosaccharide monomers joined by two glycosidic linkages and a water molecule is released when each of these linkages is formed.

**Figure 5.24**   The result of the condensation reaction between two amino acids: a molecule of water is eliminated and a peptide bond is formed.

(b) Cellulose is the principal polysaccharide of plant cell walls and consists of glucose monomers joined by glycosidic linkages.

(c) Sucrose is a disaccharide made up of one molecule of glucose and one mole of fructose; if one mole of sucrose is hydrolysed then the products of the reaction will be one mole of fructose and one mole of glucose.

(d) Glycogen is the main energy-storage polysaccharide of animals.

## Question 5.3

Collagen is a protein that forms a triple helix in which three long polymer chains are intertwined (see Figure 5.9). It functions as an extracellular support material. [Keratin is made up of *pairs* of intertwined helices; myosin, which is also mentioned in Section 5.5.1, has a more complex structure than collagen and keratin.]

## Question 5.4

(a) Protein X is most likely to be a receptor protein that is exactly the correct shape to bind adrenalin to the surface of specific cells of the body, e.g. heart muscle cells. These cells will then respond to the bound adrenalin to promote a coordinated response by the body to the stimulus. Book 4, Section 16.2.2 discusses the 'fight or flight' response to a stressful situation, which is controlled by the interaction of adrenalin with its specific cell surface receptors.

(b) A change in the amino acid sequence, i.e. the primary structure, of protein X may change its higher-order structure. If this change occurs at or near the adrenalin binding site, the binding of this hormone will be impaired. So the cells of these individuals will not respond to adrenalin or may respond less readily than those with normal protein X.

## Question 5.5

(a) True. Proteins are polymers of amino acids, so they all yield amino acids on hydrolysis.

(b) False. A given protein does not necessarily contain all 20 amino acids.

(c) False. When 100 amino acids condense, the protein thus formed has 100 monomers joined by 99 peptide bonds.

## Question 5.6

Proteins, polysaccharides and nucleic acids all have the following properties:
- they are very large molecules
- they consist of chains of monomers
- their constituent monomers are covalently linked
- weak interactions are important for their higher-order structure.

## Question 5.7

(a) Increasing the concentration of the reactants increases the probability of reactant molecules encountering each other.

(b) Increasing the temperature ensures that more encounters between molecules have sufficient energy to overcome the energy barrier.

(c) A catalyst lowers the energy barrier of the reaction.

## Question 5.8

(a) True. The ending '-ase' in amylase tell you that it is an enzyme, and all enzymes are proteins.

(b) True. The basic metabolism of all living things is the same. The metabolic reactions involved can only occur at the rate they do because of enzymes, so life depends on the activities of enzymes.

(c) False. All enzymes are globular proteins but not all globular proteins are enzymes. Receptor proteins and antibodies (described in Section 5.5.1) are not enzymes.

(d) True. Specificity is a crucial feature of enzymes.

## Question 5.9

Prolonged cooling can result in hypothermia, when the rate of enzyme-catalysed reactions will be significantly reduced to the point at which the rate is insufficient to maintain metabolism. Overheating can be even more dangerous, since the thermal denaturation of the higher-order structure of proteins can result in enzymes that will no longer catalyse reactions. Once again, metabolic reactions will stop and death can result.

## Question 5.10

(a) NAD is reduced to NAD.2H. The two hydrogen atoms are transferred from $BH_2$ to NAD.

(b) The enzyme involved has an active site tailored to bind both $BH_2$ and NAD. Presumably it is able to bind $JH_2$ less well than $BH_2$ because the 'lock and key' fit is less precise, i.e. the enzyme is very specific for the substrate $BH_2$.

## Question 5.11

(a) Myoglobin is a protein that stores oxygen, and the monomers from which proteins are synthesised are amino acids; alanine (ii) and lysine (v) are both amino acids.

(b) TAGs are made from glycerol (iii) and fatty acids such as palmitic acid (vi).

(c) Glycogen is a polysaccharide made from monomers of the monosaccharide glucose (i). [Fructose (iv) is also a monosaccharide but is not the monomer unit of glycogen.]

## Question 5.12

(a) Fibrous *proteins* (e.g. collagen) and fibrous *polysaccharides* (e.g. cellulose) both provide support.

(b) *Polysaccharides*, such as starch and glycogen, and *TAGs* serve as energy stores.

(c) Globular *proteins* called enzymes have catalytic activity.

(d) *Nucleic acids* carry genetic information.

(e) Membranes separate the cell into compartments (both surrounding and within organelles, such as those making up the mitochondria), and *phospholipids* and *proteins* are the main molecular components of cellular membranes.

## Question 6.1

Photosynthesis is essential for life on Earth because:

- it converts solar energy into chemical energy in sugars, which can be used to fuel all the energy-requiring processes of life
- it releases oxygen, which is required for respiration.

## Question 6.2

The dark reactions (i.e. the reactions in which carbon dioxide is reduced to sugar) are driven by the products of the light reactions, namely ATP (as a source of energy) and NADP.2H (for the reducing power).

## Question 6.3

M, consisting of the chloroplast membranes, contains chlorophyll (a) and all the components that carry out the light reactions which produce oxygen from water (c).

S, consisting of the solution between the chloroplast membranes, contains the enzymes required for the dark reactions which convert carbon dioxide to sugar (b).

## Question 6.4

Solar energy is transformed into chemical energy in the form of ATP in the light reactions of photosynthesis. This energy drives the dark reactions (the biosynthetic part of the process). In all other biosynthesis reactions the ATP required is generated from the breakdown of organic molecules such as glucose.

## Question 6.5

There would be little or no change. ATP levels will remain roughly constant, but there will be a greater rate of both ATP synthesis and ATP breakdown, i.e. ATP turnover, as the ATP $\rightleftharpoons$ ADP + $P_i$ system is coupled to the energy-requiring activity of working muscles and the energy-releasing process of glucose oxidation in muscle cells.

Question 6.6

(a) False. The conversion of ADP + $P_i$ to ATP is coupled to energy-*releasing* reactions.

(b) True. ATP is a carrier of chemical energy in that it transfers energy between energy-releasing and energy-requiring reactions.

(c) False. ATP is used in many processes other than biosynthesis, such as muscle contraction.

(d) True. ATP is a short-lived energy store, typically being converted to ADP within a minute.

Question 6.7

The fate of the glucose molecule is summarised in the following sequence of steps.

1    The glucose is converted to starch – the form in which it is stored in the plant.

2    The plant is eaten by an animal.

3    The starch is digested to glucose in the animal's gut.

5    It enters the cell with the help of glucose transport proteins present in the cell membrane (see Section 5.7).

Question 6.8

**Table 6.6**  Summary of glycolysis. Completed Table 6.1.

| Reaction or metabolic pathway | Part of cell/ mitochondria located in | Begins with (principal substrate) | Carbon-containing end-products | Other products |
|---|---|---|---|---|
| glycolysis | cytosol | glucose | 2 × pyruvate (3C) | 2ATP* 2NAD.2H |

* Remember that although glycolysis requires 2ATP to phosphorylate glucose, 4ATP is produced during the metabolic pathway than is consumed so there is a net gain of 2ATP.

Question 6.9

**Table 6.7**  Summary of the link reaction. Completed Table 6.2.

| Reaction or metabolic pathway | Part of cell/ mitochondria located in | Begins with (principal substrate) | Carbon-containing end-products | Other products |
|---|---|---|---|---|
| link reaction | matrix of mitochondrion | 2 × pyruvate (3C) | 2 × acetyl CoA (2C) $2CO_2$ (1C) | 2NAD.2H |

Question 6.10

**Table 6.8** Summary of the TCA cycle. Completed Table 6.3.

| Reaction or metabolic pathway | Part of cell/ mitochondria located in | Begins with (principal substrate) | Carbon-containing end-products | Other products |
|---|---|---|---|---|
| TCA cycle | matrix of mitochondrion | $2 \times$ acetyl CoA (2C) | $4 CO_2$ (1C) | 2ATP 6NAD.2H 2FAD.2H |

Question 6.11

All the carbon dioxide produced in glucose oxidation (and also in the respiration of other energy sources) is produced in the link reaction (pyruvate = acetyl + $CO_2$) and the TCA cycle (acetyl = $2CO_2$). Both of these stages occur within the mitochondrial matrix.

Question 6.12

(a) (iii) NAD.2H is converted to NAD in the electron transport chain.

(b) (i) and (ii) This is glycolysis, in which a 6C molecule is split into two 3C molecules and NAD is converted to NAD.2H.

(c) (i) and (ii) This is the link reaction, in which a 3C molecule (pyruvate) is split into a 2C fragment (acetyl) and a 1C molecule (carbon dioxide), with the transfer of two hydrogen atoms to NAD.

(d) (i) and (ii) This is the overall reaction of the TCA cycle, in which a 6C intermediate is split to a 5C compound ($+ CO_2$) and a 5C intermediate is split to a 4C compound ($+ CO_2$) and quantities of NAD.2H are made.

Question 6.13

**Table 6.9** Summary of the electron transport chain/oxidative phosphorylation. Completed Table 6.4.

| Reaction or metabolic pathway | Part of cell/ mitochondria located in | Begins with (principal substrate) | Carbon-containing end-products | Other products |
|---|---|---|---|---|
| electron transport chain/ oxidative phosphorylation | inner mitochondrial membrane | 10NAD.2H* 2FAD.2H $6O_2$ | none | 30ATP $6H_2O$ |

* Recall that each molecule of glucose leads to the production of two NAD.2H during glycolysis and two NAD.2H during the link reaction, added to the six NAD.2H produced during the TCA cycle gives us ten in total.

You will be aware that you have answered the same question for each of the 4 stages of glucose oxidation. You may find it helpful to combine your four answers into one table so you can see how the whole pathway fits together. See if you can relate the information in the combined table with the overall equation for glucose oxidation.

$$C_6H_{12}O_6 + 6O_2 \longrightarrow 6CO_2 + 6H_2O + \text{energy}$$

Question 6.14

In Stage 4, NAD.2H molecules (produced by reduction of NAD) are oxidised back to NAD, and ADP is phosphorylated.

Question 6.15

(a) Protons are pumped from the matrix, through the inner mitochondrial membrane and accumulate in the intermembrane space. Thus the proton concentration here is higher than that in the matrix, i.e. a proton concentration gradient is established.

(b) 2,4-DNP damages the inner mitochondrial membrane, thereby uncoupling electron transport from oxidative phosphorylation; NAD.2H is converted to NAD as electron transport proceeds, but there is no net change in the distribution of protons because protons would leak back into the matrix, and so no ATP is produced in the process.

(c) In the presence of carbon monoxide, the final carrier, cytochrome oxidase, cannot pass electrons on to oxygen because the binding site for oxygen is blocked. Hence electron transport cannot occur, so there is no energy made available for pumping protons and so no proton gradient is produced.

Question 6.16

(a) True. This is shown in Figure 6.7.

(b) False. The first step in amino acid catabolism is removal of the amino ($NH_2$) group.

(c) True. This is explained in Section 6.5.1.

(d) True. This is shown in Figure 6.19.

Question 8.1

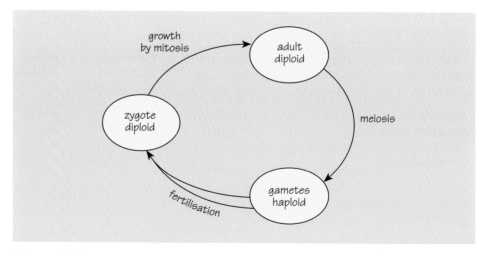

**Figure 8.17**    Completed Figure 8.1.

## Question 8.2

The missing terms are: (a) homologous; (b) karyotype; (c) meiosis; (d) fertilisation.

## Question 8.3

(a) The karyotype is the number, size and shape of all the chromosomes and is characteristic of a species. Members of a species have the same karyotype, although there may be slight differences between males and females because of the sex chromosomes.

(b) The term genotype can mean either the full complement of genes or the copies of a gene for a particular character present in an individual. The former will vary between individuals of the same species (unless they are identical twins or clones), while the latter may or may not vary.

(c) Likewise, for the phenotype – meaning either the sum total of all characters, or a particular character of an individual. The former will vary between individuals of the same species, while the latter may or may not vary.

## Question 8.4

*Experiment 1* The expected ratio is 3 red : 1 white (genotypes $1\,R\,R : 2\,R\,r : 1\,r\,r$) because all the $F_1$ would be heterozygous $R\,r$.

*Experiment 2* It would be expected that none of the $F_1$ would be pink, but rather all would be red since this is dominant to white.

*Experiment 3* The colour of the $F_1$ plants would be expected to be the same in both crosses since Mendel found that it made no difference whether the pollen grains came from the female or the male parent.

## Question 8.5

There are four possible outcomes: $P\,P$; two $P\,p$; and $p\,p$. Since three of the four possible fertilisations contain at least one $p$ allele, the probability that the offspring will contain at least one $p$ allele is 0.75 or $\frac{3}{4}$.

## Question 8.6

The completed Figure 8.12 is shown in Figure 8.18. The ratio of the genotypes of the offspring will be $1\,P\,p : 1\,p\,p$, and the phenotypic ratio will be one purple : one white.

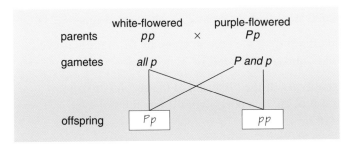

**Figure 8.18** Completed Figure 8.12, showing a cross between a pure-breeding white-flowered variety of pea and a heterozygous purple-flowered variety.

Question 8.7

The mating diagram for this cross is shown in Figure 8.19.

The genotypic ratio of the offspring is 1 $PP$ : 1 $Pp$; the phenotype of all the offspring is purple-flowered, since they all carry at least one (dominant) $P$ allele.

**Figure 8.19**  Mating diagram for Question 8.7. Our diagram is based on the style given in Figure 8.12, but you might have drawn a diagram based on the style of Figure 8.11. Both are equally acceptable.

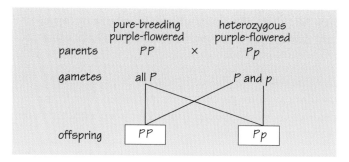

Question 8.8

You could best solve the problem by working through each step in the guidelines in turn:

1  Pure-breeding parents, by definition, must be homozygous, since they breed true; since the two varieties have contrasting characters, they are homozygous for different alleles of the gene for eye shape.

2  Using the information given in the question, the mating diagram is as shown in Figure 8.20:

**Figure 8.20**  Mating diagram for Question 8.8.

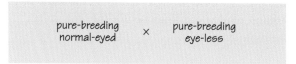

3  Next you should have assigned letters to alleles of the gene for eye shape for the parents of cross 1. Since normal shape appears in the $F_1$ generation, you deduced that normal shape is dominant to eye-less; you probably used $EE$ for normal-eyed flies and $ee$ for eye-less, but you may have chosen a different letter.

4  The mating diagram you drew should be as shown in cross 1 of Figure 8.21. (The normal-eyed $F_1$ flies must be heterozygous ($Ee$) since they are the offspring of $EE$ and $ee$ pure-breeding parents. All eye-less flies must be $ee$ because this phenotype is recessive.)

5  You should have repeated steps 2–4 for cross 2 (as shown in Figure 8.21).

6  The phenotypes of the offspring of the second cross are ($Ee$) normal-eyed (since $E$ is dominant to $e$) and ($ee$) eye-less.

7  The ratio of the two genotypes of the offspring of the second cross is 1 $Ee$ : 1 $ee$, and the ratio of the two phenotypes is one normal-eyed ($Ee$) : one eye-less ($ee$).

8  The results appear consistent with what you know of genetics, and the ratio is a familiar genetic ratio.

[You can use the guidelines again when tackling genetics problems later in this book.]

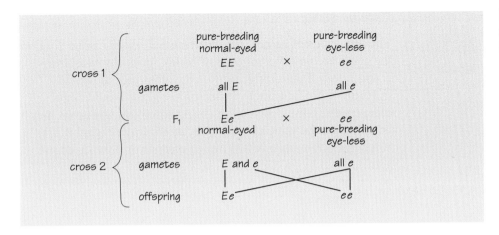

**Figure 8.21** Completed mating diagram for Question 8.8.

## Question 8.9

The deviations from a 3 : 1 ratio are due to chance. However, larger variations would be expected with smaller samples. This is what is observed in Mendel's results. In the experiment in which Mendel counted a large number of seeds (experiments 1 and 2), he obtained a ratio very close to 3 : 1. In the experiment in which he counted a much smaller sample of pods (Experiment 4), he obtained a ratio that showed a greater deviation from a 3 : 1 ratio.

## Question 8.10

The completed sentences are as follows:

(a) At the start of mitosis, the chromosomes become visible and each can be seen to be replicated along its length, that is, each consists of two *chromatids*.

(b) During mitosis, the two *chromatids* of each chromosome separate, one to one end of the *cell* and the other to the other end.

(c) The movement of the *chromatids* is facilitated by delicate threads.

(d) At the end of mitosis, the number of chromosomes in each progeny cell is the *same* as in the original parent cell.

(e) At metaphase, the chromosomes line up across the *middle* of the cell.

## Question 8.11

The completed table is as follows:

**Table 8.4** Similarities and differences between mitosis and meiosis. Completed Table 8.3.

| Feature | Mitosis | Meiosis I | Meiosis II |
| --- | --- | --- | --- |
| Members of a homologous chromosome separate | | ✓ | |
| The two chromatids of a chromosome separate | ✓ | | ✓ |
| The product of this division is two cells | ✓ | ✓ | |
| The product of this division is four cells | | | ✓ |
| The chromosomes are single stranded at the end of this division | ✓ | | ✓ |

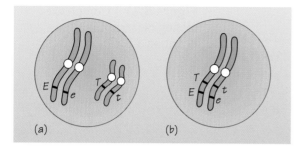

(a)    (b)

**Figure 8.22**   Answer to Question 8.12.

## Question 8.12

The four kinds of gamete produced are *E T*, *e t*, *E t* and *e T*. (a) If the genes are on different pairs of homologous chromosomes – *E* and *e* on one pair and *T* and *t* on the other pair, as shown in Figure 8.22a, at gamete formation the genes would assort independently from each other. (b) Alternatively, the genes may be linked on the same chromosome, as shown in Figure 8.22b. If the genes remained linked during meiosis then two kinds of gametes will be produced *E T* and *e t* but when crossing over occurs between the two genes then the two genotypes *E t* and *e T* will be produced.

## Question 8.13

There are two main processes that lead to the production of new combinations of alleles at meiosis: the independent assortment of homologous chromosomes and crossing over between members of a homologous pair.

[Your answer may differ from the one given here, but the meaning should be clear.]

## Question 9.1

Compare your answer with Figure 9.8.

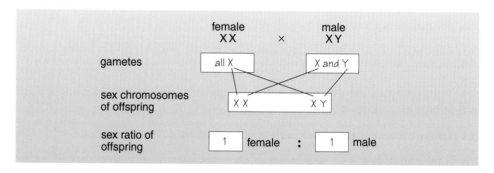

**Figure 9.8**   Completed version of the mating diagram given in Figure 9.2.

## Question 9.2

The X chromosomes carry the genes responsible for X-linked characters. A son inherits the Y chromosome from his father and an X chromosome from his mother. The X chromosome of the father will be transmitted only to his daughters and not to his sons.

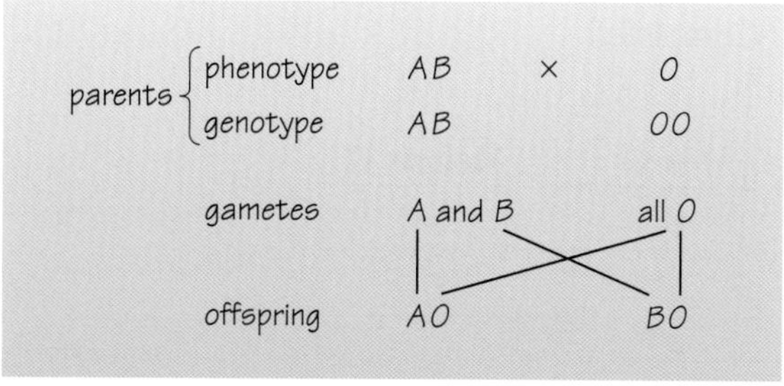

## Question 9.3

The mating diagram is shown in Figure 9.9. The children would have either the A phenotype (genotype *A O*) or the B phenotype (genotype *B O*). Thus the children have different phenotypes from either of their parents.

**Figure 9.9**   Mating diagram for Question 9.3.

## Question 9.4

(a) (ii). Both plants are presumably heterozygous and one-quarter of the offspring inherited two recessive wrinkled-pea alleles, one from each parent. This is a similar situation to the second cross of the flower-colour experiment (Figures 8.9 and 8.10) which gave a phenotypic ratio in the offspring of three with the dominant phenotype : one with the recessive phenotype (or three-quarters : one-quarter).

(b) (iii). The variation in stem lengths appears to be continuous, which suggests that several genes are involved in this phenotype, and probably environmental factors too, such as soil nutrition.

(c) (i). Since purple flower colour is dominant and neither parent has this phenotype, a new mutation in a gamete of one of the parents must be involved.

(d) (v). Only two alternative phenotypes (green and virtually white) are described, suggesting that leaf colour shows discontinuous variation; however, many genes affect the development of the green pigment, chlorophyll (Section 6.2), and if *any* one mutates, chlorophyll will not be produced.

## Question 10.1

Statements (a), (b) and (e) are correct. Statements (c) and (d) should read as follows:

(c) Each monomer is linked to adjacent monomers by covalent bonds formed by condensation reactions with loss of water.

(d) The higher-order structure is maintained by weak interactions.

## Question 10.2

(a) 100 bases would form 50 complementary base pairs.

(b) The number of nucleotides is the same as the number of bases, i.e. 100.

(c) Again, the number of deoxyribose molecules is equal to the number of bases, i.e. 100.

(d) Since C always pairs with G, the number of guanine (G) bases is the same as the number of cytosine (C) bases, i.e. 30.

(e) and (f) Sixty of the 100 bases are either C or G, so the remaining 40 are either thymine (T) or adenine (A). As A always pairs with T, then half this number, i.e. 20, are T and 20 are A.

(g) Each C–G pair forms *three* hydrogen bonds, giving a total of $3 \times 30 = 90$ for the 30 C–G pairs present; each A–T pair forms two hydrogen bonds giving a total of $2 \times 20 = 40$ for the 20 A–T pairs; therefore the total number of hydrogen bonds in the DNA fragment is $90 + 40 = 130$.

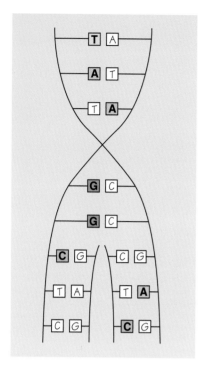

**Figure 10.11** Completed Figure 10.10, showing base-pairing in part of a double-stranded DNA molecule during replication.

## Question 10.3

(a) Figure 10.11 is the completed version of Figure 10.10. Note that sequences must be the same in the two daughter strands, so these can be deduced from the limited information provided in Figure 10.10. Here is one example. One member of the base pair at the bottom right is C. Since C always pairs with G, the missing base must be G. Because the two daughter strands are identical, the missing base pair at the bottom left must also be C–G.

(b) Since the DNA shown in Figure 10.10 is replicating, the cell must be at interphase. This is the stage between two nuclear divisions during which the DNA, and hence the chromosome, becomes replicated, and two double helices, and hence the two chromatids, are produced.

## Question 11.1

The three important differences between the structures of DNA and RNA are listed below.

(a) DNA contains the sugar deoxyribose; RNA contains ribose instead.

(b) DNA contains the base thymine (T); RNA contains uracil (U) instead.

(c) DNA is double-stranded, i.e. it consists of two polynucleotide chains wound around one another to form a double helix; RNA is mostly single-stranded.

## Question 11.2

The completed sentences are as follows (missing words are shown in italics).

(a) The enzyme *RNA polymerase* copies a stretch of DNA into RNA in a process known as *transcription*.

(b) Only the *template* strand of DNA is 'read' in the process of RNA synthesis; the other DNA strand is known as the *non-template* strand.

(c) There are three different types of RNA molecule: *rRNA*, *mRNA* and *tRNA*.

(d) The transfer of information from the mRNA base sequence to the amino acid sequence of a polypeptide is known as *translation*.

(e) The mRNA sequence has a triplet code, and each triplet is known as a *codon*.

(f) Reading of the RNA base sequence begins at a *start codon* and finishes at a *stop codon*.

(g) *tRNA* binds both an amino acid and mRNA; it attaches to the latter via its three-base *anticodon*.

(h) A ribosome has three RNA binding sites: one for *mRNA* and two for tRNA.

(i) A ribosome moves along an mRNA chain, and there are several ribosomes attached to a particular mRNA at any one time; such a string of ribosomes along an mRNA chain is termed a *polysome*.

## Question 11.3

(a) The mRNA sequence will be:

AUGGAGCCAGUAGGGA…

(b) The amino acid sequence will be:

Met–Glu–Pro–Val–Gly–…

Notice that this is only the start of the amino acid sequence. You cannot say what the last 'A' base might be part of the code for, since two-thirds of the codon is missing.

(c) The DNA sequence of the non-template strand is:

ATGGAGCCAGTAGGGA…

## Question 12.1

The original template DNA sequence coded for the following sequence of amino acids:

Met–Glu–Pro–Val–Gly–…

(See answer to Question 11.3.)

(a) The new DNA sequence is given as:

TACCTGGTCATCCCT…

After transcription, the mRNA sequence would be:

AUGGACCAGUAGGGA…

After translation, the amino acid sequence would be:

Met–Asp–Gln–stop…

The significant feature here is that a mutation has resulted in a stop codon in place of the fourth amino acid in this sequence. Since translation would terminate at the stop codon, an incomplete – and therefore non-functional – tripeptide would be produced.

(b) The new template DNA sequence is given as:

TACCCTCGGTCATCCCT…

After transcription, the mRNA sequence would be:

AUGGGAGCCAGUAGGGA…

After translation, the amino acid sequence would be:

Met–Gly–Ala–Ser–Arg–(Asp or Glu)–…

Notice that because the last codon is incomplete, you cannot be sure which of either Asp or Glu is the sixth amino acid.

The significant feature is that this mutation has brought about a large change in the resultant amino acid sequence as a consequence of insertion of a single base. Only the first amino acid is the same as in the cells that were not treated with the mutagenic agent (as in Question 11.3).

## Question 12.2

(a) The DNA of the cystic fibrosis gene contains 250 000 base pairs, so the template strand has 250 000 bases. Transcription of this would, therefore, produce a primary RNA product with 250 000 bases.

(b) Of these 250 000 bases, only 6500 remain in the mature mRNA. Therefore, the number of non-protein-coding bases is 250 000 − 6500 = 243 500. Thus the percentage of the primary RNA product that consists of non-protein-coding sequences is:

$$\frac{243\,500}{250\,000} \times 100\% = 97\% \text{ (to 2 significant figures).}$$

So 97% of the primary RNA product consists of non-protein-coding sequences (introns) which are removed during RNA splicing to produce mRNA.

(c) 243 500 base pairs in the cystic fibrosis gene are non-protein-coding (i.e. form introns). The gene contains 26 introns. Therefore:

$$\text{mean size of an intron} = \frac{243\,500}{26}$$
$$= 9400 \text{ base pairs (to 2 significant figures).}$$

## Question 13.1

The genomes and gene function in prokaryotes and eukaryotes are very different, as Table 13.3 shows.

**Table 13.3**  Comparison of genomes and gene function in prokaryotes and eukaryotes. Completed version of Table 13.1.

| Feature | Prokaryotes | Eukaryotes |
|---|---|---|
| genome complexity | simple | complex |
| site of DNA replication | cytosol | nucleus |
| site of transcription | cytosol | nucleus |
| site of translation (ribosomes) | cytosol | cytoplasm* |
| introns | absent | present |
| exons | absent | present |
| split genes | absent | present |
| repeat sequences | absent | present |
| mRNA splicing | absent | occurs |

*Strictly speaking, translation in eukaryotes occurs either on ribosomes free in the cytoplasm, or on ribosomes attached to the rough endoplasmic reticulum (see Section 4.1).

## Question 13.2

Statement (d) is the correct statement.

The two statements (a) and (c) contradict the correct statement (d). For (a), genes are not evenly spread out along the chromosomes of eukaryotes. For (c), genes are distributed at specific locations – at loci (see Chapter 8) – but the distribution is random, and the density of genes varies from chromosome to chromosome and between regions in a chromosome. (b) Although data for only three species are provided, the average gene density in humans is 7 per 1 000 000 bases (Table 13.2), which is a lower density than 7 per 100 000 bases.

## Question 14.1

Two: one that 'replaces' her in the population when she dies and one that 'replaces' one of the males with whom she has mated during her life. If any more than two survive on average, then the population would increase.

## Question 14.2

Bright coloration makes male guppies more conspicuous to predators. Thus, where predators are present, it will be the less-colourful males that tend to survive and reproduce. Putting it another way, in streams where predators are present, males have less-bright coloration, an adaptation that reduces their risk of being eaten.

## Question 14.3

The purpose of the group A ponds was to show what happened over the same period of time in the absence of predators. The change in the number of spots in the group C guppies might have taken place anyway, whether or not the predators had been introduced. The group A ponds allowed Endler to check on this possibility. [The group A ponds therefore served as 'controls' for the 'experimental' group C ponds. A 'control' is an important feature of scientific experimental procedure. It enables the investigator to be sure that any change taking place in the 'experimental' set-up is due to the factor that has been experimentally changed, and not to some other factor which has not been accounted for.]

The group B ponds allowed Endler to check whether any change observed in the group C ponds could have been due, not so much to the addition of a fish that preys on guppies, but to the addition of *any* other species of fish or even *any* other species of predatory fish (whether it preyed on guppies or not). [So again, the group B ponds served as 'controls' for the 'experimental' group C ponds.]

## Question 14.4

Factors (b), (d) and (f) would tend to promote genetic diversity. The Red Queen effect (b) means that organisms have to change just in order to survive because their physical environment and/or their interaction with other species are constantly changing, and this in turn promotes genetic diversity. Recombination during meiosis (d) is a process in which the genes and alleles in the genome of an individual are shuffled, and this, together with the combining of gametes at fertilisation, generates an enormous number of combinations of genes and alleles. Mutations (f) are the ultimate source of all variation.

Factors (a), (c) and (e) would lead to a reduction in genetic diversity. In the founder effect (a), a small population that is formed from a larger one contains less genetic variation than the larger one. A constant environment (c) would lead to all members of a species becoming adapted to it by selection of similar phenotypes with correspondingly similar genotypes. A genetic bottleneck (e) occurs when a population is reduced to a very few individuals, in which case the amount of genetic variation in the population may be much reduced, even if population numbers build up again later.

## Question 14.5

You may have thought of some of the following examples of geographical barriers:

- populations on different islands or continents separated by sea
- fish in different lakes or rivers separated by land
- populations on areas of land separated by rivers or streams
- populations living on a rocky coastline separated by areas of sandy shore
- populations living on a sandy coastline separated by areas of rocky shore
- lowland populations separated by mountains
- alpine populations separated by valleys
- rural populations separated by bands of urban development
- woodland populations separated by open fields
- areas of vegetation on a volcanic island separated by new lava flows
- areas of vegetation separated by areas covered in ice.

## Question 14.6

(a) You should be able to see that on an island such as Santa Cruz near the centre of the archipelago there are no endemic species, whereas if you move out from the centre, the number of endemic species increases.

(b) See Figure 14.9.

## Question 14.7

Factors (a), (d) and (g) will tend to hinder speciation. Speciation is prevented when there is sufficient gene flow between two populations; (a) migration and (d) hybridisation both transfer alleles from one population to another. (g) A greater than average number of offspring produced by hybrids between two populations, assuming the offspring survive and are themselves fertile, will also lead to a greater proportion of individuals carrying a mixture of alleles from both populations, i.e. to greater gene flow.

Factors (b), (c), (e) and (f) will tend to promote speciation. Speciation is promoted when gene flow between two populations is reduced. A genetic bottleneck (b) will greatly reduce the genetic variability of the population, with some alleles disappearing completely, and make the population more different from other populations of that species than it was before. In a novel environment, intense selection (c) can cause the colonising population to evolve adaptations to the new environment very quickly, and become different from other populations of that species in the process. If there are two types of female in a population, each of which prefers to mate with a different type of male (e), then this will tend to lead to two subgroups within the population, with mating mostly taking place within each subgroup, so that gene flow between them is reduced. Reduced fertility of hybrids between two populations (f) will mean that hybrids will tend to have lower reproductive success than other members of each population so that individuals carrying a mixture of alleles from the two populations will become less common, i.e. gene flow is reduced.

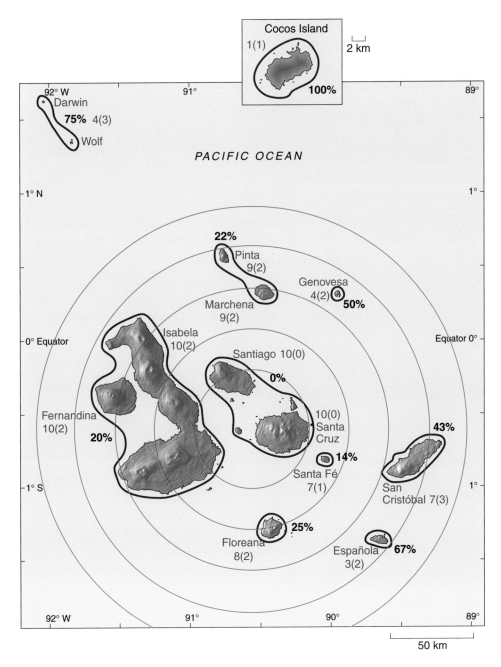

**Figure 14.9** Map of the larger islands of the Galápagos archipelago showing number of species and subspecies on each island (and the number of species and subspecies found *only* on that island in brackets). Percentages relate to the number of species and subspecies that are endemic to each island.

Question 14.8

(a) False. No evidence was presented in the text that the rate of mutation changed; if there had been some increase, it is unlikely to have been high enough to explain the dramatic increase in the *carbonaria* form from almost zero to 95% in urban areas.

(b) False. There is no evidence to suggest that moths died because of the direct effect of sulfur dioxide pollution.

(c) True. Recall that fitness is defined as the relative ability of an organism to survive and leave offspring that themselves survive and leave offspring. It is known that the frequency of *carbonaria* moths increased in industrial areas of Britain from almost zero to 95% during this time.

(d) False. It is highly unlikely that the changes were due simply to chance. Since the environment was changing and since colour form is adaptive, differential reproduction of genotypes would have occurred within the population – and this, by definition, is natural selection!

(e) True. Between 1970 and 1980 the number of the typical form was increasing and the number of the *carbonaria* form was decreasing; hence the gene pool must have changed.

## Question 15.1

Table 13.2 indicates that there are 3200 million bases (i.e. about $3 \times 10^9$ bases).

$1 \times 10^6$ base pairs gives $\dfrac{1 \times 10^6}{3 \times 10^9} \times 100\% = 0.03\%$ of the total.

# Comments on activities

## Activity 2.1

Here are suggested responses to the questions posed:

*What size container do I need?*

As long as the container has room for the contents of the soup can and approximately the same volume of air or more, its size is not critical.

*Why was it suggested that a rectangular container be used rather than (say) a cylindrical one?*

There is nothing wrong with using a cylindrical container. It is just that the maths involved in working out the volume of the air is easier with a rectangular container than with a cylindrical one. An empty rectangular ice-cream tub would be ideal for the investigation.

*How do I make sure that only air and soup are in the container at the start of the investigation?*

The container must be as clean as possible. After washing and rinsing it, it is best to leave it to dry in the air, since contamination can be introduced from cloths used for drying. In fact, it would be better if the container were left upside down as it dries to reduce the chance of fungal particles settling on the inside while it is drying.

*How do I make sure that nothing else gets inside the container once the investigation is under way?*

Clearly, the container needs to be covered during the investigation; cling film is probably the best option. The advantage of using cling film – rather than the container's own lid – is that you can see what is happening during the course of the investigation without having to lift the lid, which might introduce further contamination.

*How do I measure the volume of air in the container?*

You are going to have to measure the volume of air above the soup without disturbing the experimental set-up. It is easy to find the length and width of the container with a ruler, but how do you measure its depth? It is a good idea to use a translucent container if possible, so that you can see the level of the soup from the outside.

*Where should I leave the container for the duration of the investigation?*

The fungi are likely to grow faster if the container is left somewhere reasonably warm. Since it does not matter whether the container is kept in the light or the dark, a warm airing cupboard may be ideal.

*How long should I leave it?*

This is a difficult one to answer at this stage. However, if cling film is used and the container can be inspected (say) daily, then perhaps you do not have to decide before the investigation begins.

*How do I make sure that no one disturbs it?*

Besides putting the container in a safe place (e.g. out of reach of young children), you should label it so that it is clear what it is and who is responsible for it. (Although this may be obvious at home, it is good scientific practice to label all experiments in this way.)

*What records should I keep of the investigation?*

You should certainly record the date and time you started the investigation, and the location and conditions of the place where the container is to be kept during the investigation. You will presumably also want to record the date and time of each occasion when you inspected the container subsequently, as well as the number of fungi seen growing on the soup on each occasion and possibly a brief description of them.

*What should I do with the container and its contents afterwards?*

Although any fungi growing on the soup will have grown from fungal particles that were already floating in the air of your kitchen, it is recommended that you dispose of both the container and its contents without ever having lifted the cling film. It is for this reason that it was suggested that an ice-cream tub would be ideal (rather than a plastic lunch box that you would probably want to keep).

## Activity 4.1

(a) There are very few actual mistakes in the description. 'Growth 1 and growth 2' are generally written 'growth I and growth II' and 'intophase' should have been spelt 'interphase'.

(b) Perhaps the first criticism to be made is that the writer seems to assume that the reader knows what is meant by the term 'cell cycle' and therefore hardly explains it at all. The phrase 'takes different amounts of time' is rather vague. If anything is to be written about how long the cell cycle takes, there needs to be more detail than this. An alternative approach is simply to omit all reference to duration of the cell cycle.

The writer could have done a lot to help the reader by rethinking the order in which points are raised. For instance, replication – which takes place between growth I and growth II – is rather unhelpfully introduced right at the end. Generally speaking, if a process consists of a series of events that invariably take place in a particular sequence, then it is probably best to describe the process by following this sequence.

Note that, in this case, particular care has to be exercised to distinguish between 'cell division' taken to mean mitosis plus growth of the cell membrane across the middle of the cell, and 'cell division' taken to mean the actual separation of the parent cell into two progeny cells by the growth of this cell membrane. To emphasise the nature of this potential confusion, you will come across phrases such as 'mitotic cell division' (although mitosis is always followed by cell division). Slightly different uses of the same term or phrase are, regrettably, quite common in biology.

(c) Here is one attempt. Of course, yours is bound to be somewhat different. However, there is no reason to suppose that it isn't just as good.

> The cell cycle is the alternation of cell growth and division giving rise to successive generations of progeny cells. There is great variation in the total duration of the cell cycle and in the durations of different parts of it. The cycle consists of two parts: interphase and cell division. Interphase comprises two growth phases – growth I and growth II – separated by replication of the cell's DNA. Cell division consists of mitosis, in which a copy of each DNA molecule goes to each end of the cell, and actual division of the cell by growth of a new cell membrane across its middle.

Note that what is sometimes called a 'top down' approach has been used here. First, an overview is given of the entire cell cycle. Second, it is pointed out that the cell cycle consists of two parts. Third, these two parts are then described in more detail in the order in which they occur.

## Activity 4.2

Figures 4.29 and 4.30 are two possible diagrams. Figure 4.29 is a useful diagram because it puts the words prophase, metaphase, anaphase and telophase in the right order and links them with sketches showing what happens during each phase. This diagram is thus complete in its visual description of the process and the order of the phases.

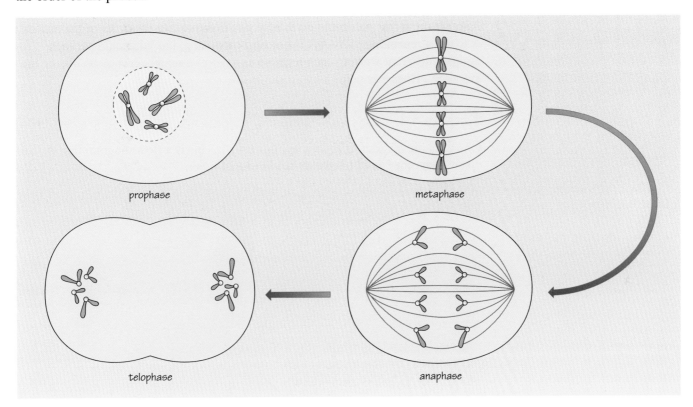

prophase

metaphase

telophase

anaphase

**Figure 4.29** A flow diagram of mitosis.

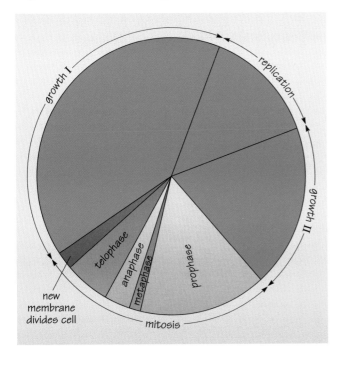

growth I

replication

growth II

telophase

anaphase

metaphase

prophase

new membrane divides cell

mitosis

**Figure 4.30** A diagram showing mitosis within the cell cycle.

315

Figure 4.30 is also a useful diagram because it makes the relationship between mitosis and the rest of the cell cycle very clear. In addition, it illustrates the passage of time. [Certain phases take longer than others. Their approximate relative durations have been shown for interest only. You were not given enough information to enable you to show these differences in your diagram.]

Your diagram is unlikely to be identical to either of the ones provided here, but does it help you to visualise the order in which the phases of mitosis take place?

Another thing that you could do to help you to remember the order of the phases is to use a mnemonic. 'PMAT' is not very promising, but you could perhaps assign a different word to each letter so as to form a sentence, such as 'Phone me any time'. Does this help?

### Activity 4.4

One possible diagram is shown in Figure 4.31. This is a flow diagram that shows clearly the order in which the different events occur.

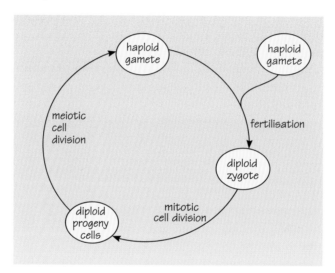

**Figure 4.31**    A flow diagram showing the order of events in sexual reproduction.

### Activity 4.5

Table 4.3 lists features relating to asexual and sexual reproduction. Note that if you were asked for a piece of writing on this topic, drawing up such a table would be an excellent early stage in the planning process.

**Table 4.3** A comparison of asexual and sexual reproduction.

|  | Asexual reproduction | Sexual reproduction |
|---|---|---|
| **Similarities:** | produces offspring | produces offspring |
|  | offspring are smaller than parent, and must grow | offspring are smaller than parent, and must grow |
| **Differences:** | one parent only | two parents |
|  | no gametes are produced | gametes are produced. These are haploid. Nuclei of two gametes fuse (fertilisation) to form a diploid zygote |
|  | meiosis absent | meiosis present at some stage in the life cycle |
|  | DNA of offspring identical to that of parent | part of the offspring's DNA is a copy of some of the DNA of one parent, the remainder is a copy of some of the DNA of the other parent |
|  | offspring identical to parent | offspring not identical to either parent |
|  | commonly occurs in plants, less-complex animals and microbes. Absent in more complex animals | occurs in the majority of plants and animals |
|  | often results in the rapid production of large numbers | less-rapid increase in numbers |

## Activity 5.1

Suggested answers are as follows, with the chemical formulae and structural formulae included for reference.

A *carboxylic acid* is an organic compound containing the carboxyl group, —COOH. Example: propanoic acid, $CH_2CH_3COOH$.

An *amine* is an organic compound containing the amino functional group, —$NH_2$. Example: methylamine, $CH_3NH_2$.

An *amino acid* is an organic compound with an amino group, —$NH_2$, and a carboxylic acid group, —COOH.

A *catalyst* changes the rate at which a chemical reaction occurs, but is itself unchanged at the end of the reaction.

An *enzyme* is an organic catalyst produced by living cells, e.g. trypsin that catalyses the breakdown of food protein in the gut.

A *covalent bond* is a strong bond in which the electrons are shared by the atoms involved in the bond, for example $CH_4$ has four covalent bonds, one between carbon and each hydrogen.

In a *condensation reaction* two functional groups from two separate monomers react with each other; a covalent bond is formed and a molecule of water is eliminated.

$$CH_3-C\overset{O}{\underset{OH}{\lesseqgtr}} \quad + \quad HO-CH_3 \quad \longrightarrow \quad CH_3-C\overset{O}{\underset{O-CH_3}{\lesseqgtr}} \quad + \quad H_2O$$

| acid | alcohol | ester | water |

An *ester* is an organic compound containing the ester group:

$$-C\overset{O}{\underset{O-}{\lesseqgtr}}$$

For example, methyl acetate, which is formed in the condensation reaction between an acid (acetic acid) and an alcohol (methanol).

$$CH_3-C\overset{O}{\underset{O-CH_3}{\lesseqgtr}}$$

*Hydrolysis* means 'splitting with water'. It is the opposite of condensation and involves breaking a covalent bond in a reaction in which water is consumed.

$$CH_3-C\overset{O}{\underset{O-CH_3}{\lesseqgtr}} \quad + \quad H_2O \quad \longrightarrow \quad CH_3-C\overset{O}{\underset{OH}{\lesseqgtr}} \quad + \quad HO-CH_3$$

| ester | water | acid | alcohol |

A *monomer* is a small molecule from which polymers are built up, for example amino acids are monomers of proteins. The monomers must have two functional groups that react to form strong covalent bonds. For example, all amino acids have an amino group at one end and a carboxylic acid group at the other, as in glycine: $H_2N-CH_2-COOH$.

A *polymer* is a large molecule built by many small molecules reacting together. Most biopolymers are a result of condensation reactions, e.g. three amino acids condense to form part of a protein:

$$\cdots NH-\underset{R^1}{CH}-\overset{O}{C}-NH-\underset{R^2}{CH}-\overset{O}{C}-NH-\underset{R^3}{CH}-\overset{O}{C}\cdots$$

Note that the bonds formed when amino acids condense in this way are called *peptide bonds*.

### Revising and integrating information

You may have found that you had to refer back to Book 4 in order to complete this activity. Revising and integrating knowledge from earlier in the course is a feature of this book. It is worth making a general point about this activity. Here the idea has been to reduce a large amount of information to a manageable quantity, with the key concepts standing out, ready to be used in Book 5. The actual examples you have chosen will probably be different, but they should be meaningful to you.

When you want to recall something, you may find that you can remember either an example, from which you can construct the description or definition for yourself, or you can remember the description. Either way will help you to interpret further examples, and to make sense of additional related information.

Reworking and extending earlier knowledge is an important way to consolidate your understanding. When you come to revise ideas from earlier in the course in preparation for the final S104 assessment, you will not want to have pages and pages of notes; gathering together important information in a table, or as a condensed paragraph, a bullet point list or a diagram, is a valuable way to home in on the core information you need. Also, working like this makes it easier to remember the concepts. This is partly because you have reworked them actively, and partly because you have assembled them in a form in which you can remember them more easily.

## Activity 5.2

(a) The following are possible interactions between the R groups.
- *Ionic interactions*: Asp (aspartate) and Lys (lysine). In this case the negatively charged carboxylate ion in aspartate can form a weak interaction with the positively charged ammonium ion in lysine.
- *Hydrogen bonds*: Ser (serine) and Thr (threonine); Asp and Ser; Asp and Thr; Lys and Ser; Lys and Thr. Here a hydrogen with a δ+ charge forms a hydrogen bond to an oxygen atom (with a negative charge) in another amino acid. Refer to Book 4, Section 4.2.3 for a recap of hydrogen bonding.
- *Hydrophobic interactions*: Ala (alanine) and Val (valine); Ala and Ile (isoleucine); Ala and Phe (phenylalanine); Val and Ile; Val and Phe; Ile and Phe. In this case amino acids with prominent hydrocarbon side chains (alkyl groups or benzene rings) can form weak interactions when these hydrophobic groups align themselves together.

(b) Hydrophobic groups (R groups of Ala, Val, Ile and Phe) are 'water-fearing' and hence are found towards the interior of the molecule. Many hydrophilic groups (R groups of Asp, Lys, Ser and Thr) are also found in the interior when the polypeptide chain folds up, where they will interact with each other (as in (a) above). However, where hydrophilic groups occur on the surface of the protein they will interact with water molecules.

## Activity 5.3

Here is one possible answer:
- *primary structure* of a protein or polypeptide is its sequence of amino acids
- peptide bonds link amino acids (amino group to carboxylate group) forming a chain
- 20 different amino acids
- some amino acids are repeated more than once and some are not present at all
- can join up in a huge number of different sequences
- amino acid sequence is unique to a specific protein
- globular proteins fold up on themselves to give three-dimensional shapes – *higher-order structure*
- the 20 different amino acids have different R groups sticking out from the polypeptide chain

- weak interactions between R groups in the polypeptide result in the higher-order structure
- some R groups form hydrophobic interactions, some form hydrogen bonds and yet others form ionic interactions with each other
- proteins fold up so that the maximum number of weak interactions are formed
- given the same sequence of amino acids, the protein will always fold up in the same way, i.e. same higher-order structure.

By producing a summary list of all the information that you would need to include in the account, the hard work is already done. You now only need to decide how to divide up the information into appropriate paragraphs, what diagrams you might like to use to illustrate your main points, and ensure that you explain any unfamiliar terms. By attempting to write your list without reference to the book in the first instance, you are able to check your understanding of the underlying science, then identify 'holes' in your knowledge and understanding, which you can rectify from re-examining the book. When you do write your completed account, you should always use your list rather than going back to the original text. This will ensure that your final account is written in your own words and is not a collection of choice sentences lifted from the book.

## Activity 6.1

The light reactions of photosynthesis are dependent on the capture of photons of light energy by chlorophyll molecules in the chloroplast. As Figure 6.23 shows, this light energy is used to split water to release oxygen and protons and electrons. The electrons are passed along a sequence of carriers in the thylakoid membrane, shown in the diagram as the structure separating the stroma of the chloroplast from the lumen. These electrons eventually combine with the coenzyme NADP and protons from the stroma to give NADP.2H.

**Figure 6.23**   Completed summary of the light reactions.

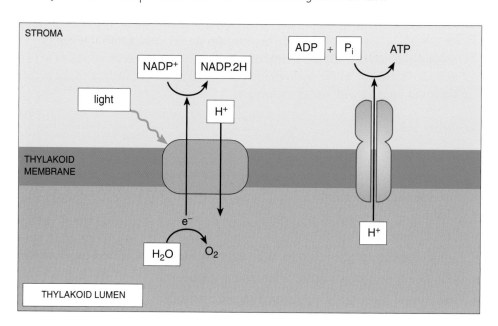

Protons are added to the thylakoid lumen as a result of the splitting of water and proton shuttling and are removed from the stroma as a result of electron transport to NADP. These processes allow the formation of a proton gradient across the thylakoid membrane, with a greater concentration of protons inside the lumen than in the stroma. Protons in the lumen are then able to flow down the concentration gradient via the ATP synthase proteins shown on the right of the diagram and manufacture ATP from ADP and $P_i$. The products of the light reactions ATP and NADP.2H are then used in the dark reactions to reduce carbon dioxide to glucose.

(*195 words*)

Notice how the above account makes several specific references to the diagram so the text and the figure complement each other and together summarise the process as clearly as possible.

## Activity 6.2

Check your completed flow diagram with the one in Figure 6.24. You might have drawn yours differently. For example, you might have drawn the reactions that occur in the TCA cycle as a cycle; we chose not to do this because we wanted to emphasise that most of the energy from the 2C acetyl group is transferred during this cycle to reduced coenzymes, particularly NAD.2H, and a small amount is harvested to produce ATP by means of substrate-level phosphorylation. The energy stored in the reduced coenzymes is released during Stage 4 of glucose oxidation via a number of steps, eventually being transferred to ATP. What is important is that your diagram shows all the steps involved in the transfer of energy to ATP, and that it makes sense to you. This is quite a difficult activity and if you got most of the steps, then you have followed the text very well. Drawing this flow diagram should have prompted you to think more carefully about the sequence of events occurring in the mitochondria. Remember that flow diagrams like this summarise a considerable number of pages of text and so are useful revision aids

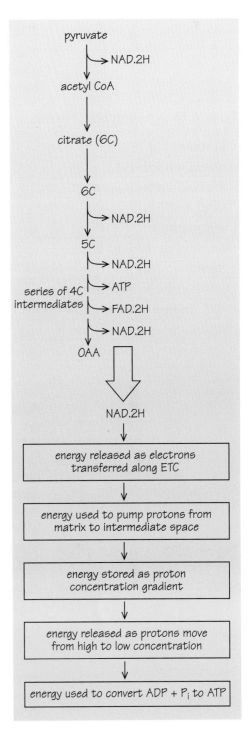

**Figure 6.24** Flow diagram summarising the transfer of energy stored in pyruvate to ATP in the mitochondria.

## Activity 6.3

The processes of oxidative phosphorylation and photophosphorylation are summarised in Table 6.10. These are similar for features with 'yes' in the table but different for all the others.

**Table 6.10** A comparison of oxidative phosphorylation and photophosphorylation. Completed Table 6.5.

| Feature | Oxidative phosphorylation | Photophosphorylation |
|---|---|---|
| type of cell found in | all cells | plant cells containing chlorophyll |
| location of process in cell | mitochondria | chloroplast |
| location of ETC | inner mitochondrial membrane | thylakoid membrane |
| energy source | carbohydrates/lipids/amino acids | solar energy |
| source of electrons for ETC | NAD.2H/FAD.2H | $H_2O$ |
| electron acceptor | $O_2$ | NADP |
| proton gradient established across a membrane | yes | yes |
| ATP synthase is site for ATP synthesis | yes | yes |
| ATP produced from ADP and $P_i$ | yes | yes |
| end-products of phosphorylation process | ATP and $H_2O$ | ATP and NADP.2H and $O_2$ |

## Activity 7.1

### Section 1    Introduction to an oak woodland

Using the virtual woodland landscape and the field guides you have found and identified a number of species that occupy an oak woodland. The species that interact with each other form a biological community. The biological community and the physical environment it occupies is an ecosystem. The oak tree itself can be regarded as an ecosystem. It provides many different environments which a wide range of species can occupy as their habitats.

### Section 2    A sparrowhawk's eye view

There are complex interrelationships within an ecosystem but by focusing on a single species it was possible to unravel some of that complexity. You were able to construct a nutritional sequence, or food chain. You first identified what the sparrowhawk eats. You repeated the process with the great tit, the food of the sparrowhawk, and completed the chain by identifying the food of the great tit as the winter moth caterpillar and that these in turn eat the leaves of the oak trees. The chain consists of two carnivores and a herbivore and begins, as all food chains do, with an autotroph.

### Section 3    How much food to raise a brood

Having identified the steps in the food chain, it may be possible to establish how many individuals of a particular species are needed to support those species that feed on them either directly or indirectly. Although the resulting pyramid of numbers is interesting it must be used with caution (e.g. consider whether individual trees or individual oak trees should form the base of the pyramid). Great care needs to be taken over data collection to ensure accurate averages are used when food chains are quantified.

## Section 4    Energy flow

Organisms in a food chain represent sources of energy for those organisms that feed on them. Thus a food chain can be converted into an energy chain and a pyramid of numbers can be converted into a (much more useful) pyramid of energy flow. Only a tiny proportion of solar energy falling on plants is captured by photosynthesis as gross primary productivity (GPP). Of this, some is used in plant respiration and only that stored as increase in plant biomass (net primary productivity or NPP) is potentially available to herbivores. For both herbivores and carnivores:

biomass consumption = energy assimilated + energy lost in faeces

and

energy assimilated = increase in biomass + energy used in respiration.

Comparatively little of any species biomass ends up as biomass increase in the next species in a food chain.

## Section 5    Food webs

This section took a broader look at the interactions between species in the woodland. Most species are part of several interacting food chains. By looking at the tit in the food chain you saw that the sparrowhawk competes with other species for this food source. You constructed a food web that explored a few of the many interactions in the woodland ecosystem. This system was used to classify the organisms into different classes, such as producer, consumer, herbivore and carnivore, and to introduce new classes of organism such as parasites, decomposers and detritivores. Most organisms harbour smaller parasites. All organisms that avoid being consumed and die a natural death are broken down by detritivores and consumers, as are faeces and other waste. Thus, the oak woodland and other ecosystems are best thought of in terms of food webs rather than food chains. The ultimate fate of all the energy captured by photosynthesis (GPP) is to be used in respiration by one of the organisms in a food web (ignoring combustion).

## Section 6    Getting the timing right

A key feature in breeding success is getting the timing right. In this exercise you identified some of the key dates in the year of the oak tree. You then identified the key stages in the life cycle of the winter moth, and the blue tit. (The blue tit occupies the same position in the food chain as the great tit, both birds being taken by the sparrowhawk.) Using the field guides you put durations to the key stages in the life cycles of the winter moth, the blue tit and sparrowhawk.

All these pieces of information were then used to investigate the optimal timing in the year for caterpillar egg emergence, and breeding for the blue tit and the sparrowhawk. You found that whilst each organism acts in its own 'best interests', its actions often have considerable consequences for other organisms in the food chain. Finally, you saw that there is a difference in timing between individuals of each species, and looked at some of the implications of changes in the weather at critical times of the year, and global warming.

323

**Activity 7.2**

1   20% of the GPP of the plants in the oak woodland per hectare per year is eventually lost to the ecosystem by plant respiration:

$0.20 \times 1.0 \times 10^8$ kJ ha$^{-1}$ y$^{-1}$ = **2.0 × 10$^7$ kJ ha$^{-1}$ y$^{-1}$**

2   Rearranging the equation GPP = NPP + R gives NPP = GPP − R:

NPP = $1.0 \times 10^8$ kJ ha$^{-1}$ y$^{-1}$ − $2.0 \times 10^7$ kJ ha$^{-1}$ y$^{-1}$

NPP = $8.0 \times 10^7$ kJ ha$^{-1}$ y$^{-1}$

We are expressing this answer to 2 significant figures even though this suggests a higher precision than is really justified from the original data. This follows best practice of greater precision in intermediate calculations.

3   10% of plant biomass (NPP) is consumed by herbivores:

$0.10 \times 8.0 \times 10^7$ kJ ha$^{-1}$ y$^{-1}$ = **8.0 × 10$^6$ kJ ha$^{-1}$ y$^{-1}$**

4   Amount of energy unassimilated is 60% of energy consumed by herbivores:

$0.60 \times 8.0 \times 10^6$ kJ ha$^{-1}$ y$^{-1}$ = $4.8 \times 10^6$ kJ ha$^{-1}$ y$^{-1}$

The question states:

biomass consumption = energy assimilated + energy lost in faeces

Rearranging this equation gives:

energy assimilated = biomass consumption − energy lost as faeces

$= 8.0 \times 10^6$ kJ ha$^{-1}$ y$^{-1}$ − $4.8 \times 10^6$ kJ ha$^{-1}$ y$^{-1}$

**= 3.2 × 10$^6$ kJ ha$^{-1}$ y$^{-1}$**

Alternatively, you may have simply calculated 40% of energy consumed by herbivores:

$0.40 \times 8.0 \times 10^6$ kJ ha$^{-1}$ y$^{-1}$ = **3.2 × 10$^6$ kJ ha$^{-1}$ y$^{-1}$**

5   Amount of energy in herbivore biomass is 15% of plant material consumed:

$0.15 \times 8.0 \times 10^6$ kJ ha$^{-1}$ y$^{-1}$ = $1.2 \times 10^6$ kJ ha$^{-1}$ y$^{-1}$

The question states:

energy assimilated = increase in biomass + energy lost in respiration

Rearranging this equation gives:

energy lost in respiration = energy assimilated − increase in biomass

$= 3.2 \times 10^6$ kJ ha$^{-1}$ y$^{-1}$ − $1.2 \times 10^6$ kJ ha$^{-1}$ y$^{-1}$

**= 2.0 × 10$^6$ kJ ha$^{-1}$ y$^{-1}$**

6   25% of herbivore biomass is consumed by carnivores:

$0.25 \times 1.2 \times 10^6$ kJ ha$^{-1}$ y$^{-1}$ = **3.0 × 10$^5$ kJ ha$^{-1}$ y$^{-1}$**

7   25% of energy consumed by first carnivores is unassimilated:

$0.25 \times 3.0 \times 10^5$ kJ ha$^{-1}$ y$^{-1}$ = $7.5 \times 10^4$ kJ ha$^{-1}$ y$^{-1}$

The question states:

biomass consumption = energy assimilated + energy lost in faeces

Rearranging this equation gives:

energy assimilated = biomass consumption − energy lost in faeces

$$= 3.0 \times 10^5 \text{ kJ ha}^{-1} \text{ y}^{-1} - 7.5 \times 10^4 \text{ kJ ha}^{-1} \text{ y}^{-1}$$

$$= 2.25 \times 10^5 \text{ kJ ha}^{-1} \text{ y}^{-1}$$

$$= \textbf{2.3} \times \textbf{10}^5 \textbf{ kJ ha}^{-1} \textbf{ y}^{-1} \text{ (to 2 significant figures)}$$

8   5.0% of the energy consumed by first carnivores is converted into biomass:

$$0.050 \times 3.0 \times 10^5 \text{ kJ ha}^{-1} \text{ y}^{-1} = 1.5 \times 10^4 \text{ kJ ha}^{-1} \text{ y}^{-1}$$

The question states:

energy assimilated = increase in biomass + energy lost in respiration

Rearranging this equation gives:

energy lost in respiration = energy assimilated − increase in biomass

$$= 2.25 \times 10^5 \text{ kJ ha}^{-1} \text{ y}^{-1} - 1.5 \times 10^4 \text{ kJ ha}^{-1} \text{ y}^{-1}$$

$$= \textbf{2.1} \times \textbf{10}^5 \textbf{ kJ ha}^{-1} \textbf{ y}^{-1}$$

9   (a)  Material such as leaf fall or wood fall from plants, faeces from animals including indigestible material such as feathers and bone.

(b)  50% of $2.9 \times 10^7 \text{ kJ ha}^{-1} \text{ y}^{-1}$ is $1.45 \times 10^7 \text{ kJ ha}^{-1} \text{ y}^{-1}$ (keeping it to 3 significant figures at present).

25% of this material is assimilated by detritivores and decomposers:

$$0.25 \times 1.45 \times 10^7 \text{ kJ ha}^{-1} \text{ y}^{-1} = 3.63 \times 10^6 \text{ kJ ha}^{-1} \text{ y}^{-1}$$

$$= \textbf{3.6} \times \textbf{10}^6 \textbf{ kJ ha}^{-1} \textbf{ y}^{-1} \text{ (to 2 significant figures)}$$

(c)  5.0% of the energy consumed is used to increase detritivore and decomposer biomass:

$$0.050 \times 1.45 \times 10^7 \text{ kJ ha}^{-1} \text{ y}^{-1} = 7.25 \times 10^5 \text{ kJ ha}^{-1} \text{ y}^{-1}$$

Using the same equation as in step 8:

energy lost to respiration = energy assimilated − increase in biomass

$$= 3.63 \times 10^6 \text{ kJ ha}^{-1} \text{ y}^{-1} - 7.25 \times 10^5 \text{ kJ ha}^{-1} \text{ y}^{-1}$$

$$= 2.91 \times 10^6 \text{ kJ ha}^{-1} \text{ y}^{-1}$$

$$= \textbf{2.9} \times \textbf{10}^6 \textbf{ kJ ha}^{-1} \textbf{ y}^{-1} \text{ (to 2 significant figures)}$$

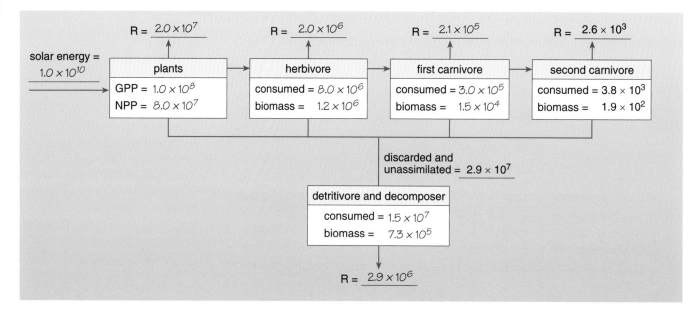

**Figure 7.6**    Energy flow through an oak woodland ecosystem. Completed Figure 7.5.

10  Of the $1.0 \times 10^{10}$ kJ ha$^{-1}$ y$^{-1}$ of solar energy incident on the ecosystem only $1.9 \times 10^2$ kJ ha$^{-1}$ y$^{-1}$ ends up as biomass in the highest carnivore. Therefore:

$$\frac{1.9 \times 10^2 \text{ kJ ha}^{-1} \text{ y}^{-1}}{1.0 \times 10^{10} \text{ kJ ha}^{-1} \text{ y}^{-1}} \times 100\% = \mathbf{1.9 \times 10^{-6}\%}$$

Photosynthesis is only 1% efficient so there is a huge initial loss of energy. Further up the trophic levels, energy is lost from the ecosystem at every trophic level, as heat from herbivore, carnivore, decomposer and detritivore respiration.

11  This loss of energy at every level to respiration explains why the numbers of organisms/biomass of organisms at each trophic level decrease as one moves from herbivore to highest carnivore. There is simply insufficient energy left at the highest carnivore level to sustain many organisms.

12  Carnivore assimilation is much more efficient than herbivore assimilation due to the nature of the food material consumed. A great proportion of herbivores' food is the plant material cellulose (the cell wall polysaccharide you met in Chapter 5) which is very difficult to digest. A lot of the energy from the plant material eaten by herbivores is therefore unavailable and passes out in the faeces. Carnivores can assimilate a much greater proportion of the energy in their food, as the high protein content is easy to digest and absorb.

## Activity 7.3

Compare your answer with the one below, written by a student. (The terms you were asked to include are printed in italics.)

> An *ecosystem* is a set of organisms linked by flows of energy and materials.

Energy enters the ecosystem in the form of solar energy, captured during *photosynthesis* by *autotrophic* organisms such as plants. These autotrophs form the lowest *trophic level* of an ecosystem.

The energy captured by autotrophs during photosynthesis is known as the *gross primary productivity* of the ecosystem. Some of the energy is lost when the plants *respire*, but the rest goes to make plant material or *biomass*. The amount of plant biomass produced is known as the *net primary productivity* of the system.

Plant biomass may then be consumed by *heterotrophic* organisms; that is, organisms that do not use solar energy directly but gain their materials and energy by consuming other organisms. Plant-eating animals, called *herbivores*, are heterotrophs and constitute a higher trophic level. The transfer of materials and energy between organisms in different trophic levels is the basis of a *food chain*. The heterotrophic organisms are able to *assimilate* some of the plant material, and the rest is discarded as *faeces*. Assimilated food is either used to build animal biomass, or is used in respiration, with the energy then being lost from the ecosystem.

Energy continues to flow through an ecosystem into further trophic levels of the food chain, consisting of the primary and higher *carnivores*, which consume other animals and are therefore also heterotrophs. Dead plant and animal material, and animal faeces, may be consumed by yet other heterotrophs known as *decomposers* and *detritivores*. The complex system involving many such transfers of energy and materials creates a *food web*. Respiration by detritivores and decomposers releases any remaining energy left in plant and animal material/faeces as heat.

To summarise, energy flows through ecosystems through a series of energy conversions; beginning with solar energy. If the ecosystem is in steady state all the energy absorbed is lost as heat as a result of respiration by all the living organisms in that ecosystem.

(343 words)

You might have made additional points, for example, that plant biomass may be burned (e.g. in forest fires) or may enter the rock cycle as part of an organic rock (such as coal) (recall your study of Book 1, Chapter 7, on the carbon cycle); in such cases the materials and energy are removed from the ecosystem.

How does your answer compare with this student's? Obviously they will be different, but they should convey the same overall meaning. If they don't, is this because you have misunderstood the meaning of one of the new terms? Look it up in the course Glossary if necessary.

If you have correctly understood all the terms, have you used them unambiguously and explained their meaning where necessary? Look at your own writing critically, in much the same way as you looked at someone else's writing critically in Activity 4.1.

Finally, look critically at the structure of your piece of writing. Did you try to order the terms in a logical fashion so that they fitted in with your plan, or did you just take them in the order they were listed in the question – alphabetically? Here is the plan from the student who wrote the answer above:

Introduction: ecosystem

Initial energy input: solar energy, photosynthesis, autotroph, gross primary productivity

First stage (plant productivity): biomass, respiration, net primary productivity, trophic level

Next stage: heterotroph, herbivore, food chain, assimilate, faeces

Next stage: carnivore, decomposer, detritivore

Next stage: food web

Conclusion: fate of energy in ecosystems

This student started by grouping the terms into what she thought were related topics, and then tried to structure her account around that list. As you can see, she had to move a few of the terms to construct her final account, but the initial ordered list gave her a good structure to build on. In fact, she ended up by writing a paragraph around each group of terms. How did you structure your account?

### Writing scientific accounts in assignments: general advice

There are many different ways of producing scientific accounts, and what matters is that you develop your own method so that you can produce accounts of the standard you want. It is probable that you will be asked to produce some extended pieces of writing in the remaining assignments of S104. It might help you to ask yourself the following questions:

*(a) What is the question asking me to do?*

The first step is to analyse the question. Underline or highlight process words like 'describe, 'discuss' or 'compare and contrast' that tell you what you have to do with the material. Then underline/highlight the words that tell you which concepts in science you will be working with.

*(b) On what science does this question depend?*

Next you need to research the science. You will find the information you want by searching in glossaries, summaries, indexes, contents pages, questions, activities, your notes, and (if you have time and if it is appropriate to the question asked) outside sources such as books, articles, internet resources etc.

*(c) How am I going to put it all together?*

We encourage you to plan pieces of written work before you start writing. However, research amongst both tutors and students reveals that the actual process of writing an account takes many different forms, and may not follow the traditional process of 'first make a plan'. The boon of being able to rearrange sentences and paragraphs with a word processor means that even a very poorly thought out first draft can still be turned into what appears to be a well-planned account.

What is essential is that you decide what to include and what to leave out, and how to link the points that you include so that they answer the question that was set. Noting down your decisions as a plan, or outline, gives you a framework within which you can construct your account. Of course, you may change your ideas about content or order as you're writing, but that will be easier to do if you have a plan in front of you. And if you have an overall structure for your answer in mind, then it is much easier to tell a coherent story, and you won't have to spend so much time rejigging your answer later. What you should be aiming for is an account that is presented in a good order, written clearly and concisely, in appropriate language, with signposts and links between the different points to make it easy to read.

*(d) How can I improve my written work?*

When you have completed your account, you may like to ask yourself, 'How well have I done?' and consider 'Why?'

Try to be constructively critical, considering both how good your account is and how it could be further improved. A similar approach can be applied to any piece of scientific writing.

In general terms, the criteria by which you should judge your work fall into three groups. First, there are the criteria by which the *science* content is judged; you should demonstrate your knowledge and understanding by ensuring the information you include is correct, relevant to any question posed and addresses all the key points. Second, there are criteria by which the *writing* is judged: the science is communicated clearly and concisely using language appropriate for your purpose and audience; that you are writing in the correct style, for example an account or a report; that the relevant information is well organised with a logical structure, including relevant figures (such as tables, graphs, or diagrams addresses that you refer to from the text) and that you reference sources of information correctly (you will build further on your experience of referencing websites and journal articles in Book 8). Third, when you are answering an assignment question, pay particular attention to the cognitive skills that you are being asked to demonstrate, where words such as describe, explain, analyse, interpret, compare and contrast, indicate how you should process your knowledge and understanding of the subject matter; if you are asked to interpret information, simply describing data is insufficient.

Of course, to work systematically and thoughtfully through your answer, improving it as you go, requires that you set aside sufficient time and that means not leaving completion of an assignment until the day before the cut-off date!

One last point; an assignment is not finished until you receive feedback from your tutor. Read this carefully and integrate any advice on how to improve your writing skills into your advice to yourself about how to tackle future writing and assignments.

## Activity 9.1

(a) The completed diagram, summarising Morgan's observations, is shown in Figure 9.10. Note that the white-eyed flies are all male (and incidentally they appear every alternate generation).

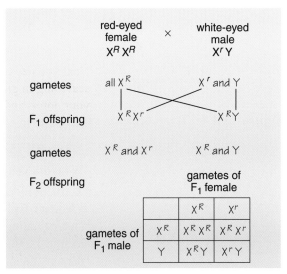

**Figure 9.10** Completed version of Figure 9.3.

(b) Half of the $F_2$ offspring would be female (XX) and half would be male (XY). All the female $F_2$ offspring are red-eyed, in a 1 $R\,R$ : 1 $R\,r$ genotypic ratio. Half of the males would be red-eyed (*R*–; they would have only one copy of the gene) but the other half would be white eyed (*r*–). The phenotypic ratio of all red-eyed flies to white-eyed flies would be 3 : 1, and the overall ratio would be two red-eyed females : one red-eyed male : one white-eyed male.

(c) Males have to inherit only one copy of the recessive allele for the phenotype to be shown, whereas females have to inherit two copies of the recessive allele, one from each parent, in order for the recessive phenotype to be manifest.

## Activity 11.1

The following is a list of key scientific points to be included, and one possible order in which they could be written up into a coherent account:

- Transcription is the process of RNA synthesis; it transfers the code in DNA to RNA.

- Hydrogen bonds are broken – the DNA strands separate; one of these is the template strand.

- Only part of the DNA molecule is transcribed.

- RNA polymerase adds nucleotides one at a time and the sugar–phosphate backbone is formed.

- Base-pairing rules of DNA to RNA.

(Note that these key points could be put together in other logical orders.)

The answer, given below, is based on the order of the key points given in the list. It would, with a suitable diagram (as used here), provide a very good answer.

Transcription is the process of RNA synthesis, in which information coded in DNA is transcribed into RNA (Figure 11.14).

The hydrogen bonds of part of the DNA double helix are broken so that the two strands separate.

Only one of the polynucleotide strands is used as the DNA template on which RNA synthesis occurs (Figure 11.14). RNA polymerase adds nucleotides one at a time according to the base-pairing rules: G binds to C, T of DNA binds to A of RNA, and A of DNA binds to U of RNA. The sugar–phosphate backbone of the RNA molecule is formed.

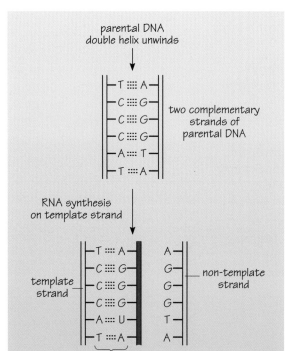

**Figure 11.14**   The process of transcription.

What did you achieve by doing this activity?

The activity asked you to think about which key points are needed to give an adequate explanation of transcription. This required you to have a thorough understanding of the process. Your order of key points may not have been identical to those given here, but if the points were similar, you have demonstrated a good understanding of transcription.

Asking you to identify key points should help you to look closely at questions and to assess what is likely to be important in the answer. This in turn should enable you to become more critical of your own written work. Also, putting the key points in a logical order is an important part of planning a piece of writing.

Finally, note that this answer summarises 2–3 pages of the book into one paragraph. This sort of summary, especially if accompanied by appropriate diagrams, is useful for revision.

## Activity 11.2

In this activity, you reviewed the structure of DNA and RNA, and the processes of DNA replication, transcription and translation. You have seen how the first two of these processes relate to the structure of DNA as a double helix, and how the information carried in DNA is translated – via mRNA – into a sequence of amino acids in a polypeptide chain. In this computer-based video sequence, the information coded in DNA is likened to the printed characters in a pile of telephone directories. In the cell, only a portion of this information (i.e. only some genes) is required to be translated into proteins. In the analogy, this portion is represented as a page in a telephone directory and the information it contains can be transferred either by being removed (torn out), in which case some of the information is lost, or by it being copied as a photocopy, in which case the information in the directories is left intact. In the cell, the information in DNA is transferred, not by being removed, but by being copied – a 'photocopy' – in the form of mRNA, and the entire information in DNA is left intact.

The notes you added to the comments column in Table 11.2 will reflect whatever you personally found useful or visually striking, and therefore will help you remember the key points of the structures and processes shown in the video sequence.

## Activity 15.1

Here is one possible explanation:

The long generation time for humans means it is unlikely that the high frequencies of the CCR5–Δ32 allele in Northern Europe derive from the selection pressure of HIV, as this virus became prevalent only from about 1970, well within the lifespan of individuals living now. As the mutant allele appeared about 2000 years ago and this mutation event is very rare, the relatively high frequencies of CCR5–Δ32 in Northern Europe are likely to have resulted from marked selection pressure, probably a lethal infection prevalent many generations ago. This infective agent, like HIV, entered the cells of the immune system via the receptor coded for by the CCR5 gene.

An epidemic of this lethal infection across Northern Europe could have been spread by Viking invasions. If the CCR5–Δ32 gene conferred immunity to the infection in a similar way to the way it does for HIV, those individuals having the CCR5–Δ32 allele would have been resistant to the infection. Most infected individuals with the CCR5 gene would have died, meaning that there were relatively fewer offspring having the CCR5 gene following the epidemic. In contrast, those individuals with the CCR5–Δ32 allele survived and their offspring inherited the mutant gene. Natural selection therefore resulted in the increased frequency of *CCR5–Δ32* in the gene pools of the populations, which has been maintained in the succeeding generations. The selection pressure for the *CCR5–Δ32* allele was very high, as indicated by the high frequencies of the mutant gene in Northern Europe, especially Scandinavia.

(*247 words*)

Since this is written by one student for another, the answer assumes an understanding of terms such as mutant, natural selection, selection pressure, immune system, gene and allele. The student starts by stating the key factor – that the association with HIV is independent of the high frequencies of the mutant allele observed in Europe. The evidence for this is then given and explained by referring to natural selection. Finally, the presence of an unknown selection pressure is suggested and an explanation for how it might have acted is provided.

[As an aside, it is possible that smallpox provided the selection pressure, and that the *CCR5–Δ32* mutant provided resistance to smallpox. It is not possible to test this hypothesis as smallpox has been eliminated from human populations and experiments with the virus are not possible.]

# References

Darwin, C. (1859) *On the Origin of Species by Means of Natural Selection, or the Preservation of Favoured Races in the Struggle for Life*, London, John Murray.

Hooper, J. (2002) *Of Moths and Men: The Untold Story of Science and the Peppered Moth*, WW Norton & Company, New York.

Linnaeus, C. (1758) *Systema Naturae* (10th edn).

Watson, J. D. and Crick, F. H. C. (1953) 'A structure for deoxyribose nucleic acid', *Nature*, vol. 171, pp. 737–738.

Wilson, E. O. (1992) *The Diversity of Life*, Cambridge, MA, Belknapp Press.

Global Conservation Organization (WWF), available online from http://www.panda.org/ [last accessed June, 2007].

# Acknowledgements

The S104 Course Team gratefully acknowledges the contributions of the S103 *Discovering science* course team and of its predecessors.

Grateful acknowledgement is made to the following sources for permission to reproduce material in this book.

## Figures

Cover: Eric Heller/Science Photo Library;

Figure 1.1: Bjanka Kadic/Science Photo Library; Figure 1.2a: Geoscience Features Picture Library; Figure 1.2b: Colorado State University; Figure 1.3a: © David Fleetham/Alamy; Figure 1.3b: Gavin Kingcome/Science Photo Library; Figures 1.3c and 1.3d: Peter Sheldon; Figure 1.4a: Heather Angel/Natural Visions; Figure 1.4b: Tim Jackson/Photolibrary; Figure 1.4c: Mike Gilliam/Ardea;

Figure 2.1: Kim, S./Flickr Photo Sharing; Figure 2.2: Pat Morris/Ardea; Figure 2.3: © Popperfoto/Alamy; Figure 2.6: Michael Fogden/Photolibrary; Figure 2.8: Photolibrary;

Figure 3.1a: © Philip Mugridge/Alamy; Figure 3.1b: Rolf Mueller/Photolibrary; Figure 3.1c: © Arco Images/Alamy; Figure 3.1d: Lawrie Phipps/Flickr Photo Sharing; Figure 3.2: G. E. Hyde/FLPA; Figures 3.3a and 3.3b: Heather Angel/Natural Visions; Figure 3.7: Dr Gopal Murti/Science Photo Library; Figure 3.8a: Ken Hudson; Figure 3.8b: Astrid & Hanns-Frieder Michler/Science Photo Library; Figure 3.11: The Linnean Society;

Figures 4.1, 4.10b and 4.10c: Mike Stewart; Figures 4.3a, 4.4a and 4.6b: Heather Davies; Figure 4.5: Dr Klaus Boller/Science Photo Library; Figure 4.10a: Andrew Syred/Science Photo Library; Figure 4.10d: D Phillips/Science Photo Library; Figure 4.11: L. Booth and H. S. Vishniac; Figure 4.12: Steve Long/University of Massachusetts Photo Service; Figure 4.17: Spike Walker/Getty Images; Figures 4.22 and 4.26: Heather Angel/Natural Visions; Figure 4.28: © Ian Walker/NHMPL;

Figure 6.3: Dr Kari Lounatmaa/Science Photo Library; Figure 6.16: © The Royal Society;

Figure 8.5: Science Photo Library; Figure 8.6a: Simon Fraser/Science Photo Library; Figure 8.6b: Dr Jeremy Burgess/Science Photo Library; Figure 8.13: Lizzie Harper/Science Photo Library;

Figure 9.1: Biophoto associate/Science Photo Library; Figure 9.4: © Juniors Bildarchiv/Alamy; Figure 9.6: Hattie Young/Science Photo Library;

Figure 13.2: Jeffreys, A. J., Brookfield, J. F. Y. and Semeonoff, R. (1985) 'Positive identification of an immigration test-case using human DNA fingerprints', *Nature*, vol. 317, 31 October 1985, Nature Publishing;

Figure 14.1: National Library of Medicine/Science Photo Library; Figure 14.2: Heather Angel/Natural Visions; Figure 14.4: Slater, P. J. B. and Halliday, T. R. (1994) *Behaviour and Evolution*, Cambridge University Press; Figure 14.7: Grant, P.R., Grant, B. R. and Petren, K. (1999) 'The allopatric phase of speciation: the sharp-beaked ground finch (*Geospiza difficilis*) on the Galápagos islands', *Biological Journal of the Linnean Society*, vol. 69, The Linnean Society; Figure 14.8: Ford, E. B. (1965) *Ecological Genetics*, Methuen and Co Ltd;

Figure 15.2: Multimedia Laboratory, University of Zurich; Figure 15.3: Klug, W. S. et al. (2006) *Concepts of Genetics*, 8th ed., Pearson Education Inc; Figure 15.4: Smith, F. D. M. et al. (1993) 'How much do we know about the current extinction rate?', *Trends in Ecology and Evolution*, vol. 8 (10), Elsevier Science; Figure 15.5: Halliday, T. (1978) *Vanishing Birds*, Sidgwick & Jackson Limited.

Every effort has been made to contact copyright holders. If any have been inadvertently overlooked the publishers will be pleased to make the necessary arrangements at the first opportunity.

# Index

Entries and page numbers in **bold type** refer to key words that are printed in **bold** in the text and that are defined in the glossary. Where the page number is given in *italics*, the index information is carried mainly or wholly in an illustration or table.